FACTORY OF STRATEGY

INSURRECTIONS

Critical Studies in Religion, Politics, and Culture

INSURRECTIONS
Critical Studies in Religion, Politics, and Culture
Slavoj Žižek, Clayton Crockett, Creston Davis, Jeffrey W. Robbins, Editors

The intersection of religion, politics, and culture is one of the most discussed areas in theory today. It also has the deepest and most wide-ranging impact on the world. Insurrections: Critical Studies in Religion, Politics, and Culture will bring the tools of philosophy and critical theory to the political implications of the religious turn. The series will address a range of religious traditions and political viewpoints in the United States, Europe, and other parts of the world. Without advocating any specific religious or theological stance, the series aims nonetheless to be faithful to the radical emancipatory potential of religion.

After the Death of God, John D. Caputo and Gianni Vattimo, edited by Jeffrey W. Robbins
The Politics of Postsecular Religion: Mourning Secular Futures, Ananda Abeysekara
Nietzsche and Levinas: "After the Death of a Certain God," edited by Jill Stauffer and
    Bettina Bergo
Strange Wonder: The Closure of Metaphysics and the Opening of Awe, Mary-Jane Rubenstein
*Religion and the Specter of the West: Sikhism, India, Postcoloniality, and the Politics of
    Translation*, Arvind Mandair
Plasticity at the Dusk of Writing: Dialectic, Destruction, Deconstruction, Catherine Malabou
Anatheism: Returning to God After God, Richard Kearney
Rage and Time: A Psychopolitical Investigation, Peter Sloterdijk
Radical Political Theology: Religion and Politics After Liberalism, Clayton Crockett
Radical Democracy and Political Theology, Jeffrey W. Robbins
Hegel and the Infinite: Religion, Politics, and Dialectic, edited by Slavoj Žižek, Clayton
    Crockett, and Creston Davis
What Does a Jew Want? On Binationalism and Other Specters, Udi Aloni
A Radical Philosophy of Saint Paul, Stanislas Breton, edited by Ward Blanton, translated by
    Joseph N. Ballan
Hermeneutic Communism: From Heidegger to Marx, Gianni Vattimo and Santiago Zabala
Deleuze Beyond Badiou: Ontology, Multiplicity, and Event, Clayton Crockett
Self and Emotional Life: Philosophy, Psychoanalysis, and Neuroscience, Adrian Johnston and
    Catherine Malabou
The Incident at Antioch: A Tragedy in Three Acts / L'Incident d'Antioche: Tragédie en trois actes,
    Alain Badiou, translated by Susan Spitzer
Philosophical Temperaments: From Plato to Foucault, Peter Sloterdijk
To Carl Schmitt: Letters and Reflections, Jacob Taubes, translated by Keith Tribe
Encountering Religion: Responsibility and Criticism After Secularism, Tyler Roberts
Spinoza for Our Time: Politics and Postmodernity, Antonio Negri, translated by
    William McCuaig

ANTONIO NEGRI

FACTORY
of
STRATEGY

Thirty-Three Lessons on Lenin

Translated by Arianna Bove

Columbia University Press / New York

Columbia University Press
Publishers Since 1893
New York   Chichester, West Sussex
cup.columbia.edu

Copyright © 2004 manifestolibri
English translation copyright © 2014 Columbia University Press
All rights reserved

Library of Congress Cataloging-in-Publication Data
Negri, Antonio, 1933–
    [Fabbrica della strategia. English]
    Factory of strategy : thirty-three lessons on Lenin / Antonio Negri ;
translated by Arianna Bove.
        pages   cm — (Insurrections: critical studies in religion, politics,
and culture)
    Translation of the author's Fabbrica della strategia.
    Includes bibliographical references.
    ISBN 978-0-231-14682-1 (cloth : alk. paper) — ISBN 978-0-231-51942-7
(e-book)
    1. Communism—Soviet Union—History. I. Bove, Arianna, translator.
II. Title.

HX312.N3513 2014
335.43—dc23
                                                2013021200

Columbia University Press books are printed on permanent and durable
acid-free paper.
This book is printed on paper with recycled content.
Printed in the United States of America

c 10 9 8 7 6 5 4 3 2 1

JACKET DESIGN AND ART: Martin Hinze

References to websites (URLs) were accurate at the time of writing.
Neither the author nor Columbia University Press is responsible for URLs
that may have expired or changed since the manuscript was prepared.

CONTENTS

CONTENTS

CONTENTS

CONTENTS

CONTENTS

PREFACE TO THE
ENGLISH TRANSLATION

These lessons were first published in 1978, around thirty-five years ago. They enjoyed their own life cycle, which I tried to describe in the preface to the second edition of 1998. Why give them another life now in an English translation that will address readers of different sensibilities, readers outside Europe (which was the field of Leninism), and younger readers, who, forty years ago, were not even born and now see Lenin's Soviet Russia as an archaeological remain? Will it be possible, even, to give Lenin a *new* life?

I would like to dedicate this book to the militants of Occupy, to the Indignados in Spain, Greece, and Europe, and to the young people who, in the "Arab Spring," have opened a new cycle of anticapitalist struggles for the emancipation of labor, social equality, and common freedom. Why would they welcome such a gift? What use could it be to them? These are the questions I will try to address here. I don't know if I will succeed, but if I do, my political conscience, work, and militancy will be strengthened and maybe renewed as a result.

My starting point is a conviction, reiterated in all the volumes I coauthored with Michael Hardt (*Empire*, *Multitude*, and *Commonwealth*), that after 1968, through 1989, and especially during the first decade of the twenty-first century, we have embarked on a new epoch in human history; the conviction that the modernity that was definitively consolidated from the eighteenth century onward and that produced the emergence of socialist movements with capitalist development and the liberal revolution has come to its end. Capitalism, in the financial forms it takes on today and the crises it relentlessly undergoes, displays all the characteristics of its terminal stage. Occupy, the new movements of the Indignados, and the Springs seem to point to the other side of the expression of this crisis and radically manifest a new mode of thinking and acting for the emancipation of the oppressed. A Paris Commune: the novelty imagined by contemporary movements is a political form, finally discovered, that realizes the economic emancipation of labor, a new form of common life that is fundamentally expansive, a new season of critique of work and domination, and a spring of democratic invention.

However, on these premises, we do not forget Lenin or Robespierre. And we keep condemning Stalin as we condemn Napoleon. We don't forget Bolivar as we don't forget Jefferson—though we condemn many of the consequences of their actions. Having said that, this is old news, and we insist on that. It's over, finished. But what has finished, really? What's finished is the way these people, to impose their ideas and build a desirable society, experienced the state. They imagined and made use of the state as a necessary and fundamental tool of political activity. Here, instead, we find a place of radical discontinuity, of the very inversion of thought and political affects that we describe when speaking of this "rupture" with modernity; and this prevents us from seeing ourselves as disciples of any one of these heroes of modernity. We no longer believe that the state can be a motor of emancipation. Instead, we believe that the state is a sad and corrupt machine, and ontologically so, one that must definitively think of itself as an ill-fated abortion, a desire that never came to fruition because the commitment to unify democracy and capitalism, freedom and sovereignty could never be actualized. Today, we are aware of the crisis and the dissolution not only of the nation-state but also of sovereignty, and of the "autonomy of the political," of that "body of the King" that from up in the heavens made power so sacred. We know that Jefferson, Robespierre, Bolivar, and Lenin too often hated that figure of power; but they always used it, they were always part of it.

But there is more to it in Lenin. Among the great politicians of modernity, Lenin is the only one who managed to posit the question of the "withering-away" and "extinction" of the state. Like Marx, he identified the profound connection between capitalism and modern sovereignty, and thus intuited the need to destroy not only capitalism but also the state. The attempt ended badly—that's the least we can say, and with no irony. Nonetheless, we do not think that the experiment "necessarily" had to end badly. As Machiavelli taught us, there is no other necessity in human history than that born out of the victory or defeat that characterizes life in the continuous struggle between political subjects, interests, ideals, and productive forces. That attempt was defeated, but what didn't disappear was its spirit, the drift that drives anyone who seeks freedom to propose a project for the dissolution of the state.

In the book we present here, forty years ago we were already trying to understand and demonstrate how Leninism was not the ferocious machine of the poor's reappropriation of wealth and of the political dictatorship of an intellectual elite over the whole of society; it was not the mere military instrument of a subversive vanguard against the ancien régime. No: instead, thanks to its revolutionary ductility, Leninism could be configured as a new "political form" able to make itself adequate to different realities, both extensively (as it in fact did in Russia, China, Latin America, and globally) and intensively (singularly adapting itself and putting itself at the service of different working-class compositions and proletariats in the various countries oppressed by capitalism where it fought and sometimes imposed itself). I owe this knowledge to Italian Marxism, to Gramsci, and to all the subsequent developments, in *operaismo*, of revolutionary internationalism. Today, however, the task at hand is different. It is not only to demonstrate how Lenin's method was effective in representing a new political figure in and beyond modernity, and how its organizational model was capable of adapting to different historical conditions through the seizure of the state. More than this, the task is to understand how the thought on the "withering-away of the state," so central to Lenin's agitation, has now become universal. Lenin as the withering-away of the state, the organized (not anarchic, but institutionally led) destruction of central power and of the "theological-political" nexus in all its forms, the reappropriation of freedom and of wealth: in this, can Lenin be a project for the future?

In the "Springs of 2011" in Arab countries, and in the Spanish Indignados revolt of M15 and then OWS, that project is present. Anticapitalism characterizes both the Arab "Springs" for freedom against dictatorial regimes and the Western ones for social justice against the financial crisis. And they are not mistaken in recognizing that the hegemony of financial capital presents itself on the one hand as "biopower" and on the other as a global, imperial power. But these "Springs" also present a series of novelties. These are:

(1) The reinterpretation of freedom as activity, as participation, and as "absolute democracy." Central to this transformation is a set of material conditions: in particular, the acknowledgment of the transformations of labor, the postindustrial conditions of productive valorization, and the hegemonic emergence of the cognitive productive force. In focusing on this new figure of the labor processes and valorization, we can appreciate how the autonomy of the work of knowledge that represents the new subjectivity of living labor materially contests and dissolves any authoritarian organization that transcends the autonomy and immanence of producing.

(2) The reinterpretation of equality and the project of building an order of the "common." On the basis of this *claim* lies the transformation of work, the hegemony of social cooperation in its postindustrial organization, and the ensuing "biopolitical" character assumed by production. A large part of this labor force has become precarious, mobile, and flexible, but from within such a condition, in the second or third generation of the precariat, the idea of an inequality of merit and of one's role in the production of wealth, the ideology of debt, and the guilt of poverty are all dissolved and replaced by a consolidated recognition of the deep and creative equality of one's common connection to work. This applies not only to advanced economies, but also to the young labor force of the Arab countries, which is highly educated and is also launched into the cognitive functions of the organization of production.

These are the fundamental and common characteristics of the "Springs." Were their hopes realized? No. Instead of spring, hell broke out. In the Arab countries, a bloodthirsty process of stabilization followed the revolt. This was a sinister repetition of the spectacles of "pacification" and "normalization" that we had witnessed in past centuries: "Order reigns in Warsaw!" Political struggles were often turned into wars of religion. We are confronted with a monstrous alternative between the preservation of neofeudal regimes and the emergence of populist right-wing regimes that are often parareligious and racist, and always nationalist.

We have seen political, diplomatic, and war initiatives marked by a nonsensical and perverse pragmatism, almost worse than previous authoritarian regimes. In fact, we are faced with a shift from old disciplinary regimes to new regimes of control and exception, as we saw in Europe between the two great wars of the twentieth century.

In the Middle East, in Europe, Spain, and Greece, the repression of the "Springs" goes through processes of global financial regulation, that is, through a supranational duress implemented through a mechanism that thrusts individual countries into the new financial structures of global capitalism.

Biopolitical accumulation and cognitive valorization, wherever they are realized, are subjected to the dominion of banks and the global command of financial rent. We can read in this process and in the extreme violence of this shift a weakening of the efficiency of capitalist domination. As it becomes increasingly parasitical, its power does not so much arise from the activity of research and the organization of society for profit, as from the passive capturing of social rent. Financial capital usurps *welfare* and privatizes the public patrimony. It now produces technical governments to develop purely predatory functions for the state. In the United States, this process is probably even more powerful and violent; complicated and exacerbated by the demise of American hegemony over the rest of the world and the crisis of its constitutional shell and the "American dream," a singular extremism has annihilated all debates between political forces and homogenizes the initiatives of power.

Has the "Spring of 2011" thus definitively come to an end? It would seem so. But the question is still open if only we see it all from other perspectives:

(1) The economic crisis is anything but over. The situation in the Mediterranean and the Persian Gulf can hardly remain stable. The new technical and political composition of the subordinate classes and the new forms of accumulation render the ideological-religious system of control, which hides the

now abyssal social differences, increasingly fragile. In this context, the "Spring of 2011" functions as a revolutionary potential, augmented only by the continuation and deepening of the economic crisis.

(2) In the West, as we have begun to see, an even more important process has been unfolding. Social and political movements—that we consider under the name of Occupy—produced a wealth of innovations with respect to the few past centuries of political history of the proletariat. In modernity, the great libertarian and socialist revolutions were characterized by the question of the seizure and use of the state. Every proletarian revolution, whether successful or not, aimed at establishing the "dictatorship of the proletariat." Today, Occupy and the Indignados produce a new form of social revolution: they propose "constituent" revolutions that build new institutions for the appropriation of wealth, and for its production and management. They propose the citizenship of the common.

(3) We have entered an epoch when the central question arising from the "Spring" insurgencies concerns the construction of multitudinal political devices and institutions of democratic management of the common. This constituent thrust necessarily entails moments of destruction of existing forms of capitalist power and demands a federal space for the activity of the subaltern classes in the global realm.

Is a libertarian Lenin right for the present, then? Can the withering-away of the state be a question on the table again? We don't know. However, just as Lenin was useful to us in our political infancy, so today, as the project of political autonomy of the new proletariat is mature, we propose his teachings anew, well aware of the provocation, and yet also capable, in the hell we are fighting in, of any alliance that can destroy the state and defend the old commitment to "peace and freedom" for every worker.

Between you and me, we are quite surprised that this language doesn't sound more archaic today, as it sometimes did in past decades. It must be that because there have been "Springs," this is how we make sense of it. But now the summer must come. We already sense the maturity of a new time of hope.

The seeds were sowed. The harvest will follow if we work our soil well.

Antonio Negri

PREFACE TO THE
SECOND EDITION

In its present form, this book dates back to 1972–1973, but some of it had been written (or at least partly written) ten years prior to that. Obviously, the present form of these essays is final. I decided against reworking any of these lessons for this edition. Why? Because in their relative naivety they are constructive, creative, and joyful.

How was the text born? Where did I get the idea from and why did my comrades at the time urge me to write it? In the 1970s, Lenin was very present in the movement, in the Italian Communist Party (PCI) as well as in the relatively distant areas of my militancy. Discussing his works and positioning the movements in relation to the Leninist tradition was essential. But the Leninist camp was divided along clear lines. I would say that there were two major interpretative trends in the workers' movement of these times in Italy. Following Togliatti, the majority of the PCI defended an orthodox adherence to Leninism that was as philologically strict as it was opportunistic. In that climate, Gramscianism served a reformist theory of social change, and the concept of hegemony was a *dispositif* of consensus meant to substitute the will to power and Leninist indication toward the dictatorship of the proletariat. (Poor Gramsci, betrayed twice: first for being an authentically Leninist thinker and then for authoring an improbably democratic theory of communism.) The second trend present in the ideological market of the proletarian and workers' movement of the 1960s and 1970s was that of other pseudo-Leninist groups. These were, above all, Marxist-Leninist (M-L); they were often organizational caricatures, symbolic rather than political, financial and appropriative rather than subversive and cooperative. In these groups and their sensibilities, the idea of Leninism had been attached to the twisted image drawn by Stalinism: Leninism entailed a delegation of revolutionary political decision to a leader or a leading group; it meant fetishism of authority and the glorification of dictatorial symbolism. In a popular way, they often represented communism as a church or, worse, as a sect, and at times as the vessel for the most unbridled populism.

Beyond the Italian borders, during the Cold War, on the international stage, forces and programs much more important than the caricatured figures of the Italian debate of the 1970s claimed to be Leninist and opposed both superpowers of that period. To them, the USSR was clearly a betrayal of Marxism. What needed to be worked out was whether a Leninist opposition to this Marxist betrayal was possible. In this context I was first and foremost interested in the current of the Bordighists, who engaged in a polemic against Stalinist voluntarism in the name of a harsh materialist objectivism. The Bordighists sought to reinterpret the history of leaps of insurrections described by Lenin in the framework of a theory of the revolutionary cycle. This theory in the first instance seemingly drifted away from the hope of a revolution, but subsequently established it as an event that was absolutely necessary. In those years, the 1960s and 1970s, some of my friends were Bordighist: a few comrades from Cremona in Italy, and Robert Paris and some others in France. To me, Bordighism responded to an open and effective demand for revolution by presenting itself simultaneously as resistance and insurrection, organization and event. Because of this, I had the impression that a theory of the subject like the one I was developing at the time could be submitted to such a *dispositif*. These theoretical alternatives to Leninism still exist today: they can be read without great political insight in Alain Badiou, for instance. But another trend interested me even more. Some friends had traveled back and forth between Europe and the United States and met the militants and theorists of the Facing Reality group. They came from the workers' rank and file of the communist left that in the United States presented itself as Trotskyism, and offered very strong subjective interpretations of Leninism, linked to and also renovating the critical Marxism of Dunayevskaia. Their subjectivism, deeply rooted in the new working class of the New Deal, was made concrete through their continuing investigation of the relationship between the technical and political compositions of industrial labor. This was a high form of subjectivism open to the technological transformations of the organization of the labor force, the sociological changes of development, and a lively project of revolutionary transition.

Italian workerism was in a different position in relation to both the domestic and the international framework. Its position in relation to Lenin was wholly revisionist when it came to his theory and entirely pretentious when it came to his revolutionary project. From this perspective, Mario Tronti's article "Lenin in England" was the starting point of our discussion. There, Tronti argued that in the situation of the 1960s Lenin's theory confronted a radical transformation, a caesura in the social composition of the proletariat. This made a revision of the revolutionary project necessary. In the 1960s, at the journal *Classe Operaia* we all accepted this framing of the question on Lenin: some friends later renounced him or forgot and gave up this research project—I have been and still am convinced that we should return to Lenin again in the same way now as we did then.

In the following lessons from the 1960s and 1970s, I began revisiting and reworking the initial premise of Tronti ("Lenin lives on and confronts a new class reality"). First, the perception of a technical change in the composition of the proletariat that a political change corresponds to, or, in other words, revolutionary revisionism, is praised as an epistemological *dispositif* and as a means to organize the continuity of a revolutionary process: this is obviously made, produced, and reconfigured through struggles, victories, and defeats, but also and primarily through the ontological mutations of its protagonist subject.

Second, the crisis of theoretical Marxism after 1956 that followed the publication of reports on Stalin at the twentieth congress of the Communist Party of the Soviet Union (CPSU) was perceived to be a positive, constructive, and creative crisis. Revolutions and their necessities, theories and their possibilities exchanged roles: at this point in time, theory drove subjectivity and disposed it to becoming adequate to a new present. Then, a strange sort of "patristic process" began: this is to say that a renewal of Marxism began to unfold, similarly to the renewal affecting Christianity in the early centuries since its birth; on the ruins and the mistakes, on the political battles and ontological developments of the subject, a new synthesis for the future was being articulated.

Third, Lenin's theory of revolution seemed to be far superior and infinitely purer than the Stalinist Thermidor. Revolutionary terror is real; it determines profound historical discontinuities and radically destroys the reproduction of the ruling classes: but it is also always mystifying when, alongside this drainage of the spirit, it reintroduces a new ruling class and new forms of command. Today, the Stalinist Thermidor is in no continuity with the Leninist revolution: a continuity of Leninism is only found in the heterodoxies of the October revolution. Lenin is continued in literature and in the imaginary with Mayakovsky, Bakhtin, and Lukács, in law with Pashukanis, in politics with Mao. Read Brecht's *Die Massnahme* (*The Measures Taken*): there, in the monstrosity of revolutionary terror, you will find reclaimed the heterodox originality of the Leninist *dispositif*. Finally, seeing how theory could, after 1956, recover the place in the development of class struggle that it was denied by Stalinist administrative practice, we rediscovered in Leninism a productive matrix of new organizational forms, an ever stronger origin of the development of revolutionary power. In the early 1970s, we were experiencing the shift from the hegemony of the mass worker and the organizational hegemony of the outside intellectual to new organizational forms of the social worker and the labor force that were internal to intellectual production: this process of mutation of political subjectivity would clearly not stop there and we knew this. In fact, we already sensed the dawn of new organizational figures in praxis and revolutionary theory. To us, Lenin served as a *methodological essay* for the analysis of the transformation of class struggle; he was the *shibboleth* of a continuous revolutionary refoundation through the transformation of subjects.

At this point I would like to digress and remember the climate, the places, and the people who surrounded the work on these lessons on Lenin. As I said earlier, some of these lessons (particularly on the Soviets) had already been developed into articles in the early 1960s. Others, on Lenin and the theory of the party, were anticipated in lectures given at the University of Rome, La Sapienza. But it was not until later, at the University of Padua's Institute of Political Science, which I chaired at the time (as a real "evil master"), that these lessons became thirty-three sessions. I am very proud of my academic work: I prepared the lectures, recounted them to very large audiences of students, and they were recorded. Then Gabriella and Elisabetta typed them up. I corrected them and prepared them for publication during the summer of 1973. I only held the course on Lenin between 1972 and 1973. The "evil master" did not repeat himself to students. There was a different course every year, and the debates at the weekly seminar at the Institute contributed to verifying the issues and fixing the points of didactic intervention for the coming year. Thinking about it now, I must admit that a seminar like that was impossible to digest for the Italian university system: it was really a Leninist seminar. In 1979 they put almost all of us in jail. But, before that, you could not imagine what, how much, and how subversive that Institute was capable of being. Luciano Ferrari Bravo, Sandro Serafini, Sergio Bologna, Guido Bianchini, Christian Marazzi, Maria Rosa Dalla Costa, Lisi Del Re, Ferruccio Gambino, and many others not unknown to the Italian intellectual chronicles of the last thirty years established themselves at the Institute. And then, many important friends and foreign comrades passed through: from Agnoli to Bruckner, from Harry Cleaver to John Merrington and Selma James, from Moulier Boutang to Coriat, to De Gaudemar. And even illustrious Italians, although they always disagreed, were compelled to confront us: from Rossana Rossanda to Trentin to Carniti; and then there were the laborites, from Giugni to Tarello to Ghezzi, all the way to the great Mancini, to Giannini, and to Caffe. And then there was the research our Institute carried out under the auspices of the Consiglio Nazionale delle Ricerche (CNR) [National Research Institute], which in those years only a few other university institutes did. We produced important works on contemporary issues, from an analysis of the structures of centralization and the administrative procedures of the European Community, to direct investigations of the transformations of labor, between factory and society, between immaterial work and social work. The Institute as a whole oversaw a couple of scientific journals published by Feltrinelli and others by CLEUP [the University of Padua's Publishing Cooperative]. The Leninist ideas of a theoretical reinvention of communism and an insurrectional overcoming of state structures toward liberty traveled and were updated amid this sea of initiatives and concrete projects.

The Institute was brought down by a repressive blitz thought up by a judge named Calogero and inspired by the occult structures of the state, of the Christian Democracy Party and the PCI. The blitz consisted in defining the Institute as the theoretical center of the Red Brigades. The heroic judge who came up with this theorem made an excellent judicial career for himself; the infamous informers and provocateurs who fabricated evidence and threw the professors of the Institute in jail are still now MPs on the reformist left (and the self-elected revolutionary left) or, obviously, on the political right. The Padua professors who supported the operation, typically inept in their work, had outstanding academic careers, even though they do not make any reference now in their curriculum (how pusillanimous!) to their work in the "April 7 affair." But they could: the political class has not changed much, its anticommunism has proliferated, and today there is not even a need for a President of the Republic (the most honorable Pertini) to legitimize infamy by approving in only two days, on April 9, 1979, the preventive arrests of April 7.

I feel no bitterness or scandal in writing this. I only feel Leninist contempt for all the charioteer flies who call themselves socialist while serving patronage. There is no time to talk about the squalor of the Italian media of those times (and of today?); but this is no scandal, because infamy serves the owners of the means of communication, and dishonesty is amply compensated by them. Here there is only the certainty and denunciation of the fact that the whole of the Italian left has been involved in the corruption of the law ever since.

Most of the thoughts, passions, and people who carried out destructive, repressive, and reactionary actions against these "thirty-three lessons on Lenin" are dead and ended up in oblivion. These lessons, however, are now being republished. The political shift, which is only stammered in these lessons on a new theory of the organization of the exploited, between the working class and new forms of the proletariat, between the working class and the postmodern multitude, has greatly progressed today. But there is something more to it: in addition to the realizations that Leninist epistemology has imposed itself and that the revolutionary changeover from one subject to another across the historical process is truly and entirely perceivable and understood by everyone, there is also the fact that this shift is now presented as the very fabric of a global revolution, of the multitude against empire. Many of the premises of these lessons have certainly changed, as have many of the conditions that underpinned their reasoning. But does it matter? By imposing themselves on history, subjective forces alter the way that we know history; the movement of reality interprets reality itself. Leninist abstraction has returned to be real because the Leninist utopia is again a desire. It is much more amusing to see the great bourgeois men of letters recover, in this period of epochal transformation, the figure of Saint Paul as a testimony of the shift. To us, only Lenin seems to possess, for communism, the qualities of a Pauline revolution. We have a remaining task: to reconstruct historical materialism and communist theory in the imperial era. I am sure that these ancient lessons can serve as a useful introduction.

Rome, September 2003

TRANSLATOR'S NOTE

The choice of some terms might seem at odds with current uses in English language. Where this is the case, it was intentional.

For instance, class composition studies in Italy make abundant use of the word "comportamento." Intuitively, the translation of this term would be "behavior," but behavioral studies do away with subjectivity, whereas when class composition analysts speak of "behavior" it is precisely to refer to that: how the masses act, whether they steal, what they sign up to, whether they are family-oriented, how they refuse or sabotage work, and all observations that point to the conditions of possibility of such micropower relations, as a starting point. In English and American, the term "behavior" is tainted with the worst positivist determinist objectivism ever dreamed up by the social sciences: from Pavlov's dogs to Skinner's pigeons, behavior points to the observable, patterned, and hence allegedly manipulable activities of animals. In its place, the translator wishes to promote the use of the term "comportment" in English, because com-portment speaks of the body and how it moves in social relations, and of conduct and how one carries oneself with others, and it's used in French and Italian to underline the elements of subjectivity in "social facts."

It is possible that other similar linguistic oddities will strike the reader: for these the translator takes full responsibility.

The translator wishes to acknowledge the work of Neal McTighe, Guio Jacinto, and Maurizia Boscagli, who have previously translated parts of this text. Their translations were not adopted here, but obviously they were consulted.

For their generous linguistic advice and support, to Steve Wright, Robert Demke, and Erik Empson, *grazie mille.*

FACTORY OF STRATEGY

PART ONE

Lenin and Our Generation

1

TOWARD A MARXIST READING
OF LENIN'S MARXISM

THIS YEAR, IN three groups of lessons, along with a few interludes and appendices, we aim to arrive at an understanding of Vladimir Lenin, though without suggesting that it is possible to arrive at any sort of conclusive reading. Primarily, we compare problems that are born from Leninism with issues that arise out of today's workers' movement. These three groups of lessons are: First, an introduction that centers on the fundamentals of Lenin's thought. We will follow how problems in Lenin's political theory are developed, comparing them with how it is that we, today, handle similar problems. The second and more-focused group of lessons will instead center on the concept of organization, particularly Lenin's thoughts about the Russian Communist Party. The third and last group puts forth, once again, the essential idea of the extinction of the state, starting with, on the one hand, Lenin's work *The State and Revolution* and, on the other, the actual current condition of the class struggle and the development of the productive forces. Therefore, we have three groups of lessons and three sets of problems, which are supplemented by notes and appendices (on Lenin's dialectics, on the Soviets, and on *"Left-Wing" Communism*), three groups of lessons that are unequal in content and disproportionate in importance. Yet the stimulus to think and act that comes from reading Lenin is so strong and enthusing that I believe we shall derive some uses from this exercise.

Let us begin, therefore, with the first point—Lenin and us, Lenin and the political experience of the movement of our times—and ask ourselves, what contribution has Leninism made to our theoretical and political formation? This question calls for a comparison and, as is the case with all comparisons, requires us to make a value judgment, one that may be expressed in radical terms: Does Lenin still mean anything to us? Is Lenin's method such that it is of value to us, or does it correspond to the practice of research and action that we have, often spontaneously, renewed and rediscovered in class struggle? Note that I do not say "spontaneously" because spontaneity is our religion, but because no one in the 1950s and 1960s ever helped us read in class struggle. To respond to these questions, it will be necessary to trace the entire development of Lenin's thought, highlighting its key points. First period: an analysis of capital; second period: the issue of organization; third period: the struggle against autocracy and therefore an organic approach to the definition of the revolutionary process; fourth period: insurrection; and fifth period: how socialism is constructed under the dictatorship of the proletariat. It will be necessary to follow this process, giving special note not so much to the content as to the relationship between strategy and tactics, which seems the most distinctive element in Lenin's thought. With regard to Marx, class struggle and the development of the productive forces determine in Lenin's thought a highly valuable tactical moment, such that Marxist thought is enriched overall by it. Certainly, Marx's writings on the Commune are an example of intelligence in the historically concrete, of the ability to seize the insurrectional moment and develop from it a theoretical stance: but it is also true that for Lenin, as Mario Tronti observes in his *Operai e capitale*,[1] the relationship between revolutionary theory and practice, between the definition of a strategy and the determination of tactical shifts, and above all the novel use of organizational mediation provide a qualitative new approach to the entire communist position.

Let us start with a purely introductory discussion: how to read Lenin today. I shall leave aside the various critical perspectives on the matter, widespread in the official communist movement. Dogmatic temptation and the most blatant opportunism are undoubtedly developed and balanced in the interpretation of Lenin as we have come to know it in the recent years of the theoretical development of the communist movement, of which we have direct experience. Lenin becomes the one who has said it all: the one who sang the praises of insurrection, but who also wrote *"Left-Wing" Communism, an Infantile Disorder*, a gold mine of maxims and countermaxims whereby theory becomes the philological aptitude for taking the most efficient shortcuts between two opportune citations.[2] However, beyond dogmatic temptation and opportunism, it is true, in fact, that Lenin's thought presents a number of formal contradictions that often have considerable relevance. Having acknowledged this, our problem is understanding if and to what extent Lenin's thought can be subjected to a Marxist analysis of Marxism. What does this mean? It means that, in principle, Marxist authors must undergo a historical, practical critique that is essential to defining and locating their thought. Marx provided, with respect to the development of his own works, a number of examples of what we know as a Marxist science of Marxism, that is, the ability to situate the variations and the necessary discontinuities of political analysis within a coherent structural design. He did so, for example, in his writings on the Commune, where the initial opposition to an in-depth study of the insurrectional process quickly turns into an analysis that is internal and participative to the process. Thought is discontinuous because reality is dialectical and movement is revolutionary and progressive:

> But the revolution is thorough. It is still journeying through purgatory. It does its work methodically. By December 2, 1851 it had completed one half of its preparatory work; it is now completing the other half. First it perfected the parliamentary power, in order to be able to overthrow it. Now that it has attained this, it perfects the executive power, reduces it to its purest expression, isolates it, sets it up against itself as the sole target, in order to concentrate all its forces of destruction against it. And when it has done this second half of its preliminary work, Europe will leap from its seat and exultantly exclaim: Well burrowed, old mole![3]

In general terms, this means that one of the most salient aspects of Marxist discourse on Marxism is the assumption of its own essential discontinuity and the discontinuity of its real referent. Only if Marxist thought presented itself as ideology would it find a fictitious inner continuity, an internal relation of filiations and its own worthy ancestors. But that is not the case: Marxist thought can only address the series of problems that present themselves anew, and the continuity it assumes can be no other than that of the revolutionary subject, both dynamic and contradictory, to which it refers. Marxism is the real continuity of a subject that puts forward subversive practice as the essence of its continuity: it is only under these conditions that theory becomes material power. Therefore the discontinuity of Marxism is a negation of ideology: it is never simply theoretical continuity, filiations, continuous processes leading from thought to thought, but always a rupture and renovation of political hypotheses confronting the needs, exigencies, urgency, and new qualities presented by a revolutionary subject. Any reading or criticism of a Marxist author can only be given as an elegy of real discontinuity, the only systematic and continuous point of reference of Marxism.

Therefore, when analyzing Lenin, the first and greatest danger is that of entering into a debate on "Leninism." Leninism does not exist, or rather, the theoretical statements contained in this term must be brought back to bear on the set of comportments and attitudes to which they refer: their correctness must be measured in the relationship between the emergence of a historical subject (the revolutionary proletariat) and the set of subversive problems that this subject is confronted with. Is this an overly drastic reduction of the historical depth of Lenin's thought? I do not think that reservations are called for on this issue. As a confirmation and example, I would like to use the discussion that Lukács, in his article from 1924, proposes about Lenin. Lukács asks himself: who is Lenin? And the answer starts this way:

> Historical materialism is the theory of the proletarian revolution. It is so because its essence is an intellectual synthesis of the social existence which produces and fundamentally determines the proletariat; and because the proletariat struggling for liberation finds its clear self-consciousness in it. The stature of a proletarian thinker, of a representative of historical materialism, can therefore be measured by the depth and breadth of his grasp of this and the problems arising from it; by the extent to which he is able accurately to detect beneath the appearances of bourgeois society those

tendencies towards proletarian revolution which work themselves in and through it to their effective being and distinct consciousness.[4]

Historical materialism or the ideas of the theorists of historical materialism must therefore be measured within a determined existence of class, in its presence, exactly as a tendency. Now, Lenin is this: he is the fullest representation of that which Lukács calls the "actuality of the revolution":

> However, there are today only few who know that Lenin did for our time what Marx did for the whole of capitalist development. In the problems of the development of modern Russia—from those of the beginnings of capitalism in a semi-feudal absolutist state to those of establishing socialism in a backward peasant country—Lenin always saw the problems of the age as a whole: *the onset of the last phase of capitalism and the possibilities of turning the now inevitable final struggle between bourgeoisie and proletariat in favor of the proletariat—of human salvation.*[5]

Lenin is the actuality of the revolution. Lenin interprets, within the determinate situation, within the determinate class relationship between a historical subject (the Russian proletariat) and the overall capitalistic power structure confronting it, the whole set of questions that the worldwide proletariat faced in that historical moment. In a Marxist way, the abstract becomes concrete, that is, the sum of all real determinations. The Leninist solution to the problem of the revolution in Russia is not, therefore, a solution that is simply linked to a definition of the relationship (between the revolutionary Russian proletariat and the semifeudal condition of the relationships of production and control). But insofar as it is, and only to the extent that it is so, it is also the solution to an overarching problem: an analysis, interpretation, and practical solution determined by a class relationship as well as an overall general contribution to the construction of the revolutionary project for all situations of a given epoch. The shift toward the last phase of capitalism is the possibility of turning the struggle between autocracy and proletariat ("the fatal moment of this nation") in favor of the proletariat and the salvation of humanity at large.

I believe that this Lukácsian position is correct and profoundly Leninist. In reality (as we shall see in future conversations discussing Lenin's texts on the subject) this sense of determinacy, of the concreteness of the situation that confronts us, this application of Marxist science as a choice of determinate relations shaped by determined power relations, constitutes the fundamental reduction that Lenin performs and imposes on the Marxist science of his time: winning this theoretical battle translated into the creation of the Bolshevik Party and the determining of the October revolution—the choice of a specific power relation between the working class and capital at a particular point in history and, consequently, the choice of organization as an awareness of this relation and of the series of nexus and articulations that begin with and point to this relation and that, starting from it, form the basis of the subversion of praxis. The choice of the subject of organization and of the subversion of praxis is sectarian and particular: it is a standpoint that does not simply wish to define the relation that from time to time is established between the working class and capitalist power, but that also aspires to become the ability to turn the relation it is grounded in upside down, to identify, at each stage, the chance to put the adversary in a crisis, to ruin its means of domination, the chance of setting into motion a violent destruction of these mechanisms. Theory develops precisely and absolutely alongside the capacity to exercise violence. Violence is the fabric in which all political relations intertwine. The state's domination is the domination of violence and legality, and all constitutional forms, the normal forms of capitalist command, are violence pure and simple. Marxism is the realization that violence inhabits not only formal relations but also the everyday relations of production and life; it is the discovery that the science of capital is the science of capitalist violence, one of the ways in which capital organizes its violence upon the subalterns. Marxism, therefore, is destruction and overthrow. Bringing this relationship between knowledge and violence directly into class analysis is a sectarian standpoint, the workers' standpoint, the point of view of Marxist theory.

From this standpoint we must immediately deem several other trends in Marxist theory unsatisfactory, where they try to expunge from their analysis the determinacy of the proletarian subject. Louis Althusser's position is typical in this regard: insofar as he tends toward a definition of theory as an interventionist practice and class stance,[6] he insistently refuses to ascribe these activities to a material subject, characterized by an inner dialectic between subjectivity and material discontinuity, between the various elements that compose it. The science of the revolutionary process refuses here to become the science of the revolutionary subject. It is easy to understand the effects of this concept: an exaltation of reflection and mediation (alternatively of the intellectual or the party) against dialectical immediacy and therefore against the concreteness (understood in a Marxist sense) of the revolutionary subject. But how can this concept pretend to be Marxist and especially Leninist when in Lenin, as we have already begun to see and as our analysis will make clearer, the crucial problem is that of the determinacy of the revolutionary subject and its temporal and spatial constitution? Obviously establishing the party is quite different from longing for it!

But going back to the problem at hand, what does it mean to subject Lenin to the very scientific model he himself helped develop? It means asking two questions. First: what is the subject that is being interpreted in Lenin's sectarian point of view, what is its theoretical scope? Second: what subject is able to and knows how to read Lenin today? And, therefore: has the subject who reads Lenin today changed by making his issues its own, or is it similar or homogeneous? On the one hand, therefore, we ask: what is the referent of a Leninist standpoint? On the other hand, what is the referent of class struggle and Marxist science today? Our referent, at present, is the revolutionary mass worker who in Europe in the 1960s, and even before that in the United States, developed an action that brought about a period of dramatic crisis in capitalist development.[7] What is Lenin's referent? It is the workers' industrial vanguard in Russia, enveloped, as Massimo Cacciari rightly notes, in its "isolation":

Lenin's discourse translates a real class structure into the terms of organization. Yet the structure imperatively asserted the *material* character of the vanguard that the industrial working class still retained, which means its isolation. The relation of production of late capitalism, and therefore the material reproduction of the labor force *and* the working class, was isolated—it was vanguard. But the possibilities of a revolutionary process directly depend on the possibilities to defend and develop mechanisms of class reproduction. The primary task of the revolutionary party is thus to prevent precapitalist relations of production from carrying out a *mass* offensive on these mechanisms. This is the meaning of Leninist strategy: to strengthen, materially and organizationally, a working class aware of its objective isolation, and to turn this isolation in the vanguard.[8]

The distance between our referent and Lenin's could not be better expressed. The composition of the contemporary working class in struggle and the composition of the entire proletariat have nothing whatsoever to do with the composition of the proletariat of the early twentieth century. Two issues follow from this: the first, a formal one, confirms what is often repeated, that is, that the continuity of the subversive subject elected as its referent by Marxist science must reckon with the discontinuity of the determination of the subject and the dialectical variation of the material forms it takes. The second issue is that failing to understand the difference between the historical relationships that shaped Lenin's proletarian subject and ours means failing to understand the dynamic law of the process. Lenin has won. It is the victory of the working class by means of Leninism that necessarily set a different and determinate dynamic of capitalist relations into motion: this entails a change and a different configuration of the subversive subject. Unless we understand this modification of the subject, we cannot comprehend the rule and form of the relations that capital establishes with the working class. The working class is outside of capital insofar as it exercises a revolutionary thrust, but to the extent that it does so, capital tries to recapture it within itself and reduce it to labor power again; at times capital even tries to comprehend it as an organized working class and make it function as such in its productive process, accepting its demands while restructuring the system of exploitation so that these demands can be incorporated and become an element of its development where they initially were an element of its rupture. This kind of relation becomes fundamental to Marxist science and is the redefinition of the determination in which the working class confronts capital. We call this relation (with all of the complexity of comportments, consciousness, and needs that it comes to acquire) the technical or political *composition of the working class*. For each historical phase of class struggle, we identify a compositional type of working class, which is at its core not only its location in the overall process of production, but also the series of experiments with struggle, comportments, and the way determinate and life needs come to be renewed and newly defined. Marxist thought addresses this object as its real referent. The object of Marxism is the constitution, modification, and recomposition of this subject, because only within this subject do real power relations measure themselves. The entire history of capital, from this point of view, becomes a history of workers' struggles and of the various political class compositions; this fabric reveals the thread of the history of capital as its effect. When we say *effect*, of course, we mean the constant action and reaction of capitalist comportment (of the structures of machinery, law, and state) with respect to the subject within which power relations come to be embodied, starting from the revolutionary axis of the refusal of exploitation. But the dialectical substance of the process does not break up into casual relations; on the contrary, it insists on the determinate causality of the working-class standpoint, of violence and higher understanding. At this point, let us return to the definition of the historical limit of Leninist thought as defined by Cacciari. Lenin's discourse translates a real class composition into organizational terms as it is specifically determined: in the Russian situation Lenin analyzed, the relations of production of late capitalism, the material reproduction of labor power into the working class, were isolated, vanguard. Lenin practically starts from this awareness of determinate class composition and its isolation, confronts it, and reverses this isolation into being vanguard, into an ability to drive the entire movement: "Lenin revolutionarily transforms the late-bourgeois anti-Enlightenment ideology of the elite and the masses."[9] On this point, it must be said that we are a planet away from Lenin's issues. The working class we struggle in no longer knows this: it has been turned into mass by the capitalist mode of production itself, transformed by the technological changes introduced by capital in order to combat those Leninist "vanguards" and beat their overbearing and victorious organized isolation; the composition of the class we struggle in is entirely different. Today's mass worker turns her deskilling, which capital imposed on her as a sign of a new isolation, into the unity of all abstract labor; it transforms the interchangeability of her tasks into chances of general mobility across sectors and territories, *and so on.*

Now we ask, given this profound and effective discontinuity in the real referent, is there continuity in the organized figure of the subversive subject? Cacciari raises this question intelligently, but this time his solution is not so felicitous. He argues that the form of extraneousness and isolation of the vanguard, which becomes the condition of the party, recurs as a formal and methodological canon when faced with a planned capitalist offensive of the kind we are witnessing today. In fact, under the circumstances, Leninist organizational dualism is exalted when confronted with the ability of capital to anticipate class movement through planning, through its mass command over society. Leninism allegedly renews itself in the face of a new capitalist offensive against the unity of class. Well, in my view, this is extremely debatable. In fact, while it is true that it is necessary to identify new and different functions of revolutionary organization within the mechanism of capitalist domination and its new configuration, within, that is, the capitalist attempt to respond to the actions of the mass worker and the crisis its struggles have provoked, these functions are still charged with a content and direction that cannot be reduced to Lenin's discourse: "With the growing integration of the masses, and, in particular, of the working class, through the strengthening of the abstract domination of an increasingly extensive system of abstract labor, the degree of abstraction of propaganda and agitation grows too. . . . Where the premises for defining a classical relationship between political leadership and mass bases are no longer there, mass propaganda and agitation must be organized differently."[10]

Therefore, if the need to develop moments of vanguard in the organizational composition of the mass worker is the focus of the theoretical interest in organization, if the mass worker who fights against a state that produces the crisis, a state that is prepared to destroy wealth in order to dominate class, grasps the urgency of an act that captures the state reaction as it develops and strikes it down as a function of the vanguard, well, then this vanguard is something very different from that seen by Lenin's theory: its foundation and its potential cannot be sociologically isolated, because this vanguard does not confront the whole "people," nor does it look at the state planner and the domination over production with confidence. Rather, through the unity of abstract social labor, it looks at capitalist violence and the capitalist capacity for the destruction of this unity and its own mode of production; it therefore wants to achieve, on this ground, maximum violence. The problem today is not how to establish different degrees of consciousness and objective power within the subject that pushes the revolutionary process forward, but rather how to move along lines that are internal to the capitalist attempt to decompose class and identify in praxis the ability to lead and drive the movement.[11] If different functions need to be assigned to a really unified and mass subject, then we need to be clear: these different functions do not arise from an inhomogeneous class, but from the confrontation with the dishomogeneity induced by capital. They are given in the subversive project of destruction, not in the project of popular recomposition of development. Only a struggle that manages to affect and destroy the relations of violence that capital necessarily exercises as a function of the mechanism of value is worth fighting today.[12] Different functions can be recognized in the vanguard only insofar as the vanguard moves directly on this terrain of violence, of power, of overall armament that capital has initiated on its side. Then, having outlined these initial problems, our question to Lenin becomes this: given that the subject we depart from is different from Lenin's, what do we care about Leninism today? And we will answer this question by looking into the Leninist relation between tactical strategy and organization to verify in a particular class composition (as correctly interpreted by Lenin) the general laws it identifies; and we will put these laws to the test of practical criticism, because only by recognizing the shifts, leaps, and discontinuity that workers' theory is forced to confront can we call ourselves Leninist and use Leninist models of organization. I think there are no other ways of linking our thought to Lenin's today.

NOTES

1. Mario Tronti, *Operai e capitale* [Workers and capital] (Turin: Einaudi, 1966).
2. [Translator's Note: We have supplied an English translation of the Italian title here. This work, however, exists in English translation. See Vladimir Lenin, *Left-Wing Communism, an Infantile Disorder: A Popular Essay in Marxian Strategy and Tactics* (New York: International Publishers, 1940).]
3. Karl Marx, *The Eighteenth Brumaire of Louis Bonaparte*, trans. Daniel De Leon (Chicago: Charles H. Kerr, 1907), 69.

4. György Lukács, "The Actuality of the Revolution," in *A Study on the Unity of His Thought*, trans. Nicholas Jacobs (London: New Left Books, 1970), 1, http://www.marx.org/archive/lukacs/works/1924/lenin/cho1.htm. The original was published in 1924.

5. Ibid. my emphasis.

6. Louis Althusser, *"Lenin and Philosophy," and Other Essays*, trans. Ben Brewster (London: New Left Books, 1978). See also Althusser, "Response to John Lewis," in *Essays in Self-Criticism*, trans. Grahame Lock (London: New Left Books, 1976). It remains certain that Althusser's theoretical position regarding certain aspects of his thought should be taken absolutely seriously. In particular, Althusser's *negation* of the "idealistic" category of the subject allows us to address the history of the workers' movement in nonideological terms; it constitutes a particularly effective *pars destruens* against all surreptitious continuities and can be used to introduce, in my opinion, the very concept of composition. On all of this, see Althusser "Ideology and Ideological State Apparatuses," in *"Lenin and Philosophy."*

7. On this point, along with M. Tronti, *Operai e capitale*, see various authors, *Operai e stato* [Workers and the state] (Milan: Feltrinelli, 1972); A. Serafini, ed., *L'operaio multinazionale in Europa* [The multinational worker in Europe] (Milan: Feltrinelli, 1974); and S. Bologna, P. Carpignano, and A. Negri, *Crisi e organizzazione operaia* [Crisis and workers' organization] (Milan: Feltrinelli, 1974).

8. M. Cacciari, "Sul problema dell'organizzazione: Germania 1917–1921" [On the question of organization: Germany, 1917–1921], introduction to the Italian edition of G. Lukács, *Kommunismus, 1920–1921* (Padua: Marsilio, 1972), 52.

9. Hans-Jürgen Krahl, *Costituzione e lotta di classe* [Constitution and class struggle] (Milan: Jaca Books, 1973), 179.

10. Ibid., 180.

11. From this point of view, it is necessary to underline the limit of the analysis of Leninism proffered by Krahl and the antiauthoritarian left. Paradoxically, their polemic against Lenin's objectivism, authoritarianism, and centralism ends up endorsing a wrong solution: the reclaiming of revolutionary consciousness as a fundamental moment of mediation in the process. Two paths emerge here: either the return to a conception of a collective party-consciousness or the spreading of consciousness to the spontaneous movement. In both cases theory becomes material power only by mediation of consciousness. This standpoint must be inverted while obviously retaining the polemical content of the antiauthoritarian approach: not the consciousness, but the prominence of working class and proletarian practice of struggle for power as it immediately emerges in the structures and development of the material unity of abstract labor needs to be affirmed. Revolutionary practice, the effort in the exercise of an armed generality in the structures of capitalist domination: this is the (superior) form of revolutionary consciousness today. In this, the ability to recompose worker's initiative must be invested. In this, the highest abstraction becomes concreteness of power.

12. On this issue, see my pamphlet "Crisi dello Stato-piano: comunismo e organizzazione rivoluzionaria" [Crisis of the planner state, communism, and revolutionary organization], in *Opuscoli Marxisti*, vol. 1 (Milan: Feltrinelli, 1974).

2

FROM THE THEORY
OF CAPITAL TO THE THEORY
OF ORGANIZATION (1)

Economic Struggle and Political Struggle:
Class Struggle

I N THIS SECTION we begin from Lenin's reading of Marx, in particular, his approach to the theory of organization as derived from a theory of capital (lessons 2–5). In the second part of our discussion (lessons 5–8) we analyze the question of the program to see how one proceeds from a theory of organization to a theory of revolution: what shifts can be dissected in Lenin, and how historically determined were they by the practice in which he operated? For ease of inquiry, we will keep this first tranche of the reconstruction of Lenin's discourse separate from the following one, and only in the end (lesson 9) will we return to the questions we have been asking on the possibility of tracing Lenin's trajectory onto a class subject that has radically changed (such as the one we face today in the historical present of class struggles and power relations).

What, then, is Lenin's historical trajectory? How does he proceed from the theory of capital to a theory of organization? In the 1890s, Lenin's point of departure is a reading and critical analysis of Karl Marx's *Capital*. In my view, few political Marxists know Marx's works and *Capital* in particular as well as Lenin did. Lenin's first works, from the 1890s, are theoretical polemics against a number of populist and generally revisionist trends in the Russian revolutionary movement. On the historical fabric of his work, I suggest you read the introduction by Vittorio Strada to *What Is to Be Done?* published by Einaudi.[1]

Strada frames his presentation with two fundamental issues: on the one hand, he recognizes the significant novelty of Lenin's intervention into the Russian populism that functioned as an ideology of revolutionary movements in Russia in the 1890s and underlines the irreducibility of Marxism-Leninism to this current; on the other hand, he specifies elements of continuity between the organizational tradition of some branches of the left of Russian populism and Lenin's thought, especially in the notion of the centralization of organization that, in the first period, was already investing Lenin's thought despite his theoretical distancing from populism. We will later return to this issue. However, beyond this historiography, we are interested in grasping the way Lenin read *Capital*. If we examine the main text of this first phase, the pamphlet published in 1894 entitled "What the 'Friends of the People' Are and How They Fight the Social Democrats," we already see a definition of some of the concepts that constitute, one might say, the quintessence of Lenin's translation of *Capital*. The first main concept, which can be reconstructed through a passage in the pamphlet, is that of determinate social formation, which Lenin sees as the essential foundation of the method of what he calls "Marxist sociology." Writing about Marx's *Capital*, Lenin claims that:

> the analysis of material social relations at once made it possible to observe recurrence and regularity and to generalize the systems of the various countries in the single fundamental concept: *social formation*. It was this generalization alone that made it possible to proceed from the description of social phenomena (and their evaluation from the standpoint of an ideal) to their strictly scientific analysis, which isolates, let us say by way of example, that which distinguishes one capitalist country from another and investigates that which is common to all of them. . . . This hypothesis for the first time made a scientific sociology possible in that *only the reduction of social relations to production relations and of the latter to the level of the productive forces* provided a firm basis for the conception that the development of formations of society is a process of natural history.[2]

The skeleton of *Capital* is not so much the critical analysis of the economic theory of capital but rather of the social relation that this theory unveils, a relation established between the social forces of production of a determinate social formation, which is the definition of the entire dialectical fabric in which the working class develops its standpoint. It would be superfluous to remind the reader here that, heretic interpretations of Marxism aside, this is the same generic concept developed in Marx's mature methodological phase expressed in the 1857 introduction. Lenin continues: "this is no longer a hypothesis: this materialist concept of history is a thesis that has already been scientifically demonstrated."[3] From a reading of *Capital* we immediately derive the possibility of operating on the field of revolutionary social democracy.

What does the concept of determinate social formation mean, then? We should not be misled by the highly naturalistic terminology used here: Lenin is paying his debt to the culture of his time, and we will later see how glad he was to free himself from it after reading Hegel. But we must underline a fundamentally Marxian gesture toward the recognition that the science of capitalist formation and development must always be brought to bear on the determinacy of the power relations between classes as they are posited inside of it. All chances of development are, for capital, a record of the solution, however determined, of a power relation in class struggle. All social relations must be referred to the struggle and the conflict of the productive forces in the relations of social production. We do not believe that the obvious discovery of this content in *Capital* is so obvious to Lenin, especially in 1894: as we have already seen, this concept is important to a Marxist analysis of Marxism. In fact, the theoretical framework of the social democracy of the Second International as a whole tended to produce a theory of capital that was extremely objectivist, in Russia as in capitalist developed countries. Marxism was not a sectarian standpoint or the form of a working-class choice; it did not present itself as the workers' view of struggle, as the ability to distinguish and demystify the power relations that confront us in order to bring them to bear on our ability to struggle against and destroy them. Marxism was not interpreted or presented as a different science, but as a "superior" one, a "more comprehensive" science of objective development.[4] Naturalism, the most extreme objectivism, was an absolutely crucial element of the debate of his contemporaries that still resonates in some of his definitions, for instance, in the scientific emphasis on the ability to reiterate, regularize, and generalize phenomena.

We probably find the only exception to this in the theory of Rosa Luxemburg, who, whether aware of it or not, is in agreement with Lenin on this methodological framework: for Luxemburg, the standpoint of classes, as forces of production, is the motor of the global movements of capital.[5] This definition of historically determinate formation provides Lenin with the prerequisites for a definition of the class composition of the revolutionary subject.

In these passages we also find an equally important methodological tool. Beyond the formal identification of the notion of determinate social formation, there is an ability to descend into this determination and discover it as a dialectical relation between the forces of the working class and capital (in every instance); in other words, this is the ability to operate what was called a fundamental scientific choice and a scientific foundation of the revolutionary subject. In addition to this, the new methodological instrument, that is, the concept of determinate abstraction, must allow for an understanding of revolutionary dialectics in the framework of a tendency, and of the insubordinate particular in the perspective of totality. In *The Development of Capitalism in Russia*, written during the exile in Siberia and printed in 1898, Lenin had already fully developed the concept of determinate abstraction. How is it defined in the early maturity of Lenin's thought? As an ability to grasp *the highest stage of development* of class struggle, and therefore the resulting capitalist development, and to tear it away from the immediate determinations that fix it, to assume its abstract concept in terms of a necessary tendency in the process. This procedure subverts the current meaning of determinations such as "abstract" and "concrete": what appears as the most abstract (capitalist development in an underdeveloped society) becomes the most concrete element in the tendency, and what is concrete and immediate is eliminated from view. The real concrete is not the immediate but the entirety of real determinations. The concreteness of an abstract definition derives from the dialectical nature of the process investigated. Concreteness is a tendential limit of the immediate determinations grasped and analyzed (and this time, these are properly abstract). In this, Lenin reiterates Marx's teachings. In Marx, determinate abstraction operates in this way: for instance, relations of production, the determinate social formations that took shape during the class struggles of the 1840s in England (which was a foundational moment for the formation of English capitalism), are assumed as an overall tendency of the process of production and class struggle in all capitalist formations. Class struggle is inherent in the concept of determinate social formation and implicates, in the description of what is immediate, a movement toward higher levels of development. Therefore, abstraction is an essential moment in the explanation of the relations that stand before us; insofar as it reveals their dynamic nature, it also carries the power of scientifically determining what will come. Lenin displays the same power of scientific reasoning.[6]

What was the situation in Russia in the 1890s? It was incredibly backward, the working class was restricted to very few areas, and the labor processes of industrial capitalism were not such that, at first sight, Russian society could be characterized as an overall capitalist society. In the face of this, enormous pressure came from agriculture, which was organized into the semifeudal structures that were common in a partly wild country that lay outside not so much the history of capital as that of civil history. However, Lenin's approach forces this reality and locks the immediacy of perception in the progressive mechanism of the tendency. The most advanced moments of the working class and capitalist production are abstracted from this context and identified and marked as moments that are absolutely fundamental for development. The power of capital had come to determine an original qualitative leap, and having accomplished this, the working class is, on the one hand, presented as an inevitable moment, as the fundamental subject of exploitation, and of the overall reproduction of the system. On the other hand, the working class is consequently, and necessarily, revolutionary. Hence, the need for capital to move forward relentlessly, because exploitation can only be consolidated and reproduced by means of constant pressure on this power of the working class that, as such, keeps refusing exploitation and thus must constantly be recomposed in the mechanism of exploitation. Lenin's definition of a working class that refuses and fights against exploitation as a key to understanding the progress of capital leads to a series of consequences: revolutionary organization and subversive action must be construed at the most advanced points of capitalist development. If capital is still a minority power, if it is only through determinate abstraction that we can derive the framework whereby "the entire agrarian system of the state becomes capitalist and for a long time retains feudalist features,"[7] the processes of augmentation of the productive forces of social labor and the socialization of labor are still unstoppable,[8] because the becoming mass of class struggle in some central nodes of the system becomes the overall motor of development. It is worth pointing out that starting from the concept of determinate social formation, and consequently using the method of abstraction and of tendency, does not require a subjective forcing of reality, not insofar as this entails that the working-class standpoint is identified and a revolutionary process is imputed to it. Lenin would be repeatedly accused of this operation; although he was friends with Plekhanov and thus a participant in the Russian theoretical current of the Second International, until 1917 Lenin was practically excluded from the international debate and assigned to the representation of an Asiatic subculture of Marxism. I think that Lenin never wrote for the *Die Neue Zeit*. In fact, the originality of Lenin's reading of Marxism is explicit in these concepts, and this notion of working class is based on the idea of determinate social formation that becomes real as a motor of an unstoppable process of tendency. A modern apologist of the Second International might repeat: economism and spontaneism! And this is true: but only in such a way is it possible to attack the standpoint of the working class, grasp its determinate existence as a sectarian judgment that participates in development, its antagonist reality as a motor of capitalist progress. From the first reading of Marx, and from the opposition, on the strength of this reading, to the theories in vogue in his times, Lenin derives the conviction that theory can only be sectarian, that no political theory is not also the theory of a class in struggle:

> Throughout the civilised world the teachings of Marx evoke the utmost hostility and hatred of all bourgeois science (both official and liberal), which regards Marxism as a kind of "pernicious sect." And no other attitude is to be expected, for there can be no "impartial" social science in a society based on class struggle. In one way or another, all official and liberal science *defends* wage-slavery, whereas Marxism has declared relentless war on that slavery. To expect science to be impartial in a wage-slave society is as foolishly naïve as to expect impartiality from manufacturers on the ques-

tion of whether workers' wages ought not to be increased by decreasing the profits of capital.[9]

To say that "without revolutionary theory there can be no revolutionary movement"[10] is the same as saying that without revolutionary movement there can be no revolutionary theory. This scandalizing conclusion is really Lenin's point of departure.

Equally scandalous in these early years of activity is Lenin's view on dialectics and substance. On these issues we discover a different Lenin, because the first thing that strikes us from reading the Lenin of this period is an exaltation of spontaneity that is not occasional, but permanent and systematic. It is worth recalling that in the 1880s and 1890s, the Russian working class had expressed an extremely high level of spontaneous combativeness: these years saw a series of processes that could be described in terms of a spontaneous circulation of struggles and the constant formation of self-organizing organisms within struggles for political and economic objectives.[11] Lenin collects these kinds of contents and describes these struggles, thus coming to conclusively express a fundamental notion that he would never subsequently repudiate: that economic struggle is political. In light of the fetishist interpretation of "Leninism," this fundamental notion would be completely forgotten. But with what insistence Lenin reiterates it! In the pamphlet *The Tasks of the Russian Social Democrats*, written in 1898, Lenin insists on the need for economic agitation to be at the basis of the political agitation of the proletariat. Each class struggle, each economic struggle, is a political struggle:

> Just as there is no issue affecting the life of the workers in the economic field that must be left unused for the purpose of economic agitation, so there is no issue in the political field that does not serve as a subject for political agitation. These two kinds of agitation are inseparably connected in the activities of the Social-Democrats as the two sides of the same medal. Both economic and political agitation are equally necessary to develop the class-consciousness of the proletariat; both economic and political agitation are equally necessary for guiding the class struggle of the Russian workers, because every class struggle is a political struggle.[12]

Lenin's position never substantially changes: economic struggle and workers' spontaneity will always be at the basis of revolutionary social democracy and its process of organization. When the latter becomes complicated, develops, and centers on political struggle, it demonstrates the maturity of the project but will still demand a great political emphasis on economic and spontaneous struggle as its first phase. In *"Left-Wing" Communism, an Infantile Disorder*, a later work in many respects, Lenin returns to this issue. In a polemic against Turati and friends in Italy, Lenin comments on an interview with Turati published in the *Manchester Guardian*, which is worth reading again because it resonates with the declarations of other *revolutionaries*—and *Leninists*—today in the current struggles. Here is Lenin's comment: "It is clear as daylight that this British correspondent has blurted out the truth, which is probably being concealed and glossed over both by Turati himself, and his bourgeois defenders, accomplices and inspirers in Italy. That truth is that the ideas and political activities of Turati, Treves, Modigliani, Dugoni and Co. are really and precisely of the kind that the British correspondent has described." That is, the ideas of good revisionists, laborists, people who will never make the revolution and only raise their voices a little to castigate struggles. Lenin continues:

> It is downright social treachery. Just look at this advocacy of order and discipline among the workers, who are wage slaves toiling to enrich the capitalists! And how familiar to us Russians all these Menshevik speeches are! What a valuable admission it is that the masses are *for* Soviet government! How stupid and vulgarly bourgeois is the failure to understand the revolutionary role of spontaneously spreading strikes! Yes, indeed, the correspondent of the English bourgeois-liberal newspaper has rendered a backhanded service to Messrs. Turati and Co., and has excellently confirmed the correctness of the demand of Comrade Bordiga and his friends of *Il Soviet*, who are insisting that the Italian Socialist Party, if it really wants to be *for* the Third International, should drum Messrs. Turati and Co. out of its ranks and become a Communist Party both in name and in deeds.[13]

In the same pamphlet, Lenin exclaims: "How stupid and vulgarly bourgeois is the failure to understand the revolutionary role of spontaneously spreading strikes!" This confirms that Lenin remains, from beginning to end, close to a fundamental theoretical statement: even at the spontaneous level and in economic struggle, the working class fights directly against the overall power structure that confronts it, and the moment of this insurgence is absolutely fundamental to the genesis, and thus the organizational development, of social democracy. "Spontaneity as the Beginning of Social Democracy" is a chapter of *What Is to Be Done?* from 1902, another work that is normally used to demonstrate the exact opposite. There are, to be fair, diverging trajectories in this work, but the question is to grasp the specificity of the shifts in the discourse, instead of moving through interpretative lines of Leninism that are terribly traditional and flatten out any development of it. *What Is to Be Done?* contains a beautiful description of the process of spontaneity of struggles as a founding moment of social democracy. "The beginning of the spontaneous upsurge" is a paragraph in the second chapter and an exaltation of the movement of spontaneous strikes in Russia, in recognition of the essential function of spontaneity as a "beginning."[14] On the other side, in the same book, we find a series of reasoning and indications that return to this moment (and we will return to it ourselves when speaking of the Leninist notion of the Soviet).

It is worth clarifying immediately that Lenin regards these initial forms of spontaneous and economic movements not only as detonators but also, and especially, as a first, indispensable element of the process of *social democratic organization*. The form of the Soviet is also directly imputed to spontaneity.[15] The organizational forms of spontaneity, the forms of organized autonomy, are assumed and privileged as moments that can never be eliminated from the process of organization. Rather than material that can be easily manipulated, these are structures that have already taken shape "organizationally" in a determinate revolutionary function, for mass organization and *also* for the beginning of the organizing process of the party. Therefore, even when he engages in an exasperated polemic with working-class codism (in *What Is to Be Done?* and *One Step Forward, Two Steps Back*), Lenin never forgets that the refusal to submit to spontaneity is not a negation of spontaneity. Quite the opposite: the refusal to submit to spontaneity emerges, affirms itself, and consolidates when spontaneity is at its highest. As he writes:

At that time, indeed, we had astonishingly few forces, and it was perfectly natural and legitimate then to devote ourselves exclusively to activities among the workers, and severely condemn any deviation from this. The whole task then was to consolidate our position in the working class. At the present time, however, gigantic forces have been attracted to the movement; the best representatives of the young generation of the educated classes are coming over to us.[16]

The main problem today is one of organization, or the ability to channel the movement toward the full consciousness of its power.

On these premises, there is a second element at the basis of Lenin's determinate approach to the problem of organization. Completing the notion that economic struggle is political struggle determines a leap onto a second and fundamental statement: political struggle is not just economic struggle. The materiality of economic struggle saw the expression of the first moments of organization and developed an entire political movement: in this essential condition, the political struggle of the proletariat finds the strength to attack the totality of the determinate social formation in which it finds itself.

This is the main passage in *What Is to Be Done?* Political struggle is not merely economic struggle: if political struggle is kept at the level of the factory, if spontaneous organization cannot fathom the power to break the indefinite process of economic struggle and overcome itself in the determination of an act of subjective will that is constituted externally in terms of a totality, well, unless this occurs, the process of organization cannot reach the level of the determinate social formation and its needs. With this, though in terms of method, we approach the core themes presented by Lenin in this period and even more so in the future. Both historically and logically, in Lenin the need for an organization of this kind emerges from the analysis of the determinate social formation and of the determinate working-class movement in the particular phase to which he directs his practical reflections. Here theory does not wish to be a negation of the spontaneity of economic struggle. On the contrary, it is its internal critique and comes from within the formidable and spontaneous mass movement that determined itself. Here—

allow me the paradox—the organization break is presented as continuity: this is a useful paradox if the need for a break in the organization presents itself to Lenin at different times as a characteristic of its pace. Therefore, only by descending deeply down to these levels of the masses, economism and spontaneism, could social democracy acquire the ability to leap and assume leadership; and this corresponds with a particular phase of the revolutionary process in Russia, because it displays a special kind of power relation between classes, a particular form of composition of the working class. To this, we will return in our next conversation. For the time being, we are interested in looking deeper into what we have named the continuity of the leap, because it is characteristically constituted inside the mass movement, exists in the spontaneous movement, and is founded on an internal reading and a critique of the spontaneous movement of the masses, and we have insisted on these points. But it is now time to analyze the characteristics of this leap forward.

The text *What Is to Be Done?* from 1902 is renowned as being fundamentally linked to the debate on article 1 of the statute of the Russian social democratic party, and is a key text because the polemic it develops would later determine a historical break in the Russian revolutionary movement. (The edition by Strada is useful because it reproduces all the materials relevant to the debate internal to Russian social democracy on the statute and *What Is to Be Done?* and thus includes all of the polemic and what led up to it in the appendix.) What does the refusal to bow to spontaneity mean? What is the ability to lead social democracy? First of all, we have some negative determinations. The first opposes the ability to lead social democracy to *fabbrichismo*, to "the 'drab everyday struggle' in the narrow confines of factory life."[17] The second is the refusal to permit any principle of "tactical-process," any organizational determination that would programmatically become confused with the development of the struggles themselves:

> The fundamental error committed by the "new trend" in Russian Social
> Democracy lies in its bowing to spontaneity and its failure to understand
> that the spontaneity of the masses demands a mass of consciousness from
> us Social Democrats. The greater the spontaneous upsurge of the masses,

the more widespread the movement becomes, so much the more rapidly, incomparably more rapidly, grows the demand for greater consciousness in the theoretical, political and organizational work of Social Democracy.[18]

The third negative determination is the struggle against particularism and localism.[19] In the positive determination of Lenin's refusal to bow to spontaneity, his position is to place a strong emphasis on the centralization of the revolutionary movement.

Political struggle is not only economic struggle. The centralization of the revolutionary movement here is based on the ability to politically unify, from above rather than outside, the diversity of class stratifications, and to turn the urgency of this unification into a *consciousness* of the proletariat as a whole. At this level of development of the productive forces, spontaneity determines a diversified consciousness and a discontinuous level of organization. Effective unification can only be accomplished by a conscious unification and a conscious and external leadership.

The break in the continuity Lenin operates here must be seen in light of the methodological presuppositions discussed earlier. They embed Lenin's discourse in a determinate class composition as defined through a process of determinate abstraction; they thus make it possible to grasp the active motor of the overall process and the power relations that define it, inside a necessary tendency. The relationship between the mass movement and the leadership is posited starting from the determinate reality of the revolutionary relations of the process, from the overall composition proposed by the organization. The concept of determinate social formation, insofar as it results from the principles of determinate abstraction and tendency, dialectically turns into a concept of organization, mediating the specificity of the power relations it conceals while subverting and destroying them. Organization is the reflex of a determinate social relation because the latter is traversed by class struggle, insofar as the revolutionary proletariat is animated by the will to turn all existing power relations on their head and initiate its process of liberation. In the next conversation, we will try to analyze closely the conditions of the political composition of class in which this theoretical process of Leninism becomes defined.

NOTES

1. V. Strada, introduction to the Italian edition of Lenin, *What Is to Be Done?* (Turin: Einaudi, 1972).

2. Vladimir I. Lenin, "What the 'Friends of the People' Are and How They Fight the Social Democrats," in *Collected Works* (Moscow: Progress Publishers, 1894), 1:138.

3. Ibid., 139.

4. On the effects of this attitude up to our times, see Hans-Jürgen Krahl, *Costituzione e lotta di classe* [Constitution and class struggle] (Milan: Jaca Books, 1973), 340–341: "The assumption of a dialectics of nature that makes historical materialism ontological turns the revolutionary theory of the proletariat into a contemplative conception of the world, and impoverishes it by reducing it to a small property of sectarian groups, inheriting all the petty bourgeois forms of decadence of the antiauthoritarian movement that Marxist-Leninist groups fought so hard against. In these conditions, the cadre-school becomes a surrogate of praxis for individuals and groups who always only organize themselves, whatever they do, and Mao's generic statements preclude them from access to the knowledge of the capitalist world they are surrounded by. The closed canon of systematic statements and rigid disciplinary organization are expressions of a surrogate of the strategy of formations, of the needs for security and for connection that prevent the development of productive revolutionary collectives and emancipating needs for liberation, and of revolutionary needs for a political struggle that always demands action and is always full of risks. The contemplative dogmatists of M-L groups resemble those of whom Brecht says 'it seems they only want to make a revolution to impose dialectical materialism.' The ontology of a revolution announced as an 'objective law independent of man's will' repeats, word by word, the quid pro quo of the Second International and Soviet Marxism, the equivalence of a second nature of the capitalist social formation to a first nature that labor must appropriate. The critique of the ideology of the second nature and the importance of an autonomous proletarian consciousness and will as factors of the revolution are a significant contribution to the theory of revolution made by György Lukács in his early works."

5. On Luxemburg's method, see J. P. Nettl, *Rosa Luxemburg* (London: Shocken Books, 1989).

6. For a thorough analysis of the issue of determinate abstraction in Marx's and subsequent thought, see the following works: A. V. Ilyenkov, *Dialectics of the Abstract and the Concrete* (Moscow: Progress Publishers, 1982); L. Colletti, *Marxism and Hegel*, trans. L. Garner (London: Verso, 1979); J. C. Michaud, *Teoria e storia nel Capitale di Marx* [*Theory and history* in Marx's *Capital*] (Milan: Feltrinelli, 1960).

7. V. I. Lenin, preface to the second edition of *The Development of Capitalism in Russia*, in *Collected Works* (Moscow: Progress Publishers, 1977), 3:30.

8. Ibid., 3:50.

9. V. I. Lenin, *The Three Sources and Three Component Parts of Marxism*, in *Collected Works* (Moscow: Progress Publishers, 1968), 19:23.

10. V. I. Lenin, *The Tasks of the Russian Social Democrats*, in *Collected Works* (Moscow: Progress Publishers, 1972), 2:343. On the relation between Lenin and the Second International in general, see G. Hayot in *Rivista storica del socialismo* [Socialist historical review] 29 (September-December, 1966). But on the intensity of the misunderstanding and ideological distortions of the Russian situation in the German and international public opinion, see L. Stern et al., *Die russische Revolution von 1905–1907 im Spiegel der deutschen* (Berlin: Rutten & Loning, 1961).

11. For an overview of the wave of struggles at the turn of the century and the formation of Russian social democracy, see O. Anweller and K. H. Ruffmann, *Kulturpolitik der Sowjetunion* (Stuttgart: Alfred Kroner Verlag, 1973), a text we will return to when analyzing the Soviet. See also V. Zilli, *La rivoluzione russa del 1905: La formazione dei partiti politici, 1881–1904* (Naples: Istituto italiano per gli Studi storici, 1963); T. Dan, *The Origins of Bolshevism* (London: Schocken Books, 1965); S. Schwarz, *The Russian Revolution of 1905: The Workers' Movement and the Formation of Bolshevism and Menschevism*, trans. G. Vakar (Chicago: University of Chicago Press, 1967).

12. Lenin, *Tasks of the Russian Social Democrats*, 2:332.

13. Lenin, *"Left-Wing" Communism, an Infantile Disorder* (Peking: Foreign Language Press, 1970), 199.

14. Lenin, *What Is to Be Done? Burning Questions of Our Movement* (Peking: Foreign Language Press, 1973), 35.

15. Lenin, *First All Russia Congress of Soviets of Workers' and Soldiers' Deputies*, in *Collected Works*, vol. 25, trans. S. Apresyan and J. Riordan (Moscow: Progress Publishers, 1974).

16. Lenin, *What Is to Be Done?*, 107.

17. Ibid., 88.

18. Ibid., 64.

19. Lenin, *Tasks of the Russian Social Democrats*, 2:342.

3

FROM THE THEORY OF CAPITAL TO THE THEORY OF ORGANIZATION (2)

The Working-Class Character of Organization:
The Party as Factory

I N THE PREVIOUS lesson we saw how the methodological framework Lenin provides for his reading of *Capital* and the relation he establishes between the theory of capital and the theory of the working-class movement led to a series of consequences that form the basis of the discussion on organization, using concepts such as determinate social formation. We saw how this discourse unfolds through an appreciation of the movements of spontaneity and economic struggle, which would become fundamental to Lenin's thought throughout his experience. We have also seen how a descent into the concreteness of the composition of the working class and the proletariat as a whole would be crucial to his overall theory. But we also recognized that one of the most characteristic moments in Lenin's discourse is how the tendency to dwell and penetrate the concreteness of the revolutionary subject also immediately points to a need for a qualitative leap; that is to say, that the continuity of class struggle in its spontaneous form, with its insistence on the immediate needs of the proletariat, must, at some point, be overcome. The adherence to this concreteness of the working-class movement is as important, since one must not be subjugated by it but must put forward an overall intelligence and ability for the working class to lead itself and, insofar as this comes from its outside, to lead the whole proletariat. The path is straightforward: the shift to the issue of external leadership emerges out of a close class analysis from within, and arises from an increasing awareness of the internal political needs of class, starting from organized autonomy. The courage and the difficulty of walking and having walked this path push for its verification and extension to organization: "We are marching in a compact group along a precipitous and difficult path, firmly holding each other by the hand. We are surrounded on all sides by enemies, and we have to advance under their almost constant fire. We have combined voluntarily, precisely for the purpose of fighting the enemy, and not to retreat into the adjacent marsh."[1]

This first decisive leap occurs around the beginning of the twentieth century and needs to be analyzed closely in order to unravel its implications. To sum up the presuppositions of this conceptualization, the first issue we need to be aware of is the depth and constancy of Lenin's perception and insistence on the spontaneity of class processes. The second issue is the logical character of Lenin's style, his ability to proceed from within the context of problems, to appreciate them with great analytical strength, and to then break, through an internal decision, with the continuity of the issue in a manner that is adequate to the problems that arose. The third moment of note that confirms the continuity of the shift is the absolutely *working-class character* of Lenin's *notion of an organization that is external to class*. In this lesson I would like to dwell on this point.

Let us look at another text that introduces this working-class character of external organization. We have seen that *What Is to Be Done?* is the main text establishing a discourse on organization, and how this text is not only born out of a need for theoretical analysis, but also immediately tied to a political debate internal to the discussion on the first statute of the party.[2] Here, Lenin's polemic is waged against everyone who does not see the shift toward organization as a shift to a degree of centralization of the movement, and thus as the determination of an external direction of the mass movement and the enucleating of a moment of political leadership in the form and content of both strategy and program. On this, there is a beautiful passage, worth reading:

> The *Rabocheye Dyelo*'s assertions—which we have analyzed above—that the economic struggle is the most widely applicable means of political agitation and that our task now is to lend the economic struggle itself a political character, etc., express a narrow view not only of our political, but also of our organi-

zational tasks. The "economic struggle against the employers and the government" does not in the least require—and therefore such a struggle can never give rise to—an all-Russian centralized organization that will combine, in one general onslaught, all and every manifestation of political opposition, protest and indignation, an organization that will consist of professional revolutionaries and be led by the real political leaders of the whole people. This is but natural. The character of any organization is naturally and inevitably determined by the content of its activity. Consequently, the *Rabocheye Dyelo*, by the assertions analyzed above, sanctifies and legitimizes not only the narrowness of political activity, but also the narrowness of organizational work. In this case too, as always, it is an organ whose consciousness yields to spontaneity. And yet the worship of spontaneously developing forms of organization, failure to realize how narrow and primitive is our organizational work, what amateurs we still are in this most important sphere, failure to realize this, I say, is a veritable disorder from which our movement suffers. It is not a disorder that comes with decline, it is, of course, a disorder that comes with growth. But it is precisely at the present time, when the wave of spontaneous indignation, as it were, sweeps over us, leaders and organizers of the movement, that a most irreconcilable struggle must be waged against all defence of backwardness, against any legitimization of narrowness in this matter, and it is particularly necessary to rouse in all who take part in practical work, in all who are preparing to take up their work, discontent with the amateurishness that prevails among us and an unshakable determination to get rid of it.[3]

The polemic is first and foremost leveled against those who believe there to be no need for centralized organization in Russia because the organization of the movement across Russia could only occur through the development of struggle: this is the theory of "organization as process," that is, of an organization that comes into being directly within the process of struggles rather than by means of an act of political decision that transcends the process itself. Lenin's adversaries defend not only a theory of organization in process, but also a theory of struggle in process, that is, a struggle that arises from, spreads, and develops without internal moments of general unification, general collision, or reunification into one struggle. Third moment: Lenin's adversaries deny the possibility of a professional revolutionary organization where the effective political leaders of the whole people can meet. Beyond a theory of organization as process, beyond a theory of organization as struggle, there is a theory of leadership as process, whereby leadership cannot be a stable and professional struggle of political cadres, because these could never coincide with the effective political leaders of the masses. In the cited passage, following a convincing line of argumentation, Lenin strongly reiterates the urgent need "to establish *an organization of revolutionaries* capable of maintaining the energy, stability and continuity of the political struggle."[4]

What interests us here is the rule defined in this passage and in Lenin's work of this period as a whole. The rule of the shift to organization is that the more spontaneous and economic struggles develop, the more the need for a shift to a level of organization increases. Lenin shows no indulgence in notions of organization based on the theory of reflux of struggles, of "resistance," and so on. On the contrary, the function of mass offensives and the ponderous wave of spontaneity impose a dialectical shift to organization. The image of this formidable billow, this impetuous growth of spontaneous struggle, reflects the mechanisms of argumentation of the spontaneists; but it also overwhelms them, because, here, to asseverate rather than deny the analysis of spontaneity, Lenin decides to impose the shift to organization. Organization is the verification of spontaneity, its refinement, while a code-driven attitude to spontaneity and organized primitivism, elevated and branded as an elegy of spontaneity, is a grave digger in this phase. Reality is dialectic; spontaneity is the dialectical basis of the shift to organization: when this shift does not take place, spontaneity itself is wretched and neutralized. Spontaneity, in this case, becomes organizational impotence. Its development prevents its own chance to configure itself as the totality of the revolutionary process. Organization is spontaneity reflecting upon itself. Otherwise it is impotence and defeat that try to justify themselves.

In those years the polemic continues on all aspects pertaining to spontaneism as organizational opportunism. The time and themes of the polemic return in a passage from *One Step Forward, Two Steps Back*:

We fought opportunism on the fundamental problems of our world conception, on the questions of our programme, and the complete divergence of aims inevitably led to an irrevocable break between the Social-Democrats and the liberals who had corrupted our legal Marxism. We fought opportunism on tactical issues, and our divergence with Comrades Krichevsky and Akimov on these less important issues was naturally only temporary, and was not accompanied by the formation of different parties. We must now vanquish the opportunism of Martov and Axelrod on questions of organisation, which are, of course, less fundamental than questions of tactics, let alone of programme, but which have now come to the forefront in our Party life.[5]

Questions of organization are less essential than those of program and tactics, Lenin says! Only if we understand correctly the relationship established here between, on the one hand, dialectical theory and the definition of the determinate social formation and, on the other, the theory of the working-class movement can we appreciate this statement, so unusual and unacceptable to the organization fetishism typical of the Leninist tradition. The fact is that the material referent of the movement, the scientifically recordable spontaneity of the working-class science of program and tactics, is more important: it *logically* precedes the problem of organization. Organization is the completion of a material referent, and its question can become or, as in the time Lenin analyzes, be *historically* primary.

Since we looked at the specificity of Lenin's shift to the issue of organization, it is now time to consider the working-class character of organization itself. Initially, we investigated the relationship between spontaneity and organization and what determines the singular moments of their synthesis. We then saw that social democratic organization is formed within a determinate social formation and defined by the parameters and relations that working-class knowledge describes. The rule of the shift to organization is verified in this context: in more general and abstract, but no less valid, terms, we will see that this rule expresses a variable relationship between spontaneity and organization marked by a greater or lesser intensity that depends on the power relations between classes in struggle. That is, the force of the dialectical shift is directly proportional to the strength of capitalist power and inversely proportional to the strength and maturity of the working class. The whole of the relations Lenin describes through the category of determinate social formation is grasped in the concept of *class composition*, closer and more suited to us, which develops Lenin's lesson in this direction. The political composition of the proletariat is understood as the determination of the needs, comportments, and degrees of political consciousness manifested in the working class as a subject at a given historical juncture. The concept of determinate subject is understood to be the working class as it confronts a whole series of power relations that connects it, as a subject, to other emerging social strata of the proletariat, as well as to other forces that face the proletariat, be they irreducibly antagonistic or susceptible to accepting the revolutionary hegemony of the working class. In other words, the political composition of the proletariat is the dialectical fiber sustained by the revolutionary subject, which Maoism defines through "class analysis." In Mao's works, this analysis is a grounding necessary for all political work to determine, from the standpoint of the revolutionary subject, the interweaving of the different components of the proletariat into power relations and to include, from the standpoint of antagonism, the other side of the dialectical relation. From the perspective of organization, class analysis functions as a way of determining the location of the organizational subject and the dimensions of its political impact on society as a whole. Obviously, there is a huge difference between the notion of class composition and the series of relations found in Maoist class analysis: the content of subjectivity we attribute to the working class in highly developed capitalist countries and its ability to situate itself in class divisions actively and hegemonically are infinitely superior to the possibilities of Maoist theory. But this is also further proof of the validity of the Leninist rule of organization. The difference is explicit in the fact that from the Maoist perspective the subject carrying out the analysis is essentially the subject of the organization, a party point of view dialectically linked yet external to class, whereas as far as we are concerned the kind of maturity and subjectivity that we can attribute to a working class that composed itself in mature capitalist development entails a subjectivity and higher analytical consciousness capable of developing the analysis immediately from inside class. (This working-class subjectivity was named, in slightly polemical terms, "working-class science" to recognize an effective tendency.)

The application of the Leninist rule of the shift to organization in Lenin himself presented specific characteristics too. The definition of the duality and externality of the point of view of the party and leadership in relation to the class movement is, as we have seen, in a direct relationship with the growth of the spontaneous struggles that are a permanent and not sporadic object of Lenin's analysis throughout the 1890s. But the shift from this very high level of spontaneity, from this diffuse subjectivity and appreciation of working-class strength as a hegemonic subject, is later mediated toward the point of view of organization and its externality as a function of leadership and political recomposition, through the exaltation of some of the characteristics that are proper in a (given) political composition of class. The first specific characteristic directly involves the recognition of the absolute need for an organizational centralization of social democracy in Russia, a need evidenced both by the autocracy in Russia and by the conspiratorial tradition of the movement. From this first standpoint, Lenin appreciates and validates an element of the tradition of the struggles and the evaluation of their particular conditions. In the struggle against autocracy, the pursuit of the greatest effectiveness of struggle and terrorism, insofar as these had been the fundamental weapons of the populist movement, and, in the beginning, of social democracy itself, had entailed from the very first moments of emergence of revolutionary organization in Russia a maximum level of centralization and the use of conspiratorial rules. Here there is a fundamental difference between the rise of social democracy in Russia and Western European countries, for instance. In Western Europe, social democracy is essentially born out of the lever of the union, from a diffuse process subsequently unified by intellectual groups or intellectualized workers' vanguards that constitute the party through various attempts at aggregation. In the specific conditions of the revolutionary process in Russia, in a regime of autocracy, this process is completely different: despite its far reaching character, the movement never manages to give itself forms of legal organization that go beyond spontaneity. Spontaneous revolts and riots develop without managing to group up: here, in a preliminary way, the idea of an absolute need for a central nucleus of leadership is formed precisely as an appreciation of the specific character of the struggle against autocracy and against the ferocious centrality of repression. The formation of a central nucleus is a response to a series of comportments filtered by the need for struggle and already becomes part and parcel of the comportments of the revolutionary movement.

The second specific characteristic of the rule of organization in Lenin's Russia is also linked to the specificity of the political composition of class struggle there, the proof and character of the party form as external leadership: it is the working-class character of organization. Lenin's merit is to have powerfully revealed this specificity of organization. One might say that the more the action of the vanguard needs to be defined in an external, generic, and recompositional form, the more Lenin insists on this character of organization. For him, the model of organization is the factory in the fullest meaning of the term. The power of capital is invading Russia and transforming it in a formidable and dramatic way. Adopting a Marxian outlook, Lenin follows the two faces of capitalist development: on the one hand, the cold-blooded smirk at the formidable power of capital as a productive force, for its authentic revolutionizing of social conditions, through the growth of the productive forces; on the other hand, an implacable hatred for the exploitation and wage subjugation of labor. In Russia, the drama of development is greater when the first phase of industrialization is both primitive and extensive. The formation of the Russian social democratic party occurs within the process described by Lenin in *The Development of Capitalism in Russia*, published in 1898. What is the factory in this context? It is the place of the formation of the first nuclei of the working class, where, aside from exploitation, they learn organization, this superior form of labor organization, which despite exploitation presents a higher degree of rationality and sophistication of production through labor cooperation. These are the characteristics that the organizational model of the party must concentrate on. The party, too, must be able to organize and form the multiplicative character of revolutionary labor, exalting and subverting against capital the very thing that it determines as a growth of the productive power of socialized labor. The party is a factory; it is an enterprise of subversion, an ability to impose a multiplier of productive rationality onto the revolutionary will of militants and the spontaneity of the masses. The party turns this primary matter, which is workers' insubordination, into the accumulation of revolution, into a generic power to attack the adversary.

Lenin's insistence on professionalism, centralization, and the division of labor in the party is fundamental and continues in *What Is to Be Done?, One Step Forward, Two Steps Back,* and the rest of his works from these years. A few references will suffice to grasp the overall spirit of his discourse. On the professionalism and centralization of the party: "no revolutionary movement can endure without a stable organization of leaders that maintains continuity. . . . Such an organization must consist chiefly of people professionally engaged in revolutionary activity."[6] On centralization and the division of labor: "specialization necessarily presupposes centralization, and in turn imperatively calls for it."[7] "Conspiratorial organization" of combat.[8]

Above all, in the following passage the Leninist model of the party is clearly outlined:

For instance, this same "Practical Worker" of the new *Iskra* with whose profundity we are already familiar denounces me for visualising the Party "as an immense factory" headed by a director in the shape of the Central Committee (No. 57, Supplement). "Practical Worker" never guesses that this dreadful word of his immediately betrays the mentality of the bourgeois intellectual unfamiliar with either the practice or the theory of proletarian organisation. For the factory, which seems only a bogey to some, represents that highest form of capitalist co-operation which has united and disciplined the proletariat, taught it to organise, and placed it at the head of all the other sections of the toiling and exploited population. And Marxism, the ideology of the proletariat trained by capitalism, has been and is teaching unstable intellectuals to distinguish between the factory as a means of exploitation (discipline based on fear of starvation) and the factory as a means of organisation (discipline based on collective work united by the conditions of a technically highly developed form of production). The discipline and organisation which come so hard to the bourgeois intellectual are very easily acquired by the proletariat just because of this factory "schooling." Mortal fear of this school and utter failure to understand its importance as an organising factor are characteristic of the ways of thinking which reflect the petty-bourgeois mode of life and which give rise to the species of anarchism that the German Social-Democrats call *Edelanarchismus,* that is, the anarchism of the "noble" gentleman, or aristocratic anarchism, as I would call it. This aristocratic anarchism is particularly characteristic of the Russian nihilist. He thinks of the Party organisation as a monstrous "factory"; he regards the subordination of the part to the whole and of the minority to the majority as "serfdom" (see Axelrod's articles); division of labour under the direction of a centre evokes from him a tragi-comical outcry against transforming people into "cogs and wheels" (to turn editors into contributors being considered a particularly atrocious species of such transformation); mention of the organisational Rules of the Party calls forth a contemptuous grimace and the disdainful remark (intended for the "formalists") that one could very well dispense with Rules altogether.[9]

This is no simple polemic! In fact, this concept of the party and organization as a factory is adequate to the actual level at which the project of Leninist organization develops, reproducing the technical and political composition of the proletariat; it develops by making itself adequate to an ideology of organized labor typical of the large factory and of the class vanguard in Russia, also taking into account the internal and determinate characteristic of the shift we have described, where in fact capital and the organization of the factory are a formidable step forward in the formation and consolidation of an industrial proletariat as a material vanguard of the struggle. What develops in this shift is not only the material activity of the working class, but also its highest level of subjectivity as class, and therefore as comportments, needs, and quality of life. In this we find an application of some of the fundamental criteria of historical materialism, from which Lenin's definition of the party grasps a level of class composition in an absolutely correct manner. At that level of composition, the factory is able to form a conscious vanguard, exalting the organizational moment and providing the conditions for emancipation, in a way that is all the more clear as the exploitation that a backward society such as Russia is subjected to gets deeper. For this reason, on the issue of organization for Lenin, the very interiority of the standpoint of the working class determines the need for external leadership. For this reason, the working-class character of Lenin's analysis demands as its conclusion and consequence the definition of a relation of organization and leadership that is external to the proletariat as a whole. For this reason, Lenin's adherence to an overall situation of the Russian proletariat and to the definition of the levers that will destroy this system determines that conception of the party. The way Lenin speaks of the party as a generalized necessity is similar to the way he speaks of the material economic needs and demands of the masses: "We emasculate the most vital needs of the proletariat, namely, its political needs"[10] unless we develop a struggle for this kind of party.

I believe that it is not abstract phrases or models we need to learn from Lenin, but more importantly, this mode of relating to the revolutionary process and working-class subjectivity; we need to ask ourselves how the working class is composed today, what the need is for an organization that arises from its determinate composition, which is undoubtedly different today from what Lenin described. However, the object of this lesson is not to answer this question: what matters is that we start a series of verifications beyond the texts to gather some general ideas on the process of organization, going through Lenin's discourse as it moves from the theory of capital to the theory of organization. This task can only be accomplished if we believe that "in its struggle for power the proletariat has no other weapon but organisation."[11]

NOTES

1. Lenin, *What Is to Be Done? Burning Questions of Our Movement* (Peking: Foreign Language Press, 1973), 10.
2. See V. Strada, introduction to the Italian edition of Lenin, *What Is to Be Done?* (Turin: Einaudi, 1972).
3. Lenin, *What Is to Be Done?*, 122.
4. Ibid., 129.
5. Lenin, *One Step Forward, Two Steps Back: The Crisis in Our Party*, trans. A. Fineberg and N. Jochel, in *Collected Works* (Moscow: Progress Publishers, 1965), 7:404.
6. Lenin, *What Is to Be Done?*, 152–153.
7. Ibid., 160.
8. Ibid., 167.
9. Lenin, *One Step Forward*, 7:391–392.
10. Lenin, *Two Tactics of Social Democracy in the Democratic Revolution* (Peking: Foreign Language Press, 1965), 102.
11. Lenin, *One Step Forward*, 7:415.

4

IN LENIN'S FOOTSTEPS FROM THE THEORY OF CAPITAL TO THE THEORY OF ORGANIZATION

Annotations

WE HAVE NOW come to the first point of verification in our debate. What this entails is an attempt to determine not so much the correctness of Lenin's journey from the theory of capital to the theory of organization, in its historically determined moment or, to use his terms, in its determinate social formation, but rather a definition, problematic as it may be, of the correspondence between Lenin's discourse and the problems that the theory of class struggle presents us with today. We will later apply this kind of analysis to another fundamental shift in Lenin, that from the theory of organization to the theory of insurrection (in lessons 5, 6, 7, and 8). But let us now deal with the first question.

Undoubtedly, on this issue, the main question, in *What Is to Be Done?* and in the outline of a theory of the party, concerns the shift from economic to political struggle, from particularity to generality, from the process of struggle to the external consciousness of the political generality of the conflict. We have already seen how this shift occurs in a given political composition of the Russian working class, how it is placed in that particular phase of class struggle and the power relations between those classes, and correspondingly in the structures of production as they are based on a dialectics of antagonism. *On the one hand,* there is an ongoing process of industrialization and the formation of some class vanguards, which are splitting; *on the other hand,* there is the rest of the country, involved as it is in the difficult labor of exiting semifeudal or precapitalist modes of production, a working class limited but now able to assume and configure, in itself, and by virtue of its contradictory relation with the overall development of society, a concept of organization as a general interpretation of the needs of society as a whole. This workers' vanguard actually finds itself in the position of having to interpret the need for a shift to a higher level of labor organization and a more advanced reconfiguration of social relations: while fighting against exploitation, the working class posits itself as the interpreter of this development. This historical paradox of the revolution common to all underdeveloped countries finds its most extreme expression in Lenin's Russia. The fight against exploitation is here a fight for development, a struggle to build the conditions of liberation from exploitation and, simultaneously, a struggle against exploitation, against labor, to build a communist society. It is precisely in such dramatic relation that the correspondence between Lenin's thought and a determinate class structure finds its place: the workers' consciousness is external to class and to the whole of the proletariat. In this determinate situation, the need for an overall recomposition of development and of the struggle against exploitation cannot be carried forward by a vanguard without an external project and leadership: but this externality is still entirely workers' based—it is the recording and subversion of a situation that capital exploits for its own development and the development of exploitation, and that must instead be assumed in the theory of the party as the driving force of the revolution. Here again the proletarians storm the heaven. The problem seems unsolvable within the everyday of political discourse: and yet, the determined moment in Lenin's discussion, where the correctness of his treatment of the determinate social formation and the status of class struggle of his times is shown, is this giant effort to subvert a given structure that is consolidated in the capitalist mode of production, in the determinate phase of Russian development, and to subvert it in order to turn it, instead, into the key to the subversion and destruction of the overall command of this development. Lenin proceeds from an assumption of the particular class interest: this deep assumption of the "general" is imposed by an adherence to the class particular.

Let us now move on to the second problem: does Lenin's discussion, which is correct in relation to its given social situation, correspond to our needs? Evidently, for it to correspond to our needs, there would have to be a significant degree of homogeneity between the kind of political class composition that Lenin's analysis is situated in and the kind of political class composition that Marxist analysis operates in today. In fact, we can immediately note some instances of great heterogeneity that emerge from a material analysis of facts, with respect to both working-class comportments and the overall analysis of the power relations, and hence the needs, organizational forms, and even mechanisms that spontaneity assumes in the current situation. With particular reference to the same core problem, two thematic doubles are completely reconfigured in our situation: these are the relationship between the particular and the general, and the relationship between the economic and the political. Undoubtedly (from the standpoint of the working class, but even more so from the standpoint of capital), whereas in the context of Lenin's times and their class composition these doubles presented themselves as alternatives within which the subjective will to impose an organizational shift needed to be exercised, now their antagonistic form has dissipated. This is to say that today at a stage of capitalist development where control needs to extend not simply to the level of the factory but to the level of society as a whole, today in a phase of capitalist development where the process of valorization and realization of capital requires conditions that involve society globally, the very terms of the socialist project (particular and general interest, private and public, and so on) fade and tend to merge into nothingness. The factory walls, as they are empirically given, crumble. The specific process of factory exploitation extends over the whole of society, and capitalist exploitation actually turns the form of control of the relation between factory and society into a continuum: control is such that this continuity is verified and consolidated.[1] If we read the problem of continuity between the economic and the political not only from the standpoint of capital but from that of the workers, we grasp it in the same terms, with an accentuation that is typical of the sectarian position of the workers against capital: thus we identify the reasons for the terrible precariousness of capitalist domination today. Because in fact, insofar as this continuity was determined, insofar as factory control has had to spread to the whole of the social process of valorization of capital, insofar as the economic revolt could be immediately configured as a political struggle, this attacks not only the field of the relation of exploitation in the factory, but the whole of the social conditions that allow for the determination of the exploitation in the factory.

Only a few years ago, these elementary truths seemed hidden, but they are now assumed even by the official working-class movement, whatever distortions they are submitted to. Reformism assumes the continuity between economic and political struggle as its necessary foundation, mystifying in this continuity the antagonistic character of workers' struggles. However, in Italy and all of the countries of developed capitalism (and the demonstration of this comes from the workers' struggles of our times), we know that where the last and most general phase of subsumption of labor under capital occurs (to say it in Marx's terms), capital covers the whole of society and there are no longer any forms of production or cooperation that are external to capitalist domination. The totality of capitalist domination over society in this phase is realized, to say it with Marx, as "real subsumption."[2] The situation that Lenin describes in *The Development of Capitalism in Russia* can be defined as the last phase of the "formal subsumption" of labor under capital, where by formal subsumption we mean a mode of production that without being directly capitalist entails the hegemony of the capitalist world over the market and the circulation of commodities, though they are still produced in various and diverse ways. This is the situation in Russia that Lenin analyses, where there is still a vast amount of precapitalist forms of production despite the tendency of capitalism to dominate them.

But this is no longer the situation we experience, despite the fantasies of the most fervid apologists of the orthodoxy of the situation Lenin describes. Instead, our condition is defined by a relationship of direct domination of capital over society through a series of mechanisms that can be described analytically, though the materiality of this description is always changing, as a relation that sees the spread of capital over the globe and the whole of the social fabric, so that, conversely and consistently, there is a need for an objective and determinate recomposition of class, which is regarded as an essential premise of the analysis. Therefore, from this standpoint, one of the most specific and fundamental presupposition of Lenin's discourse does not apply. The shift from particularity to generality, from economic to political struggle (with its wealth of implications), loses the meaning it had in Lenin's thought.

Of course, for Lenin the shift from economic to political struggle does not exclude the possibility that at some junctures the economic struggle is as valid as the political one; but the problem lies elsewhere: the problem is that for Lenin, beyond a certain limit, political struggle is no longer economic, and in general, political struggles are not only economic struggles. Conversely, today, in our situation, economic and political struggles are completely identical, and this assumption leads to crucial changes both in terms of the theory of organization and, as far as questions we will later analyze are concerned, from the theory of the revolution to the theory of the dictatorship of the proletariat. These are changes that affect the whole of Leninist theory and, above all, as we will see in part 4, the conception of the withering-away of the state. Here we begin to express ourselves on this issue.

At this point, it is legitimate to ask what we agree with Lenin on. From the standpoint of opportunism, so long as we deny any equivalence between the determinate social formations Lenin operates in and our current situation, the problem is solved: when reformists predicate the pacifist path to socialism, the reforms of structures, and the other weapons that belong to the arsenal of their lies, they claim to be in agreement with Lenin's *method* and that the problem can be solved by substantiating this method with the differences that emerge in determinate historical situations one by one. In my view, this distinction between method and substance, methodological and material determinations, is one of the biggest theoretical betrayals of the whole tradition of theory, especially of Marxist practice. The distinction between method and substance, between form and content, is entirely one with idealist thought and belongs to an essential theoretical need of capital to mark distinctions in the continuity of its own domination of the variety of contents on which it exercises itself. Unsurprisingly, bourgeois law, a fundamental and privileged instrument of the capitalist organization of society as well as a theory of the *form* of domination, often relies on its ability to develop vast and adequate modes of application to different contents that the new comportments of the working class and the new forms of insubordination present it with. The law is a fluid and effective form placed to cover up the holes that, in the compact system of bourgeois domination, are opened by workers' subversion. Only capital, insofar as its development and domination over development are determined by the workers' struggles, finds this distinction between form and content of any use.

To use the distinction is useless and unpleasant. Therefore, the answer to the question of how Leninist we are is far from being that Lenin's method is fine but we don't like the substance of his discourse. On the contrary, we answer that our agreement with Lenin can only be found starting from the totality of the standpoint of the working class that is proper to this determinate social formation, without even raising the question of continuity or discontinuity with the Leninist tradition. Our Leninism is an outcome, not a premise; the entire Marxian tradition is premised on class struggle, not the assumption of theoretical questions: theories that arise from and place themselves outside the struggle and the determinate relations in which it develops, theories that do not turn into a revolutionary material force, have no place in the Marxian tradition. Theoretical problems, when isolated from the determinate location of each social force in the development of struggles, have no place in the Marxian tradition. Therefore, the only answer that can be given to the question of how far we are Leninists today is that we are Leninists insofar as from within our contemporary determinate situation we affirm a class standpoint geared toward subversion. Clearly there can be times when Lenin's discourse is summed up and valued, but as the outcome of a confrontation, not as a premise.

At this stage, we can see things from a second perspective, with reference to a problem that was recently raised in a debate among reformists. The debate concerns the concept of determinate social formation and the polemic that split Sereni from Luporini:[3] moving from a comparison between Marx's and Lenin's category of "forms" of "economic formations," they both note their difference, but Sereni characterizes the Leninist category in the traditional terms of Gramscianism, that is, in terms of political science, whereas Luporini defines it in more modern, structuralist terms, as the definite index of a synchronic analysis. Going back to the questions we have raised in this conversation, let us ask, for us and in relation to these analysts, what the value is of the category of "determinate social formation," and in what ways we can adopt it in our stock of knowledge in the struggle. Initially, when compared with the pacifying and naive historicism of Sereni, Luporini seems to be right. After clarifying the difference between the concept of determinate social formation and the concept of economic formation in Marx, Luporini claims that in Marx the shift from different forms of production (from Asian to feudal, capitalist, and communist) entails a continuing progress and is thus based on a historicist projection (that also corresponds to his general notion of development), whereas in Lenin, there is a deeply different, punctual, and scientifically fixed determination. In this, we believe, Luporini tries to come close to the concept of political class composition that emerges from more *recent* Marxian research (especially that which originated in Italy with *operaismo*, but also including some motifs of structuralism in its historical genesis). Our agreement with Luporini, however, ends here; in fact, from this point onward our views go in opposite directions, because the expunction of the methodological elements of historicism cannot allow for a split between the Marxian and the Leninist category: while historicism separates the two, dialectics unites them. Moreover, if the Leninist concept of determinate social formation is different from that of "historical formation" used by Marx in the analysis of the overall economic development (from the Asian mode of production up to communism), we still nonetheless find the notion of determinate social formation in Marx, often confused and at times juxtaposed with that of historical formation, but always present. In this debate, albeit not always explicitly, Marx presents a series of elements that entail constructing a concept of working class and its composition; these are, if not more mature, very close to Lenin's definition—it is their premise, in fact. There are two moments worth focusing on in this respect: the first concerns the definition of the wage and the relationship between the constitutive moments of the wage (both quantitative and qualitative) and its composition, that is, the quality determined by the working class. The second moment can be traced in the theory of class antagonism and its effects on institutions, which Marx discusses mainly in his historical writings.

On the first issue, Marx offers a clear exposition, from the early writings up to the *Grundrisse* and *Capital*: that is, the determination of the relationship between wage levels, technical levels, political levels, and the subjective quality of class, and therefore the analysis of the constant transformation that class is subject to and of which it is a subject. If the wage corresponds to determinate needs and has paid for that essential aspect for the capitalist system that is the

reproduction of the workforce, if the definition of the wage includes "historical and moral" elements and these constantly change, then with it changes the
quality of the workforce reproduced and the very mechanism of reproduction.[4] These dialectical elements together make up the historically changeable
structure that characterizes the very substance of the concept of class and are
the foundation of its dialectical reality and, consequently, also the dialectical
mechanism of the revolutionary development of its composition. Marx outlines, in generic terms, a progressive trajectory from structure to structure. For
instance, the English proletariat of the middle nineteenth century is radically
different from the proletariat as we know it today, when among the costs of
the reproduction of the workforce a certain use of social goods needs to be
taken into account, and the relationship between the satisfaction of needs and
the demand for power must be identified. In any case, here we can read the
following: (a) a homogeneous use of the concept of composition, insofar as
both structures are defined by a dialectical whole of materially differentiated
components; (b) the dialectical moment of development, where the subjective
composition of the proletariat finds, in an open-ended relation between needs
and struggle against exploitation, the space for a demand for power. *The concept
of composition (of determinate social formation with reference to class) becomes an
operative concept here.* In Marx's theory of the wage, the relationship between
the satisfaction of needs and the demand for power becomes less and less
important: at the pace of development today we come to a situation where the
working class (to use the prophetic terms of the *Grundrisse*) is recomposed
not only in terms of a homogeneous offer of social labor (abstract labor), but
also as a "historical individual," the indispensable foundation of the production of all possible wealth, where the relation between labor supply and reproduction of life, as well as the demand for power, is turned on its head, when
compared to the forms of composition of the early nineteenth century. This
perspective in the *Grundrisse* comes to define the working class that no longer
satisfies needs but demands power because its role is so radically essential and
necessary to the process of production that any class movement affects the
whole power structure, determining and undermining its existence.[5]

But this is not enough. In a way that is parallel to it, in his so-called historical writings Marx returns to the analysis of the relation of class composition;

this time he confronts it with a series of institutional moments and builds the foundation of an analysis of the political structures and the composition of the revolutionary subject. If, for instance, we consider his writings on Bonaparte and the Commune, we find a precise and internal analysis not only of the development of class, but also of the power relations that characterize this development, of the historical and political realm where this determinate working class can develop. If it can develop, organization needs to make itself adequate to this possibility and become more and more internal to the kind of development potential described. This is the case both in the event of defeat and in that of victory.[6] The definition of the goals of the proletariat, both material and political, is already there in the classical perspective of Lenin: in Marx's description of the determinacy of the composition and the situation, the notion of a shift from the call for social republic to insurrection and the Commune is verified in and through the same methodological terms we can recognize in Lenin.

So to return to the thread we left halfway through this discussion, we initially saw, in the verification of the validity of Lenin's thought, how a series of statements, especially on the double thematic opposition of particular and general as well as economic and political, no longer applies to the current class composition. We have argued that what we were interested in grasping, to the extent to which we are Leninist, was the operability of the concept of composition, and we subsequently showed, against some contemporary positions, that the concept of composition and the political choices it calls for as such entail and unfold in a complete continuity from Marx to Lenin. Here we reinstate the first conclusion, after this further proof of the orthodox continuity of the methodology we refer to. We cannot imagine a Marxian orthodoxy consisting in anything other than an ability to grasp the revolutionary process and the material laws of development starting from the movement and the struggle and immediately from the organization of refusal, hatred, and the negation of the present state of things. There is no possible continuity of themes unless we characterize and locate the will to insubordination in the political composition of this insubordination. From here derives the specific determination of the proletarian subject; and only starting from this subject can any theoretical proposal begin to be of value, insofar as it is translatable into a practical proposal, played, won, or lost within the specific class struggles.

The acceptance of these presuppositions is a fundamental aspect of this problem in relation to reading Lenin: not to distinguish between method (form) and substance (content), but on the contrary, to assume, from the outset, the same intensity of the practical standpoint that characterized Marx and Lenin and to immediately turn science into the expression of the proletarian subject. Some will accuse us of idealism, and so on. We will remind them that the subject is defined by its material composition: materiality of struggles, wage, institutional location. We are proud of our materialism when confronted with all the old positions that can only praise Leninism in terms of "class consciousness." (Where the other pole of the dualism, the material one, ends up they never tell us: they lost it on the way.) And we are also proud of our materialism in the face of the more recent structuralist apologies for Lenin, which separate the analytical from the subjective moment, the science of the acting materiality from the class struggle.

NOTES

1. For all of these, see Raniero Panzieri, "Sull'uso capitalistico delle macchine nel neo-capitalismo," *Quaderni Rossi* 4 (1964): 257–288.
2. Karl Marx, "Results of the Direct Production Process," in "The Process of Production of Capital," draft of chapter 6 of *Capital* (London: Penguin, 1976).
3. See, in particular, Luporini, "Marx According to Marx," *Critica Marxista* 10 (1972): 48–118, 291–295.
4. Here there is an obvious reference to Marx's analysis of the working day and wages in *Capital*, vol. 1. As for the definition of the general parameters of the concept of political composition of the working class, see my article "Partito operaio contro il lavoro," in Sergio Bologna, Paolo Carpignano, and Antonio Negri, *Crisi e organizzazione operaia* [Crisis and workers' organization] (Milan: Feltrinelli, 1974), 99–160.
5. Karl Marx, *Grundrisse*, trans. M. Nicolaus, ed. Q. Hoare (London: Penguin, 1973).
6. Hans-Jürgen Krahl, *Costituzione e lotta di classe* [Constitution and class struggle] (Milan: Jaca Books, 1973), 183ff.

5

FROM THE THEORY OF ORGANIZATION TO THE STRATEGY OF THE REVOLUTION (1)

Proletarian Independence

W E HAVE SEEN how the analysis of the subject imposes crucial elements on the Leninist model of organization. In particular, the location of the workers' vanguard in relation to the totality of the proletariat determined the externality of revolutionary consciousness. We particularly insisted on Lenin's definition of organization and how his thought is deeply inserted into the reality of the mass development of class struggles; an aspect we have analyzed in this respect is often neglected in the interpretation of Lenin's thought, and that is his emphasis and insistence on the processes of spontaneity, the importance of economic struggle, and its definition, in some respect, of economic struggle as an already political struggle. The second element we insisted on is how, by inserting himself in this kind of process, and by defining the specificity of the Russian proletariat and its working class, Lenin defines a model of organization that corresponds to these characteristics. We concluded that the kind of Leninism we are interested in is that which is able to make this organizational process functional to the particular composition of the working class under each condition inside the "determinate social formation."

In this new series of conversations, I would like to try to clarify a further problem, that is, how in Lenin the shift from the theory of organization to the strategy and tactics of insurrection, and thus revolution, is defined.

In this respect, we immediately need to clear up our ideas, and reiterate that in Lenin, strategic determinations are strictly linked to the "determinate social formation," that is to say, again, to the place of the revolutionary class subject in the overall power relations with other classes and against the present power structures. There are two main problems in Leninist strategy: the problem of the relationship between democracy and socialism, struggle for democracy, and struggle for socialism; and the problem of alliances, in particular, the alliance between the working class and peasants. Both problems are precisely located in Lenin's definition of historically determinate formations in which he operates. The methodological criteria that will emerge from the kind of analysis we intend to carry out are likely to be as relevant as the outcomes of the investigation of our first question were: the definition of the shift from the theory of capital to the theory of organization. In this case too we will equip ourselves with a series of tools that can be renewed by our analysis of the contemporary situation. Again, the two questions that arose in the first part of our conversations will be asked again: First, what is the real dimension of Lenin's discourse on the shift from the theory of organization to the strategy for revolution? And second, how far can Lenin's discourse be made adequate to our determined situation?

At the center of these questions is the concept of determinate social formation, the concept of the workers' subject in the Russian situation. We have seen how this subject turns itself into a revolutionary organization, and the whole of Lenin's theory until 1905 and the first great experience of the struggles of the Russian proletariat on the terrain of insurrection revolves around the question of organization. From 1905 onward, particularly in the text *Two Tactics of Social Democracy in the Democratic Revolution*, Lenin begins to ask the question of a definition of strategy in more complex and definitive terms with respect to the annotations he previously developed, which remain subordinated to the solution of the organizational problem and thus to a definition of the ability of conflict of the proletariat as an organization, as an effective instrument in hitting with an intensity that is equal and contrary to the power of the state. The subversion of this standpoint and the theoretical completion of this perspective are made possible and accelerated by the fact that "revolution undoubtedly teaches with a rapidity and thoroughness which appear incredible in peaceful periods of political development. And, what is particularly important, it teaches not only the leaders, but the masses as well."[1]

Here we find the first fundamental concept for Lenin on this question: that organization is the essential condition for strategy. There can be no strategy without organization, and Lenin will keep reiterating this point from 1905 onward. The reason is clear if we go back to Lenin's definition of organization as a weapon adequate to the emergence of the proletarian subject in the historically determinate situation: in that situation, organization was the only means for the class movements to take on an internal identity, compactness, and some degree of self-consciousness. If the proletariat corresponded to what the analysis of the historical situation demonstrated, it was very fragmentary; if the proletariat could only change with great effort, on the back of the experiences of the vanguards of industrialization on the one hand, and of economic-political struggles of revolutionary vanguards on the other, if all of this was true, then evidently only the organization, that is to say, the hegemony of these advanced sections of the workers over the whole of the proletariat, only the imposition of the standpoint of the workers' vanguards on the whole proletariat, could constitute an effective force to hurt constituted power and become credible to the masses in the course of the revolutionary process. Organization is the condition for strategy because organization is the moment of determination not only of the strength of the proletariat but also of its awareness, insofar as in organization the proletariat recomposes itself. In the Russian conditions of economic development and class struggle, only organization can reunite the proletariat. This is fundamental for Lenin and needs to be remembered in the context of its link to the concept of historical formation and its determination of the proletarian situation: one of dispersion and precariousness that can only be solved through the leading function of the vanguard, as consciousness, and as a moment of internal unification of the proletariat. Therefore, organization is the condition for strategy.

But what is this strategy? In 1905 the social democratic strategy and the Bolshevik one especially essentially point toward the shift to democracy that follows socialism. The main concept Lenin bases himself on is that the strength of the proletariat must, in the strategic perspective, first and foremost determine the capitalist conditions, from the economic point of view, and democratic conditions, from the institutional one, such that its growth can be ensured and strengthened, so as to secure a chance for the proletariat to present itself as a socially hegemonic class and to make itself a candidate as a politically leading class in the course of the revolutionary process. Lenin proposes and subsequently defends this strategy, as he normally does, in the years between 1905 and 1917, though perhaps it is a reductive strategy; it certainly reflects the kind of analysis that concerns the determinate social formation proportionally to specific tasks and forecasts that the organized proletariat will accomplish them. The building of the conditions for the unity of the proletariat is the main task Lenin assigns to social democracy in this phase, and it only becomes possible when the party, the organization of the proletariat, manages to determine its strategy in such a way that it leads the stages of a unified process and thus determines in it new conditions for the shift toward a superior phase of the struggle. The rallying cries of the revolution of 1905 carried forward by social democracy, especially its Bolshevik faction, continue to build the unity of the revolutionary process. This is regarded, on the one hand, as a recomposition of the proletariat under the leadership of the working class and, on the other hand, as the possibility that the party can provoke, push forward, and lead this proletarian unity toward the next stage of the revolutionary struggle for socialism.

For this to happen, further political conditions need to be met. We have seen how organization is the condition of strategy and what this strategy is, but what are the conditions for organization to be *effectively* the condition of this strategy? That is to say, what is a strategy that, while allowing for the shift from the struggle for democracy to the subsequent struggle for socialism, is also able to really determine the continuity of this process and win on this terrain? The first of these conditions is independence, the guarantee of the independence of the proletariat as the hegemonic class of the revolutionary process. The constant relation between the development of proletarian struggle and the goal of the democracy that follows from it must find within itself and in this very same shift the key to the discontinuity of the further leap onto the struggle for socialism. The party is both the continuity of the struggle for democracy and the condition for the unification of the proletariat and of socialist struggle. It is therefore an agent of both continuity and discontinuity in the revolutionary process. The struggle for democracy is a determination of power relations that are advantageous for the proletariat, but insofar as these power relations are given, the proletarian party must turn from the guarantor of the autonomy of the proletariat, from the guarantor of the continuity of the process, into the motor of the discontinuity and rupture of the same process. In *Two Tactics*, Lenin explicitly returns to the decisions of the Third Congress of POSDR (Workers Party of Social Democratic Russia) to clarify that while it is admissible for social democracy to participate in the provisional revolutionary (bourgeois) government, "an indispensable condition for such participation is that the Party should exercise strict control over its representatives and that the independence of the Social-Democratic Party, which is striving for a complete socialist revolution and, consequently, is irreconcilably hostile to all bourgeois parties, should be strictly maintained."[2] "Independence of social democracy": this means that the shift of the social democratic party, of the organized vanguard of the proletariat, through the democratic phase is not a tactical and instrumental objective, but one stage in the construction of a power relation and an effective advancement of the unity of the working class, and only in this strategic and yet conditional way is participation in the bourgeois democratic representation permitted. The referent, the rule of the strategy, is wholly internal to the organization of class struggle. The limits and prospects of the strategy are completely defined by the main goal, which is to preserve the independence of the proletariat. The motor of the strategy is, again, the vanguard, for its need to form itself and lead the shift to insurrection. Importantly, for Lenin this is not a formal problem:

> The final political result of the revolution may prove to be that, in spite of the formal "independence" of Social-Democracy, in spite of its complete organizational individuality as a separate party, it will in fact not be independent, it will not be able to put the imprint of its proletarian independence on the course of events, will prove so weak that, on the whole and in the last analysis, its "dissolving" in the bourgeois democracy will nonetheless be a historical fact.[3]

To clear all doubts, he pushes for an understanding of the synthesis of the shift with strategic prospects in strict and rigid terms. On the one hand,

> the proletariat expects to find its salvation not by avoiding the class struggle but by developing it, by widening it, increasing its consciousness, its organization and determination. Whoever degrades the tasks of the political struggle transforms the Social-Democrat from a tribune of the people into a trade union secretary. Whoever degrades the proletarian tasks in a democratic bourgeois revolution transforms the Social-Democrat from a leader of the people's revolution into a leader of a free labour union.[4]

This is the most important affirmation of the political independence of the proletarian project. On the other hand,

> Social-Democracy has fought, and is quite rightly fighting against the bourgeois-democratic abuse of the word "people." It demands that this word shall not be used to cover up failure to understand the class antagonisms within the people. It insists categorically on the need for complete class independence for the party of the proletariat. But it divides the "people" into "classes," not in order that the advanced class may become shut up within itself, confine itself to narrow aims and emasculate its activity for fear that the economic rulers of the world will recoil, but in order that the advanced class, which does not suffer from the half-heartedness, vacillation and indecision of the intermediate classes, may with all the greater energy and enthusiasm fight for the cause of the whole of the people, at the head of the whole of the people.[5]

This is the most radical interiorization of the synthesis of democracy and revolution, shift and prospect: the independence of the proletariat fully subsumes under itself, controls, and dominates the shifts that it is forced to concede. This is a Marxian and Leninist triumph of the revolutionary dialectics. Whether this is valid is a different question: there, in that situation, it succeeds; whether it does in general, we will see later.

Let us come to the second question that interests us, that is, if the independence of the proletariat is a condition of and must be a character of organization, then without organization there is and cannot be the independence of the proletariat. On this issue, Lenin carries out an extremely acute analysis of the existing interrelations between spontaneity and the lack of proletarian independence. Here he develops his definitive critique of anarcho-syndicalism, in a much more persuasive form than he would after 1917, because here the analysis is materialist and centered on the relation between struggle and economic cycles. In the conditions of the development of revolutionary struggle in Russia, the absence of an organizational project and of an adequate organizational reality always risks breaking the framework of development where workers' autonomy wishes to affirm the independence of the proletariat. This is due to the weakness of the given power relation with respect to other strata of the proletariat and the class adversary. In this sense, the autonomous, spontaneous struggles from below end up being completely absorbed in the cyclical nature of proletarian struggle in general, irrespective of their importance in determining these cycles themselves. Autonomy and the independence of the proletariat end up disappearing or become subordinated to this cyclical movement. Only if organization is posited as the condition of the whole shift can the organic cycles of workers' struggle create an upward rupture in a situation that is deficient overall from the standpoint of power relations. Organization must determine the independence of the proletariat as a rupture of the spontaneous cycles of struggle; thus, starting from spontaneity, it must propose a shift from defense to attack, from insurrection to socialism. The theory of organization thus becomes the strategy of the revolution insofar as the notion of the independence of the proletariat manages to turn from a condition of organization into the form of organization, into the ability of organization to lead the whole development of struggle (or at least control class relations) and link it to this kind of process. The nexus between the resulting democracy and socialism is not only objectively discontinuous: the discontinuity must be interpreted subjectively and dominated in order to be recomposed organizationally. One of the most interesting aspects of Lenin's discourse emerges at this juncture: the working-class character of organization breaks the cyclical and mystifying continuity of the revolutionary process. Let us read another passage from *Two Tactics*:

The long reign of political reaction in Europe, which has lasted almost uninterruptedly since the days of the Paris Commune, has too greatly accustomed us to the idea that action can proceed only "from below," has too greatly inured us to seeing only defensive struggles. We have now, undoubtedly, entered a new era: a period of political upheavals and revolutions has begun. In a period such as Russia is passing through at the present time, it is impermissible to confine ourselves to old, stereotyped formulae. We must propagate the idea of action from above, we must prepare for the most energetic, offensive action, and must study the conditions for and forms of such actions.[6]

In these aspects of Lenin's thought, there is a fundamental shift from a theory of organization to a strategy for the revolution. We have seen how crucial the relevance of the theory of organization to the theory of the specific composition of the working class and proletariat was. Now we see how the strategy of the revolution is really presupposed in organization, a kind of organization that registers and exasperates, and thus preliminarily determines, the absolute autonomy of the proletarian interest. This autonomy and independence the proletariat carries not only against capital but also within its own organization, as struggle and as a condition for organization. If we wish to speak of Leninist duplicity, let us do so, but this duplicity is wholly dialectical and manages to develop, with great consistency, the most difficult shift of socialist and partly of Marxian thought: the shift from the theory of development to the theory of the destruction of development.

NOTES

1. Lenin, *Two Tactics of Social Democracy in the Democratic Revolution* (Peking: Foreign Language Press, 1965), 1.
2. Ibid., 11.
3. Ibid., 50.
4. Ibid., 122.
5. Ibid.
6. Ibid., 19.

6

FROM THE THEORY OF
ORGANIZATION TO THE STRATEGY
OF THE REVOLUTION (2)

The Factory of Strategy

I N THE LAST conversation we saw how the issue of the shift from the question and practice of organization to the question of strategy needs to be brought to bear on the definition of the political composition of the working class and the proletariat in Russia, grouped under the scientific category of determinate social formation, and how the concept of the independence of proletarian organization (which was the condition of strategy) was also based on the same category. Where the working class was a socially distinct vanguard within the proletariat, the externality of the process of organization and the need to impose the recomposition of the proletariat from above amounted to a need and desire for a theoretical isolation of the vanguard from the process of masses in conditions of emergency. We have also seen how a series of internal shifts essentially centered on two questions: that of the shift from the resulting democracy to socialism, and that, which will be discussed later on, of alliances, especially of workers and peasants. These questions were related to the kind of structure described. We also underlined how the concept of the independence of the proletariat as a condition for organization and the concept of organization as a condition for strategy constitute an essential moment that unfolds at a necessary pace and is objectively rooted.

Now we come to another concept emerging in those years from Lenin's theoretical and practical labor. This is the notion that the working-class character of organization is, for him, the essential qualification of strategy. Let us read, again, the text previously cited from *Two Tactics*:

> The proletariat expects to find its salvation not by avoiding the class strug-
> gle but by developing it, by widening it, increasing its consciousness, its
> organization and determination. Whoever degrades the tasks of the politi-
> cal struggle transforms the Social-Democrat from a tribune of the people
> into a trade union secretary. Whoever degrades the proletarian tasks in a
> democratic bourgeois revolution transforms the Social-Democrat from a
> leader of the people's revolution into a leader of a free labour union.[1]

In such a framework, we find the correct notion of the shift from democracy to socialism. One fights for democracy because in the bourgeois republic the proletariat can materially recompose more rapidly and easily, but this does not entail the reduction of the tasks of the proletariat and its party to those of the democratic revolution: on the contrary, "the proletariat expects to find its salvation not by avoiding the class struggle but by developing it, by widening it." In the bourgeois democratic revolution, the task of the proletarian party is not merely to consolidate the structures that transform the previous historical formation, positing the conditions for power relations to be subverted; the real objective is actually that of pushing the revolution forward toward determi-nate working-class contents, the interests of the working class that are finally hegemonic. Here then we move, in this prospective, from the concept of the independence of the proletariat in the democratic phase of the revolution to the concept of the leadership of the working class of the mature revolutionary process. This leadership is the hegemony of the interests of the working class in its specificity, which must initially be represented by the independence of organization, and is here shown to be an ability to actualize this dialectical shift, to dominate the series of democratic stages in the most radical deepen-ing of the revolutionary process, in the withering-away of the state, in the destruction of the machine of power that has been built around wage labor.

We can immediately highlight a paradox here, which we will return to at the end of our reading: *Lenin moves from spontaneity to spontaneity*. In fact, Lenin starts in the 1890s with a deep analysis of the spontaneous class movements, in a correct conceptual framework of the circulation of struggles, of their consolidation, and of the formation of the proletariat into class through this spontaneous mechanism; subsequently, from this he moves to an extremely rigid conception of external organization; finally, in the last pre-revolutionary phase, he recovers the formidable notion of the withering-away of the state, that is, the figure of a free community of free men and women who destroy all the conditions through which capital, by exploiting them and chaining them to labor, dominates them. From spontaneity to spontaneity: if this is Lenin, it is perfectly understandable that during the Second International, any possibility of expressing his thought was practically closed off to this Asian Marxist barbarian.

But let us see how this concept of workers' leadership is materially expressed in this period and how it concretely and politically develops. One of the densest writings of this period is *The Lessons of the Revolution*.[2] The text was written in 1910; having reflected on and developed the events and lessons from the revolution of 1905, here Lenin theoretically outlines the concept of the workers' leadership of organization: "Five years have elapsed since the working class of Russia, in October 1905, dealt the first mighty blow to the tsarist autocracy. In those great days the proletariat aroused millions of the working people to struggle against their oppressors. In the space of a few months of that year the proletariat won improvements which during decades the workers had been vainly waiting [for] from the 'higher authorities.'"[3] What are the lessons of the revolution? "Both the victories and the defeats of the revolution taught the Russian people some great historical lessons. In honouring the fifth anniversary of 1905, let us try to ascertain the main substance of these lessons. *The first and main lesson* is that *only* the revolutionary struggle of the masses can bring about worth-while improvements in the lives of the workers and in the administration of the state."[4] The economic struggle of the masses is a political struggle, we would say: again, at the basis of all of Lenin's analysis lies this indistinct political and economic mass struggle directly leveled against the state structure:

No "sympathy" for the workers on the part of educated people, no struggle of lone terrorists, however heroic, could do anything to undermine the

THE FACTORY OF STRATEGY

tsarist autocracy and the omnipotence of the capitalists. This could be achieved only by the struggle of the workers themselves, only by the combined struggle of millions, and when *this* struggle grew weaker the workers immediately began to be deprived of what they had won. The Russian revolution was confirmation of the sentiments expressed in the international hymn of labour:

No saviours from on high deliver,
No trust have we in prince or peer;
Our own right hand the chains must shiver,
Chains of hatred, greed and fear!

The second lesson is that it is not enough to undermine and restrict the power of the tsar. It must be *destroyed*. Until the tsarist regime is destroyed concessions won from the tsar will never be lasting.[5]

This is a strong and immediate attack on any reformist proposal to change or restructure the Tsarist power, and an insistence on the principle of democracy. Here the role of class vanguard is fully emancipated. But the last and fundamental principle is that:

The tsarist autocracy has also learned a lesson from the revolution. It has seen that it cannot rely on the faith of the peasants in the tsar. It is now strengthening its power by forming an alliance with the Black-Hundred landlords and the Octobrist industrialists. To overthrow the tsarist autocracy will now require a much more powerful offensive of the revolutionary mass struggle than in 1905. Is such a much more powerful offensive possible? The reply to this question brings us to the *third and cardinal* lesson of the revolution. This lesson consists in our having seen *how* the various classes of the Russian people act. Prior to 1905 many thought that the whole people aspired to freedom in the same way and wanted the same freedom; at least the great majority had no clear understanding of the fact that the different classes of the Russian people had different views on the struggle for freedom and were not striving for the same freedom. The revolution dispelled the mist. At the end of 1905, then later during the First and Second Dumas, *all* classes of Russian society came out openly. They showed themselves in action, revealing what their true ambitions were, what they could fight for and how strongly, persistently and vigorously they were able to fight. The factory workers, the industrial proletariat, waged a most resolute and strenuous struggle against the autocracy.[6]

And he continues:

In militancy the working class of Russia was in advance of all the other classes of the Russian people. The very conditions of their lives make the workers capable of struggle and impel them to struggle. Capital collects the workers in great masses in big cities, uniting them, teaching them to act in unison. At every step the workers come face to face with their main enemy—the capitalist class. In combat with this enemy the worker becomes a *socialist*, comes to realise the necessity of a complete reconstruction of the whole of society, the complete abolition of all poverty and all oppression. Becoming socialists, the workers fight with self-abnegating courage against everything that stands in their path, first and foremost the tsarist regime and the feudal landlords.[7]

Most importantly, Lenin's analysis of the revolution leads him to exalt the working-class character of organization, because only the working class can represent the essential moment, the founding stone of the real independence of the proletariat, and it can do this for any condition of organization. All of this is clear in Lenin's analysis of the revolution of 1905, which is where the shift from the issue of organization to that of strategy occurs.

It would be unnecessary to insist on what Lenin's analysis identifies as the parallel condition: "The degree of economic development of Russia (an objective condition) and the degree of class consciousness and organization of the broad masses of the proletariat (a subjective condition inseparably connected with the objective condition) make the immediate complete emancipation of the working class impossible."[8] Here we find, again, Lenin's determination to develop his thought with an awareness of the given condition of the Russian development and its determinate power relations. Within these relations a series of horizontal and vertical shifts are defined, both in terms of alliances and in terms of strategic gradualism (from democracy to socialism). However, Lenin's thinking is always driven by a particular priority: the working-class character of organization, insofar as this character must function as a qualification of strategy.

On this issue, another important element is the concept of alliance that Lenin expresses in this phase, especially in reference to peasants. I cite from the pamphlet *Social Democracy's Attitude Towards the Peasant Movement*,[9] which is Lenin's comment on a resolution approved by the Third Congress, where the working-class character of organization and the workers' hegemony over organization are expressed with extreme clarity precisely in relation to the peasant movement. Commenting on a letter sent to the party newspaper, Lenin writes:

> A question of theory has in this connection been raised by the author of the letter, whether the expropriation of the big estates and their transfer to "peasant, petty-bourgeois ownership" should not be specifically qualified. But by proposing such a reservation the author has arbitrarily limited the purport of the resolution of the Third Congress. There is *not a word* in the resolution about the Social-Democratic Party undertaking to support transfer of the confiscated land to petty-bourgeois proprietors. The resolution states: we support . . . "up to and including confiscation," i.e., including expropriation without compensation; however, the resolution does not in any way decide to whom the expropriated land is to be given. . . . We must help the peasant uprising in every way, up to and including confiscation of the land, *but certainly not including all sorts of petty-bourgeois schemes*. We support the peasant movement to the extent that it is revolutionary democratic. We are making ready (doing so now, at once) to fight it when, and to the extent that, it becomes reactionary and anti-proletarian. The essence of Marxism lies in that double task, which only those who do not understand Marxism can vulgarise or compress into a single and simple task.[10]

The relation to the peasants is clearly expressed, but we also find another concept here: the dialecticization of the objective and the subjective elements of the theory of the party is founded on the reality of the determinate social formation, but it is not the reflection, once and for all, of determined conditions to which the strategy of organization must make itself adequate. In fact, the working-class leadership is a struggle against the objective conditions. The latter are changed in the revolutionary process, and on the basis of these changes, in the field of alliances, we see a shift, for instance, from the call for an establishment of peasants revolutionary committees to what can be a new phase of revolutionary struggle between the agricultural workers and peasant owners: "We stand for uninterrupted revolution. We shall not stop half-way. If we do not now and immediately promise all sorts of 'socialisation,' that is because we know the actual conditions for that task to be accomplished, and we do not gloss over the new class struggle burgeoning within the peasantry, but reveal that struggle."[11]

The stages of development of the revolutionary process are dominated by the permanence of the organization only insofar as this presents a working-class character. In this respect, we come to appreciate the significance of the revolution *from above* so strongly advocated by Lenin. Organization is the highest level of awareness of the tendency, and in this perspective it is strongly opposed to the objective conditions that come to limit the effective communist task.

From the next conversation onward, we will see how the communist contents of Lenin's strategy are already defined at this juncture. But for the time being we will highlight some aspects of this shift. For instance, this communist finality here appears in the form of an *unending revolution*, recalling Marx's writings, in particular the historical texts. Phrases and concepts, such as the continuous reduction of the margins of the defense of democracy, are recurrent:

> The idea of seeking salvation for the working class in anything save the further development of capitalism is *reactionary*. In countries like Russia, the working class suffers not so much from capitalism as from the insufficient development of capitalism. The working class is therefore *decidedly interested* in the broadest, freest and most rapid development of capitalism. The removal of all the remnants of the old order which are hampering

the broad, free and rapid development of capitalism is of decided advantage to the working class. The bourgeois revolution is precisely a revolution that most resolutely sweeps away the survivals of the past, the remnants of serfdom (which include not only autocracy but monarchy as well) and most fully guarantees the broadest, freest and most rapid development of capitalism. . . . It is of greater advantage to the bourgeoisie if the necessary changes in the direction of bourgeois democracy take place more slowly, more gradually, more cautiously, less resolutely, by means of reforms and not by means of revolution; if these changes spare the "venerable" institutions of serfdom (such as the monarchy) as much as possible; if these changes develop as little as possible the independent revolutionary activity, initiative and energy of the common people, i.e., the peasantry and especially the workers, for otherwise it will be easier for the workers, as the French say, "to hitch the rifle from one shoulder to the other," i.e., to turn against the bourgeoisie the guns which the bourgeois revolution will place in their hands, the liberty which the revolution will bring, the democratic institutions which will spring up on the ground that is cleared of serfdom.[12]

Also recurrent are calls for the implacable pressure of the working class to deepen and intensify class struggle starting from consolidated stages:

Without falling into adventurism or going against our conscience in matters of science, without striving for cheap popularity we can and do assert only one thing: we shall bend every effort to help the entire peasantry achieve the democratic revolution, *in order thereby to make it easier* for us, the party of the proletariat, to pass on as quickly as possible to the new and higher task—the socialist revolution. We promise no harmony, no equalitarianism or "socialisation" following the victory of the *present* peasant uprising, on the contrary, we "promise" a new struggle, new inequality, the new revolution we are striving for. Our doctrine is less "sweet" than the legends of the Socialist-Revolutionaries, but let those who want to be fed solely on sweets join the Socialist-Revolutionaries; we shall say to such people: good riddance.[13]

These phrases and concepts literally refer to a series of expressions found in Marx's writings on 1848 in France. The methodology is identical. What matters, from the communist perspective, is demonstrating how the advancement of struggles simplifies the terrain of the conflict and recuperates its antagonistic nature: adequate to revolutionary practice, the analysis leads a dialectical and dynamic reduction of class struggle to its essential terms, the working class and the bourgeoisie. Only on the basis of this fundamental reduction can the working class seize the opportunity of carrying forward the will to destroy the entirety of the capitalist mode of production and its state, having accomplished the intermediate stages of the revolutionary process. From this standpoint, Lenin's methodology and Marx's coincide because they keep establishing a relation between theory of class composition, theory of organization, and theory/strategy of revolution.

But there is something more to the Lenin of these years: the issue of the revolution from above. This is not simply a question of the total comprehension of the process and of the organizational ability of the working class to lead it; it is not simply about the ability to set into motion the mechanisms of the permanent revolution at each moment. The question is one of the subjective ability of the class vanguard to be the point of the diamond, an effective military force to lead this process. Revolutionary subjectivity is not a subjectivity of understanding and of leadership posited outside of the masses and able to drag up from above a *project* of unending revolution: it must also be a capacity for rupture and attack, a force of traction from above, and in this case a physical military *power*.[14] *The Lessons of the Moscow Uprising* was written in 1906.[15] Here the relation between working-class leadership and insurrection (that is, the ability to promote the process of insurrection as a subjectivity that is present inside the level of the mass) is clearly outlined. As a conclusion to our discussion so far, we can see that starting from the theoretical concept of determinate social formation and arriving at the concept of insurrection is not a process that developed in the abstraction of analysis. The abstraction was determined in a working subjectivity that was given within the mass movement and determined and measured practically, at all stages of its development. Lenin's thoughts on this are very clear and do not need much comment.

The publication of the book *Moscow in December 1905* (Moscow, 1906) could not have been more timely. It is an urgent task of the workers' party to assimilate the lessons of the December uprising. . . . The principal forms of the December movement in Moscow were the peaceful strike and demonstrations, and these were the only forms of struggle in which the vast majority of the workers took an active part. Yet, the December action in Moscow vividly demonstrated that the general strike, as an independent and predominant form of struggle, is out of date, that the movement is breaking out of these narrow bounds with elemental and irresistible force and giving rise to the highest form of struggle—an uprising.[16]

The party was wrong because it did not manage to put itself in the lead of the process and subjectively reflect the leap forward of the masses:

Thus, nothing could be more short-sighted than Plekhanov's view, seized upon by all the opportunists, that the strike was untimely and should not have been started, and that "they should not have taken to arms." On the contrary, we should have taken to arms more resolutely, energetically and aggressively; we should have explained to the masses that it was impossible to confine things to a peaceful strike and that a fearless and relentless armed fight was necessary. And now we must at last openly and publicly admit that political strikes are inadequate; we must carry on the widest agitation among the masses in favour of an armed uprising and make no attempt to obscure this question by talk about "preliminary stages," or to befog it in any way. We would be deceiving both ourselves and the people if we concealed from the masses the necessity of a desperate, bloody war of extermination, as the immediate task of the coming revolutionary action.[17]

This is the first lesson of the Moscow uprising, the second is as follows:

The December events confirmed another of Marx's profound propositions, which the opportunists have forgotten, namely, that insurrection is an art and that the principal rule of this art is the waging of a desperately bold and irrevocably determined *offensive*. We have not sufficiently assimilated this truth. We ourselves have not sufficiently learned, nor have we taught the masses, this art, this rule to attack at all costs. We must make up for this omission with all our energy. It is not enough to take sides on the question of political slogans; it is also necessary to take sides on the question of an armed uprising. Those who are opposed to it, those who do not prepare for it, must be ruthlessly dismissed from the ranks of the supporters of the revolution, sent packing to its enemies, to the traitors or cowards; for the day is approaching when the force of events and the conditions of the struggle will compel us to distinguish between enemies and friends according to this principle. It is not passivity that we should preach, not mere "waiting" until the troops "come over." No! We must proclaim from the house-tops the need for a bold offensive and armed attack, the necessity at such times of exterminating the persons in command of the enemy, and of a most energetic fight for the wavering troops.[18]

The third lesson of the Moscow uprising concerns the form of struggle: the "new barricade tactics," guerrilla warfare, and artillery in crowds. The party must take up this practice through a study of the Moscow experience, and spread it among the masses to develop it further.

The last important lesson from the Russian revolution of 1905 concerns the working class, again, and its creative activity in the insurrection. With this, the whole series of concepts that link the independence of the proletariat in strategy to the question of organization finds its definitive working-class qualification. Workers characterize organization as a technical structure of leadership and overall mediation in class relations (the times and phases of strategy and alliances): now they are also hegemonic in organization as a weapon and creative activity of insurrection.

NOTES

1. Lenin, *Two Tactics of Social Democracy in the Democratic Revolution* (Peking: Foreign Language Press, 1965), 122.
2. V. I. Lenin, *The Lessons of the Revolution*, trans. C. Dutt, in *Collected Works* (Moscow: Progress Publishers, 1967), 16:296–304.

3. Ibid., 16:296.
4. Ibid., 16:299.
5. Ibid.
6. Ibid., 16:300.
7. Ibid., 16:301–302.
8. Lenin, *Two Tactics of Social Democracy*, 16–17.
9. Lenin, *Social Democracy's Attitude Towards the Peasant Movement*, trans. A. Fineberg and J. Katzer, ed. G. Hanna, in *Collected Works* (Moscow: Progress Publishers, 1972), 9:230–239.
10. Ibid., 9:235–236.
11. Ibid., 9:237.
12. Lenin, *Two Tactics of Social Democracy*, 45.
13. Lenin, *Social Democracy's Attitude*, 237.
14. On the Moscow insurrection in 1905 and on the military organization, but especially on the organization of the revolutionary appropriation and expropriation of the Bolsheviks, which is a very important issue for present class struggles, see J. Baynac, *Kamo: L'uomo di Lenin* (Milan: Bompiani, 1974), especially the bibliography.
15. Lenin, *The Lessons of the Moscow Uprising*, trans. C. Dutt, in *Collected Works* (Moscow: Progress Publishers, 1965), 11:171–178.
16. Ibid., 11:171.
17. Ibid., 11:173–174.
18. Ibid., 11:176.

7

FROM THE THEORY OF ORGANIZATION TO THE STRATEGY OF THE REVOLUTION (3)

Organization Toward Communism

W E WILL NOW conclude our analysis of the shift from the theory of organization to the strategy of the revolutionary process as outlined by Lenin. We have already insisted on several points, in particular on the independence of the proletarian party as a condition of any strategic proposal, and secondly on the fact that the revolutionary character of organization derives, in its historically determinate formation, from its working-class character and therefore from the particular dialectics established between the workers' leadership of organization and the general determinations of the social formation, both at the level of alliances and at the level of timing, forms, and objectives of the revolution. On this issue, the significance of the shift from progressive democracy to socialism is defined, as is the relation with peasants as a separate class. In this conversation we would like to explore how the content and tendency of strategy in Lenin are characterized in terms of communism; that is to say, despite the determination that theory is forced to take on from the social formation, Lenin's project never loses from sight the highest goal of the revolutionary process, which is communism. The building of communist society—to each according to their needs—is still the fundamental point, whatever the conditions, shifts, and analyses that given power relations demand.

Lenin as a whole, and in particular the Lenin of the years we are analyzing, the decisive years of the formation of the Bolshevik program immediately after 1905, continues to insist on the permanent character of the revolutionary action of the vanguard. Each single objective, when reached and consolidated, must be burned by the revolutionary party. Guaranteeing the continuity of this process is the independence of the proletariat, the independence of the political and material needs of the proletariat: the party, time after time, uses each situation to consolidate and strengthen itself, to establish the springboard for a further leap forward. The notion of the democratic-bourgeois dictatorship of the proletariat, a fundamental concept from the standpoint of permanent revolution, is located in this framework.

Why the democratic-bourgeois dictatorship of the proletariat? In the writings from 1905, in a ferocious polemic against Mensheviks, Lenin insists on the concept of dictatorship. What were the terms of the polemic? In *Two Tactics of Social Democracy*, from 1905, Lenin attacks the Mensheviks on the question of dictatorship and the form of management of the progressive bourgeois democracy in Russia. In his attack, Lenin refers to a book by Franz Mehring, one of the few good interpreters of Marx's discourse in the Second International.[1]

Returning to the history of Marx's activity as told by Mehring, Lenin reconstructs the shift of Marx's discourse on democracy, in 1848 and the years after the revolution of 1848, especially through the work carried out in the *New Rhine Newspaper*. Lenin demonstrates that Marx correctly grasps the German revolutionary process of 1848 at various moments. First moment: an adherence to the concept of formal democracy in the hope that the democratic revolution, as such, could lead the process from within the very forms of democracy itself: the constituent, the establishment of free parties, and so on. Second moment: Marx's clear suggestion that the simple form of democracy, without the ability to "impose democracy," and thus a form of dictatorship with bourgeois contents, is completely in vain. What is meant by "bourgeois contents"? In the German case of 1848, these are the expropriation of landowners, the imposition of small peasant property, an alliance between the bourgeoisie and peasant small-property owners. If such an alliance is not built, it is because the revolutionary process, that is, the critical consciousness of the proletarian party (the League of Communists), is unable to lead the movement and impose this shift. The third moment is therefore Marx's awareness of the absolute need for the proletariat to sustain the bourgeois-democratic phase by coercive means, and his awareness that this necessary phase of recomposition of the proletariat, by overcoming a whole series of material and economic delays to the constitution of a vanguard class, is led by the proletarian party in terms of dictatorship. The theory of the working-class leadership of the process turns into the outline of a process with intermediate phases (the formation of a free labor market and free peasant ownership), which the imposition of the law of capital onto all precapitalist social strata must go through. This is the constitution of a process of capitalist development within which the working class is constituted as such, and thus becomes capable of putting forward its own communist goals. But this can only occur through the material coercive force of the proletariat for the achievement of bourgeois-democratic ends. Bourgeois democracy is not only one of the forms of development of class domination; the question is who is in charge of the dictatorship, who holds the levers of power, whether it is the proletariat or, as in the German case, the bourgeoisie: a shy bourgeoisie unable to lead a revolutionary process and correspond to its own interests will necessarily need to ally with reactionary classes and carry out (within the bourgeois democracy itself) the most ferocious repression of the revolutionary force.

The same example applies to the Russian one: Lenin immediately uses it in the last chapter of *Two Tactics of Social Democracy*. When the revolutionary process fails to hit the state form and appropriate the material means of domination that the state avails itself of in a centralized way, then the revolution fails too. The democratic form, as such, allows for various alliances, but in particular it permits the repressive turn of the bourgeoisie when it is unable to correspond to its own interests of development. Instead of this, it is necessary to set in motion an impetuous capitalist development, and this means recomposing the working class and approach in Marxian terms, the "catastrophe" of capital.

This is a first standpoint that must be strongly underlined. The communist tension running through Lenin's discourse on the strategy of the revolution is expressed in the concept of permanent revolution as a revolution capable of burning, in each instance, the single shifts to which it is coerced, a permanent revolution that is determined by an act of workers' political will and decision. The political decision of the vanguard of the organized proletariat posits and then burns each single moment of the development that contains the struggles. The concept of the bourgeois-democratic dictatorship as a moment of the workers' revolution and a form that proletariat power takes on at a specific phase of the Russian revolution radically expresses the notion of the continuity of revolution. This notion concretely returns to Marx's discourse on communism, as it had emerged in the writings of 1848 through an effort to discover the mechanisms of revolutionary development, and as it had then been fully affirmed, as we will later see in our discussion on the Soviet, in the writings on the Commune from 1871. Marx states that it is always the working class that imposes the bourgeois republic, but only to the extent that this seizure is held by an adequate level of dictatorship and that organization is a nonreversible outcome.

In a backward situation and a determinate social formation such as that registered in Marx's historical writings (in 1848 and 1871 in France and Germany) or that registered by Lenin's writings on Russia in 1905, this shift is necessary but must also always be burned. Why? Because

> it is our interest and our task to make the revolution permanent, until all more or less possessing classes have been forced out of their position of dominance, the proletariat has conquered state power, and the association of proletarians, not only in one country but in all the dominant countries of the world, has advanced so far that competition among the proletarians in these countries has ceased and that at least the decisive productive forces are concentrated in the hands of the proletarians.[2]

The history of the Commune verifies this as an indication in the form of working-class power with this objective: "Its true secret was this. It was essentially a working-class government, the produce of the struggle of the producing against the appropriating class, the political form at last discovered under which to work out the economical emancipation of Labour."[3]

These Marxian concepts are constantly reiterated and exalted by Lenin. From the theoretical point of view, this leads to a series of important consequences. Until now, we have seen how the determinate social formation and class composition are the condition for the creation of a working-class and proletarian type of organization. We have seen how Lenin's concept of organization emerges from the recording of a given situation and from its transformation into a series of operative concepts. At this point, there is a typical Leninist shift and an inversion of the discourse: the discourse on workers' dictatorship in the phases of transition is in fact an introduction of the concept of organization, the force of organization that can modify class composition and thus the given social condition. The shift we have described in a linear way so far, from composition to organization to strategy, is now forcedly resolved and subverted. Lenin is convinced that where the proletariat organizes itself it manages to produce a power effect that determines the inversion of the relationship between class composition and organization. *The independent variable is no longer class composition but organization.*

Voluntarism, subjectivism, and Asian barbarism: Lenin's adversaries have declared this a betrayal of Marxism in the most bizarre ways. But we could really say the opposite: it is precisely in this dialectics, established in each instance, between the ability of revolutionary subjectivity to recognize itself in the given conditions and its capacity to modify the conditions as they are given in this relation that the "mysterious curve of Lenin's straight line" takes its shape, as Bebel used to say. The character of Marxist objectivism and materialism is never a static conception of reality (which is codism), but rather the ability of a material subject to recognize itself in its material needs and to constitute them into immediately revolutionary causes. It is simultaneously the principle of the subversion of praxis and the principle of collective and constitutive praxis. The reality confronting us, from nature, to history, to institutions, is changeable, as are the tools of interpretation and understanding of the violence of the relationship that one is subjected to every day. This is the field where Marxist materialism finds its clearest explanation. This dialectics between the objectivity of the premise and the subjectivity of the conclusion, the inversion of the relation between material class composition and the ability of organization, is Lenin's innovation on Marxism: the theoretical hegemony is ascribed to a material subject that changes its reality by interpreting and using its constitutive material interests; these are no ideals, but actual facts that do not go beyond the generalized needs of the proletarian masses.

From this standpoint, the goal of communism traverses the whole of Lenin's perspective without ever becoming an ideology: it is always interpreted through material shifts; it is not a dream or a utopia, but always a relation between means and ends, between materiality and subjective tendency.

Let us see where Lenin's notion of the revolutionary perspective matures. Fundamental to it are passages of *The State and Revolution*, but former theorizations can also be found in *The Task of the Proletariat in Our Present Revolution*.[4] The text is written in April 1917, at the beginning of a period between a first phase of bourgeois democracy and a second one of proletarian revolution, when the Bolsheviks seized power. It is important to read it because it sums up, concisely, the main issues of Lenin's discourse on the state and on the permanence of the revolution and its final goals. The section is entitled "A New Type of State Emerging from Our Revolution." Lenin writes:

> The Soviets of Workers', Soldiers', Peasants' and other Deputies' are not understood, not only in the sense that their class significance, their role in the *Russian* revolution, is not clear to the majority. They are not understood also in the sense that they constitute a new form or rather a new *type of state*. The most perfect, the most advanced type of bourgeois state is the *parliamentary democratic republic*: power is vested in parliament; the state machine, the apparatus and organ of administration, is of the customary kind: the standing army, the police, and the bureaucracy—which in practice is undisplaceable, is privileged and stands *above* the people. Since the end of the nineteenth century, however, revolutionary epochs have advanced a *higher* type of democratic state, a state which in certain respects, as Engels put it, ceases to be a state, is "no longer a state in the proper sense of the word." This is a state of the Paris Commune type, one in which a standing army and police divorced from the people are *replaced* by the direct arming of the people themselves. It is *this feature* that constitutes the very essence of the Commune, which has been so misrepresented and slandered by the bourgeois writers, and to which has been erroneously ascribed, among other things, the intention of immediately "introducing" socialism. This is the type of state which the Russian revolution *began* to create in 1905 and in 1917.[5]

In the same context, he proposes to change the name of the Russian social democratic party, of the Bolshevik faction, to the communist party, in a section called "What Should Be the Name of Our Party, One That Will Be Correct Scientifically and Help to Clarify the Mind of the Proletariat Politically?" This section is extremely important and fully clarifies the continuity of the communist project and the insistence on the communist content of past experiences and of all of Lenin's actions.

> I now come to the final point, the name of our Party. We must call ourselves the *Communist Party*—just as Marx and Engels called themselves. We must repeat that we are Marxists and that we take as our basis the *Communist Manifesto*, which has been distorted and betrayed by the Social-Democrats on two main points: (1) the working men have no country: "defense of the fatherland" in an imperialist war is a betrayal of socialism; and (2) the Marxist doctrine of the state has been distorted by the Second International. The name "Social-Democracy" is scientifically incorrect, as Marx frequently pointed out, in particular, in the *Critique of the Gotha Programme* in 1875, and as Engels re-affirmed in a more popular form in 1894. From capitalism mankind can pass directly only to socialism, i.e., to the social ownership of the means of production and the distribution of products according to the amount of work performed by each individual. Our Party looks farther ahead: socialism must inevitably evolve gradually into communism, upon the banner of which is inscribed the motto, "From each according to his ability, to each according to his needs." That is my first argument. Here is the second: the second part of the name of our Party (Social-Democrats) is also scientifically incorrect. Democracy is a form of state, whereas we Marxists are opposed to *every kind of state*.[6]

To sum up, in the determination of the shift from a theory of organization to a revolutionary strategy, where the latter is rooted in the analysis of the particular determinate social formation of Russia, Lenin insists on the independence of the proletariat as a party and on the workers' leadership of that party, seeing this as a substantial guarantee of the continuity of the revolutionary design. But this is not sufficient: the organizational project is developed with allusions to the contents of communism and to the issue of the withering-away of the state, which becomes a key issue sustained throughout the whole of the revolutionary process. Lenin states that Marxists recognize the actual need for a state, and thus for a dictatorship in the particular phases that the revolution goes through; they especially recognize where the contents of the struggle, needs, and power of the masses can only produce a bourgeois-democratic determination of the contents of the revolutionary process. However, all of this must constantly be burned and overcome: the permanent revolution is the goal of communists. The communist party is different from other forces in the management of the intermediate phases of the revolutionary process of the proletariat because it is able to impose, within each moment, the goal of withering away the state.

As we have already done after the first part of our conversations, on the theory of organization, we will have to see where this Leninist shift from the theory of organization to the strategy of the revolution finds its place in the current composition of the working class, and how far Leninism can be used in the determinate social formation of current class struggles.

NOTES

1. Lenin, "The Vulgar Bourgeois Representation of Dictatorship and Marx's View of It," in *Two Tactics of Social Democracy in the Democratic Revolution* (Peking: Foreign Language Press, 1965), 135–145.
2. Karl Marx and Fredrick Engels, "Address of the Central Authority to the League," in *Marx and Engels Collected Works* (Moscow: Progress Publishers, 1978), 10:281.
3. Karl Marx, "The Civil War in France," in *Marx and Engels Collected Works* (Moscow: Progress Publishers, 1986), 22:334. On the way the problem of the Paris Commune and the state was approached by Lenin prior to 1917, see A. Tovaglieri, "Il problema dello stato in Lenin prima del 1917" [The question of the state in Lenin before 1917], *Rivista di storia contemporanea* 3 (July 1972): 289–314.
4. Lenin, *The Task of the Proletariat in Our Revolution*, trans. B. Isaacs, in *Collected Works* (Moscow: Progress Publishers, 1964), 24:55–91.
5. Ibid., 24:67–68.
6. Ibid., 24:84–85.

8

IN LENIN'S FOOTSTEPS FROM
THE THEORY OF ORGANIZATION
TO THE STRATEGY OF REVOLUTION

Annotations

W E WOULD LIKE to present a conclusive judgment on the theory of organization, or rather, on the relation between the theory of organization and the strategy of revolution that we have outlined so far. Let us summarize the main issues on which we have concentrated. We have seen that organization is the condition for strategy, from at least 1903, throughout the period of theoretical development of *What Is to Be Done?* and the revolution of 1905. The concept of organization is linked to a determinate analysis of the Russian situation, and defined as the condition for all possible strategies insofar as the independence of the working class is configured autonomously. Only in this situation can the party of the working class constitute itself as a dynamic element inside a social structure that is extremely differentiated, and impress a permanent character on the revolution by overcoming each single stage and power relation forced by the lack of homogeneity internal to the process (the need for alliances, the relation between the working class and peasants, and overall differences and unbalances in development). The vanguard represents the ability to make the process permanent; the concept of vanguard is therefore the concept of the party, as an independence of judgment and the working class's continuous ability to lead the differentiated proletariat. Therefore, there can be no strategy unless the different shifts in alliances occur, unless the different moments of the building of the struggle between progressive democracy and socialism unfold up to the allusion to communism, the dictatorship of the proletariat, the destruction of the state. That is to say, unless the process is based on a dynamic relation established by the workers' party to all other classes, starting from its independence, autonomy, and overall ability to command. The second element we have insisted on is the working-class character of strategy and organization, which is another way of saying the same thing: the most advanced capitalist form, the factory form, must be assumed within the workers' organization as a moment of rationalization and efficiency. The guarantee that the proletarian organization will win and will, in the meantime, command the permanent process of revolution through successive stages goes through the efficiency of the command internal to the organization. Lenin derides anyone who accuses the Bolshevik formula of the party of resembling the factory, and also anyone who affirms that the dignity and radical nature of the workers' revolutionary party are based on this, on being a guarantor of the production of organization according to the most advanced forms of production: this is the working class way of repeating, for the party, the formula of production. Here it must be pointed out that the Leninist party never had anything to do with the kind of communist party of the Third International and the communist reformism it produced. The difference lies in the working-class character of organization that Lenin always and decisively insisted on, from both the strategic point of view and the organizational one. The third observation we made concerns the programmatic content of the Bolshevik Party and how it directly points toward communism. The aim of the program is permanent revolution, a struggle that tends toward the constant traction of the revolutionary process and the burning-off of the levels at which it stops. The analysis we dedicated to this shift, for instance, from the issue of progressive democracy to the issue of socialism (which we will return to when we deal with the withering-away of the state), presents a fundamental case: the destruction of the wage system, the destruction of the system of capital, of the capitalist mode of production, and this is always taken into account in the Leninist party, even when the particular phases in which the working class and the party struggles are forced to oblige a series of intermediate solutions. These intermediate solutions, as soon as they are posited, must be dominated by the party from the standpoint of its overall independence, intelligence, and goals to lead the class struggle forward toward the objective need for the end of the capitalist mode of production, as the outcome of a conscious will of the proletariat in struggle.

Let us now ask, as we have already done in previous conversations on our interpretation of Lenin's thought, how far this kind of analysis of the path that leads from the theory of organization to the strategy of revolution is valid for us today. We will examine the issues proposed by Lenin one by one.

The first concerns the concept of organization as a condition of strategy. We have seen why organization becomes the condition for strategy: it does so because in the objective conditions of the revolutionary process there was great fragmentation of classes, and thus there needed to be a determination of the shifts that developed at the pace of alliances between different social strata. The political and social situation of the Bolshevik Party in Russia really lacked homogeneity: the independence of the organized proletariat therefore demanded an organizational engine to posit and dissemble the knots of the overall social relation. In our current condition, seen from the standpoint of the objective conditions of the revolutionary process and thus of the organization of the party, the situation is radically different from that recorded in Lenin's analysis. The concept of the party, in order to be functional in terms of working-class science, must always refer to the concept of class composition. Class composition is the determinate degree of unity of the workers' interests and the relations between workers and proletariat that evolve historically, as well as a reflection of the power relations enacted or withstood by the working class in relation to other social classes. The analysis, in Marxian terms, not only goes through the sociological survey of existing social relations (the position of the class in the organization of labor and the prominent figure of this integration), but above all grasps the translation of existing social relations into movements of struggles of the proletariat, into subjective consciousness, levels of organization, and comportments. Class composition therefore means technical composition plus social composition plus political composition, and the whole is dialectically united. Today, the recomposition and requalification of the working class in relation to other proletariat strata are radically different, in our analysis, from that recorded by Lenin. The basis of this unitary recomposition of class essentially stems from the changes in qualifications and the demise of objective divisions in the labor force. These changes were imposed by the capitalist mode of production in the phase of development typical, to use Marx's terms, of the period of "real subsumption" of labor under capital. Marx distinguishes between two broad phases. The first is called the "formal subsumption" of labor under capital. Here capital becomes the master of society by organizing labor, insofar as the latter is separated and tied to conditions that capital has not put in place. Capital conquers and organizes the labor conditions that preconstitute its development: this is the phase of "formal subsumption." The "real subsumption" of labor under capital occurs when capital moves to a phase where all labor conditions (from the extraction of surplus to accumulation) are preconstituted by capital itself. At this stage capital is the master and commander of the circuit within which only the fact that it creates the conditions for work makes it possible for there to be work. Salaries that are independent from capital and its money form, incomes and forms of labor independent from large industry no longer exist: capital has completely conquered society and imposed on it a gigantic progress. Marx claims that this determines the emergence of the new collective individual capable of communism. And this is the point: communism is imposed first and foremost by capital as a condition of production; it is a gigantic development of the productive capacities of man, who becomes social and needs others to survive and create—no longer to vegetate and procreate, but to build. Building this man in alienation, capital offers a formidable potential for wealth and happiness. While being formed, this new world is monstrously exploited, and the exploitation of the system is directly proportional to its potential.

The Leninist party is linked to the phase of formal subsumption of labor under capital and to the recuperation and unification of a series of different strata, forms of labor, forms of subsistence, forms of income and struggle. The peasants' revolt, the revolts of the nonindustrial proletariat, the early workers' revolts are described by Lenin in his writings from the 1890s and in *The Development of Capitalism in Russia* from 1898, where the notion of formal subsumption of labor under capital is fully developed. Lenin states clearly that Russia is a capitalist country insofar as capital subsumes under its own organization different, previous, and ancient forms of production, not because capital dominates production and reproduction in the whole of the mechanisms of accumulation. The shift from the formal to the real subsumption of capital is crucial to the context of the issues of the Leninist party and the development of capitalism in Russia, because the latter is only possible in a democratic-progressive or socialist form.[1] This is done with great clarity, and Lenin's greatness consists in his ability to accept all these conditions and bring them forward without ever being touched by the opportunism of those who believe that each of these shifts is sufficient; on the contrary, he does so with the ability to place in this paradox the working class will to destroy labor and the wage system, so that only the construction of capitalism can give us truly revolutionary conditions, and only the strength to traverse this infernal purgatory of an accomplished capitalist production can build the new potential communist humanity. This is the figure of the Leninist party, and it is valid in that determinate social formation. Today the conditions for this question are radically different, and the issue of the communist revolution is born out of the recomposition of class that capital carried out, here as in socialist countries, on the basis of a real subsumption of labor under capital as the fundamental and primary condition and the starting point of the analysis. In Marxian terms, the problem of organization must found itself on the recomposition and homogeneity of the working class that the capitalist process is determining. Beware, capitalism does not determine it out of will, but out of necessity, because in each shift lies the motor of profit. But profit, like all others Marxian categories, is a political relation insofar as it is extorted from other men; and when this political relation becomes capitalist development, its progress is necessarily dialectical, determined by a huge number of visible and invisible struggles, because this extortion of labor from the masses is constantly fought against, and only (technological and political) changes, continuous and systematic innovation, and progress in the modes of extortion can, time and again, defeat this kind of determinate workers' resistance. In fact, all the great shifts in the capitalist mode of production have occurred at this threshold between formal and real subsumption and can be explained in terms of workers' struggle. This exemplification can be made at least at three great moments. One of them is recorded by Lenin and consists in the first introduction of mass machinery and the assumption of the professional worker as a fundamental figure to the capitalist organization of labor.[2] The second moment occurs during what we have described elsewhere as the great crisis of 1929, with the introduction of systematic deskilling, the construction of the assembly line, and the most radical imposition of abstract labor: it is the period of the mass worker.[3] We are currently going through the third moment: the phase of automated production and the shift of the form of command over production, the expansion and hierarchization of these relations of command and organization over the whole of society, beyond the enormous step forward in the productivity of human labor and thus the increased potential for the growth of the collective ability of the proletariat to produce wealth and invention, while the condition of the proletariat is made more miserable from the point of view of the relations of appropriation of the overall wealth.[4] When compared to Lenin's times, today the path that leads from the theory of organization to the strategy of the revolution is much more stringent and unison: it traverses a unified working class that is attacked in the realm of the social, and it excludes alliances that cannot be brought back to bear on the identity of workers' interests, proposing a field of attack that is immediately unified by the goal of communism. In a Marxian sense, organization must always "reveal" the free activity of class and is prefigured in it. Prefiguring today means reading the near possibility of communist libera-tion of the unified working class in the enormous productive potential that it represents. Organization lives this class composition immediately and orga-nizes a perspective of power.

Second problem: we have said that in Lenin the working-class character of organization and strategy is fundamental, even in the contradictions that the party form repeats. The working-class character of organization here directly means vanguard. Now we need to ask whether this subjective character, as well as the condition of vanguard interpreted by Lenin's organization, is changed by the real subsumption of labor under capital today. In fact, we need to rec-ognize that the experience of proletarian and workers' struggles in this phase provides a set of subjective conditions to propose, again, the question of orga-nization and strategy for the revolution (in our determinate social formation). But these conditions have radically changed in relation to those in which the Leninist party came into being. The very concept of vanguard has changed. In

Lenin's conception of the party, the vanguard can only be exalted in an intimately dialectical and deeply contradictory situation, where the working class, the proletariat, and other social strata are tied together in a circuit where the rhythm of alliances is absolutely central, and the shift from the phase of the struggle for progressive democracy to that of the proletarian dictatorship for socialism is typical of it. Subjective will and the ability to pull and collide, as well as to use the margins left open by autocratic domination, are all essential aspects of it. Revolutionary opportunities are built in the reign of tactics; they are the overall contradictions of the system finding residual spaces where the subjective autonomy of the vanguards can initiate its process. Insurrection is an art, an ability of the vanguard (as subjective power) to utilize the series of open spaces and incentivize a mechanism of relative necessity. The working-class character of organization is thus turned into revolutionary professionalism. The revolution is "from below" because the general conditions of the revolutionary process are posited from above, or from outside the vanguard's ability to determine them. But if today class composition has advanced to the levels we have described, if the homogeneity in the relation between working class and overall proletariat is so close, what does this all mean? What are the subjective conditions of organization today? Is it still possible to imagine a kind of vanguard that, while positing the problem of insurrection, is itself simultaneously capable of recuperating, and imputing to itself, a full identification with the needs of the masses and the very movement of the united masses, rather than a mere ability to generically represent them? In fact, the notion of vanguard has changed and become a concept of "mass vanguard"; subjectivity has become an objective element itself. Mass vanguard becomes the objective condition on which to ground any notion of organization. From this standpoint, the determining and most important problem arises: that is, the problem emerging from the singular and dramatic objectivism of Leninist theory, its desire to reflect the determinate composition of class, while simultaneously trying to force it and transfigure it into a "communist" organization of the party.

Lenin thinks that the concept of organization comes, so to speak, after the concept of class composition; but in the project he develops, as a whole, the moment he relates some elements of composition to the form of organization he forces the situation and pushes it to the limit of an inversion of the relation between composition and organization. Now, starting from this limit of Leninism, we must go back to this problem and see how far struggles, in the specific kind of organization that class has given itself, have changed the very composition of class. We must verify whether the concept of organization has become so internal to the composition of a given class that there is now an infinitely more dialectical, immanent, and articulated relation between class composition and organization than the one Lenin could think of at the limits of his project. Despite the tension of his project toward its limits, in Lenin, objectivism and subjectivism always risk separation (and classical examples of this separation were offered in the problems of the Third International). Here, on the other hand, each step forward in the proletarian organization is directly and immediately a modification of class composition, a further inherence of the subjective aspects in the class composition. Lenin previews an inversion as the theoretical fulfillment of the theory of organization, embodied in the life of the actual working class. On this, some steps forward in the theory of organization can certainly be made today, considering the wealth of our experience in the past few years.[5] In any case, isn't it capitalist command itself that intuited the new form of the relationship between the capitalist cycle and subjective changes in class composition? This can be largely proved, as can the manner in which, starting from this awareness, the forms of control and domination of capitalism change to record the enormous structural and subjective power conquered by the working class.[6] Taking the discussion further, we ought to not only consider the changes in the objective conditions of a theory of the party, but also see the changes in the subjective conditions in order to proceed to a deeper analysis of the working-class character of organization founded on the new concept of mass vanguard and internally correlated to class movements as such.

The third element that we have underlined in our analysis of the Leninist shift from the theory of organization to the strategy of the revolution was the communist content of this project. For it, the permanent revolution here burns all of the stages and, through a paradoxical inversion of economic need, points to the overcoming of all of the intermediate stages precisely when the revolutionary movement centers on the intermediate stages: from progressive democracy to socialism, from socialism to proletarian dictator-ship, to the issue of the withering-away of the state and the allusion to com-munism. Our research will proceed and deepen on these issues: we will ask how the essential content of the program is presented in a different form today, whether the permanent revolution is not more dense and less paradox-ical now, and, if communism is the minimal program of proletarian struggle, whether the issue of the withering-away of the state should not be imme-diately grasped as the issue of the withering-away of labor and whether in working-class and proletarian struggles today the problem of the workers' dictatorship and the destruction of the bourgeois state is not immediately configured as one of the building of communist society. But this is the issue of our comment on *The State and Revolution*.

NOTES

1. A note on this point: in *Notebooks on Imperialism*, Lenin analyses all of the organiza-tional forms of labor in the work of Taylor, Gilbreth, and their German commentator Seubert. His strong interest in these works does not prevent an immediate under-standing of the anti-working-class nature of the Taylorist system. Overall, however, Lenin has an objective attitude to it and records it with interest. Hence the ambiguity of his attitude; but isn't ambiguity inevitable in a theory of two stages? In his analysis of Seubert's work, Lenin insists on describing Taylorism as "labor science" and on the need for a democratic base for such reform to be possible (contrary to the rigidity of the workers stratification in Germany). In his analysis of Gilbreth's work, one can primarily detect the working-class attitude of Lenin's initial approach: but the ambi-guity emerges again when he expresses such interest in the scientific analysis of labor and the means to augment productivity, especially in the conclusion to the notes: "magnificent example of technical progress of capitalism towards socialism." Other references to Taylor show Lenin's insistence on the "progressive" character of his work (as technical progress and socialization of labor).

2. On this, see Sergio Bologna, "Composizione di classe e teoria del partito alle origini del movimento consiliare" [Class composition and theory of the party in the early Council movement], in *Operai e stato* (Milan: Feltrinelli, 1972); B. Pribicevic, *The Shop-Steward Movement in England* (Oxford: Oxford University Press, 1955); K. H. Roth, *Die "andere" Arbeiterbewegung* (Munich: Trikont, 1974); and the works on IWW by Gisela Bock, Paolo Carpignano, and B. Ramirez. In addition, on this and related issues, see the collection *Contropiano* (Florence: La Nuova Italia, 1968–1971).

3. On this, see, again, Roth, *Die "andere" Arbeiterbewegung*; and various authors, *L'operaio multinazionale in Europa* (Milan: Feltrinelli, 1974); various authors, *Arbeiterkampf in Deutschland* (Munich: Trikont, 1973); A. Negri, *Crisi dello Stato-piano, comunismo e organizzazione rivoluzionaria* (Milan: Feltrinelli, 1974); and Negri, *Proletari e stato* (Milan: Feltrinelli, 1976).

4. See Carpignano's and Negri's essays in S. Bologna, P. Carpignano, and A. Negri, *Crisi e organizzazione operaia* [Crisis and workers' organization] (Milan: Feltrinelli, 1974). Two works will also be very useful in this respect: L. Ferrari-Bravo, ed., *Imperialismo e classe operaia multinazionale* [Imperialism and the multinational working class] (Milan: Feltrinelli, 1977); and, on the current class composition in America, F. Gambino, "The Significance of Socialism in the Post-War United States," in *Why Is There No Socialism in the United States?*, ed. J. Hefer and J. Rovet (Paris: Éditions de l'Ecole des Hautes Etudes en Sciences Sociales, 1987), 297–309. Both works were part of the collection *Materiali Marxisti* printed by Feltrinelli, edited by the Collective of Political Science in Padua.

5. To dwell on these points, any analysis should prove itself through the study-inquiry of the structural comportments of the working class. Absenteeism, sabotage, and the workers' use of mobility are all elements on which power concentrates, which are irreducible to the socialist perspective that is in other respects alive in the movement. But the analysis cannot develop solely as an allusion or in a purely analytical mode. In fact, at a consolidated level of historical experience, even the greatest nodes of the struggles of the working class on the international stage (workers' struggles in the United States and Great Britain, the French May, the Italian Autumn) reveal a "turn" that intervened to change the political composition of class. Complete studies are not available, and it is our generation of researchers who should accomplish them.

6. We don't wish to insist, here, on the new Sraffian's mystification of political economy; and we are looking instead at the science of the state in strict terms: for a further analysis, see the first two issues of *Kapitalistate* (1973) and their bibliographies, as well as, more generally, the works of Baran-Sweezy, Habermas, Hirsch, Agnoli, Miliband, Offe, Poulantzas, Preuss, and others. Moreover, on the more strictly economic issues, as an introduction, see F. Botta, ed., *Sul capitale monopolistico* (Bari: De Donato, 1971); and Botta, ed., *Il dibattito su Sraffa* (Bari: De Donato, 1974). Finally, see my survey of the current tendencies of state theory from the working-class perspective: Negri, "Su alcune tendenze della più recente teoria comunista dello stato: rassegna critica" [On some tendencies in the most recent communist theory of the state: a critical survey], *Critica del Diritto* 3 (1974).

9

INSURRECTION AS ART AND PRACTICE OF THE MASSES

WITH THIS LESSON, we reach the conclusion of the first part of our discussion and can outline some of the problems that we raised and will return to in the course of our future conversations. These problems concern: Lenin's political practice in the Soviets and their relation to the party; Lenin's dialectical methodology in relation to Marxist tradition; the problem of the withering-away of the state, posited in *The State and Revolution* and also confronted in other preparatory texts on Marxist state theory; finally, the questions raised by the polemic on extremism. The first part of the debate that we conclude here only aimed to outline the "frame of reference" and to point out the overall theoretical and historical dimensions where Lenin's thought is located, as well as to specify some more current questions.

In the last conversation we distanced ourselves from a series of Leninist assumptions on the theory of organization, especially concerning the relation between the theory and form of organization and determinate class composition in Lenin's period and in ours, which demanded that we distance ourselves with the banal but true recognition that it is unimaginable to return to the theory of the party in the current class composition and to repeat in a pedestrian fashion Leninist theory. It follows from this that it is impossible to recuperate Lenin's strategy of the revolutionary process because all the conditions, both objective and subjective, and the contents of the revolutionary

shift as it can be defined today from within the struggles and needs of workers have deeply changed. But we need to pay careful attention to the debates
of the past few years on this, because the positions that are critical of Lenin
already and immediately return to revisionist plans and end up consolidating
positions of reflux, which is a complete misunderstanding of the objective
of workers' struggles and a pure and simple opportunism. Contrary to these
positions, we believe that reading Lenin while questioning his thought and
criticizing it when necessary can be expedient as a way of recovering a solid
ground for revolutionary action. Having distanced ourselves from Lenin, we
can now verify some of the elements that are valid as determinations of a
continuous weaving of revolutionary practice, or, if you prefer, of a theory of
revolution as science rather than ideology; we can verify the extent to which
recalling Lenin can configure a point of reference for working-class theory.

Now, a fundamental moment in Lenin's thought needs to be underlined
and recuperated: this concerns the (wholly correct, in terms of Marxian theory) relation between composition, strategy of revolution, and party organization. But the dialectics Lenin establishes between these moments is entirely
resolved in the ability to subvert the objective conditions within which revolutionary practice unfolds, and to turn them into subjective conditions of the
party, in the will of the party, to grasp determinate conditions and operate on
them. Therefore, Leninism does not consist in raising the "question of the
state"; Leninism is raising the "question of the withering-away of the state"
in a definite context, according to workers' needs when these are embodied
in the comportments of the masses and have become their practice. Leninism is the ability of the party (or in other words, of the subjective will that
has become collective brain) to seize these needs and turn them, by means of
adequate organizational tools, from the impotence of demands to the power
of a confrontation, a subversion and an attack on the structures of the state, on
the practice of the exercise of power. This will of subversion and power is what
characterizes, effectively, Leninism and turns it into a permanent category, a
discriminator between who is revolutionary and who is not.

I believe that, taking this fundamental character of Leninism as a point of
departure, and seeing how it has penetrated into the masses, we can revalu-
ate a set of questions, though they pertain, in Leninism, to a particular class

composition. Let us see how. For instance, let us look into the discourse on insurrection as an art: this is, perhaps, one of the most provoking aspects, if you like, or one that at least seems to be the most related to the particular position of the party in relation to the masses in a situation where there is very little homogeneity among the various strata of the proletariat and where the possibility of immediately ascribing communist contents to the struggle is the furthest. Because of this, the action of the party needs to be seen as the action from below of a subjective vanguard that mediates, in itself before the masses, the continuity of the revolutionary process and thus demands to be delegated to represent the masses. Insurrection as art is the ability to grasp the opportune moment when the subjective will of the party can be made to react, and this moment, rather than deriving from the strength of class struggle, is determined by composite factors that are contradictory and, in any case, out of the direct control of the working class. We criticized this notion from our perspective, one that sees a renewal of the revolutionary process when confronted with a higher degree of class homogeneity and a series of comportments that do not allow for representations of working-class interest, a situation where the working class creates a block on itself and directly builds the conditions and contradictions of capitalist development rather than simply using them. However, beyond this and the fact that this new standpoint on insurrection eliminates the "transcendence" of the party in relation to the organisms and movements of the masses (even when, in the case of the Soviet, they configure instances of power), we could still read, in Lenin, the strong tendency toward a situation where this insurrectional movement subverts this relation of representation and decision, composition and organization: in Lenin, we find a faith in the prospect that the moment of insurrection can see organization (as subjective will), affect the objective comportments of the masses, and change them, while identifying with them. The inversion of the relation between composition and organization thus turns upside down the meaning of the theory of the party, and "tends to" anticipate Marx's forecasting of the maturity of communism and of the masses for communism. This hope exalts the Leninist notion of insurrection as an "art," and elides its irrationalist character while materially filling it with subjective impetus. If we read Lenin's *Marxism and Insurrection*, we find, on the one hand, the greatest example of the discourse on insurrection as art (bearing in mind that it was written in September 1917, between the first and the second phase of the revolution), a letter to the central committee of the Russian social democratic workers' party written at a time when Lenin was forced into hiding, an extremely acute moment of struggle faced with an attempt of reactionary forces to recuperate it. On the other hand, the very incidence of the concept of insurrection on the relation between composition and organization makes it possible to conceive of an inversion of this very relation:

> Marxists are accused of Blanquism for treating insurrection as an art! Can there be a more flagrant perversion of the truth, when not a single Marxist will deny that it was Marx who expressed himself on this score in the most definite, precise and categorical manner, referring to insurrection specifically as an art, saying that it must be treated as an art, that you must win the first success and then proceed from success to success, never ceasing the offensive against the enemy, taking advantage of his confusion, etc., etc.? To be successful, insurrection must rely not upon conspiracy and not upon a party, but upon the advanced class. That is the first point. Insurrection must rely upon a revolutionary upsurge of the people. That is the second point. Insurrection must rely upon that turning-point in the history of the growing revolution when the activity of the advanced ranks of the people is at its height, and when the vacillations in the ranks of the enemy and in the ranks of the weak, half-hearted and irresolute friends of the revolution are strongest. That is the third point. And these three conditions for raising the question of insurrection distinguish Marxism from Blanquism. Once these conditions exist, however, to refuse to treat insurrection as an art is a betrayal of Marxism and a betrayal of the revolution.[1]

Many other passages in the text could be cited to this purpose. But it will be sufficient and useful to pause at this section because it has often been recalled as a refrain of the left communism of the 1920s, when what was known as the "theory of the offensive" was first confronted with the emergence of the Soviet bureaucratic party. That theory was rightly defeated,[2] not so much because of its adventurism or the inadequacy of the political project it sustained: these were inherently contradictory aspects, and thus precarious, open to criticism and modifications. What was not open to change and needed to be defeated was the irrationalist and nonmaterialist notion of the revolutionary process and of insurrection in particular. How could it be doubted that in Lenin's position the concept of "insurrection as art" was completely dialectical in relation to the basic relationship between organization and composition? Let us return to the text we quoted: here Lenin founds the notion of insurrection on the dynamic relationship between the movement of organization and the revolutionary movement of the oppressed masses. Only by deepening this relation can the revolutionary moment explode; it does not do so by means of acts of will or idealist considerations! The inversion of the relation between composition and organization is a material and wholly determinate function. In order to succeed, the revolution must not base itself on a conspiracy or on a party (indeed!), but on the vanguard class: here the inversion of the relation between class composition and organizational process is given, as is its material form. The moment the working class reaches this level of realization of the revolutionary process, it has changed itself and its composition, as well as its relation to the party. The occurring inversion is an index, in Lenin, of a degree of uncertainty, which is immediately repressed and turned into theory, and which is felt when the continuity of the project faces this innovative power, the overall determinate invention of the revolutionary process of a class. Therefore, rather than insurrection as art, it is the materiality of the process of the masses and the class that wins!

Having said this, let us return to the debate on Leninism that is a permanent feature in the political comportments of the revolutionary vanguards. Leninism as a method we have seen and already specified in two elements: the relation between theory of composition, strategy, and organization, and the possibility of inverting this relation in a subjective practice. In this sense, Leninism is a method:

Our theory is not a dogma, but a *guide to action*, said Marx and Engels; and it is the greatest mistake, the greatest crime on the part of such "patented" Marxists as Karl Kautsky, Otto Bauer, etc., that they have not understood this, have been unable to apply it at crucial moments of the proletarian revolution. Political activity is not the pavement of the Nevsky Prospect (the clean, broad, smooth pavement of the perfectly straight principal street of St. Petersburg)—N. G. Chernyshevsky, the great Russian Socialist of the pre-Marxian period, used to say. Since Chernyshevsky's time Russian revolutionaries have paid the price of numerous sacrifices for ignoring or forgetting this truth. We must strive at all costs to prevent the Left Communists and the West-European and American revolutionaries who are devoted to the working class paying as dearly for the assimilation of this truth as the backward Russians did.[3]

In fact, the nonassimilation of this fundamental and elementary concept has cost us very dearly indeed: Marxism is a method that makes sense, the method of the destruction, at all costs, of the state, the method that leads from class composition to organization, and to the inversion of this relation in the destruction of the state (in the destruction of labor itself).

But let us move deeper into the method. Marxist method is a practical and revolutionary method. Theory is the practice of mass. This is not an issue for intellectuals; it is always a mass method, a political method.

The whole point now is that the Communists of every country should quite consciously take into account both the main fundamental tasks of the struggle against opportunism and "Left" doctrinarism and the specific features which this struggle assumes and inevitably must assume in each separate country in conformity with the peculiar features of its economics, politics, culture, national composition (Ireland, etc.), its colonies, religious divisions, and so on and so forth. Everywhere we can feel that dissatisfaction with the Second International is spreading and growing, both because of its opportunism and because of its inability, or incapacity, to create a really centralized, a really leading centre that would be capable of directing the international tactics of the revolutionary proletariat in its struggle for a world Soviet republic. We must clearly realize that such a leading centre cannot under any circumstances be built up on stereotyped, mechanically equalized and identical tactical rules of struggle. As long as national and state differences exist among peoples and countries—and these differences will continue to exist for a very long time even after the dictatorship of the proletariat has been established on a world scale—the unity of international tactics of the Communist working class movement of all countries demands, not the elimination of variety, not the abolition of national differences (that is a foolish dream at the present moment), but such an application of the fundamental principles of Communism (Soviet power and the dictatorship of the proletariat) as will correctly modify these principles in certain particulars, correctly adapt and apply them to national and national-state differences. Investigate, study, seek, divine, grasp that which is peculiarly national, specifically national in the concrete manner in which each country approaches the fulfillment of the single international task, in which it approaches the victory over opportunism and "Left" doctrinarism within the working-class movement, the overthrow of the bourgeoisie, and the establishment of a Soviet republic and a proletarian dictatorship—such is the main task of the historical period through which all the advanced countries (and not only the advanced countries) are now passing. The main thing—not everything by a very long way, of course, but the main thing—has already been achieved in that the vanguard of the working class has been won over, in that it has ranged itself on the side of Soviet government against parliamentarism, on the side of the dictatorship of the proletariat against bourgeois democracy. Now all efforts, all attention, must be concentrated on the next step—which seems, and from a certain standpoint really is—less fundamental, but which, on the other hand, is actually closer to the practical carrying out of the task, namely: seeking the forms of transition or approach to the proletarian revolution. The proletarian vanguard has been won over ideologically. That is the main thing. Without this not even the first step towards victory can be made. But it is still a fairly long way from victory. Victory cannot be won with the vanguard alone. To throw the vanguard alone into the decisive battle, before the whole class, before the broad masses have taken up a position either of direct support of the vanguard, or at least of benevolent neutrality towards it, and one in which they cannot possibly support the enemy, would be not merely folly but a crime. And in order that actually the whole class, that actually the broad masses of the working people and those oppressed by capital may take up such a position, propaganda and agitation alone are not enough. For this the masses must have their own political experience. Such is the fundamental law of all great revolutions, now confirmed with astonishing force and vividness not only in Russia but also in Germany. Not only the uncultured, often illiterate, masses of Russia, but the highly cultured, entirely literate masses of Germany had to realize through their own painful experience the absolute impotence and spinelessness, the absolute helplessness and servility to the bourgeoisie, the utter vileness of the government of the knights of the Second International, the absolute inevitability of a dictatorship of the extreme reactionaries (Kornilov in Russia, Kapp and Co. in Germany) as the only alternative to a dictatorship of the proletariat, in order to turn them resolutely toward Communism.[4]

Here, again, the mass method is one of the elements that Leninism innovates the most. Leninism, as a method, as a mass method, and as mass practice, insofar as Leninism entrusts the fate of the revolution to the ability of the masses to make themselves immediate agents. In this new meaning, the complexity of the process is regained, and the threshold concept of insurrection as art understood:

History generally, and the history of revolutions in particular, is always richer in content, more varied, more many sided, more lively and "subtle" than even the best parties and the most class-conscious vanguards of the most advanced classes imagine. This is understandable, because even the best vanguards express the class consciousness, will, passion and imagination of tens of thousands; whereas revolutions are made, at moments of particular upsurge and the exertion of all human capacities, by the class consciousness, will, passion and imagination of tens of millions, spurred on by a most acute struggle of classes. From this follow two very important practical conclusions: first, that in order to fulfil its task the revolutionary class must be able to master *all* forms, or aspects, of social activity without any exception (completing, after the capture of political power, sometimes at great risk and very great danger, what it did not complete before the capture of power); second, that the revolutionary class must be ready to pass from one form to another in the quickest and most unexpected manner.[5]

This is a quotation from *"Left-Wing" Communism, an Infantile Disorder,* which is directly linked to the writings from 1905 on insurrection around the

Third Congress of the Russian social democratic party, and is thus connected to the notion of a shift from legal to armed struggle, which is one of the main points of Lenin's analysis of the situation that immediately followed 1905 and during the period of repression, and in other moments and situations Lenin theorizes its political contents. For instance, repression must only be faced with armed struggle, which would actualize the tools and processes of proletarian justice that attack where capital is no longer presented as development but as crisis and dysfunction. But Lenin's political choice in the particular does not interest us: we are interested in the general, in the methodological proposal it contains. What interests us is, again, this ability to substitute one form of struggle with another, the ability to develop (from the side of the vanguard) a wide articulation of the adequate instruments within the tension proper to the revolutionary process, and the capacity to use Marxism as a method that can grasp all of the given alternatives: this is the innovative relevance of Lenin's discourse.

Having said this, a last observation is needed. We have seen how Lenin is largely interested in the determinate form of organization, and could see this even more if we were to study Lenin as a party organizer.[6] In this case, we could verify how Lenin's discourse always finds its own determinate practical mediation in forms of organization that are, time and again, adequate to the revolutionary process, that are, so to speak, time and again chased, defined, led. Curiously, on this basis, Leninism has often been presented as a list of precepts, a sort of key to the solution to any problem (a false key, if it opens all doors). It has been presented, in other words, as formalism, in terms opposed to those we heard him speak. At the Third International, it was typical of the process of Bolshevization to try to impose a series of firm precepts on all parties that referred to themselves as part of the Bolshevik revolution; this might have been necessary, insofar as these firm points made it possible to discriminate between the authentic revolutionary forces and the forces that were not so or that, at least at the level of ideology, were trying to introduce a series of erroneous and backward positions inside the movement. In fact, this Bolshevization functioned as a formal kind of rigor and precepts that cut some vanguards off at the legs and made it impossible for them to make themselves adequate to the particular situations they were meant to intervene in. The extreme example is probably the vicissitude of the communist party in the United States of America, where an imposing force of communists coming from a formidable class experience like that of the IWW, with capable cadres and a very long experience of struggle, was castrated by the campaign for Bolshevization, by an incredibly slavish repetition of the model, which led, for instance, to the exclusion of African-American members from the organization (in the name of a politics of nationality that repeated something that might have been valid in Russia, even though in the United States class unity was given and blacks and whites worked on the same assembly line).[7] Well, all of this comes from the formalistic use of Leninism as a set of precepts. Ours is not a recrimination among intellectuals. In fact, this absurd formalism functioned as a material force, castrating effective revolutionary powers, eliminating their chance to express themselves and interpret the class needs of more advanced degrees of capitalist development. This is no recrimination: it is another indication of method, but this time, a wholly Leninist one. First comes mass practice, everything else follows. Theory either is verified in the practices of the masses or does not exist. There is no fetish we sacrifice to, even if it is called Lenin. Lenin is useful, essential, and fundamental: but he lives in the history of the workers' movement only insofar as he corresponds to the needs and practices of the masses. This is Leninism.

And perhaps the concept of insurrection as art—this ambiguous limit of privileging, on the one hand, the party (even against the party if necessary) and, on the other hand, the activity and practice of the masses—indicates this to us. It shows that in Lenin there is never a moment when all the real contents of the practice of the masses and of the needs of the proletariat are mechanically subordinated to the demands of the party: the opposite is always the case. The Leninist party manages to melt with the masses and determine thus the inversion of the relation between composition and organization only at times: beyond these times, there is no illusion that the fusion will happen, but there is an awareness of the tendency and the limits of the action of the party. The party is necessary but not sufficient: what is both necessary and sufficient is the revolutionary practice of the masses. If we keep these elements in mind—on the one hand, the relation between the theory of class composition, strategy, and organization in the process that moves from the determination of the situation to the organization of the party, and on the other hand, the possibility of inverting this relation in the practice of the masses, in the emergence of the most acute revolutionary contents—we can determine the permanence of the Leninist method as an organic experience of the movement, as an element of the political composition of the working class that cannot be destroyed today. In Lenin, the transition to the highest stage of the recomposition of the proletariat is experienced as a hope, a project, and a risk. The ambiguity deriving from this is often heavy. But if we assume as an index of this ambiguity the couple "insurrection as art–practice of the masses," we can have no doubts about the meaning of Lenin's tremendous solution.

NOTES

1. Lenin, *Marxism and Insurrection*, trans. Y. Sdobnikov and G. Hanna, in *Collected Works* (Moscow: Progress Publishers, 1964), 26:22.

2. Current thoughts on the theory of the "offensive" can be found in the articles G. Daghini, "Motivazione, irrealtà e il tema della praxis" [Motivation, unreality, and the issue of praxis], *Aut-Aut: Rivista di filosofia e di cultura* 107 (1968): 7–43; and G. Piana, "Sulla nozione di analogia strutturale in 'Storia e coscienza di classe'" [On the notion of structural analogy in *History and Class Consciousness*], *Aut-Aut: Rivista di filosofia e di cultura* 107 (1968): 101–103. General information on the theory of communism of the German left can be found in G. E. Rusconi, *La teoria critica della società* (Bologna: Il Mulino, 1970).

3. Lenin, *"Left-Wing" Communism, an Infantile Disorder* (Peking: Foreign Language Press, 1970), 68.

4. Ibid., 95–97.

5. Ibid., 100–101.

6. On Lenin's biography, see the work of L. Fischer, *The Life of Lenin* (New York: Harper and Row, 1964); A. B. Ulam, *Lenin and the Bolsheviks* (London: Secker and Warburg, 1965); S. Cohen, *Bukharin and the Bolshevik Revolution* (Oxford: Oxford University Press, 1971); L. Trotsky, *My Life* (New York: Charles Schribner's Sons, 1930); M. Gorky, *Autobiography of Maxim Gorky: My Childhood, in the World, My Universities* (New York: Citadel Press, 1949); and N. Krupskaya, *Reminiscences of Lenin* (Moscow: International Publishers, 1970).

7. In particular, see T. Draper, *American Communism and Soviet Russia* (New York: Viking, 1960).

PART TWO

Lenin and the Soviets in
the Russian Revolution and
Some Remarks on Sovietism

10

THE SOVIETS BETWEEN
SPONTANEITY AND THEORY

A HISTORICAL ANALYSIS of Lenin's judgment on the Soviet in the various phases of the Russian revolution, a judgment that is essentially unitary but deeply complex, must preliminarily reflect on the singularity of Lenin's method. Lenin's method seems to give prominence to practical-theoretical reflections on each aspect of the analysis, especially the issue of the doctrinarian Marxist tradition and the theoretical analysis of the specific development of the real movement of class and capital in Russia. Lenin eviscerates these analytical aspects, reshapes, and renovates them while always subjecting them to the sectarianism of the practice that innervates his notion of the party and to which he responds. The usefulness of this method, its constant flexibility of approach to particular situations, and the politically and theoretically creative motives it keeps contributing to the workers' science of revolution are manifest in his analysis of the Soviets and in how this analysis becomes an instrument of agitation and organization for the revolution.

The historical tradition of proletarian struggles that Lenin politically reinterprets offers a great number of council experiences. The councils were the direct expression of the exploited class, and were rooted in that class and organized in radically democratic forms; they were the result of a revolutionary struggle and marked its most acute phases. In particular, the tradition offered at least three typical models of Soviet organization: the council as an organ of the leadership of revolutionary struggle (the councils of soldiers in the English Revolution); the council as representative of the interests of the proletariat in the structure of bourgeois republican power (the Luxembourg Commission of 1848); and the Communard council as "class organized in state power." The analysis and the ideological projects of socialist theoreticians had been based on these examples. It was no accident that anarchic populism had exalted the council moment of the mass management of the struggles, up to the utopia of a "federalism of the barricades," whereas the Proudhonian tradition retraced the foundation and decorum of a pluralist ideology in the democratic radicalism of the councils.

As for Marx, the question is immediately simplified in an ironic remark on the vanity of any institutionalization of the councils and, in general, any proletarian self-government in the world of capitalist production. Marx saw the Luxembourg Commission as "a socialist synagogue" (which it was), and thought that the project of a democratic organization of labor was merely a support for the capitalist organization of labor, and thus nothing but a sign of immaturity and political impotence.[1]

But in the same text Marx already outlines a definition of the relation between the struggle of the working class and the political movement of capital. Beyond the mystifying effect of the reformist institution, there is the fact that the proletariat had won it as a concession from the bourgeoisie. The workers "imposed" the bourgeois republic, and "the February Republic was forced to proclaim itself a *republic surrounded by social institution.*"[2] The result, as soon as the proletariat imposed it, was dissolved and gradually became the substance of the reformism of capital.

For the proletariat this is now nothing but the new starting point for a workers' struggle at a higher level:

It is our interest and our task to make the revolution permanent, until all more or less possessing classes have been forced out of their position of dominance, until the proletariat has conquered state power, and the asso-ciation of proletarians, not only in one country but in all the dominant countries of the world, has advanced so far that competition among the proletarians of these countries has ceased and that at least the decisive productive forces are concentrated in the hands of the proletarians.[3]

Only in this framework, therefore, can a Marxian rediscovery of council power be justified. And the history of the Paris Commune verified this hypothesis: "its true secret was this. It was essentially a working-class government, the result of the struggle of the producing against the appropriating class, the political form at last discovered under which to work out the economical emancipation of labor."[4] The revolutionary power of the working class is configured in the continuity of the struggle and only in that continuity, as its product. There should be no descending to utopian positions, but rather, an affirmation of the councils as organizations of struggle in the permanent process of the workers' revolution and as the initial figures of revolutionary class government.

Lenin's interpretation of the council tradition integrates and validates Marx's discussions. Lenin does not assume Marx's interpretation as a doctrine: its theoretical validity must be analyzed and proved in light of the singular revolutionary pragmatism that, given the scientific investigation of the specific conditions of the revolutionary movement in Russia, seeks to illustrate the theoretical lessons of the classics through a series of strategic and tactical determinations.

We should first look at Lenin's analysis of the revolution of 1905:

The peculiarity of the Russian revolution is that it was a bourgeois-democratic revolution in its social content, but a proletarian revolution in its methods of struggle. It was a bourgeois-democratic revolution since its immediate aim, which it could achieve directly and with its own forces, was a democratic republic, the eight-hour day and confiscation of the immense estates of the nobility—all the measures the French bourgeois revolution in 1792–93 had almost completely achieved. At the same time, the Russian revolution was also a proletarian revolution, not only in the sense that the proletariat was the leading force, the vanguard of the movement, but also in the sense that a specifically proletarian weapon of struggle—the strike— was the principal means of bringing the masses into motion and the most characteristic phenomenon in the wave-like rise of decisive events.[5]

On the one hand, there was an extraordinarily backward economic situation that made a bourgeois revolution inevitable; on the other hand, as extraordinary a degree of political maturity and combativeness in the proletariat made its hegemonic function possible in the course of the revolution. Lenin's position on the revolution in Russia, and consequently on the revolutionary organization of social democracy, is characterized by a constant confrontation between these two terms. Given the degree of development of Russian capital, the revolutionary objectives of a radically democratic management of capital can thus be assumed by the proletariat and by the industrial working class as its leader, but only on the condition that the party is "independent" and its leadership "hegemonic." This condition transforms the character of Plekhanov's analytical premise and dissolves its economist residues. The Menshevik affirmation of the necessarily bourgeois character of the ongoing revolutionary phase, the programmatic deductions about the type of political organization of the Russian proletariat, the implications of the democratic function concerning the role of proletarian organizations once a bourgeois republic is achieved: all these issues are confronted and overcome in Lenin's definition of the relation between democratic revolution and workers' struggle, and by the subsequent definition of the structure and the tasks of the party. In fact, the interest of the working class is only occasionally, albeit necessarily, tied to the aim of a democratic-bourgeois revolution: therefore it must be guaranteed that its "substitutive" function can be soon overcome in the further stages of its progress toward communism. As already seen in Marx, the relation between the objective determination of the movement and the general meaning of the revolutionary struggle is all resolved in favor of the second. And Lenin's theoretical and practical struggle to emphasize and practically impose these objectives and the corresponding organizational conditions on Russian social democracy has this same significance. This leads directly back to the indications contained in the "Address of the Authority to the League."[6]

Such an approach to the strategic and organizational problem of the revolutionary movement in Russia has direct implications when Lenin confronts the problems of the mass organizations, that is, the problems that pertain to the form of organization of alliances that, according to the plan of the democratic revolution, are the necessary premises for the development of the

movement, and should not jeopardize but help the uninterrupted development of the struggle toward more advanced aims. Now, mass organizations,
as well as the entire movement, must be led by revolutionary social democracy
and destroyed by it insofar as, in the course of the movement, the democratic
aims of the revolution are in their turn realized and overcome. When this
is not possible, social democracy will negate the function exercised by such
organisms, even if they are mass and popular organizations. Their inevitable
destiny, once they are excluded from the permanent action of the workers'
struggle and the leadership of its avant-garde, will be that of becoming an
integral part of the development of capital: at best, merely a useful tool for
its internal reform. Hence, Lenin's suspicious and fiercely polemical attitude
from the beginning, his bitter denunciation of all forms of mass organization
that tend to become institutional outside of the revolutionary process and
that therefore subordinate the permanent and real aims of the class movement to the provisional organizational ends of social democracy.

Nor are the Soviets an exception to this. In fact, from their first emergence,
Lenin correctly defines them as mass democratic organizations "a million times
more democratic than any bourgeois democracy," and their function is judged
on the basis of the general strategic and tactical criteria of revolutionary social
democracy. Therefore, the Soviet can be praised as an instrument of proletarian
struggle, and Lenin will gradually prefigure in the Soviet the organization of the
dictatorship of the proletariat, at least insofar as the Soviets can be hegemon-
ized by the independent organization of the working class. When these original
and radically democratic instruments deviate from the project of a "revolution
all the way" and when revisionary forces tend to make them function within the
political dialectic of capital (insofar as they manage to do so), Lenin unleashes
a polemic to demystify these organisms and proposes the sacred sectarian alternative: either the liquidation of the Soviet as a reformist tool or its conquest of
the movement as a moment of revolutionary organization.[7]

The working class in struggle in the course of the revolution of 1905
invented the Soviets. In fact, we can recognize many anticipations of their
organization in the history of the Russian working class. Given their fragmentary and inorganic character and the strong and continual autocratic
repression waged against them, the movements of the Russian working

class had basically been spontaneous ever since the first wave of industrial-ization in the 1870s. The process whereby struggles took on a mass charac-ter that unfolded during the second industrial wave starting in 1895 did not really change the spontaneous character of the movement: rather, the process restructured the movement by imposing necessary forms of self-organization on it. Thus in this phase, strike councils and workers' resistance funds were often created. Already in 1895, in the Morozov textile factory in Tver, a per-manent strike council was set up; in 1895, there is the first appearance of the Ivanovo-Voznesenk council in the textile area around Moscow: its new for-mation in 1905 will be considered as the official date of the birth of the Sovi-ets. The Soviets of 1905 are rooted in a long tradition of struggles and experi-ences of the Russian working class, and are thus intrinsically characterized by it. If "the history of the Russian revolution is the history of the Russian mass strikes,"[8] then the genesis of the Soviets is itself internal to this type of struggle, which rediscovers the unifying effectiveness of the continual process of the revolutionary working-class struggle beyond the merging of economic and political elements, through the circulation and succession of ever new forms of management, and in a political structure that is defined step by step. This does not mean that 1905 does not represent the true moment of the birth of Russian Sovietism. Only then did the fast generalization and spreading of the struggle—its immediately political character (at least from October onward)—and the insurrectional forms that it took on free the Soviet from the extraordinariness of the previous experiences and attribute to it a defini-tive figure of a fundamentally expansive dynamism.

We do not need to mention here the various phases of the revolutionary struggles that continued to grow from January until October and December. The activities of insurrection took place mostly in Moscow and its surround-ings, where between May and July the Ivanovo-Voznesenk Kostroma Soviets and the Moscow printers were set up, but the insurrection then spread to other areas, until, in October, it reached St. Petersburg, where the local Soviet was created on October 13:

The Soviet came into being as a response to an objective need—a need born of the course of events. It was an organization which was authoritative and yet had no traditions; which could immediately involve a scattered mass of hundreds of thousands of people while having virtually no organizational machinery; which united the revolutionary currents within the proletariat; which was capable of initiative and spontaneous self control—and most important of all, which could be brought out from underground within twenty-four hours.[9]

Recognized by the local working class, which adhered to the strike, the Soviet of St. Petersburg assumed the leadership of the revolutionary movement. In St. Petersburg it spread to all the representatives of the capitalist factories of the capital, and was recognized by all unions and the different sections of social democracy. The example of the St. Petersburg Soviet inspired the setting-up of Soviets in all the major cities in the country and expanded and unified the movement everywhere. In Siberia the first Soviets of soldiers were born.[10]

The Soviets, mass workers' organizations formed by responsible and revocable representatives, thus constitute the center of revolutionary organization in the last stage of the insurrection. They appropriated the slogans of social democracy—"eight-hour working day and constituent assembly"—and fought their democratic battle with proletarian tools. The ambiguity of the relationship between the immediate aims of democratic reform and radical revolutionary refusal, one that workers' spontaneity always carries with it, is thus typically configured in the Soviets, the direct product of the workers' spontaneity. Nor could it be otherwise, given the democratic, and not always radically democratic, aims imposed by the level of capitalist development. On the other hand, the form of the workers' self-government was necessarily ambiguous, even though insurrectional, due to the persistence of the institutions and the power of the bourgeoisie, since there remained, for the bourgeoisie, wide margins of reformism, and this was inevitable due to the backward situation of the development of capitalism in Russia. In fact, the form of insurrection does not by itself guarantee the effectiveness of an organizational tool when the content of the demand is still situated at the margins of not so much the immediate possibilities of the concession to bourgeois power as its own necessary development. In an exemplary manner, the ambiguity of the Soviets expressed itself in their being at the same time organs of

insurrectional struggle and organs of internal self-government of the proletariat: in this, the initiatives and the resolutions of the St. Petersburg Soviet
are very significant. In any case, the destiny of the Soviet rested squarely on
the solution to this ambiguity; depending on the prominence given to one or
the other aspect, different revolutionary programs arise, while the exaltation
of one or the other aspect of the structure and the function of the Soviet follows on from different analytical premises.

It is not necessarily the case that the Menshevik slogan of "revolutionary self-management" had an impact, even a secondary one, on the formation
of the Soviets, including St. Petersburg's. But this slogan had certainly been
around for a long time and was now widely spoken (at the Menshevik Conference of April 1905, for example), adequate as it was to the definition of the
strategic and tactical aims of that faction. The main argument was that the
backward character of Russian capitalism would keep the proletariat from the
immediate total or partial seizure of power. Nothing was left but to exploit
the situation to "build and strengthen the class party," to reach conditions
that would allow for its free development, and therefore to build an analogous
development of instances of revolutionary struggle within the social and state
structures of capital.[11]

The idealization of the strategy of German social democracy clearly
played a predominant role in this context and exercised an important theoretical influence on Menshevism. Apart from this, however, in the definition of the Menshevik strategy the type of relation, which was fixed in an
almost mechanical identification, between the growth of the subjective and
the objective aspects of the revolutionary process was determining, as was that
between the undoubtedly correct recognition of its material conditions and
the recognition of class movements, where the latter was entirely subordinated to the former and perhaps even too disenchanted. From this point of
view, the ripening of the economic material conditions for the shift to socialism implied a parallel, mechanical ripening of subjective forces: social democracy had to recognize and record and follow this process accurately. If one
spoke of "proletarian dictatorship," it was as a "dictatorship of the majority,"
of the "huge majority of people." Now, this situation had to be attended to: to
prepare it was only the guarantee that overthrowing czarist autocracy would

create the conditions of the autonomous political growth of the proletariat in its autonomous party and union organizations, a growth meant to determine the shift to socialism. This democratic and majoritarian yet peaceful shift was still secondary then. For the Mensheviks, the Soviets fit this pattern perfectly. They prefigured a widespread process of the organization of democratic bases and found this process in a moment of great revolutionary tension (the fight against autocracy), so that beyond this limit they could verify the presumed hypothesis with all the prestige and power they derived from having determined their first revolutionary instance. Typical of the Mensheviks of that year was an exaltation of the Commune as a "dictatorship of the majority" and as an instrument of "revolutionary self-management" from which the program of "democratic self-management" is drawn.

Even to the Bolshevik organizations, the birth and the spreading of the experience of the Soviets seemed at times to verify the Menshevik program. There was a widespread attitude either of suspicion that the Soviets might reproduce irresponsible, chaotic, and irrecoverable forms of labor organization incompatible with the organization of the party, or of polemical underestimation of the Soviets as mere union organizations. In St. Petersburg, where the memory of the workers' organizations of Gapon was still fresh, Soviets were even in danger of being boycotted. Only Trotsky's intervention on Krassin managed to ward off the risk. And this attitude spread from the center to the periphery. The Bolsheviks remained, except in rare cases, foreign to the formation of the Soviets.

In fact, the revolutionary committees that Lenin had proposed as instruments to impose insurrection and achieve the objective of a "provisional revolutionary government" had little in common with the Soviets. In these committees, the party clearly has a leadership function. Precisely because of the direct action that the party exercises in them, they can guarantee both of the necessary objectives of the insurrection: the development of the permanent revolution and, in it, the development of the movement toward the immediate seizure of power. Lenin's interpretation of the rise and spreading of the Soviets did not contradict the Bolshevik line. The Soviets were "peculiar mass organizations," spontaneous forms, and organizations of insurrection.[12] They were first and foremost the outcome of workers' spontaneity, and spontaneity was not a problem: it was the normal condition of class existence and expression and had to be recognized, followed, affirmed, and overcome. It is contradictory, instead, to consider the Soviets as organs of revolutionary self-government in the Menshevik sense: doing so turns spontaneity, the keystone of insurrection, into the worst kind of democraticist utopianism and eliminates the function of the party.

"While quite correctly condemning a passive boycott, the *Iskra* contraposes to it the idea of the immediate 'organization of revolutionary self-government bodies,' as a 'possible prologue to an uprising.'"[13] Thus the neo-Iskrists wished to fill the country with a network of organs of revolutionary self-government:

> Such a slogan is absolutely useless. Viewed in the light of the political tasks in general it is a jumble, while in the light of the immediate political situation it brings grist to the mill of the *Osvobozhdeniye* trend. The organization of revolutionary self-government, the election of their own deputies by the people is not the prologue to an uprising but its *epilogue*. To attempt to bring about this organization now, before an uprising and apart from an uprising, means setting oneself absurd aims and causing confusion in the minds of the revolutionary proletariat. It is first of all necessary to win the victory in an uprising (if only in a single city) and to establish a provisional revolutionary government, so that the latter, as the organ of the uprising and the recognized leader of the revolutionary people, should be able to relegate it into the background by proposing a slogan demanding the organization of a revolutionary self-government is something like giving advice that the fly should first be caught and then stuck on the fly-paper.[14]

Opportunism breaks the continuity of the insurrectional process and stops it around the absurd project of building self-government, which is not possible without first destroying autocracy. Beyond the utopian and dangerous program of the Mensheviks, against the attempts of absorbing the entire movement of liberation into one single stream of democraticism, the value of the spontaneous experience of the Soviet is still upheld. Insofar as it is spontaneous, it must be won over to the rules of the political organization of the proletariat. In December 1905, when the Executive Council of the Soviet of the Workers'

Deputies refused to admit the anarchists, Lenin used the opportunity to stress the position of the Bolsheviks: "If we were to regard the Soviet of Workers' Deputies as a parliament of labor, or as a sort of proletarian organ of self-government, then, of course, it would have been wrong to reject the application of the anarchists." But the Soviet was not a parliament. It was "a fighting organization for the achievement of definite ends, . . . an undefined, broad fighting alliance of socialists and revolutionary democrats."[15] As such, it had to refer to the standards of the socialist international organization, insisting in particular on the exclusion of the anarchists. Its end was only insurrection.

NOTES

1. Karl Marx, "The Class Struggles in France," in *Marx and Engels Collected Works* (Moscow: Progress Publishers, 1978), 10:55. In the six lessons that make up part 2 of the present book, the first three (chapters 10–12) refer to an article I wrote and published in *Classe Operaia* [Working class] 11 (1965): 26ff.; and in *Crisi dello stato piano, comunismo e organizzazione rivoluzionaria* [Crisis of the planner state, communism, and revolutionary organization] (Florence: CLUSF, 1972), 93–128. Lessons 13–15 are new.

2. Marx, "The Class Struggles in France," 10:55.

3. Karl Marx and Fredrick Engels, "Address of the Central Authority to the League," in *Marx and Engels Collected Works* (Moscow: Progress Publishers, 1978), 10:281.

4. Karl Marx, "The Civil War in France," in *Marx and Engels Collected Works* (Moscow: Progress Publishers, 1986), 22:334.

5. Lenin, *Lecture on the 1905 Revolution*, trans. M. S. Levin, J. Fineberg, and others, in *Collected Works* (Moscow: Progress Publishers, 1964), 23:238–239.

6. See Lenin, "Preface to the Second Edition," in *The Development of Capitalism in Russia*, trans. J. Fineberg and G. Hanna, ed. V. Jerome, in *Collected Works* (Moscow: Progress Publishers, 1961), 3:31–36; see also, especially, his polemical writings and interventions in the internal debate of the party prior to the first Russian revolution: Lenin, *The Tasks of the Russian Social Democrats*, trans. G. Hanna, in *Collected Works* (Moscow: Progress Publishers, 1972), 2:323–351; Lenin, *What Is to Be Done? Burning Questions of Our Movement* (Peking: Foreign Language Press, 1973); and Lenin, *One Step Forward, Two Steps Back: The Crisis in Our Party*, trans. A. Fineberg and N. Jochel, in *Collected Works*, vol. 7 (Moscow: Progress Publishers, 1965).

7. Lenin, *The Proletarian Revolution and the Renegade Kautsky* (Peking: Foreign Languages Press, 1972).

8. Rosa Luxemburg, *The Mass Strike, the Political Party and the Trade Unions*, trans. P. Lavin (Detroit: Marxist Educational Society of Detroit, 1925), 32.

9. Leon Trotsky, "1905," trans. A. Bostock, in *Our Revolution* (London: Vintage, 1907), chap. 8.

10. The most recent and informed research on the Soviet is undoubtedly: C. Anweiler, *Die Ratebewegung in Russland, 1905–1931*, vol. 5, *Studien zur Geschichte Osteuropas* (Amsterdam: Brill, 1958). This study has been used throughout our lessons here.

11. J. Martow, *Geschichte der russischen Sozialdemokratie* (Berlin: Buchhandlung und Verl. Politladen, 1973), 110ff.

12. See Lenin, *Lecture on the 1905 Revolution*.

13. Lenin, *The Boycott of the Bulygin Duma, and Insurrection*, trans. A. Fineberg and J. Kratzer, ed. G. Hanna, in *Collected Works* (Moscow: Progress Publishers, 1972), 9:184.

14. Ibid.

15. Lenin, *Socialism and Anarchism*, trans. A. Rothstein, in *Collected Works* (Moscow: Progress Publishers, 1972), 10:72.

11

LENIN AND THE SOVIETS
BETWEEN 1905 AND 1917

L
ENIN'S REFUSAL TO accept the either-or alternative between Soviet or party, his claim that the Soviet is the organism immediately instrumental to insurrection while to the party is entrusted the permanent and final ends of the revolutionary movement in a polemic and demystification of the Menshevik program, and the ambiguity of the Soviet we mentioned earlier are all further clarified by his writings of the period of 1906 to 1907, the year of the bourgeois recovery. While during the most acute period of struggle, when the Soviets were directly invested and configured by the workers' struggle, the risk of their being entrapped in the institutional mechanism of bourgeois democracy could be considered merely theoretical, now, in a phase of the ebb of struggle and of bourgeois recovery, this had become an immediate danger. This process of the sterilization of the Soviet foreshadowed its elimination, not only as the instrument of struggle but also as an instrument of political representation in democracy. To think that there could have been a different development was to yield to the worst constitutional illusions and to conceive once again, in Proudhonian terms, the Soviet as a constitutive moment of pluralist democracy. And this was twice illusory: first of all with respect to Russian capital, which could not even imagine forms of popular self-man-agement functional to democratic development; second, in more general terms, because such constitutionalism, if it were possible, far from changing

the power of the bourgeoisie, would have merely strengthened it. The Soviets were, in sum, the products and organs of the workers' struggle and could not be anything else. Outside this way of understanding them there is only utopianism and the betrayal of the struggle, if not pure and simple opportunism.

> The Mensheviks are opposed to electing deputies to the Duma, but wish to elect delegates and electors. What for? Is it in order that they may form a People's Duma, or a free, illegal, representative assembly, something like an All-Russian Soviet of Workers' (and also Peasants') Deputies? To this we reply: if free representatives are needed, why bother with the Duma at all when electing them? Why supply the police with the lists of our delegates? And why set up new Soviets of Workers' Deputies, and in a new way, when the old Soviets of Workers' Deputies still exist (e.g., in St. Petersburg)? This would be useless and even harmful, for it would give rise to the false, utopian illusion that the decaying and disintegrating Soviets can be revived by new elections, instead of by making new preparations for insurrection and extending it.[1]

In November 1905 Lenin had actually hinted at the possibility that the Soviets might assume the function of provisional revolutionary government.[2] Insofar as they widened their representation and rooted themselves in the struggle and in the struggle became recognized as leaders of the people's majority (as was the case), Lenin suggested the possibility of making the Soviets function as a largely representative basis of a provisional government that would replace the Duma, which was itself the result of revolutionary struggle too. Considering the Soviets as the embryo of a provisional revolutionary government was well suited to Lenin's scheme: the ambivalence of the spontaneous character of the emergence of the Soviet and of the mass democratic elements of its current form could in fact be resolved by this newly assumed role. Even better: just as the Soviet assumed the function of a provisional revolutionary government, the ambiguity could be resolved in them.

Anticipating a conclusion about Lenin's consideration of the Soviet of 1917, we can already say that it is here that Lenin begins to define the Soviets as an instrument of proletarian dictatorship. But we want to mention Lenin's position on the Soviet of November 1905 also because it confirms, in the way he establishes a flexible parallel between the Soviet and instruments of democratic representation in general, that he conceives of the Soviet as nothing more than an organ of revolutionary struggle. From this point of view, even the Duma, if it is to exist, must paradoxically Sovietize itself since it too cannot escape the laws of revolutionary struggle that give it its function:

> The objective cause of the downfall of the Cadet Duma was not that it was unable to express the needs of the people, but that it was unable to cope with the *revolutionary* task of the struggle for *power*. The Cadet Duma imagined that it was a constitutional organ, but it was in fact a revolutionary organ (the Cadets abused us for regarding the Duma as a stage or an instrument of the revolution, but experience has fully confirmed *our view*). The Cadet Duma imagined that it was an organ of struggle against the *Cabinet*, but it was in fact an organ of struggle for the *overthrow* of the entire old regime.[3]

But the Duma was not an instrument of "workers' power"! In fact, any organization can carry out the revolutionary task when, formed and sustained by the workers' struggle, it rids itself of the bourgeois democratic content of the revolution. Class struggle and the generality of its revolutionary determination and refusal are primary; everything else is secondary, or at least conditioned. "Workers' power" is the power of struggle; it is a moment and a stage in the seizure of "state power": it cannot be conceived separately from the totality of the movement or, even less, institutionalized outside of it. If then the Soviets are preferable to other tools of struggle, it must be because of a pragmatic assessment of their effectiveness.

The ambiguity of the relation between "Soviet as self-government" and "Soviet as organ of struggle" of the proletariat that is established within the relation between democratic struggle and socialist struggle is here fully resolved. In the conclusive remarks of his speech on the Soviets of the first Russian revolution, Lenin can thus, on the one hand, exalt the Soviets for their very spontaneous capability as organizers of struggle and, on the other, warn against their fetishization and the risk of overvaluing them:

The role played by the Soviets of Workers' Deputies . . . in the great October and December days surrounded them with something like a halo, so that sometimes they are treated almost as a fetish. People imagine that those organs are "necessary and sufficient" for a mass revolutionary movement at all times and in all circumstances. Hence the uncritical attitude towards the choice of the moment for the creation of such bodies, towards the question of what the real conditions are for the success of their activities. The experience of October-December has provided very instructive guidance on this point. Soviets of Workers' Deputies are *organs of direct mass struggle*. They originated as organs of the *strike* struggle. By force of circumstances they very quickly became the organs of the *general revolutionary* struggle against the government. The course of events and the transition from a strike to an uprising *irresistibly* transformed them *into organs of an uprising*. That this was precisely the role that quite a number of "soviets" and "committees" played in December, is an absolutely indisputable fact. Events have proved in the most striking and convincing manner that the strength and importance of such organs in time of militant action depend *entirely* upon the strength and success of the uprising. It was not some theory, not appeals on the part of some one, or tactics invented by someone, not party doctrine, but the force of circumstances that led these non-party mass organs to realize the need for an uprising and transformed them into organs of an uprising. At the present time, too, to establish such organs means creating organs of an uprising; to call for their establishment means calling for an uprising. To forget this, or to veil it from the eyes of the broad mass of the people, would be the most unpardonable shortsightedness and the worst of policies. If that is so—and undoubtedly it is—the conclusion to be drawn is also clear: "soviets" and similar mass institutions are in themselves *insufficient* for organizing an uprising. They are necessary for welding the masses together, for creating unity in the struggle, for handing on the party slogans (or slogans advanced by agreement between parties) of political leadership, for awakening the interest of the masses, for rousing and attracting them. But they are not sufficient for organizing the *immediate fighting forces*, for *organizing an uprising* in the narrowest sense of the word.[4]

Whether the Soviet would be favored over other organs of the revolutionary struggle will simply depend, as we said, on pragmatic considerations. The question is more or less closed here. In the years following 1905, in the process of general strengthening of the Bolshevik tactics and strategy, the Soviets are seldom discussed again: this confirms that the pragmatic criterion tied to the tactical contingencies of the insurrection was sufficient to decide on their value, and such judgment could not be prejudiced in the counterrevolutionary phase. Nonetheless, some premises on the effectiveness of the Soviets were developed on the basis of the most recent experience. First of all, the Soviets were mass organizations that the bourgeois tradition had not yet burned out. In fact, it was possible to rather unscrupulously establish an analogy between the functions of the Soviet and those of the Duma as a basis and organ of the provisional revolutionary government; however, it was impossible not to recognize that, beyond this rather theoretical analogy of their functions, their genesis, organizational nature, and reality were profoundly and irrefutably original, something that could perhaps be newly deployed at the resumption of open struggle.[5] Lenin can see this: sometimes he prefers to be silent about this originality of Sovietism, at least insofar as it seems invalidated by "anarcho-syndicalism."[6] On the other hand, on the rare and less official occasions that he confronts the problem during these years, he explicitly wonders, given these facts, whether and how the Soviets could become centers of revolutionary socialist power.

After 1905, however, the problem is not that of further defining the relation between Soviet and party. The problem is now that of keeping the struggle open and relaunching it in a permanent manner. Permanent revolution remains in fact the strategic line of the Bolsheviks: "After the democratic revolution we will fight for the shift to the socialist revolution. We are for the permanent revolution. We will not stop half-way" in the hope, in 1905 and today, that "the revolution in Russia would have given the signal to begin the socialist revolution in Europe."[7] But only the party is suited to this end, and Lenin insists over and over again on the necessity of the "autonomy" and "independence" of the party of the proletariat.

Beyond the *practical* problems of the relation with the Soviets in the insurrectional phase, however, Lenin's defense of the Bolshevik view of the party reopened the *theoretical* problem of this relationship—implicitly, if you like, but continually, as a moment of a broader discussion on the relation between political direction and mass organisms, and on the alliances of the proletariat in the process of the democratic revolution and, beyond this, toward socialism. It was inevitable to reopen this problem because it was the central, most decisive, and ambiguous one, and was always imposed on workers' theory by the actual reality at that level of capitalist development. Now, the particular form of the debate was determined by the wild number of writings produced on the Russia of 1905 by the Second International. The Soviets were launched on the international scene and debate of the workers' movement and thus gave rise, perhaps more than within Russian social democracy, to occasions for further thematic investigations and political conflict. Here it is not important to follow the lines of the polemic, particularly its reformist tendencies. It is sufficient to keep in mind two positions, which were similar though somehow antithetical: that of Rosa Luxemburg and that of Leon Trotsky. Lenin's thought can be clarified by comparing it with these two.

To Luxemburg, the Soviets appear as the living proof of the validity of the theses she proposed earlier around the polemic on the *Massenstreik* in Belgium. Russia was a "grandiose example" of the fact that "the living, dialectical explanation makes the organization arise as a product of the struggle."[8] The Russian proletariat, even though politically immature and of recent formation, had learned how to impose its own political experience and move to a "comprehensive network of organisational appendages" through struggle. In such a network, all the forces of struggle circulated and were constantly relaunched in a continual interchange; therein the nexus between union struggle and political struggle finds a way to achieve full expression. As for the Soviets, they are represented as propelling elements of this revolutionary procedure: they are rooted in the life of the masses and carry them all to the movement. Organs of insurrection on one hand, and the prefiguring of the uninterrupted development of the workers' struggle from democratic radicalism to socialism on the other: the Soviets are the real embodiment of Marxism among the masses. In Trotsky, this same emphasis on the spontaneity of the formation of the Soviets and their democratic radicalism in the life of the masses is very present: the Soviets are thus seen as the "typical organization of the revolution" because "the organization itself of the proletariat will be its organ of power."[9] This concept of the dictatorship of the proletariat, directly exercised by the Soviets without the mediation of the party, is the corollary of an affirmation of spontaneity and the result of his experience in the Soviet of St. Petersburg, which was an executive organ and centralizer of the revolutionary struggle as well as, at the same time, the instrument of the democratic and socialist self-management of the masses.[10]

Trotsky's and Luxemburg's views share some features and not others; in fact, they are even antithetical in some respects. Among these, we place a special emphasis on Luxemburg's appreciation of the expansive nature of the Soviets, as opposed to Trotsky's privileging of the centralizing phase of their revolutionary functions. In the slogan "all power to the Soviets," he in fact sees prefigured, according to the schema of democratic centralism, the coming revolutionary movement and even its tactical phases, as well as the fundamental structure of the socialist state. But both their analyses exalt the spontaneity in the genesis and development of the Soviets, their radical democratic rootedness in the life of the masses, and, finally and consequently, the theoretical foregrounding of a continuity between democratic struggle and socialist struggle that both the structure and the functions of the Soviets allegedly manifest.

Lenin rejects both their positions. He has the conditions of the movement in Russia in mind, with all the ambiguity presented by revolutionary struggle in the context of backward capitalism. He does not rhapsodize over the forms that the struggle can assume, but rather subordinates such considerations to the concrete determinations that result from it for workers' science. What can the theory of the organization process mean in the Russian situation? It is simply the return of the movement to generic popular positions, a danger and an obstacle to the irresistible will to create an autonomous revolutionary class organization that now and here cannot be but minoritarian: only such an organization can guarantee, as an institutional end to the organization itself, beyond the conditions determined by the present democratic phase of the movement, the conquest and the destruction of autocratic or democratic bourgeois power. And isn't there a danger, in the affirmation of the democratic nature of the Soviet, of subordinating the hard work of organizing the party to a simple prefiguring of the future or, worse, of hiding its necessary role as *vanguard* for the sake of an illusory and utopian revolutionary unanimity? Certainly, neither Luxemburg nor Trotsky would accept, or did accept, these criticisms. In their writings the affirmation of the leadership function of social democracy never seems to vanish. After all, they had good reasons, in the polemic, to accuse Lenin of "ultra-centrism" for his concept of the party, maintaining that because of it, he tended to underestimate, however programmatically, any potentially democratic aspect of the life and the basis of revolutionary organizations; and after 1917 Luxemburg increased the tone of her polemic against him. But Lenin's argument revealed the substance of the description and the subsequent theory of the Soviet that characterized Luxemburg and Trotsky: his polemic was in this respect extremely pertinent and recognized in the expansive model of the former as well as in the intensive model of the latter both a theoretical overestimation and a fundamental strategic error. For Lenin, the overestimation consisted in entrusting to spontaneity functions that did not belong to it. It might well be that spontaneity plays an eminent role (more than once Lenin the "romantic" and the "anarchist" had acknowledged and celebrated it) but not always and not automatically. If there is a rationality underlining the history of spontaneous struggles, it is that either capital or class determines their most aware or political qualities. And the party is all here: a class-based party that recuperates from the spontaneity of the struggles the workers' longing for an alternative organization and that structures class autonomy and consciously plans its expressions. This is a vanguard party, *always* vanguard because it permanently goes beyond the material limits that the capitalist structure imposes on class movement. And here, after the overestimation, however motivated, of spontaneity, lies the frank error of Luxemburg and Trotsky: that of considering the revolutionary process as a continuity that does not find any solutions, and in particular, solutions between economic demands and political demands. Yes, Luxemburg and Trotsky had beaten, in a classical manner, the reformism of the workers' movement and international social democracy, and they had demystified each one of its characteristics: now, and even more so where the situation and chances of struggle were backward, it was necessary to beat the reformism of class movements. The party was created and functioned to this end. Therefore the dyad *class autonomy–class organization* could never be broken. By autonomy we mean: negatively, the isolation of class from the people, the need for working-class struggle to keep overcoming the given material limits from the concrete tactical determinations of the movement; positively, the imposition of the problem of its organization. No organization without autonomy: Lenin opposed this statement to any theory of democratic organization. But without organization, class autonomy is always episodic and in danger of being crushed, especially at a backward level of capitalist development, by the reformism of capital and within the wide margins that are conceded to it, and it is thus in danger of becoming defeated as a workers' struggle. And Lenin opposed this statement to all hypotheses of procedural organization.

What about the Soviets? Only the party can decide how to use them. It is not a matter of underestimating the tool that spontaneity has typically offered to the revolution, but of situating and affirming it in the tactics and strategy of the party.

NOTES

1. Vladimir I. Lenin, *Should We Boycott the State Duma? The Platform of the Majority*, trans. A. Rothstein, in *Collected Works* (Moscow: Progress Publishers, 1972), 10:98.
2. Lenin, *Our Tasks and the Soviet of Workers' Deputies*, trans. A. Rothstein, in *Collected Works* (Moscow: Progress Publishers, 1972), 10:17–28. See also Lenin, *Lecture on the 1905 Revolution*, trans. J. Fineberg and others, in *Collected Works* (Moscow: Progress Publishers, 1964), 23:236–253.
3. Lenin, *The Dissolution of the Duma and the Tasks of the Proletariat*, trans. C. Dutt, in *Collected Works* (Moscow: Progress Publishers, 1965), 11:117.
4. Ibid., 11:124–125.
5. Lenin, "Soviets of Workers' Deputies," in *A Tactical Platform for the Unity of Congress of the R.S.D.L.P.*, trans. A. Rothstein, in *Collected Works* (Moscow: Progress Publishers, 1972), 10:156.
6. Lenin, *Ueber die parteilosen Arbeiterorganisation im Zusammenbang mit den anarcho-syndakalistiscen Stromunger im Proletariat*, in *Samtliche Werke* (Wien: Verlag für Literatur und Politik, 1929), 10:522ff. On this series of problems, one finds good suggestions in A. G. Meyer, *Leninism* (Cambridge, Mass.: Harvard University Press, 1957).
7. Ibid.
8. Rosa Luxemburg, "Cooperation of Organized and Unorganized Workers Necessary for Victory," in *The Mass Strike, the Political Party and the Trade Unions* (Detroit: Marxist Educational Society of Detroit, 1925).

9. Leon Trotsky, "Discorso davanti al tribunale: 19 Settembre 1906" [Courtroom speech: 19 September 1906], in P. Broue, *Le parti bolchevique* [The Bolshevik Party] (Paris: Éditions de Minuit, 1963), 74.

10. Leon Trotsky, *Der Arbeiterdeputiertenrat und die Revolution*, in *Die Neue Zeit* 2 (1906–1907): 76–86.

12

THE SOVIETS AND THE LENINIST INVERSION OF PRAXIS

O N THE PREMISES of these previous lessons, we must now assess Lenin's theoretical and tactical judgment on the Soviets in 1917. Forgetting his judgment of these years often leads to the temptation of finding contradictions or, at least, solutions of continuity within a position that rediscovers, thanks to its adherence to a method, a singular consistency and unity: in Lenin's case, this method is the sectarianism of subversive praxis, the connection of each theoretical statement to its proletarian verification, which is always part of the project of permanent revolution.

The first motif in Lenin's judgment on the Soviet in 1917 is a strong emphasis on the spontaneity of the phenomenon: "The Soviets arose without any constitution and existed without one for *more than a year* (from the spring of 1917 to the summer of 1918)."[1] It must immediately be recognized that such exaltation of spontaneity is all but generic and populist: from the outset, Lenin sees the spontaneous development of proletarian organization as an element characteristic of the specific class situation, and uses this exaltation as the occasion to define the nature and dynamic of the revolution: "The Soviets are not important for us as forms. What interests us is which class they are the expression of."[2] Nor is he interested, as Plekhanov was, in seizing the movement of the "creation of the people in the revolution";[3] instead, Lenin wishes to fix in the Soviets the immediate expression and political form of class insubordination to the general experience of exploitation: "The imperialist war was bound, with objective inevitability, immensely to accelerate and intensify to an unprecedented degree the class struggle of the proletariat against the bourgeoisie; it was bound to turn into a civil war between the hostile classes."[4] The Soviet is the spontaneous outcome of this situation: "the embryo of a workers' government, the representative of the interests of the entire mass of the *poor* section of the population, i.e., of nine-tenths of the population, which is striving for *peace*, *bread* and *freedom*."[5] Since the beginning of the war Lenin had foreseen this intensification of class struggle, and his activities within the Second International were the result of this foresight. During the war, on the basis of his forecasts, he had fiercely attacked all attempts at making the working class in the factory jointly responsible for the production of war and refused to accept, in exchange, the "factory constitutionalism" that the opportunists of the Duma promised.[6] That was not the time to verify his analysis: his forecast proved correct at the highest level of revolutionary insubordination. Thus the constitution of the Soviets, as the center of the militant insubordination of the proletariat to the exploitation by capital that in the imperialist war reached simultaneously its apotheosis and its limit, was spontaneous. His evaluation and subsequent exaltation of spontaneity offer the grounds for a definition of the very high degree of development of the revolutionary consciousness of the Russian working class, and of the material conditions of the political planning of the shift from the first to the second phase of the revolution.[7]

This definition of spontaneity is not surprising. It is not really contradictory, but rather, a necessary, if not sufficient, element of the political design of the proletarian revolution. We have seen how this is a typically Leninist method. The difference here is only one of intensity in the definition: spontaneity here has grown to the point of being the *embryo* of revolutionary government; it is so *self-conscious* that it allows a shift to the construction of socialist power. Since 1902, Lenin had been describing the process of workers' spontaneity as the growth to a higher and higher level of mass revolutionary consciousness.[8] Here the process reaches its apex; spontaneity defines the situation and materially conditions its extremely advanced developments.

Here also the supposed contradictoriness between Lenin's judgment on the Soviets in 1917, the tasks he later ascribes to them, and his previous comments no longer applies. Once again, the new configuration of the nature and tasks of the Soviets derives from his definition of the level reached by spontaneity, which is in turn an expression of the level reached by class antagonism, and by the relevant planning of the *leap* beyond the first phase of the revolution. Developing the indications of the *Letters from Afar*, Lenin in the *April Theses* recognizes the Soviets of the Workers' Deputies as "the *only possible* form of revolutionary government. . . . Not a parliamentary republic—to return to a parliamentary republic from the Soviets of Workers' Deputies would be a retrograde step—but a republic of Soviets of Workers', Agricultural Labourers' and Peasants' Deputies throughout the country, from top to bottom."[9] From "organ of the insurrection" to "organ of the insurrection and power of the proletariat": this transformation of the function of the Soviet derives from a real, material development of revolutionary objectives: "We must know how to supplement and amend old 'formulas,' for example, those of Bolshevism, for while they have been found to be correct on the whole, their concrete realisation *has turned out to be* different."[10] The fact is that the mechanism of the permanent revolution had found a new terrain, a more advanced perspective to follow. To the old Bolsheviks who relied on the formulas of 1906, Lenin responds with an analysis of the new situation of 1917. The party must be able to grasp the new situation pragmatically: there is thus no contradiction in modifying the tactical indications of the party; there is, if anything, a constant verification of the strategic line and a necessary adjustment of its intervention. The correct relation between spontaneity and consciousness and between class and organized class movement that the party must establish in any new situation finds expression, from February 1917 onward, in an exaltation of the revolutionary function of the Soviet and, beyond this, in its theoretical function as the foundation of a new type of state.

Lenin's analysis correctly diagnosed the new reality of the Soviets: in addition to the mass success of their birth and their immediate propagation in the first week of the February insurrection, and given the evidence of their terrific organizational capability, which was expressed in the constitution of an "executive committee" with executive functions for the entire movement, the Soviets also enjoyed specific political conditions that were profoundly different from 1905, the memory of which, however, still had enormous influence on the genesis of the movement. These political conditions were essentially the following: the undoubtedly socialist political character of the entire movement and the particular definition of its mass character. Differently from 1905, now the Soviets were really born with the victory of an insurrection: rather than an old autocratic apparatus that needs to be destroyed, they were confronting the new government of the bourgeoisie; therefore, their task became immediately socialist. Moreover, the Soviets defined themselves as "organs of radical democracy," of masses and class, whose task was to express an alternative political potential with respect to the power of the bourgeoisie, irrespective of the strategic aims of the forces operating in them. And their mass character was also different from 1905: not only because of the sheer size of the phenomenon, not only because the Soviets widely spread to the army, which armed the Soviets and unified the political and military organization of the proletariat, but above all because of the political radicalization of the masses. Lenin would give all his attention to this latter element when in the following months the St. Petersburg Soviet, influenced at the formal political level by its function of "controller" of the bourgeois government, clashed with the Soviets of the periphery, which were, on the contrary, extremely permeable and increasingly led by the radicalism of the masses toward further revolutionary movements. Lenin wished to push this process to the end.

As a result of the situation, the Soviets constitute a pole of the so-called dual power that characterizes the first phase of the Russian revolution. But there are different ways of seeing "dual power": either as a system of power redistribution in a *democratic* phase of the revolution, or as a first result of the development of the permanent revolution toward socialist objectives. In the first case, the Soviet is defined as the "organism for the control of revolutionary democracy," and is therefore simply obliged, negatively, to guarantee against counterrevolutionary resurgences and, positively, to ensure the democratic development of the institutions and politics of the executive. This is the Menshevik and social-revolutionary position founded on the well-known theses on the nature of the revolution in Russia: but even the old Bolsheviks are not foreign to this position and prior to Lenin's return they seem to accept, albeit with many ambiguities, these formulas about the Soviets.[11] Only the opening of the April crisis, Lenin's return, and the struggle around the "theses" provoked a first settling in this situation.

The personal unity of the leaders of the Soviets and the ministry evidently shows that the bourgeoisie intended to resolve the dualism of power through class leadership, and therefore reveals their necessarily contingent character. It is clear that "dual power" is not a juridical relation that can be institutionalized but a mere relation of forces between opposite classes; it is "not a constitutional fact but a revolutionary fact." It cannot but be resolved in the victory of one of the two rivals: "we cannot transform civil war into a component of the State regime." Any conciliatory position, at this point, is impossible and, from the class standpoint, merely opportunistic. The ambiguity of dual power must therefore be confronted and resolved from the workers' standpoint: first and foremost, the proletarian moment of the antithesis must be emphasized and thus exalted until it founds the dictatorship of the proletariat in its Soviet form.[12]

The Bolshevik strategy, which initially implies the dissolution of "dual power," is articulated along three lines: strengthening and extending the power of the Soviets, their conquest by the party, and the socialist transformation of the state through the Soviets. The Bolsheviks dedicated themselves to the first task with all the strength of their organizational capability. In the cities they reconnected the action of the Soviets to the struggle for an eight-hour working day, thus accentuating the proletarian character of Soviet organization in their slogans. But above all in the countryside, where they carried forward extremely refined slogans, they contributed to the spreading of Sovietism and the radicalization of the movement.[13] The results of their action would soon come: in May, workers and sailors proclaimed the proletarian republic in Kronstadt. But simultaneously to these peaks of radicalization, in the same period, the process tended to flow back: "dual power" definitely wore the mask of bourgeois power insofar as the Mensheviks and revolutionary socialists accepted government responsibilities. At this point the very slogan "All power to the Soviets" began to appear outmoded and the "peaceful way," which beginning with the first consolidation of the Soviets could be imagined as feasible, became entirely illusory:

> The slogan calling for the transfer of state power to the Soviets would now sound quixotic or mocking. Objectively it would be deceiving the people; it

would be fostering in them the delusion that even now it is enough for the Soviets to want to take power, or to pass such a decision, for power to be theirs, that there are still parties in the Soviets which have not been tainted by abetting the butchers, that it is possible to undo what has been done. . . . The substance of the situation is that these new holders of state power can be defeated only by the revolutionary masses, who, to be brought into motion, must not only be led by the proletariat, but must also turn their backs on the Socialist-Revolutionary and Menshevik parties, which have betrayed the cause of the revolution. . . . Soviets may appear in this new revolution, and indeed are bound to, but *not* the present Soviets, not organs collaborating with the bourgeoisie, but organs of revolutionary struggle against the bourgeoisie.[14]

The June crisis then made it all the more urgent to Bolshevize the Soviets. Here we are touching on one of the most characteristic aspects of Lenin's method. Not even then did the theoretical relation he established between Soviet and party change. On the contrary, as soon as the Soviets ceased to be part of the revolutionary movement and abandoned their antagonistic power to settle into a democratic development, the party needed to intervene and bring them back to play their class function. After June, in a phase of recovery for the bourgeoisie, the Soviets were reconfigured again as nothing more than "organs of insurrection": this was their task and objective of the moment. The events of 1905 seemed to repeat themselves, renewed by workers' science in the urgency of class conflict. The party, the subjective organization, became primary at this point in the relation between revolutionary class and the Soviet; when its organized expression broke down, the party intervened to reestablish this relation. The Bolshevization of the Soviets was not, here, simply the attempt to use them to seize the majority (and the majority, in any case, between July and October is already won); it was, above all, a demand to relaunch, in the Soviets and the masses, the revolutionary struggle and to radicalize it on immediate objectives of power. The Bolshevik action in the summer of 1917 succeeds in this task: this is the necessary and sufficient premise for October.[15]

In these years, Lenin's theoretical contribution to the definition of the Soviet is just as important. His position in *The State and Revolution*, where the

Soviet is seen both as the organ of the dictatorship of the proletariat and as an instrument of the communist abolition of the state, is universally known.[16] There is no need for us to repeat the fundamental arguments of that book here. Instead, it is useful to consider its close relation to Lenin's revolutionary practice, in particular the practice of 1917, which is the ever present counterpoint to his studies on the nature of the bourgeois state, the Commune, and the communist withering-away of the state. It might be legitimate to suggest that without this preliminary further investigation of the problem, the *Letters from Afar* and, even more so, the *April Theses* would have never been written. In addition, had the imperialist war not pushed, on the one hand, the class struggle in single countries and, on the other, the process of rationalization and centralization of the executive power of the bourgeoisie, Lenin's intensive study of the question of the state in Marx's and Engels's writings (as well as Pannekoek's, Kautsky's, and Bucharin's), beginning in 1916, could not have led him to such a radical recognition of the teachings of the classics on the nature of the state.[17] Now Lenin sees the withering-away of the state as the task of the proletarian revolution and as a material possibility at a certain stage in the development of class struggle.

Our presuppositions aside, Lenin's analysis of this complex problem certainly derives, first and foremost, from his political judgment of the present and future effects of the imperialist war. At this juncture, the growth and rationalization of the powers of the executive, their immediate functionalization, beyond any mystification, into "pure" capitalist ends of mercantile domination, motivate and develop the perfecting of the bourgeois state machine, which in its classist foundation is a mere instrument of accumulation and exploitation. The imperialist war is like a cross section and macroscopic exemplification of capitalist development in its political form, and is the motor of its extraordinary acceleration. Faced with this material development of the structure of bourgeois power, Lenin's program to transform the imperialist war into a civil war opens up to an analysis of the problems of the state and the relationship between it and the victorious working-class struggle.

The analysis of the development of capital attempted in *Imperialism* must now find its correlative at the level of class science. Therefore, in *The State and Revolution* the central object becomes a commentary on the famous pages where Marx posits a relation between workers' revolution and reformism, with its internal restructuring of the power of capital and its political machine, to conclude that "all revolutions perfected this machine instead of breaking it."[18] Now, the internal restructuring of power that the war imposes on the bourgeoisie stretches to the limit its present capabilities of internal reform. In Russia, the last step in the reform in the capitalist order of power is provoked by and follows the February revolution:[19] now the workers' struggle is confronted by an adversary that has already become reunited. At this threshold, the problem of the destruction of the bourgeois state machine is simply open; here the ambiguous relation, already discovered and theoretically defined by Lenin, between democratic revolution and socialist revolution dissolves. The dictatorship of the "proletariat organized as ruling class" does not repeat the reformist development of the modernization of state functions, but rather, "immediately" opens the process of their withering-away.

In Lenin the analysis always functions as the direct premise of a revolutionary slogan. The Soviets are completely reabsorbed in this theoretical scenario: they constitute that "superior form of the state" that reproduces the experience of the Paris Commune. Therefore, they are not the mere destruction of the *bourgeois* state machine: rather, they represent the first condition of and the first moment in the process of the withering-away of the state as such. In the third of the *Letters from Afar* from March 1917, this evaluation of the Soviets and the subsequent program, with an explicit reference to the experience of the Commune, is already hinted at.[20] The *April Theses*, the article on dual power, and the successive resolutions up until October keep defending this program.[21] And the theory seems to support the Bolshevik praxis in the days of October, when the party destroyed any residual democratic slogan and invested all its power in the second congress of the Soviets.

But what was the relation, at this point, between the party and the Soviets? The correct relation, defined and verified by Lenin in the course of his long political battle, was one of subordination of the Soviet to the party, of the mass movement, however high its level of development, to the conscious leadership of its vanguard. Now, notwithstanding all appearances, this relation was practically maintained and imposed in the most acute period of the revolutionary struggle: between February and October, the party gradually seized the leadership of the movement. This seizure of the struggle was the work of the party and not of the Soviets; if they had a role in it, it was only in their form. But then does Lenin's strong emphasis on the Soviets and the model of the Paris Commune have a purely *ideological* rather than scientific significance? Why does he allow such a utopia to live on in theory without recognizing the inadequacy of the Soviets in determining, at that level of development, the material basis of the dictatorship of the proletariat itself and the communist process of the withering-away of the state?

In fact, we ought to note that Lenin's theoretical analysis had largely overestimated the actual level of development of capital and the degree of political formation of the Russian working class. Unsurprisingly, after the July crisis of 1917 the strong theoretical emotion that invested Lenin and made him see the imperialist war as the last act of the internal reform of capital and pushed him to understand that beyond this threshold the process of reunification of the working class and its vanguard was open (and that the ambiguous mechanism of the dualistic growth of the working class was dissolved) is placated when he is forced to confront such a different experience, to see that capital still has wide margins of resistance and recovery, and that it thus starts a counteroffensive against the first workers' revolution both within the Russian borders and at an international level. Yet besides this, the subsequent development of the revolutionary movement in Russia more decisively evidences the elements of political inadequacy on which Lenin's theoretical hypothesis was based. While the Soviet effectively begins to function as an "organ of proletarian dictatorship," it is nonetheless the party that actually exercises power, in the form and only in the form of the Soviet. The Soviet tends to be reduced to a democratic instrument of the "organization of consensus," and as such it is once again interchangeable with other instruments of advanced democracy. Therefore, far from being configured as a moment of the process of the withering-away of the state, the Soviet ends up being, in the best of instances, an "organ of the administration of the state." The fact is that we must rebuild; and again, we must push accumulation forward until it becomes materially possible to have a unified working class that knows and is able to manage social production. In this context, for Lenin the Soviets are wholly situated within the process of social production: they must organize production, push for emulation, and increase productivity. They are primarily organs of democratic management of production.[22] One might suspect at this point that the attempt of some bourgeois ideologues to argue that the Soviet is merely a model of enlarged and extremely advanced parliamentarism is quite valid.[23]

Lenin desires this insofar as it is necessary; he does not mystify the reality that confronts him: he recognizes the *democratic* character of the Soviet form of management of production and power, speaks of it as "the beginning of the socialist form of democracy."[24] Fully aware of the huge tasks that await the revolution, he gives minimal objectives to the Soviets: the power of the Soviets is a "machinery that will enable the masses to begin right away learning to govern the state and organise production on a nation-wide scale."[25] But if this is the situation, it must be further pushed forward by the class vanguard. The identification of the party with class and the inversion of the relationship between party and Soviet must be accomplished. Until the party does not succeed in this, it needs the state. State and party are, in fact, equally the result of the capitalist division of labor; only a high level of worker unification and class recomposition can therefore allow the overcoming of the state, the return of the Soviet to its function, and the beginning of the process of the communist withering-away of the state. We must get to this level: the revolutionary proletariat has not inherited it from capitalism, to the extent that its recent struggle has not imposed it on capital. Paradoxically, the situation confirms Marx's claim that "All revolutions perfected this machine instead breaking it." At this level of development, Sovietism perfects it even further: "But the revolution is thorough. It is still journeying through purgatory. It does its work methodically." For the revolutionary process to continue, it must be sustained in a high moral and political climate: after 1918, Lenin's work is fully committed to this.[26]

Lenin's propaganda on the Soviet experience in the world is, from this point of view, highly significant. Yes, Lenin perfectly understands that the success of the revolution in Russia is conditioned by the international spreading of the movement. But we are not simply dealing with the material conditions of resistance in the Soviet experiment in Russia; it is not simply a question of defending the October revolution. It is also a question of the relation of the development of the Russian revolution toward its most advanced objectives. In this perspective, Lenin's writings of the Third International are not meant so much to generalize the determinate figure of the Soviet as a practical form of proletarian dictatorship as to unify the various and at times autonomous council experiences in one single political design, in one single revolutionary tendency capable of overcoming, by far, the limitations of the movement.[27] Only in this way will it be able to beat the democratic resurgence that threatens the revolutionary institutions of the working class in Russia and elsewhere. For example, as the chief agent of the counterrevolution, European social democracy tries to block the movement on positions of democratic reformism. Therefore, it deprives the council form of its revolutionary content and tries to institutionalize it as the basis of bourgeois power, renovated according to Enlightenment principles. Here Lenin once again unleashes his polemic against any theorization of "dual power," constitutionally mummified (and therefore beaten) outside of the general revolutionary class struggle: against the proposals of the "yellow" International to legalize the Soviets, to grant to them state rights, and to introduce systems of direct democracy; against Hilferding's and Kautsky's proposals to give importance and a constitutional function to the *Räte* as control organizations of production; and against any proposal, in sum, that wants to consider the Soviets as organs of democratic representation rather than a class dictatorship grafted onto the international process of the revolution. Communists must always say no; the movement must continue and go beyond itself.[28]

This also means that the answer to the question on the *ideological* character of Lenin's theory of the Soviet is negative. The Soviet in Russia does not fulfill its tasks because it is rooted in and constrained by a backward situation. But the value of Lenin's political project lies beyond its application to Russia: there, it functioned as a utopia, as the ideal motor of a great revolt, but Lenin never used theory to mystify reality and his effort to avoid an ideology of the Soviet allows us to appreciate it scientifically as the hypothesis of a resolution of the ambiguity of workers' struggle, as the projection of a definitively resolved and unbreakable relation between the class and its movement. It is our task to recover the political use of the theory of the Soviet when we are able to inflict the most total class response to the highest moment of capitalist development. From this standpoint, Lenin's debate on the Soviet is still a great hypothesis for working-class science today.

NOTES

1. Lenin, *The Proletarian Revolution and the Renegade Kautsky* (Peking: Foreign Languages Press, 1972), 60.

2. Lenin, *Sämtliche Werke* (Wien: Verlag für Literatur und Politik, 1929), 20:1, 322.

3. Lenin, *Marxism and the State: Preparatory Material for the Book "The State and Revolution"* (Moscow: Progress Publishers, 1978), 87.

4. Lenin, *Letters from Afar*, trans. M. S. Levin, J. Fineberg, and others, in *Collected Works* (Moscow: Progress Publishers, 1964), 23:299.

5. Ibid., 23:304.

6. Lenin, *Several Theses Proposed by the Editors*, trans. J. Katzer, in *Collected Works* (Moscow: Progress Publishers, 1964), 21:401–404.

7. This program is already outlined in the first of Lenin, *Letters from Afar*.

8. Lenin, *What Is to Be Done? Burning Questions of Our Movement* (Peking: Foreign Language Press, 1973).

9. Lenin, *The Tasks of the Proletariat in the Present Revolution*, trans. B. Isaacs, in *Collected Works* (Moscow: Progress Publishers, 1964), 24:23.

10. Lenin, *The Dual Power*, trans. I. Bernard, in *Collected Works* (Moscow: Progress Publishers, 1964), 24:38.

11. On the polemic of April 1917 between Lenin and Kameney, see the valuable information in C. Anweiler, *Die Ratebewegung in Russland, 1905–1931*, vol. 5, *Studien zur Geschichte Osteuropas* (Amsterdam: Brill, 1958), 193ff.

12. See L. Trotsky, *The History of the Russian Revolution*, trans. M. Eastman (New York: Simon and Schuster, 1932), 1:166ff. See also Lenin, *The Lessons of the Revolution*, trans. C. Dutt, in *Collected Works*, vol. 16 (Moscow: Progress Publishers, 1967).

13. Lenin's contribution on the struggle in the countryside during this period can be found in Lenin, "The Agrarian and Rational Programmes," in *The Tasks of the Proletariat in Our Revolution*, trans. B. Isaac, in *Collected Works* (Moscow: Progress Publishers, 1964), 24:71–73; Lenin, "Resolution on the Agrarian Question," in *The Seventh (April) All-Russia Conference of the R.S.D.L.P.*, trans. B. Isaac, in *Collected Works* (Moscow: Progress Publishers, 1964), 24:290–293; and Lenin, *First All-Russia Congress of Peasant Deputies*, trans. B. Isaac, in *Collected Works*, vol. 24 (Moscow: Progress Publishers, 1964).

14. Lenin, *On Slogans*, trans. S. Apresyan and J. Riordan, in *Collected Works* (Moscow: Progress Publishers, 1974), 25:187, 188, 191.

15. On the Bolshevization of the Soviet in this period, see Lenin, *Marxism and Insurrection*; Lenin, *Advice of an Onlooker*; Lenin, "Meeting of the Central Committee of the R.S.D.L.P.(B.), October 10 (23), 1917"; and Lenin, "Letter to the Central Committee of the R.S.D.L.P.(B.)," in *Collected Works*, trans. Y. Sdobnikov and G. Hanna (Moscow: Progress Publishers, 1964), 26:22–27, 179–181, 188–190, and 223–227, respectively.

16. V. I. Lenin, *The State and Revolution*, trans. S. Apresyan and J. Ryordan, in *Collected Works*, vol. 25 (Moscow: Progress Publishers, 1964).

17. See Lenin, *Marxism and the State*. In the same volume, see Kautsky's text as studied by Lenin. See also A. Pannekoek, "Massenaktion und Revolution," in *Die Neue Zeit* 30 (1911–1912): 541–550, 585–593, 609–616; N. Bucharin, "Der imperialistiche Raubstaat," *Die Jugendinternationale* 6 (December 1, 1916).

18. Lenin quotes from Karl Marx, *The Eighteenth Brumaire of Louis Bonaparte*, in *Marx and Engels Collected Works* (Moscow: Progress Publishers, 1979), 11:185–186. And he continues to quote: "But the revolution is thorough. It is still journeying through purgatory. It does its work methodically. By December 2, 1851 it had completed one half of its preparatory work; it is now completing the other half. First it perfected the parliamentary power, in order to be able to overthrow it. Now that it has attained this, it perfects the executive power, reduces it to its purest expression, isolates it, and sets it up against itself as the sole target, in order to concentrate all its forces of destruction against it. And when it has done this second half of its preliminary work, Europe will leap from its seat and exultantly exclaim: Well burrowed, old mole! This executive power with its enormous bureaucratic and military organization, with its extensive and artificial state machinery, with a host of officials numbering half a million, besides an army of another half million, this appalling parasitic body, which enmeshes the body of French society like a net and chokes all its pores, sprang up in the days of the absolute monarchy, with the decay of the feudal system, which it helped to hasten." The first French revolution developed centralization as well as "at the same time the extent, the attributes and the agents of governmental power. Napoleon perfected this state machinery. The Legitimist monarchy and the July monarchy added nothing but a greater division of labor, . . . in its struggle against the revolution, the parliamentary republic found itself compelled to strengthen, along with the repressive measures, the resources and centralization of governmental power. All revolutions perfected this machine instead of breaking it. The parties that contended in turn for domination regarded the possession of this huge state edifice as the principal spoils of the victor."

19. Lenin, *First All-Russia Congress of Soviets of Workers' and Soldiers' Deputies*, trans. S. Apresyan and J. Riordan, in *Collected Works*, vol. 25 (Moscow: Progress Publishers, 1974).

20. Lenin, "Concerning a Proletarian Militia," in *Letters from Afar*, 320–332.

21. See Lenin, *The Dual Power*; Lenin, "A New Type of State Emerging from Our Revolution," in *The Tasks of the Proletariat in Our Revolution*, 67–70; and Lenin, *First All-Russia Congress of Soviets of Workers' and Soldiers' Deputies*.

22. Lenin, *The Immediate Tasks of the Soviet Government*, trans. C. Dutt, in *Collected Works* (Moscow: Progress Publishers, 1965), 27:235–277.

23. For all of them, see H. Kelsen, "Democracy," in *General Theory of Law and State*, trans. A. Wedberg (Cambridge, Mass.: Harvard University Press, 1945), 284–299.

24. Lenin, "The Development of Soviet Organization," in *The Immediate Tasks of the Soviet Government*, 27:272–274.

25. Lenin, "Report on the Review of the Party Program and on Changing the Name of the Party," in *Extraordinary Seventh Congress of the R. C. P. (B.)*, trans. C. Dutt, in *Collected Works* (Moscow: Progress Publishers, 1965), 27:134.
26. See especially Lenin, "The Development of Soviet Organization."
27. Lenin, *First Congress of the Communist International*, trans. G. Hanna, in *Collected Works* (Moscow: Progress Publishers, 1966), 28:453–477.
28. Ibid.

13

THE REFORMIST CHANGE
OF PRAXIS

Soviets Today?

IT IS STILL controversial to say that the Leninist concept of the Soviet is not ideological, that the nexus between the party and the organisms of the masses is an open one, and that the relation between the ability of the party to be effective and the power of the masses to innovate can be turned around. The fact is that the Soviets that emerged from the October revolution were institutionalized, and their development was subservient to the needs of the development of capitalism in Russia (though in a popular and state form). Instead of becoming a force of innovation of the masses in the path toward communism, the Soviets were actually the place where the masses got mobilized toward production and socialism. One might say that it was necessary to go through the stages of a "revolution from above," find a solution to underdevelopment, and build an adequate "foundation"; but once these stages were overcome, the Soviet was worn out and incapable of redefining itself as the organ and expression of class power.

The discussion among communists about how and *why* this happened must obviously start from the *fact* that it happened. For historical materialism, the irreversibility of this constituted praxis is a principle as fundamental as that of the reversibility of constitutive praxis we have insisted on.[1] Neither tearful lamentations on the "cult of personality" nor metaphysical disquisitions on the "Stalinist deviation" (in the sense of a reproduction of the *subjectivist* social relations)[2] can provide a solution to our problem. The indication of a resolution to this problem can be found in the Maoist polemic against fixing the process of socialism building and the shift to communism, and in the definition of a more grave error, which is the scission between this material construction of socialism and the permanent revolutionary transformation of the forces of production. The dictatorship of the proletariat, in that situation, institutionalized the relations that were recuperated in the revolutionary phase and made them rigid in a view of the material basis as the determining force, as the only variable of the process: a huge force of transformation was blocked, and the dictatorship of the proletariat was not seen as the subject of a permanent revolution. The most heinous economism, managed by ex-Mensheviks turned into technocratic planners, made its triumphal entrance into the state of the Soviet. The *dominant* role of class struggle up to the point of transition to a new stage was thus negated or mystified.[3]

The reformist practice of capital comes to terms with the Soviets on the basis of its awareness of the blockage of the revolutionary experience of the Russian Soviets and their recuperation into the structures of a rigid planning. It is not because it knows of the *mere institutionalization* of the Soviet that capitalist practice seeks to control it (attacks on institutionalization as such are the prerogative of anarchists and have little to do with the analysis of the complexity of the advancement of revolutionary power); instead, capital draws important lessons from the *form of this institutionalization*. The Soviet is institutionalized as participation in the organization of production, as support to the ideology of labor, as an instrument of planning. From this perspective, for the first time in the history of capital, at the mass levels of industrial production (and thus well beyond any cooperative, artisan, or peasant experience), the Soviet offers an example of how the workers' variable can be enclosed in the viscous figure of the commodity and, there, as commodity, become socialized and dominated. In other words, capital recuperates the dynamic and participatory form of the institutionalization of the workers' variable within the necessity of organizing labor and the capitalist goals of production. The first indications we have of this process are fragmentary but visible in the theory of the enterprise, at least in the socializing and strongly ideological version of it offered especially by the first, and not last, constitutionalism of Weimar.[4] A second and less ideological phase is the triumph of planning policies inspired by Keynes that followed the crisis of 1929. Here participation is played out in terms of the great proportions of income distribution. The capitalist planning state inevitably bends to the need to confront the situation of power relations among classes, but only to bring them to a halt and make them rigid, inside its structure and finality. The evidence of this is that the monetary and fiscal instruments are punctual correlatives of a maneuver on workers' forces and represent determinate levels of mediation and participation, in Keynes as in other planning economists and politicians.[5] Today, in the history of the reformist modification of praxis, we can see a third phase of adjustment and resizing of workers' participation. In any case, workers' struggle has made it impossible to capture and compress the instance of power and communism in the webs of capitalist planning. Only a relation that runs deeper in the life of the masses, a deep interpretation of the capital relation that defines it, in the very dialectics of the capitalist standpoint, as a *relation*, can win. For instance, Sraffa's economic intuitions, geared to eliminate any substance or necessity from the concept of capital and to allow for a contracting of its figure and function, manifest the conditions of a deep interiorization of the working class role for the purpose of capitalist development (even at zero profit).[6] In this perspective, council communism has a new and unexpected prescience: the capitalist need for an effective interiorization of the relation of control, the bourgeois ideological itch of pluralism and participation, the reformist flaw of social democracy, and the cynical residue from the Third International have all had a field day with this opportunity to establish a balanced state of labor. The capitalist by remembering and the reformist social democrat by forgetting that labor still means exploitation. But what can one do when the theory of the enterprise becomes yellow, when the tools of Keynesianism for implementing monetary and fiscal regulation do not work? The state of labor and the corporation today, with its fundamental unionist and participatory character, is the only practicable way.

Let us return to our Soviet. On the one hand, the Soviets were closed because of the exhaustion of the revolutionary potential of socialist countries; on the other hand, the form of their inclusion in capitalist (socialist) relations of production ended up representing a superior form of labor organization and of capitalist domination of it. Why, then, raise the question of the Soviet today? Why do we claim that the Soviet, the *Leninist* discourse on the Soviet, is still a lively hypothesis for working-class science? Last but not least, why does the question of the councils keep being put forward by workers in struggles?

We have seen that in the experience of the Russian revolution, the Soviets represented, on the one hand, a spontaneous form of workers' organization of the control of production, a *constitutional* form; on the other hand, they were an organ of the struggle against autocracy and capital, an organ of *insurrection*. These two aspects are intimately linked in the specific political composition of the Russian working class and proletariat in the revolutionary period. Lenin's effort is progressively commensurable with this reality. During the initial phase, the distinction between the participative (and Menshevik-style reformist) side of the Soviet and the insurrectional one is particularly marked: the distinction accentuated, at the price of a regression of the revolutionary objective, the radically democratic and socialist characters of the process. When the perspective of communism, linked to the catastrophe of imperialism, seems close enough, in Lenin we find a more intimately comprehensive and unitary appreciation of the revolutionary character of the Soviet: from the standpoint of the vanguard itself, the Soviet is the moment when the masses are granted a delegation so that the great leap forward of insurrection can be accomplished. It can be derived from this that the concept of the Soviet is obsolete, undoubtedly in its first version, because of the formal character of the Soviet insurrectionist function and given that its contents cannot be other than social-democratic. But it is also obsolete in its second version because the mechanism of *constitutional* integration, first in socialist then gradually in capitalist reformist terms, has hinged on it most heavily.

On this second version, it is worth noting that the bourgeois democratic dictatorship exercised today in the forms of planning and the government of multinational enterprises not only incorporates the socialist participation of the masses but also tends to eliminate any weak point and any determination or coagulation of a form of insurrectionary mass. The autocratic state—and, following it, all other state forms, including the Keynesian one—was presented as exercising control in forms that were based on the *generality* of the power relations between classes: these could become, and did become under the pressure of workers' offensives, points of rupture. Instead, the post-Keynesian, trade unionist, corporative state of the enterprise tends to the rest of the functions of control that interiorize and found themselves on the *individuality* of groups and power relations. The Soviet attacks the state along horizontal lines, turning its mass of power into insurrectionary power, playing the massification of class action against the generality of the dimensions of the capitalist relation. It operates along the *horizontal lines* of the mass against the state. But what does this mean today? Hasn't the state substantially changed in order to respond to the latest international wave of workers' struggles that were communicated along the horizontal lines of the masses against the weakest points of capitalist planning? Rather than from the generalization and circulation of struggles as typified in the Soviet experience and its repetition, the working class can expect the buildup of a determinate moment in the process of insurrection from the recognition of new power mechanisms, on which to build insurrectionary action. This action is built *along vertical lines*, with the ability to create an offensive on the points where class action coagulates and becomes mass, cumulates and multiplies: with the awareness that the bourgeois democratic dictatorship has no missing links and soft bellies, but guarantees the permanence of its power through heightening the vertex of the state and through repressive anticipations. The socialist and reformist integration of the Soviet is constitutional insofar as we recognize the structural nature of the intervening changes with adequate intensity and depth. The specter of Soviet action was reincarnated too many times, and the contemporary state is organized accordingly. As usual, the action of capital follows the struggles: this is not to recognize them through mere reference, but to clearly admit that we are aware of the force employed by capital in this shift from a dramatic perception to a structural modification of the state.

The debate on the Soviet and the fascination this organization of struggles inspires are in many respects obsolete. As for students' enthusiasm for council communism, it is vain and ridiculous. But is this recognition enough to eliminate the question of today's Soviet? No, we don't think it is.

We will start with a general remark: whatever its ambiguities, the Soviet (and the Commune before it) is a "recovered form" of working-class action. This is to say, in these cases the Marxist inversion of praxis reached the apex of tension and revealed the fundamental features of communism: they are class institutions, for the class, in the class. Therefore, they are the institutionalizations inside capital of what capitalism can only institutionalize for the purposes of domination, the consolidation of struggle for the purposes of power, and the irreversibility of struggles from the standpoint of struggle itself, of the process of destruction of the existing. These formidable experiences of the proletariat contain all of the problems that the revolutionary action against wage labor has always raised. It is the momentary (if you like) but complete solution to the relation between class and power. (Lenin apparently drank champagne when, while counting the days of the seizure of power, he realized that it lasted longer than the seventy-two days of the Commune.) From this general perspective, we need to study the Soviets time and time again.

But another, more particular remark is called for, one concerning the political composition of the working class today. As we have often claimed, the concept of class composition is formed on parameters that refer both to the productive process and to the political experience of class. It is worth dwelling on this second aspect and trying to demonstrate the hypothesis that the more class massification increases and the more its "social individuality" is determined, the greater the importance of the political moments of class composition. This derives from the continuity of the process of subjective development of class, from the affirmation of more favorable class relations; but it is also, under these conditions, facilitated by the capitalist reform of the global structure of society, when it follows the struggles and the need to reabsorb part of their momentum, always in the form of a compromise. Just as the mechanism of the circulation of capital is often subverted into a mechanism of circulation of struggles, so must the very mechanism of reformist stabilization become a mechanism of political augmentation of class composition, in a way that is contradictory and often antagonistic, but always real. From this standpoint, it must be said that a series of features of Soviet struggles has become irreversibly embodied in the current comportments of the working class and thus in its composition. An autonomous assembly at the factories of FIAT, Alfa, Renault, and Ford spontaneously repeats the revolutionary will of the Soviets of St. Petersburg; in fact, it extends, individualizes, enriches, and confirms it in the refusal of delegation, through militancy, and the overall project-driven form of its organization. From large to small factories, the proletariat fights everywhere, whether visibly or not, and there the Soviet project lives in its ingenious and multiplied power. No proletarian hope can fail to consciously comprehend a Soviet comportment.

How can one claim, then, that the model of the Soviet revolution involves, in its obsolescence, all the debates on the Soviet and forces us to answer the question of the Soviet today negatively? Won't this question be raised again by the Soviet form of the masses? When the reformist transformation of praxis acts so deeply that it destroys the realization of the functions carried out by the Soviets in their classical version, won't there still be a need for recuperating and defining these same functions in the current composition of the working class?

The next two conversations will return to these issues and consider the Soviet as an "organ of struggle" and an "organ of power" in relation to the current class composition.

NOTES

1. My methodological reference here is to the work of Hans-Jürgen Krahl, *Costituzione e lotta di classe* [Constitution and class struggle] (Milan: Jaca Books, 1973).
2. See Althusser, "Response to John Lewis," in *Essays in Self-Criticism* (London: New Left Books, 1973).
3. On this, see C. Bettelheim, *Class Struggles in the USSR, 1923–1930* (New York: Monthly Review Press, 1998).
4. On this, see F. Cavazzuti, *La teoria dell'impresa* [The theory of the enterprise] (Bologna: Il Mulino, 1962).
5. For my take on the theory of this trend of political economy, see Negri, *Operai e stato* [Workers and the state] (Milan: Feltrinelli, 1972).
6. On Sraffa, see Sraffa, *Production of Commodities by Means of Commodities: Prelude to a Critique of Economic Theory* (Bombay: Vero, 1960).

14

VERIFYING THE QUESTION OF WHETHER THE SOVIET IS AN ORGAN OF POWER

F OR LENIN, THE Soviet was primarily an organ of power. In a long polemic that directly hinges on an analysis of Russian revolutions and is nurtured by a return to the theory of the experience of the Paris Commune,[1] Lenin progressively sizes down the figure of the Soviet, the particular content of its power, and the form of management of the power that pertains to it, and links different aspects to the overall issue of strategy and organization. The outcome is a concept that is adequate to the definition of the political composition of class, a very dynamic and open one that qualifies the political question in general terms. In this dynamism is formed the singular dialectics of the Soviet and the party: we said, "Lenin from spontaneity to spontaneity," from the appreciation of the spontaneous emergence of struggles to the inversion of the relation between the party and the activity of the masses. The concept of the Soviet mediates this Leninist path and makes it consistent with all the general indications emerging from his thought. In this framework, the seizure of power is a seizure of the power of the state, through the horizontal spreading of points of contestation and demands that cumulate and define the need for power against a central power that descends from above and against autocracy, namely, repression and violence. Seizing power means destroying the centralized and fetishist image of it through proletarian dictatorship, and spreading the exercise of power among the organized masses.

But, today, what is the new reality of power that confronts working-class struggle?

Allow me to use an image to try to define some differences that arise from an analysis of the concept of Soviet and its comparison with the exigencies of class struggle today. In Lenin, and in the whole of Marxist debates on the state between the Second International and the Third, power is conceived of as state power. It is conceived of as *a vertex*, as opposed to civil society. From this vertex descend the lines of command, above civil society, against the working class. Today, this is no longer the image of power. Starting with the state planner, rather than a vertex, power is a *plenum*, a fullness of power, an equal and massive extension of command, not above but across and through civil society. The two Marxian hypotheses—that of the maturation of capital as exclusive of social organization and that of the identification of the overall tendency of capital and the state (as organically fused organization and command)—seem to have come to fruition. But it is important, here, to fully use the dialectical potential of Marx's teachings: this fullness of power is *both* a fullness of capitalist power and a full potential of workers' power, because the capitalist unification of society and its totalizing organization reproduce the entire potential of class antagonism in the social fabric as a whole, which is essential to the definition of capital.

If we move from the abstract image to the historical contextualization of these concepts, we find positive proof. The accentuation of the capitalist domination of society and the tendency to superpose the sphere of capitalist organization onto that of the state are historically marked by the affirmation of the workers' movement, as a force that widens and determines the always-higher character of workers' power in society. Power has become full, but it is a fullness of control over a reality that is largely determined by working-class struggle, a fullness of reforms, of quantities of wages that are extorted from the masters. So advanced is the process and so irreversible its force that many power determinations can only be defined anew today. For instance, even the most radical and drastic tools in the hands of capital that were used to hit workers' power and reduce the spaces of its exercise can no longer be used today! Such as the crisis and its catastrophic proportions! The capitalist resort to using restructuring radically also seems to have little success, and if it is successful, the permanence of workers' struggle during processes of restructuring runs the risk of producing a situation where working-class power is actually enhanced in the end. Moreover, the very quality of power, from the workers' perspective, appears to have changed. This fullness of power can be a fullness of possibility that forcibly exploits by directly reclaiming as much as a determinate level of technical and political class composition allows. The process appears to be antagonistic, but this reinforces, or can reinforce, the workers' presence in the society of capital, against this dirty society, insofar as the antagonism of interests and tendencies of opposing forces organize their armament in the battle.

In Lenin's conception of the Soviet, this was absent and could not be predicted. The theory of the dualism of power is short-lived: it must inevitably be resolved because its aim is *directly* the seizure of the state, the vertex of command. Today, the dualism of power is imposed by the very structures of the constitution: both material and, in its dark figures, formal,[2] it exists in the legal processes of labor and hundreds of other situations—the dualism of power is affirmed as an overall historical situation. Today, the Soviet character of the masses reaches its most advanced expression in the moments of direct appropriation but is still configured as the permanent antagonism of everyday movements. This situation irremediably distances us from Lenin and his Soviet hypothesis. In our situation, two different political compositions of the working class and the proletariat are distant and qualitatively separate, in radical terms.

Nonetheless, the Leninist Soviet is still present in our imaginary. Why? Let us look into this from a different standpoint. We have discussed the irreducibility of the political composition of the class that Lenin referred to and the one we observe today. But Lenin's hypothesis is not simply a reference, adjustment, and dynamic reflection of class composition; it is also, above all, an attempt of revolutionary subversion of praxis. All the aporiae that derive from class composition for Lenin, the scission imposed by the misery of the proletariat, are gathered and recast in the subversion of praxis. Lenin's thought is a huge effort to mediate dialectically and from the working-class standpoint a series of problems internal to a Menshevik and reformist gradualism that he sees as treason and mystification: the question of the state, the party, revolution, and transition (and, respectively, of development, the relation between the vanguard and the masses, insurrection and the dualism of power, and socialism, and so on). Doesn't Lenin look for the revolutionary solution to these aporiae in the Soviet? Doesn't he look there, with his trust in the practice of the organized masses of the Soviet, for the *contemporaneity*, the solution to the state question, to the relation between vanguard and masses, to the permanence of the revolutionary process, and to the beginning of the communist transition—this *contemporaneity* that alone can liberate, mediate, and overcome the aporiae and delays present in class composition? Don't this hope and this project lead from the tendency to reduce the capitalist crisis to a "fatal moment" found in *Imperialism*, in the *Letters from Afar*, and in *The State and Revolution*?

The critique of Leninism has not confronted the Leninist definition of class composition but ferociously attacked this formidable power of dialectical inversion of praxis. In fact, while conceding that the analysis of class composition was correct, the critique of Leninism has derived from Leninism the impossibility of a revolutionary leap. This critique reaches its apex when bourgeois sociology (a Marxian heresy erected and generously funded for anti-Leninist purposes) underhandedly tries to define the state and the transformation in terms similar to those proposed in Lenin's theory of organization of strategy and revolution, but only to fix them mechanically, to exclude their role as means and instruments, to eliminate all *illusions* that praxis can be overturned. In Max Weber, the De Maistre of the contemporary counterrevolution, the sectarian opacity of the reactionary standpoint reaches the height of an ideological subversion of Leninism. He tries to bring the model of the Bolshevik revolution to bear on that of the bourgeois revolution, and turns the question of power into a technical question of its rational management. At this level, the concept of the party (a technocracy of the proletariat) is exalted while the process of revolutionary legitimation is thrown into the nettles of irrationality and charisma.

The bourgeois form of rational management of power is superposed on, and thus detached from, the irrational tumults of proletarian contents. The Leninist tool is thus stuck on it as a project, and the bourgeoisie is reassured where in principle the laws of power tout court can only survive untouched.

This "hairpiece" image had some fortune even in the ranks of the vanguard of the workers' movement, where the fetishism for the party form and the illusion that the question of the state is to be confronted from the perspective of the possibilities it provides at the level of composition has found some followers: little stands between Lenin and Weber; Lenin's toolbox is Weberian; the falsification has come to these levels.

But in fighting these falsifications we recover Lenin's topicality. As we have shown, Lenin's realism does not consist in his definition of the adequate instruments of a given class composition, but in his ability to cast these tools in the determinacy of the revolutionary process. Leninism emphasizes the contemporaneity of the solution to the problem of insurrection, the seizure of power, and transition, which is the opposite of what bourgeois ideology does. The Soviet hypothesis is the central point of this emphasis, of contemporaneity, and of the totality of the communist revolution. In this sense, the hypothesis of the Soviet as an organ of power is fully topical because it points to the masses as the locus of any possible source of legitimacy of power, it brings the forms and contents of the revolutionary process to bear on the unity of the activity of the masses, and its hope to change the state and its strength to destroy it rely on the permanence of the mass movement.

Finally, the Soviet hypothesis is topical because, given the historical unfolding of the dualism of power and our new class composition, a Soviet form has emerged that is organic to the masses and their comportments.

Let us go back to the beginning of our discussion, to the problem of the actual meaning of the quality of "organ of power" that is attributed to the Soviet. We go back to this question having argued, on the one hand, that there is a distance between today's concept of power and the one that lived through the class composition of Lenin's times and, on the other hand, that there are fundamental analogies with Lenin's definition of the Soviet as the privileged moment and gathering point for the instruments and goals of the process of communist revolution. In other words, this notion of the Soviet has partly detached us from and partly drawn us closer to Lenin. Now the conversation can continue to offer new elements, if not solutions, to our discussion.

A further relevant consideration emerging from our discussion is that when confronting Lenin the actual reality of power displays a character of enormous complexity. When confronted with the actual figure of workers' power as the Soviet form that lives in the masses, it has to resolve a particular and wholly original aporia. This fundamental aporia is the seemingly contradictory fact that, on the one hand, the spreading of the Soviet form to the masses leaves less and less room for a traditional notion of the function of the party, while on the other hand, its function of rupturing power relations as they spread throughout the entirety of capitalist integration is more and more required and increasingly necessary if reformism is not inevitable, if the intensity of the antagonism determined by the development of social capital and capitalist dictatorship is fully appreciated. This is a very new aporia, because in Lenin's context the generality of antagonism is carried forward by the party while the singularity of the insurrectionary process of the offensive is carried forward by the masses organized in Soviets. Today the situation is reversed: the strategy of the masses is undoubtedly the determining element; the generality of antagonism is implanted in the masses. Seeing this situation as unsolvable would contradict the very image of the Soviet of the masses and the instances of the appropriation of and need for communism. In this case, the fullness of power would not turn, as capital demands, into a quagmire for mass action, and one would have to outline the laws of workers' power that determine the shift from the management of power to the struggle for power.

We don't have recipes for the solution to these problems, although we could posit it in Leninist terms as the relation between the Soviet as an "organ of power" and the Soviet as an "organ of struggle." But for Lenin, the analysis of class composition led to the identification of the laws of mediation embodied in the figure of the party, whereas our analysis of the laws of workers' power, which is steeped in the actual reality of class composition, led us to a first negative solution: the traditional figure of the party is not an adequate term for the solution to the problem. The aporia remains: the question of what is to be done is far from resolved, but since practice is pressing, indeterminacy is offensive and intolerable. We can only face the second side of the question and return to the debate on the Soviet as an "organ of struggle" to grasp the unity of the strategic project of proletarian struggle again. For now, the debate has confronted us with a fabric of workers' power that is irreversible and drawn toward communist ends. What now? Have reformism and the bourgeoisie not managed to break the resolute efficiency of this proletarian power in the field of attack? What if the bourgeois counterattack, led at the cost of subtracting economic development from the armory of the reasons for the legitimacy of bourgeois power, was not irresistible? What if it widened the scope of workers' power, as it seems to do? What are the new laws that enable class to express struggle, to concentrate tactically on the center of power? What is the overall meaning of the Soviet form in our time?

Allow me a last observation before moving on to dealing directly with these questions. Because of the appreciation of the quality and size of workers' power, from the awareness of the centrality of the question of transition and the insistence on the need for finding a contemporary solution to these problems, one is led to believe that the Leninist inversion of praxis might be becoming obsolete. The effort to speak in terms of insurrection, the attention to the mechanisms of refusal of labor, the permanence of the revolutionary process all seem to make the question of the seizure of power perfunctory. However, this is false and mystifying, because nothing in the current expression of workers' power as an irreversible fabric of the activity of the masses would occur if it wasn't sustained and led by the will for dictatorship, the solution to the antagonism that class experiences in the capital relation.

NOTES

1. On this, see especially Lenin, *Marxism and the State: Preparatory Material for the Book "The State and Revolution"* (Moscow: Progress Publishers, 1978).
2. On the notion of "constitution," see Negri, "Stato e politica" [State and politics], in *Scienze Politiche: Feltrinelli-Fischer Encyclopaedia*, ed. Antonio Negri (Milan: Feltrinelli, 1970).

15

THE SOVIET FORM OF THE MASSES AND THE URGENCY OF WORKERS' STRUGGLE

"ALL POWER TO the Soviets." The resonance of this slogan marked the beginning of insurrection: from the dualism of power, to the storming of the Winter Palace, to the dictatorship of the proletariat. The antagonism of the capital relation not only needs to be dominated from within, from the organization of Soviets as organs of power, but must also be destroyed by the Soviets' initiative as organs of struggle and insurrection. This is the red thread in Lenin's teachings. But what does it mean to us, confronted with the political composition of the working class as it is now? What does insurrection mean?

Two aporiae have emerged from our conversations. The first concerns the nature of power. It seems that the spreading and socialization of power makes it harder to define it. The working masses have seized decisive margins of power, but this does not help them as such to solve the problem of power. The first fundamental aporia thus lies between the spread, the extension, and the socialization of *power* and *insurrection*. Precisely insofar as it is extensive, totalitarian, and involves the whole of society, the capital relation makes it difficult to conceive of the prospect of its destruction as a relation. The second aporia concerns the fact that, while it is possible to identify the classical relation of rupture, it is less possible to determine its decisive point of mediation. The Soviet form of the masses does not leave room for mediating delegations in the revolutionary process. The second fundamental aporia is thus found between the *Soviet of the masses* as *the socialization of workers' power* and *mediating organ of insurrection*.

If we remain close to the Leninist formulation of the question of insurrection (the theory implicit in "all power to the Soviets"), it seems that these problems and aporiae cannot be solved. In Lenin, the call for the seizure of power seems decisively linked to an ideological notion of "power." For Lenin, power is a *nondialectical*, natural absolute. His definition of power is singularly close to that of bourgeois theories of power.[1] The fact that the dualism of power can only live in the short term is, for him, a clear consequence of this notion of power. Even in Trotsky, the idea of the dualism of power is shaped by the bourgeois notion and exemplified in the events of the English and French bourgeois revolutions.[2] Our aporiae cannot be solved on the premise of this notion of power. But the experience of power proper to workers' activity is very different today: power is experienced as a dialectical absolute that unfolds in the long term of the dualism of power, as a struggle that subverts the capital relation by introducing the workers' variable as a conscious will of destruction. I don't know whether Mao Zedong ever thought about this, but I believe that the reception of his thought can be largely attributed to this reading of workers' vanguards.

On these premises, the concept of insurrection, in its classical form, is less useful to the workers, but this does not mean that the awareness of power and the wish to seize it and take its exercise to its most explosive and destructive conclusions has waned. On the contrary, the first aporia is actually solved in the concept of power as a dialectical absolute. Similarly to Marx's definition of capital, power is dialectical because it is always a relation of forces, but absolute because conflict reaches its internal solution and finds "who is winning the war" on its path.[3] Naturalness and historicity, each in their absoluteness, here find their real locus. The consequences of a realistic and working-class notion of power (of the dualism of power) can be huge. Revolutionary action, from this perspective, can be carried forward free from illusions, whether insurrectional or gradualist and reformist: the dialectics of the masses, the Soviet form of the masses, reveals the naturalist and formal rigidity of both perspectives. The gradualism of power, of its seizure and management, is the gradual nature of the destruction of capitalist power and capital relations.

From the solution to the first aporia there emerges an indication of the solution to the second aporia between the Soviet form of the masses and the overall mediation of the process. But this aporia cannot be solved in classical terms either. Not only is the working class not prepared for a complete mediation, but there is not even a chance of mediation. Any mediation represents an attempt to restore an image of power as a nondialectical absolute. This must be rejected as much as the capitalist image of power, because in its struggle for power, class needs not *one* instrument of mediation, but *many* punctual and continuous functions of the management of its civil war. In order to overcome the second aporia and solve the problems it raises, we need to understand that the current figure of power relations between classes forces us to change our concept of *insurrection* and that of permanent *civil war*.

It might seem that we have completely and definitively departed from Lenin's thought and that ours is a left version of the particular "Italian ideology" of communism that so insisted, with greater or lesser loyalty to Gramsci, on the notion of hegemony, *and so on*. But this is not the case. Our firm and conscious adherence to the concept of the decisive centrality of working-class action, our awareness of the mechanisms that are recomposing the proletariat into a working class, and the urgency of communism clearly distance us from the sweet-toothed hypotheses of hegemony that, as far as we know, have been a necessary ground for reformism (necessary because their reference point was not the working class but "civil society").[4] In fact, we are still and decisively on Lenin's grounds because we continue to refer to his theory and method beyond the distinctions of contents and changes in class composition. On this issue, two remarks will suffice: the first refers to the way Lenin looks to the management of the spaces of power seized after the defeat of the revolution of 1905 *in the absence* of an impending insurrection.[5] Alongside his polemic against the *liquidation* of the party and in favor of its permanence, we read an insistence on the transformation of the prospect of insurrection into a prospect of civil war. Civil war is a fact of power insofar as it prevents the adversary from implementing restoration and assumes destruction as the center of its project. The organization of civil war is a fact of the masses: the Soviet and the

vanguards that composed it must be recuperated into this destructive function of the masses and not into impossible attempts at democratic reintegra-
tion. The theory of civil war as class and mass practice (and we insist on this
mass practice at the exclusion of individual ravings and deliriums on violence)
is clearly alluded to in this period. Of course, it is a minor moment in Lenin's
thought, conceived *in the absence* of a closely impending insurrection (and, in
this respect, we find more intense connotations in Mao). But we had to recall
this moment because it shows that this line of thinking was present in Leninism and obviously linked to the analysis of class composition, however weak
this composition was.

However, there is another, more important aspect that makes Leninism
seem topical and current. This is the dialectical concept of revolutionary inversion of praxis, which is so fundamental in so many respects. The shift from the
long-term dualism of power and from the mass Soviet to civil war is where we
find a Leninist inversion of praxis. We name this shift a deepening of "class
consciousness," though the vagueness of the term brings together material
elements: the given class composition, the structure of power relations, and
the need to overturn them, to *start* overturning them and open a wide cycle of
struggles. From within the composition, the actual will of civil war becomes
the Leninist key to the solution to the problem. Only the recuperated contradiction between the mass Soviet and its offensive functions can bring about a
leap forward: the inversion of praxis entails taking on the contradiction not as
an unsolvable aporia but as a practical function of attack, as the mass twisting
of reality.

The shift from the theory of insurrection to the practice of civil war is
Leninist, and it confronts the composition we face today. So we recuperate the
determinations of our situation. On what and against what does this inversion of praxis occur? First, on the vertical articulations of the fullness of capitalist power and their newly separated bodies, on repressive anticipations, on
the entire set of instruments of civil war of the masters against class. And this
is only in relation to the tactical objectives. But action and the adequate forms
of organization are qualified through strategic objectives, where the debate
broadens to immediately refer to the struggle against labor, the destruction of
the capitalist organization of labor, and thus the mass nature of the commu-

nist project, as a minimal objective, in class. The disarticulation of command and the struggle against work are the determinate content of contemporary civil war and represent the Leninist key to the inversion of praxis.

We will dwell on these issues in other conversations, especially in our analysis of *The State and Revolution*. Now, to conclude this group of conversations on the Soviet and Lenin, let us briefly reconstruct our thesis. Lenin offers a straight route from spontaneity to the Soviet, traversing the party and insurrection, against autocracy. For us, this route goes from the Soviet of the masses to the proletarian organization of the end of labor, through a civil war against the current form of bourgeois dictatorship. Here lies the verification of our Leninism and Lenin's topicality. The translations and transformations that some concepts have undergone are based on a web of methodological tools definitively consecrated in Lenin. Class composition, its determinateness, the concept of permanent revolution, and the inversion of praxis: these are the parameters by which our operations are determined. Today the interiorization of the class struggle against the system of capital has become so deep and implacable that the struggle against the capitalist organization of social labor has become the central political and theoretical medium of all passages. From the concept of insurrection to that of civil war against labor: this is an example of the application of the Leninist method to our times, even if we formally seized power, because this would not be a definitive fact. The interest of class is to manage the process of the extinction of labor. So, a working-class and proletariat dictatorship against labor—a dictatorship that is not simply accomplished through decrees, although the workers' force of invention would produce decrees that are immediately decisive—is exercised through the continuation of an implacable war, inside the whole sociality of capital. After the workers' struggle the masters turned their state into a powerful and mobile machine; they built a series of moments of absorption and integration geared toward preventing a global fracturing and the workers' construction of a similar power. Here the notion of domination and power tends to translate everything, with no "last instances," into the objectivity of the capitalist organization of social labor. And here, the concept of insurrection is interiorized by the whole of the working class, which is not waiting for decisive explosions but constantly instantiating moments of rebellion. We need to rebel, go against the current, and destroy: these are not individualistic slogans, but the watchwords of the proletariat, repeated time and again.

What about the Soviet? This "recovered form" of workers' struggle is full of theoretical and practical virtualities. In the mass movement and the movement of struggles, the Soviet is an effective organ of power. It will be the organ of civil war insofar as the struggle of power opens up to the great strategic objectives of communism. The whole of workers' realities swarms with these points of organization; it is a reality of organization. Workers' power is growing and it is only a beginning, but our gaze already extends afar. The Soviet form of the masses as a whole of red bases and initiatives of struggle against work is accumulating and creating terrible offensive functions. In this, Leninism not only lives, it is revived. How beautiful to see things growing instead of simply turning to the study of our fathers!

NOTES

1. In particular, see the fascist work (though it is not only so) of Carl Schmitt, *The Concept of the Political*, trans. G. Schwab (Chicago: University of Chicago Press, 1996).
2. See, especially, Leon Trotsky, "Introduction," in *History of the Russian Revolution*, trans. M. Eastman (Chicago: Haymarket Books, 2008).
3. In the definition of power provided by Schmitt.
4. On this, see N. Bobbio, "Gramsci and the Concept of Civil Society," in *Which Socialism?* (Cambridge: Polity Press, 1986).
5. See Lenin's writings from 1907.

PART THREE

Interregnum on the Dialectic

The Notebooks of 1914–1916

16

DIALECTICS AS A RECOVERED FORM OF LENIN'S THOUGHT

WE BEGIN BY studying a group of Lenin's writings written between 1914 and 1916, two large collections of readings: the *Philosophical Notebooks* and the *Notebooks on Imperialism*.[1] The *Philosophical Notebooks* contain notes from readings that are cited in full with Lenin's comments, general opinions, comparisons, and evaluations to the side. In particular, the most interesting part of the *Philosophical Notebooks* is the section on his reading of Hegel's *The Science of Logic*. Lenin completed this reading between September 1914 and December 17 of the same year. Then, from December to May he read Hegel's *Lessons on the History of Philosophy* and the *Philosophy of History*, providing commentary on both. In May 1915 he began a second set of readings on all the material available to him in that period regarding imperialism, which is collected in another series of notebooks that we'll soon discuss, the *Notebooks on Imperialism*. Lenin continued this work until mid-1916 when he began to write "The Popular Essay" in *Imperialism: The Highest Stage of Capitalism*, published in 1917.[2]

Let us first try to understand why and in what context Lenin engaged in a certain type of study (especially one on "the science of logic") that was apparently very far from his primary and immediate interests as a revolutionary leader. At the beginning of the great imperialist war, Lenin was living in Krakow, the Polish region of the Austro-Hungarian Empire. Here he found himself in great difficulty as a political exile, still intending to remain in Krakow, given the ease of direct contact with Russia. Nonetheless, he was forced to move to Switzerland, and after several peregrinations he established himself more permanently in Zurich. Once in Zurich, he had much material available to him because he could work in the largest libraries of this cultural center. He was completely politically isolated. In this situation he chose to withdraw into his studies, constrained by the lack of any chance of influencing others. On the other hand, during the first part of the war, the entire Bolshevik organization was radically dissolved in Russia, and efforts to put it back on its feet failed. Nearly all the Bolshevik cadre had been scattered and had no possibilities or even capability of reestablishing a central organization. The first volume of Carr's *The Bolshevik Revolution* contains a brief description of the conditions in which Lenin worked and the extremely precarious circumstances of the Bolshevik organization in Russia during that period.[3] These external factors—isolation due to the impenetrability of the front from all propaganda and agitation, as well as the destruction of the Bolshevik organization—offered Lenin the opportunity to apply himself to studying theory: first, essentially, Hegel's theories and then issues of imperialism.

Even so, the externality of the occasion became an extremely important moment in the overall succession of Lenin's thought. We have already seen the first phase of Lenin's development and decided that perhaps Lenin was one of the few people who, in those years, managed to read Marx's works in an original and lively but also absolutely faithful way, drawing extremely precise conclusions and definitions, programs and strategies. In particular, we have insisted on the definition of the nexus between class composition, organization, and insurrection as a definition of a path that revolutionary theory had to renovate from time to time. We have also seen some substantial methodological developments, such as the discussion on the Soviets, as an example of the creative mechanism of Leninist theory. But we have also seen how, before 1905, the relationship drawn between composition, organization, and insurrection was fairly rigid and how only in the heat of the battle was this relationship shaken up, opening the other path (opposed but nevertheless complementary) of theoretical considerations, the path that indicated a different order for the process: insurrection, organization, composition. In short, from 1905 on Lenin asserts that in the acute revolutionary phase, the proletariat organization can, from within the insurrection, assume an impactful force and a capacity of rupture such that it conditions the same composition of the working class. The organization, as the organization of the armed insurrection, as the capacity of destroying the power of the adversary class, can configure a situation in which the class composition of the proletariat frees itself of its misery to define itself as an innovative, creative moment, as a force that, through struggle, prepares the passage to communist society. Already indicated in 1905 was the possibility that the dictatorship of the proletariat could, as an organizing fact, as a fact of power, transform the same class composition and give us a figure of the liberated proletariat capable of constructing communism, of permanent revolution, the theoretical objective of communist discourse. That which the organization *mediates* can be made *unmediated* in the working class's comportment once the adversary class's power is overthrown, once the working class and the proletariat, as such, take upon themselves entirely the duty and the weight of the construction of a revolutionary society.

We'll now see just how important this dialectical shift is. We are actually dealing with a dialectical shift of determined negation by the proletarian composition just as it was and as it had to be driven "from on high" toward the insurrectional moment, "artfully" played in order to open the insurrectional process: now the negation transforms through the insurrectional moment that precarious reality of the proletariat into a material force capable of constructing a continual revolutionary process. All well and good, this dialectical shift begins to take on full theoretical shape in Lenin through his study of Hegelian logic on the one hand and imperialist theories on the other.

There is one fact that has continued to amaze me since I learned it: there are two of Mao's works from 1937, one "on contradiction," the other "on practice," both found in the first volume of the *Select Writings* of Mao Zedong,[4] in which the only citations that appear are from Lenin's *Philosophical Notebooks*. This is extremely interesting when we think that Lenin's *Philosophical Notebooks* were published in 1934–1935: they immediately ended up in Mao's hands, who was at that time barricaded in the mountains of Yan'an. The great Chinese revolutionary leader immediately appreciated the tremendous importance that the theoretical consciousness of the dialectical leap had taken on in Lenin. It is perhaps not by chance that this extraordinary and immediate theoretical consonance took place, if it is true, as we will see in the later sections of these conversations; it is also not by chance perhaps that it is nearly impossible to read *The State and Revolution* without thinking of Lenin's study of Hegel's thought, and that it is impossible to position the dialectical problem of transition without knowing Mao's dialectics. It is not by chance, but it is, however, extremely interesting, especially if we keep in mind that throughout the history of Marxism, both the relationships between Marx and Hegel and in particular the relationship between Marxists and Hegel have been contradictory. As we know, Marx and Engels were Hegelians. That is, they participated in the Hegelian school of thought. Their philosophical formation took place within the so-called Hegelian left, a school that was very composite and difficult to unify in precise terms. Marx and Engels's points of reference are fundamentally two: one known to all, Ludwig Feuerbach, the other less known, Moses Hess, who, however, had perhaps more influence on Marx because he had transformed Feuerbach's theological criticism into a materialist critique of the structure of the state and integrated a communist thematic in the realization of mankind as a universal genre within the Hegelian left.[5] Beyond this influence during the period of Marx's formation, there is a relationship with Hegelian methodology that continually reappears. Regarding his cocotte with Hegel in the chapter on commodities in *Capital*, Marx justifies himself. This does not take away from the fact that even in completely different moments during the development of Marx's thought the recovery and utilization of operational models from Hegelian logic always remain absolutely important. For example, in a letter to Engels from 1858, the moment at which Marx was working on his theory of profit, Marx writes: "by pure accident I came into possession of Hegel's *Logic*, I leafed through it and it proved to be very useful in chasing off all of the theories of profit ever developed."[6] There is, therefore, a relationship with Hegel, by means of the Hegelian school initially, but always profound, that Marx continued to recover and that in the preface to the second edition the first book of *Capital* he openly defended,[7] declaring to have refused to treat Hegel as the German

Enlightenment treated Spinoza, "like a dead dog." The relationship between Hegel and Marx clearly exists; we will not discuss it here at length.

Let it be sufficient to say that it is a relationship as close as it is instrumental. In reality, Marx rehabilitates a few of Hegel's fundamental instruments and his sense of dialectical logic. Sayings such as "Marx overturned Hegelianism" or "He put reason back on its feet" and so on explain absolutely nothing. The important aspect is the continuity of a very profound theoretical reversal within which certain fundamental methodological instruments still have value (and we will see which ones precisely by analyzing the reading that Lenin offers of Hegel, a reading that is extraordinarily similar to Marx's own reading). Several methodological instruments are adopted, absorbed, and developed, in a position rendered completely different by the theoretical referent's materiality: the bourgeois spirit in Hegel, the working-class subject in Marx and Engels. It is not, therefore, an abstract and illusionistic reversal of the *human* dimension that differentiates the methodological use of the dialectic in Hegel and in Marx, but rather the radical historical difference of the *subject* to which it refers. The dialectic conjoins Hegel and Marx, 1848 separates them. At this point, after the Second International Congress, it is worth saying that the theoretical development of scientific socialism in Europe during the latter years of the nineteenth century sees Hegel expelled and discarded from the Marxist's theoretical purview. (And all this was done in deeply incorrect terms, which were dominated by a mechanical and highly improbable *Weltanschauung*; Lenin did not know Hegel, if not in a summary and traditional manner, until he, at a mature age, already an experienced Marxist, confronted these writings on the science of logic.)[8] Now, therefore, Lenin's discovery of Hegel has a tremendous flavor of originality and demonstrates an extraordinary capacity to overcome cultural fetishes, which the tradition of scientific socialism had constructed and overturned in Lenin by way of a destructive evaluation and the consequent expulsion of Hegel from Marxism's theoretical context.

A strange but significant phenomenon is that after these Leninist *Notebooks* on Hegel, the theoretical in communist thought (except for the brief parenthesis of leftist communism in Germany, the heroic one represented by Lukács, Korsch, and a few others, and the already mentioned Maoist reading) practically expels Hegel once again from its philosophical development. In the Soviet Union the study of Hegel is taken up only in an already advanced period of de-Stalinization, exactly as in other countries where communist forces develop theoretical work. It is only in this latter period that interest in the relationship between Hegel and Marx and (especially at this point) between Hegel and Lenin emerges once again.

Having said this, let us take up again this argument's principal thread and let us formulate a theoretical hypothesis that might guide our reading of Lenin's *Conspectus of Hegel*. Now, the hypothesis is that by way of his reading of and the commentary on *The Science of Logic*, with the mastery of several logico-dialectical instruments, Lenin is placed in the theoretical condition of giving scientific form to one of his earlier intuitions: the possibility of overturning the series composition, organization, insurrection into its opposite and its parallel: insurrection, organization, composition. On the other hand, Lenin is placed in the condition of acting almost in a more consequent manner, which is to maintain through this theoretical attitude (acquired in that kind of purgatory that was for him an isolation from class struggle) a relationship with experience, with an anticipatory foresight of revolutionary development. It would be difficult to be able to understand the journey that Lenin takes when he makes his *April Theses* public, or the political shift he imposes between April and October, or the entire interpretive direction that he gives to the Russian revolutionary process if we didn't have in mind the theoretical attitude acquired through these studies during his most acute isolation. This theoretical attitude will show Lenin (in April 1917, against all the Bolsheviks, in a minority position within the party and the Bolshevik political office)[9] insisting continuously nonetheless on the liquidation of the democratic phase, on the insurrection as a fundamental moment, on the importance of insurrectional determination in the composition of class, on the proletariat dictatorship as the first phase of socialist development, overturning the same Bolshevik orthodoxy, which instead saw the opposite process: organization, democratic revolution, and organization toward socialism, and therefore *insurrection*. The ability to accelerate and anticipate events, which even Lenin had already expressed in 1905, at this point takes on a more explicit and knowledgeable form, through which the possession of these methodological instruments for reading is not irrelevant. What Lenin was not able to express theoretically (what he had simply alluded to in revolutionary practice in 1905), he was able in 1917 to say with both full knowledge and anticipatory power. Lenin succeeded in making the dialectics into a real-history reading instrument, a scientific tool with the same precision of a microscope or a rifle.

The theory links defined, objective causes with defined, subjective effects. Why the dialectics is read by Lenin in these terms, and how he reads the historical comportments of the masses, is paradigmatic in the comportments of the working class and therefore has the capacity to interpret, to penetrate, to anticipate the comportment of the class and the masses according to scientific criteria. Does this signify an abandonment of the materialist foundation of Marxism in Lenin's plans? Absolutely not. In reality, either materialism is considered the comprehensive horizon of our knowledge, based on human, collective, working-class praxis, which, when modifying nature and relationships of power, constitutes history, or it is considered an attitude that we do not know what to do with, that is old and mechanistic. Materialism is a theory that leads back to the real world, to the concrete before us, to the material force of the relationships of production in the entire human realm. Yet materialism reduces the world to this, insofar as mankind, as a collective praxis, as an ensemble of productive forces, continually reshapes, transforms, and revolutionizes the world in a practical relation. Dialectics is the law of this relationship; it is therefore the fundamental rule of the science that investigates the relationship between human productive collectivity and the transformation of nature and society. It reveals power relationships as attempts to block (on behalf of the power constituted through exploitation, through all the laws of command) this infinite, immense creativity, which resides in the collective praxis. This is why this "strange" chapter in Lenin's thought is important; it is an emergency that takes on a universal value in an exceptional circumstance of isolation and defeat, in the purgatory that this great political leader found himself having to cross.

All of the sudden, during these years, through the *Notebooks on Imperialism* that immediately followed the reading of and commentary on *The Science of Logic*, Lenin found a way to perform an initial experiment on dialectical laws. The second great experiment was the April 1917 event, and the third was the publication of *The State and Revolution*. But why do the *Notebooks on Imperialism* and, more broadly, his writings on imperialism represent a fundamental element of this practice? The primary theses set forth in *Imperialism: The Highest Stage of Capitalism* are well known. In it, Lenin asserts that capitalistic development entails ever greater forms of economic concentration within individual metropolitan countries. This consequently determines the necessity of exporting goods and capital, but especially capital, such that it determines the inevitable competition on the world market between imperial powers, resulting in violence and war. Why is metropolitan capital forced to export? It must do so because the rate of profit in single countries falls as concentration, driven mechanization, and industrialization increase. Let us remember how the law of the tendency for the rate of profit to fall expresses itself: if the value of commodities is determined by the relationship between necessary labor (that is, labor that reproduces the worker for the power he must concede), and surplus labor, then this relationship becomes unbalanced by an augmentation of surplus labor with respect to necessary labor—however much work productivity increases, and therefore however much fixed capital (that is, machinery) increases, the general level of technico-scientific preparation of society and thus of the whole workforce increases, and thus more economies of scale are born, that is to say, large concentrations and thus the economy of the productive process, and so on. What does this mean? It means that commodities lose value, their value being tied to living labor, to the aspect corresponding to the necessary labor, which is exploited: if surplus labor rises disproportionately, and subsequently surplus value, and thereafter, through certain mediations, profit as a mass, then the relationship between the part of living labor which has been transferred to the commodities falls; and because it falls, so does the rate, which is the proportion relative to extorted labor.[10] Capital must overcome this situation, and to do so it must enlarge its market, that is, it must find labor to which it can apply its ability to extract surplus labor. Once it arrives at a certain point of concentration and therefore at a certain point of labor productivity and socialization of productive forces, capital is compelled to seek new markets, but not simply new markets in which to sell, but rather capital markets, as a possibility of extracting even more surplus labor, as much as possible, always more; this precisely determines the phenomenon of colonization that Lenin studies in his *Notebooks*.

What does the dialectic shift in this study consist of? First, it consists in the understanding of the dramatic transformation by which capital, insofar as it accomplishes its civilizing function, is constrained—this is Marx when he continually insists on the sign of destruction that capitalist development moves within and produces and reproduces with wealth itself ("from this viewpoint the law of tendential fall in the profit rate is in general the most important aspect of the political economy").[11] In the second place, the dialectic shift consists in the understanding expressed by Lenin that the contradictions determined within this type of process (even though they were inter-imperialist contradictions in the first place) can be immediately utilized by the class point of view as a declaration and sign of capitalism's inevitable fall. Third, and this is the most important point, consciousness is determined in Lenin both by the enormous concentration of capitalist power in the figure of single imperialist states and by the enormous power of destruction that an imperialist clash unleashes. This consciousness turned in the decision of a revolutionary deadline, by word of order, not against war, but for the workers' and revolution's use of war against imperialism, for communism.[12]

Certainly all of this represents a specific situation: today Lenin's *Imperialism* is a work that faces considerable limits. In particular, we have had to see capital renew itself dialectically and overcome some of these contradictions: consequently, today the imperialist theories need to be renewed. Yet we must say that Lenin's reading of imperialism is absolutely correct for his time and suitable to reality, just as much as this reading is directly addressing the definition of that dialectic shift, which is the insurrectional shift. The awareness of Russian imperialism's inability to sustain, at the degree of relative development at which it had arrived, the enormous weight of that war which determined its inability to sustain relationships of power within Russia, for Lenin becomes an expected outcome of the revolutionary journey.

Having said this, there is nothing left to do but begin reading some of the most important passages of the *Philosophical Notebooks* and the *Notebooks on Imperialism* in order to further concretize what has been said thus far in this conversation.

NOTES

1. Vladimir Ilyich Lenin, *Philosophical Notebooks*, trans. C. Dutt, ed. S. Smith, in *Collected Works*, vol. 38 (Moscow: Progress Publishers, 1976); Lenin, *Notebooks on Imperialism*, in *Collected Works*, vol. 39 (Moscow: Progress Publishers, 1968).

2. The chronology of Lenin's studies on Hegel's works is established in Luigi Colletti's introduction to his translation of the *Notebooks on Philosophy*. Vladimir Ilyich Lenin, *Quaderni filosofici*, trans. Luigi Colletti (Milan: Feltrinelli, 1958), clxvii–viii. The chronology for the readings on imperialism is found in Garritano's introduction of his translation of the work: Vladimir Ilyich Lenin, *Quaderni sull'imperialismo*, trans. Giuseppe Garritano (Rome: Editori Riuniti, 1971), v–vii.

3. Edward Carr, *The Bolshevik Revolution, 1917–1923*, vol. 1, *A History of Soviet Russia* (London: Macmillan, 1958).

4. On practice and contradiction, see Mao Tse Tung, *Scritti Scelti*, vol. 1, *1926–36* (Roma: Rinascita, 1955), 363–384, 385–434, respectively.

5. For more on the formation of Marx and Engels's thought, see the first two volumes of Auguste Cornu's fundamental work: Cornu, *Karl Marx et Friedrich Engels: leur vie et leur oeuvre*, 4 vols. (Paris: Presses Universitaires de France, 1955–1970).

6. Marx and Engels, *Carteggio* (Roma: Rinascita, 1950–1953), 3:154–155.

7. Marx, *Il Capitale*, vol. 1, bk. 1 (Roma: Rinascita, 1956), 23.

8. Lenin's *Materialism and Empirio-Criticism*, published in 1908, in particular shows a scanty knowledge of Hegelian thought.

9. See Carr, *The Bolshevik Revolution*, 75–79; L. Cortesi, "Intorno a Stato e rivoluzione di Lenin," *Rivista storica del socialismo* 21 (January-April 1964): 181.

10. On the tendency for the rate of profit to fall, see my article in *Crisi e organizzazione operaia* and the Marxist steps cited therein. Additionally see R. Rosdolksy, *The Making of Marx's Capital* (London: Pluto Press, 1992).

11. Marx, *Il Capitale*, vol. 3, bk. 1, p. 213.

12. On Lenin's work during the years of the renewed revolutionary movement on the eve and the beginning of the first imperialist war, see his writings published in *Opere scelte* (Moscow: International Publishers, 1946), 1:507.

17

LENIN READS HEGEL

W E HAVE TRIED to define the situation in which Lenin's notebooks on dialectics and imperialism were written. Let us now begin to study the nucleus of his *Notebooks on Philosophy*, or, more properly, his notebooks on dialectics. The core of these notebooks consists in Lenin's commentary on Hegel's *The Science of Logic*. The particular condition by which Lenin's study is constrained—at times these notebooks seem more of an escape from the misery of his times than a theoretical necessity—fortunately and dramatically reacts thanks to our author's overall commitment. His study of dialectics assumes an absolutely fundamental role. Dialectics finally provides a theoretical form to the Leninist ability of political inversion and reversal, an indication measured against the exigencies of the time, always followed by the support of a theoretical system. Here the paradox of Lenin's thought is revealed and given a specific form: all of the shifts and inversions of the political line never seem opportunistic, nor are they a mere reduction of political will to the necessity of the facts that emerge from time to time. This is because there is continuity in his discourse, which is always tied to a particular class composition: Lenin's discourse weaves the organizational and political consequences of class composition. But this is not all. Until this reading of Hegel, Lenin's political intention was crippled and lacked an adequate theoretical substrate. Lenin interprets the general exigency of revolutionary thought in this way: as we have noted, it is not surprising that the situation repeated itself and that by 1937 another great leader of the workers' movement, Mao Zedong, used these writings (published during the early 1930s in Russia) in his important polemical thoughts on method (his writings on practice and on contradiction), which ascribe to Lenin's reading of Hegel an essential foundation of Marxist theoretical discourse.

So, Lenin comments on Hegel's *Science of Logic*. Alongside the *Phenomenology*, which represents the summit and conclusion of the first period of his philosophy, this is Hegel's most important work.[1] In the context of the development of Hegel's thought, we will try to clarify the concepts in which he grounds the science of logic and which Lenin clearly highlights in his commentary. Hegel is an idealist philosopher. An idealist philosophy is typically characterized by the affirmation that reality (being and the existence of truth) lies in the idea and that thought finds forms of realization that are more or less pure, more or less real. Idealism claims that the real world and truth inhabit a realm outside of the things offered to experience: in the mechanism of Plato and Neo-Platonism, which is the tradition of idealism and religious idealism, the real world is a mere projection of the ideal world and can participate in it to a greater or lesser extent. However, it never fully achieves truth, nor can it do so. Hegel reaffirms the principle that truth resides in the idea but distinguishes himself from all previous idealisms because for him, although each appearance of truth in the world is, indeed, transitory and partial, the movement of the idea and thought reaches totality, as a movement and as a production. Therefore, ontologically, while each fact is particular and a limited representation of the idea from the standpoint of the concrete, from the standpoint of the totality of the movement and dialectical phenomenology, the world is the totality of the idea. Idealism thus becomes *dialectical*: for Hegel and the Hegelians dialectics is an actualization of thought that tends toward the construction of its real totality. While at the beginning of the process being and thought do not coincide and being and truth do not initially overlap, the whole constitutes itself, in its natural and historical forms, in its relation to reality as it is given and its relation to reality as it is built through action, will, and freedom. Totality comes into being through the movement. And this leads to a further consequence: the proper definition of the mechanism of dialectics. If each appearance of being is both true and untrue, that is, true insofar as it participates in the totality and untrue insofar as it is not the totality of the truth, the entire mechanism that produces the true and thus the reconstruction of the world is one of affirmation as well as negation: an affirmation of the part of being that insists on each appearance of reality and a negation of its particularity, because each determination of the being that appears will have to be negated time and again in order to reach the totality. Only the whole is the truth, but totality must be seized within this dialectical process. From this standpoint, logic as science is none other than the methodology of a reinterpretation of all the passages through which from determinate affirmation one reascends to the truth of the whole. So, if this determinate affirmation is also the representation of a particular being, because each affirmation must be determinate and insist on an object of which it declares or negates something, then the science of logic will not be a formal science that simply studies the relations between the predicates of things, but a substantial and ontological science that follows the reality of the process through which objects come to constitute themselves in the totality.[2]

This is the overall framework of development of Hegel's logic. The aim of Marxists seems to be to take this logic and stand it on its feet, to overturn it. Let's see. Hegel's logic, according to Marx, is a perfect tool for its inner rigor, but its defect is that it stands on its head; it pivots on the notion of absolute thought and its hegemony over reality. The young Marx, in his 1844 *Manuscripts*, tries to overturn the terms of the science of logic and of Hegelianism in general.[3] His goal was to stand it on its feet and take as foundational the truth of singular and collective human interests rather than the truth of the abstract and the ideal, to see how dialectics can run through these interests and immediate needs and determine them in a mechanism of recomposition, to recognize on the one hand the moments when these interests are affirmed as collective ones, as reconstructions of an entity of *species being*, and on the other hand the moments when, in this movement, human interests reveal profound contradictions, fundamental antagonisms, and blockages to this anthropological perspective. But Lenin goes a step further and adds to what we later found in Marx's early writings, which were not known in Lenin's times and which were only published a century later, in 1932, by the Marx and Engels Institute of Leningrad.

What principles emerge from Lenin's reading of *The Science of Logic* in a persistent, precise, almost pounding way? What is the innovative motif of his reading of Hegel with respect to Marx? What is the relevance of the reading to the concrete development of his revolutionary thought? The elements that will be noted in our clarifications of these questions are many. Let us see them one at the time.

First of all, the main aspect of Lenin's reading is the claim that in the process of consciousness the form cannot be distinguished from the content of knowledge: there is no abstract logic that can be applied to different contents in different historical epoch. Logic, that is, the criteria of truth that we use, is completely conditioned by the whole historical reality, by the totality in which we are immersed. This hypothesis can be found at the outset of Lenin's commentary: "But it can be only the nature of the content which stirs in scientific cognition, while at the same time it is this very reflection of the content which itself initially posits and produces its determination."[4] It keeps coming up in Lenin's text and also represents one of the fundamental aspects of Hegel's own thought. This is no less than Hegel's anti-Kantian stance, and must be noted loudly and clearly, because it is the motif, or the red thread, of Lenin's philosophical reinterpretation, the element that makes his approach consistent with the materialist foundations of Marxist theory. The issue of the unity of form and matter and of knowledge and conceptual development is analyzed in different moments of Lenin's commentary: as the identity of form and matter (logic and epistemology) and the unity of the objective and the subjective in the process of cognition and of freedom and necessity in the process of the will. Alongside this question, Lenin also recovers from Hegel's work a very vigorous attack on all variants of subjectivist and formalist theories of knowledge.[5] He concludes:

Essentially, Hegel is completely right as opposed to Kant. Thought proceeding from the concrete to the abstract—provided it is correct (NB) (and Kant, like all philosophers, speaks of correct thought)—does not get away from the truth but comes closer to it. The abstraction of matter, of a law of nature, the abstraction of value, etc., in short all scientific (correct, serious, not absurd) abstractions reflect nature more deeply, truly and completely. From living perception to abstract thought, and from this to practice,— such is the dialectical path of the cognition of truth, of the cognition of objective reality. Kant disparages knowledge in order to make way for faith: Hegel exalts knowledge, asserting that knowledge is knowledge of God. The materialist exalts the knowledge of matter, of nature, consigning God, and the philosophical rabble that defends God, to the rubbish heap.[6]

From this first element of Lenin's reading of Hegel, two issues emerge. In some respects, as we noted in our discussion of his polemic against Russian Neo-Kantianism in *Materialism and Empirio-Criticism*, one might be forgiven for thinking that Lenin is very well disposed to accept Hegel's argument against Kant. But Lenin finds Hegel "genial" in a further respect, when he reclaims, against traditional materialism, a concept of matter that tends to merge with and touch upon that of life, while retaining a huge ontological, all-encompassing foundation that is sensitive to the intervention of praxis. We will later see how he develops these issues, but for now, we will underline that in Lenin, Hegel's lesson is applied to the terms of mechanistic materialism and enables an expulsion, or rather, a control and recomposition, of the mechanistic component of the materialist bourgeois revolution. In this first approach, we already see the problem Hegel raises for Lenin and its philosophical definition: this is the question of the dialectical inversion of subject and object that purports a radical hegemony of the concept of the real.

On this material premise, a second order of problems opens up to Lenin: the definition of dialectic as the science of the essence and of connection. From Hegel, Lenin draws the intuition that the path of consciousness traverses the negation of the simple and the immediate only to recompose them in a process that leads to the construction of the composite real. The true proceeds through the discovery of the essence as a real connection and by deepening the levels of being that come to be gradually involved: "Negation of the simple, *movement* of the mind: it is along this path of self-construction alone that Philosophy can become objective, demonstrative science. The 'path of self-construction' = the path (this is the crux, in my opinion) of real cognition, of the process of cognizing, of movement from ignorance to knowledge."[7]

Concreteness fades from the working web of allusions to immediacy, which becomes abstract and as wide as the series of elements that it needs to comprehend: from this perspective, dialectics operates an inversion and redis-covers the abstract apprehension of many connected aspects as the unity of the connection and the concreteness of the essence: "Then logic gives 'the essential character of this wealth' (*des Reichtums der Weltvorstellung*), 'the inner nature of spirit and of the world.' . . . A beautiful formula: 'Not merely an abstract universal, but a universal which comprises in itself the wealth of the particular, the individual, the single' (all the wealth of the particular and sin-gle!)!! Très bien!"[8] Here, Lenin notes, "Cf. *Capital.*" Of course, the principle of determinate abstraction that Lenin had *instinctively* applied since his writings in the 1890s is here discovered in its logical structure! But it goes on: Lenin is led to dwell on this dialectical tension with a sort of enthusiasm. The whole of world development must be comprehended in this process, materialistically, and rigorously so: "Nonsense about the Absolute. I am in general trying to read Hegel materialistically. Hegel is materialism that has been stood on its head (according to Engels), that is to say, I cast aside for the most part God, the Absolute, the Pure Idea, etc."[9] Lenin keeps returning to the issue of the necessary nexus of reciprocal determinations in the whole:

> If I am not mistaken, there is much mysticism and leeres pedantry in these conclusions of Hegel, but the basic idea is one of genius: that of the univer-sal, all-sided, vital connection of everything with everything and the reflec-tion of this connection, *materialistisch auf den Kopf gestellter*, Hegel in human concepts, which must likewise be hewn, treated, flexible, mobile, relative, mutually connected, united in opposites in order to embrace the world. Continuation of the work of Hegel and Marx must consist in the dialectical elaboration of the history of human thought, science and technique.[10]

And as an aside, this: "And purely logical elaboration? It *must* coincide, as induction and deduction in *Capital.*"[11] Subsequently, Lenin embarks on a long discussion of the logic of phenomena where he recognizes as correct the relation Hegel posits between definition of essence and connection of appearances (their unity) and thus the relation between essence and law.[12] In the discussion that follows, he tends to reduce the concept of cause and effect and even the concept of mediation to the categories of connection:[13] "The unfolding of the sum-total of the moments of actuality N.B. = the essence of dialectical cognition."[14] So we arrive at the threshold of a definition of a universal relationism that can be identified by the parameters of the all-sidedness of the concept of truth, the universal interdependence of concepts, and the mediatory and transacting operability of the elements. Let us open a parenthesis here. Lenin opens one too. Borne along by enthusiasm for a logic that seems to translate the materialist notion of relation (which is natural and historical, but real) into a concept of dialectic, he still senses that the operation is insufficient and slightly inconclusive. He seems disappointed not to find the Hegel he had expected: "The essence here is that both the world of appearances and the world in itself are moments of man's knowledge of nature, stages, alterations or deepening (of knowledge). The shifting of the world in itself further and further from the world of appearances—that is what is so far still not to be seen in Hegel."[15] Well, the world does not fall out of sight, but what needs to be explained is how the dialectics, to give reason to the whole of reality, cannot simply assert that "every notion occurs in a certain relation in a certain connection with all the others." If that is the case, "what constitutes dialectics?"[16] In fact, although it excluded and overcame rigid mechanisms, it did not provide a new definition of the concept of matter, nor did the reduction of all categories of change to those of relation give meaning to the leaps, to the novelty produced, to the dialectical synthesis, especially when faced with praxis. The outcome of this part of his reading of Hegel is a sort of *Spinozism* that innovates on the notion of reality but is incomplete and one-sided.[17] The problem is primarily logical in the proper sense. As a student of Marx, Lenin thought it necessary to make sense of the logical move that is the productive leap of knowledge from determinate abstraction to the method of the tendency. As he writes: "*Aphorism*: It is impossible completely to understand Marx's Capital, and especially its first chapter, without having thoroughly studied and understood *the whole of* Hegel's Logic. Consequently, half a century later none of the Marxists understood Marx!!"[18]

N.B. Concerning the question of the true significance of Hegel's Logic: The formation of (abstract) notions and operations with them *already includes* idea, conviction, and *consciousness* of the law-governed character of the objective connection of the world. To distinguish causality from this connection is stupid. To deny the objectivity of notions, the objectivity of the universal in the individual and in the particular, is impossible. Consequently, Hegel is much more profound than Kant, and others, in tracing the reflection of the movement of the objective world in the movement of notions. Just as the simple form of value, the individual act of exchange of one given commodity for another already includes in an undeveloped form *all* the main contradictions of capitalism, so the simplest *generalization*, the first and simplest formation of *notions* (judgments, syllogisms, etc.) already denotes man's ever deeper cognition of the *objective* connection of the world. Here is where one should look for the true meaning, significance and role of Hegel's Logic. This N.B.[19]

Here lies the problem. The uncertainty of dialectical relationism needed to be matured and overcome to discover the key to the dynamic transformation of the logical and real connection. The series essence-connection-movement needed to be translated into essence-movement-production because only the latter could represent dialectics at a higher level and directly turn it into a tool not only of materialism but also of the proletariat. "'The truth of Being is Essence.' Such is the first sentence, sounding thoroughly idealistic and mystical. But immediately afterwards, a fresh wind, so to speak, begins to blow: 'Being is the immediate.'"[20] Here the two series are still indistinct, but the immediate is already in the position to triumph over mediation (as simple relation) and manifest itself as an "inner pulse," "self-movement and vitality." This occurs as soon as Lenin shifts his analysis to Hegel's "principle of contradiction." Here the dialectical framework is presented as expansive, fresh, and warmed by a reality that has recovered the key to its self-determining qualitative movement.

Movement and "self-movement" (this N.B.! arbitrary (independent), spontaneous, internally-necessary movement), "change," "movement and vitality," "the principle of all self-movement," "impulse" (*Trieb*) to "movement" and to "activity," the opposite to "dead Being," who would believe that this is the core of "Hegelianism," of abstract and *abstrusen* (ponderous, absurd?) Hegelianism?? This core had to be discovered, understood, *hinüberretten*, laid bare, refined, which is precisely what Marx and Engels did.[21]

To sum up, the first set of problems Lenin confronts in his reading of Hegel is the definition of the unitary fabric of dialectical knowledge of the real. A second set of problems lies in the definition of a dialectical tool of reduction of the complexity of the real to connection. But in his analysis a third set of questions emerges concerning the dialectical definition of the true as movement and production.

This comes with a fourth set of problems, the critique and the inversion of the spiritual foundation of Hegel's logic, but the third set of questions concerning the definition of the dialectics as production is the highest point of Lenin's analysis. To conclude, we will underline the formidable originality of this reading of Hegel. It is both fresh and warm, and its depth is unequalled, especially when, as we shall see in the next conversation, Lenin uses a paradoxical practical translation of dialectics that allows him (and later Mao) to turn it into a weapon of the proletariat. In this step, the entire probability of Lenin's interpretation of dialectics reaches an intensity that is even greater than the use Marx made of it.

NOTES

1. G. W. F. Hegel, *Science of Logic*, trans. A. V. Miller (London: Allen & Unwin, 1969); and Hegel, *Phenomenology of Spirit*, trans. A. V. Miller (Oxford: Clarendon Press, 1977). I suggest the Italian translations by A. Moni (1925) and E. De Negri (1960).
2. Those who want to make contact with Hegel's theory can do so by reading, in particular, G. Lukács, *The Young Hegel: Studies in the Relations Between Dialectics and Economics*, trans. R. Livingstone (London: Merlin Press, 1975); K. Rosenkranz, *Hegels Leben* [Hegel's life] (Berlin: Verlag, 1944); E. Weil, *Philosophie politique* [Political philosophy] (Paris: Vrin, 1971); T. W. Adorno, *Three Studies on Hegel*, trans. S. W. Nicholsen (Cambridge, Mass.: MIT Press, 1994); and B. De Giovanni, *Hegel e il tempo storico*

della societá borghese [Hegel and the historical time of bourgeois society] (Bari: De Donato, 1970).

3. K. Marx, *Economic and Philosophical Manuscripts*, trans. M. Mulligan, in *Marx and Engels Collected Works* (Moscow: Progress Publishers, 1965), 5:229–348.

4. Vladimir Ilyich Lenin, *Philosophical Notebooks*, trans. C. Dutt, ed. S. Smith, in *Collected Works* (Moscow: Progress Publishers, 1976), 38:87.

5. Ibid., 38:89–94.

6. Ibid., 38:171.

7. Ibid., 38:88.

8. Ibid., 38:98–99.

9. Ibid., 38:104.

10. Ibid., 38:146.

11. Ibid., 38:148–155.

12. Ibid., 38:159.

13. Ibid., 38:158.

14. Ibid., 38:153.

15. Ibid., 38:197.

16. Ibid., 38:167–175.

17. Ibid., 38:180.

18. Ibid., 38:178–179.

19. Ibid., 38:129.

20. Ibid., 38:141.

21. Ibid.

18

BETWEEN PHILOSOPHY AND POLITICS

The Weapon of Dialectics

W**E HAVE DISCUSSED** how the needs internal to materialist and Marxist argumentations led Lenin to an interpretation of dialectics that was initially charged with relationist, Spinozian, and almost mechanistic elements, and how these elements gradually came to fade from it. But this was not a straightforward process: Lenin seems to force the originality of his approach after feeling rejected by the formidable power of the productive standpoint in Hegel's dialectics. In fact, in the first part of his commentary, whenever relationism is overcome and turned into an argument on production, with adequate ontological support, Lenin looks for a cover, which is also a mystification or insufficient appreciation of the move.

Let us analyze some of the writings. In his study of the "general concept of logic," Lenin comes across the question of the "necessity of connection." On this issue, Lenin observes, "Hegel puts forward two basic requirements: 1) 'The necessity of connection' and 2) 'the immanent emergence of distinctions.' Very important!! This is what it means, in my opinion: 1. Necessary connection, the objective connection of all the aspects, forces, tendencies, etc., of the given sphere of phenomena; 2. The 'immanent emergence of distinctions,' the inner objective logic of evolution and of the struggle of the differences, polarity."[1]

Lenin strikes the right chord there but then he stops. Even his discussion of Hegel's doctrine of being[2] comes to similar impasses: the power of self-productive being modifies the nexus being-connection and turns it into productive power. But this emerges from Lenin's analysis with great effort, and Lenin keeps attributing to being the character of Spinozian compactness; rather than the productive moment, he emphasizes terms such as "life" and "vitality." The latter are far from being synonymous with production, because production entails the qualitative leap and the productive inversion of the relation between immediacy and mediation. Even when, toward the end of the first book of *The Science of Logic*, Lenin comes across the notion of gradualism and a specific attempt to reason through dialectics of quantity and quality,[3] his comments go no further than a generic emphasis on the discontinuity of the dialectical process. *Natura facit saltus*: but the affirmation and emphasis on such affirmation do not result in a leap of the overall discussion.

It is important to recognize these initial difficulties because in these we register a sort of irreducible dualism between dialectical materialism and political initiative in Lenin's philosophical thought, where the former functions as a mere theoretical reflection of the connections between phenomena (with *theory* emphasized) that lies outside of the ability to bring reality to bear on a creative subject. This dualism reveals that Lenin is a *Spinozist* as well as a political pragmatist; it also reveals a conviction that there is no reunifying concept in materialism, that each concept tending toward the unitary compression of the process is idealist, and that every notion of subjectivity, understood as the imputation of the connection to a productive substrate, must be expunged from theory. Althusser[4] and some of our authors[5] definitely support this interpretation. This is not the place to discuss the consequences of their positions; but briefly, for Althusser, this standpoint does not allow for an advancement of theory and leads to the blindest opportunism, as it ties the concept of the political to a preconceived autonomy and independence of the party, which logically follows from the dualism that intervenes to isolate the mass movement from political judgment.[6] What interests us here is showing how this dualism is only an initial difficulty in the process of Lenin's reading, and how, contrary to Althusser's opinion, in these notebooks Lenin recovers a unity in his standpoint through the definition of dialectics as a weapon of the revolutionary subject.

The initial ambiguities begin to acquire some clarity when Lenin confronts the study of subjectivity in the context of Hegel's doctrine of the notion.

Lenin's attack on Kantian subjectivism and formalist theories of knowledge and his defense of Hegel's approach to the question of the relation between the content and form of knowledge clearly represent a step forward; not only is the nexus of essence-consciousness-movement made dynamic, but in the relational circularity of the process Lenin also starts emphasizing the primacy of the productive subject of knowledge materialistically: "The laws of logic are the reflections of the objective in the subjective consciousness of man."[7] This is only a first suggestion, but soon enough, in his comments on the most important part of The Doctrine of the Notion, section three on The Idea, Lenin's argument acquires greater depth: "Eternal life = dialectics."[8] Here we go again, and it seems to be only momentarily beyond the Spinozist universal relationism we have discussed. But this is not the main meaning of the term "dialectics." On the contrary, in this text and from here onward, dialectics seems to be seen as a process, with all that this term adds to the originality of the essence. The "quiet death of the object," of essence, is taken over by the process of cognition, by the enrichment of human knowledge, as a subjective activity, as work.[9] Thus the productive conjunction of subject and objects begins to find its proper name, to discover the material specificity of its dialectical nature: "Truth is a process. From the subjective idea, man advances towards objective truth through 'practice' (and technique)."[10] Praxis emerges as a specification of dialectics as it overcomes, comprehending it, the notion of the essence as connection and mediation: praxis is the motor and the verification (mediation) of the dialectical process.

So we arrive at one of the most important moments in Lenin's reading of Hegel. The meaning of praxis is crucial; it is a discovery of the radical and material and yet dynamic and productive character of mediation between the constitutive activity of the subject and the emergence of an immediate reality. Dialectics is no longer circular; its continuity is a relation of intellectually correlated moments constituted in praxis. Dialectical continuity and discontinuity find their constitutive motor in praxis. In these pages, Lenin insists on and emphasizes Hegel's own definition of praxis, the materialist character of this definition, and the importance of immediacy (as objective irreducibility) in Hegel's description of praxis. These are strong arguments. He concludes: "Practice is higher than (theoretical) knowledge, for it has not only the dignity of universality, but also of immediate actuality."[11] Moreover, "Theoretical cognition ought to give the object in its necessity, in its all sided relations, in its contradictory movement, an- und für-sich. But the human notion 'definitively' catches this objective truth of cognition, seizes and masters it, only when the notion becomes 'being-for-itself' in time sense of practice. That is, the practice of man and of mankind is the test, the criterion of the objectivity of cognition. Is that Hegel's idea? It is necessary to return to this."[12]

And he immediately returns to it: "Marx, consequently, clearly sides with Hegel in introducing the criterion of practice into the theory of knowledge: see the *Theses on Feuerbach*."[13] Finally, the concept of the syllogism of action is addressed: "Cognition . . . finds itself faced by that which truly is as actuality present independently of subjective opinions (*Setzen*). (This is pure materialism!) Man's will, his practice, itself blocks the attainment of its end . . . in that it separates itself from cognition and does not recognize external actuality for that which truly is (for objective truth). What is necessary is the union of cognition and practice."[14]

> The "syllogism of *action*." . . . For Hegel action, practice, is a "*logical syllogism*," a figure of logic. And that is true! Not, of course, in the sense that the figure of logic has its other being in the practice of man (= absolute idealism), but vice versa: man's practice, repeating itself a thousand million times, becomes consolidated in man's consciousness by figures of logic. Precisely (and only) on account of this thousand-million-fold repetition, these figures have the stability of a prejudice, an axiomatic character. First premise: The *good end* (subjective end) versus actuality ("external actuality"). Second premise: The external *means* (instrument), (objective). Third premise or conclusion: The coincidence of subjective and objective, the test of subjective ideas, the criterion of objective truth.[15]

At this stage, Lenin's dialectical and productive subjectivism leaps forward: he confronts the "theory of reflection" as a materialist theory of knowledge, providing a coherent interpretation of it as a constitutive theory of the object in materialist terms. In this passage he describes the theory of reflection as constitutive. From an objective and passive moment, rooted in the subordination of the world of ideas to the world of things ("the dialectics of *things* produces the dialectics of ideas, and not vice versa"),[16] Lenin gradually moves to a reading of reflection as something that occurs inside the dialectical process and that is a productive and constitutive moment of it. The concept of praxis, in the dialectical framework, destroys the objective fixity of reflection and subordinates it to verification and technique, which determines its constitutive function: "Life gives rise to the brain. Nature is reflected in the human brain. By checking and applying the correctness of these reflections in his practice and technique, man arrives at objective truth."[17] "The activity of man, who has constructed an objective picture of the world for himself, *changes* external actuality, abolishes its determinateness (= alters some sides or other, qualities, of it), and thus removes from it the features of Semblance, externality and nullity, and makes it as being in and for itself (= objectively true)."[18] "The result of activity is the test of subjective cognition and the criterion of *objectivity which truly is*."[19]

None of the supporters of the "theory without a subject" will be scandalized, I believe, if in conclusion we mention this final part of Lenin's commentary that sums up the proper character of dialectics as interpreted in *The Science of Logic* and definitively grasped in Leninism: "Important here is: 1) the characterization of dialectics: self-movement, the source of activity, the movement of life and spirit; the coincidence of the concepts of the subject (man) with reality; 2) objectivism to the highest degree ('*der objektiviste Moment*')."[20]

Finally, Lenin adds a *general observation*:

It is noteworthy that the whole chapter on the "Absolute Idea" scarcely says a word about God (hardly ever has a "divine" "notion" slipped out accidentally) and apart from that—this NB—it contains almost nothing that is specifically *idealism*, but has for its main subject the *dialectical* method. The sum total, the last word and essence of Hegel's logic is the dialectical method—this is extremely noteworthy. And one thing more: in this *most idealistic* of Hegel's works there is the least idealism and the *most materialism*. "Contradictory," but a fact![21]

To conclude our analysis of Lenin's *Notebooks on Philosophy*, let us return, step by step, to his polemic against the idealist elements of *The Science of Logic* and to the need to subvert them: "Engels was right when he said that Hegel's system was materialism turned upside down."[22] There is only too much to choose from: in the whole of the commentary, Lenin punctually denounces all the moments where idealism is emphasized, while signaling Hegel's intolerable *abstruseness*: "mysticism," "dialectical games," "theological vanity," "nonsense on the absolute" "- objectivism + mysticism and betrayal of development," and so on. These are only some of the epithets that accompany Lenin's description of dialectics as "the eve of" the overturning of dialectics.[23] But it is not important to chase these kinds of remarks here. These comments are pretty ordinary in the Marxist tradition.

What matters is to try to briefly sum up the extraordinary significance of this reading of dialectics for Lenin. We have already noted that dialectics provides Lenin with a proper configuration of the development of his thought, from the issue of class composition to the overbearing urgency of the question of the inversion of the relation between composition and organization to insurrection for communism. But there is more to this: Lenin's reading of Hegel adds a new and more valuable aspect to the most appropriate Marxist interpretation of Hegel (which is Marx's). This is an awareness of the ontologically dominant role of collective praxis, of workers' and revolutionary praxis. At this stage, we can definitively see materialism as a working-class science of revolution, free from the mechanistic tradition, and as the embodiment of a revolutionary and operative realism. Dialectics becomes the *weapon of the proletariat*, finally equipped to sustain its experiences. The subversion of Bolshevik praxis between April and October becomes clearer in light of this theoretical experience. Mao's interpretation is situated in this Leninist tradition on the issue of insurrection and proletarian dictatorship and its transformation into a practice of permanent revolution. This question is really nurtured by the formidable theoretical lesson of *The Science of Logic* as reinterpreted by Lenin. Without this belief in the radically innovative power of praxis, gradualism and reformism would be invincible. Without this ability to turn determinate abstraction and the method of the tendency into a resolute power of collective praxis, the human universe would be presented as a law that is implacably adverse to the oppressed. Without the force of a theoretical project that brings the shifts of praxis to light, the mass reappropriation of the joy of managing power would become impossible. All of this is part of Lenin's practice of reading Hegel, in this formidable rediscovery of Marxist methodology that is different from Marx in one respect: the theoretical weapon is now close to becoming a practical and material one.

When Lenin boarded the security train that would take him from Switzerland to Russia, he carried three sets of notes: on dialectics, on imperialism, and on the state.[24] The content of these notebooks would not be the focus of his attention, of course![25] But Lenin had built his "encyclopedia of collective praxis" on these great issues. In the set of arguments on dialectics, he rediscovered the power of innovation of the masses, as the original moment and fundamental pulse of the movement. In his notes on imperialism, he found the antithesis, the negativity of the capitalist process and all the rigidity of its composition and material tendency: capitalist negation had reached its threshold of tension in the containment of the class movement; it had set into motion a self-destructive mechanism within itself. In the notes on Marx's theory of the state, Lenin applied dialectics to a conclusive relation: it had seen revolutionary destruction develop with the movement of the masses as a longing for and demand of communism. On the basis of this development of Lenin's thought, the analysis is unified around the highest concept of productivity of class and mass action. The concept of organization emerges different, subverted, and far from that of previous Bolsheviks and *What Is to Be Done?* From now on, organization means the overall dialectics of the revolutionary movement. The concept of timing is also renewed because it is entrusted to the synthesis of destructive elements that are driven and determined by the imperialist mechanism and the activity of the masses. The communist synthesis operates at the highest level, that of the comprehension of the movement in its creative totality.

If we briefly return to the positions of contemporary commentators on the *Philosophical Notebooks*, Althusser in particular, we can certainly recognize that there is, in Lenin, an aspect of that theoretical attitude they reclaim for theory today; this attitude is one of total openness from the working-class standpoint, of a lack of definitive hypotheses, and of a tendency to open the concept to a future projected toward thresholds that current praxis cannot reach. However, we will also underline that in contemporary theory, this limitlessness and structural objectivism is empty (and so is the theory that, to eliminate this sense of vertigo, we must call for a Party!), whereas for Lenin the openness is subjectively structured by the collective praxis of the masses, and limitlessness and structural objectivism are burned by the self-generating impetus and constant self-renewal of the movement. On a strictly logical level, we find the same shift: from determinate abstraction to the tendency toward the realization of the moment, the process is renewed and always filled with a concrete and determinate activity that cannot be avoided, that alone gives meaning to the process itself. The concept of organization and the communist program experience this tension and continuity of the masses.

Let us conclude with an example. The content of Lenin's analysis of "imperialism" is well known, and we have often discussed it. Now, what makes these writings so immediately connected to the practice of the masses? Is it the theoretical, objectivist outlook? Is it the determinacy of the polemical stance against the workers' aristocracies and their sociochauvinist posturing? (To say it with Althusser, is it the "structuralism" of theory or the "class struggle" of philosophy?) Surely it is not. These writings become fundamental to the preparation of the October revolution because they identify an objective tendency, the capitalist crisis at the highest level of perfecting the machine of repression against the workers within the war among imperialists, and lead it back to the workers' subject, indicating times and objectives. The reference to the workers' subject gives meaning both to theory and to theoretical polemics, because the workers' subject is the subject of theory. Were this not the case, were it not for the ability of theory, without pretenses, to say *who*, to *whom*, and for *what*, it would all be in vain. "The inevitability of the revolutionary upsurge from the development of imperialism": this theoretical claim is also the affirmation of the working-class subject.

The dialectical intermezzo of the years 1914 to 1916 ends on a positive note. Lenin provides a theoretical configuration and continuity to the excavation in the thread on revolution that he always followed: a new weapon and theoretical consciousness for the movement. Leninist dialectics is a fundamental lesson to us.

NOTES

1. Vladimir Ilyich Lenin, *Philosophical Notebooks*, trans. C. Dutt, ed. S. Smith, in *Collected Works* (Moscow: Progress Publishers, 1976), 38:97.
2. Ibid., 38:87ff.
3. Ibid., 38:113.
4. L. Althusser, *"Lenin and Philosophy," and Other Essays*, trans. Ben Brewster (London: New Left Books, 1978); and Althusser, "Response to John Lewis," *Essays in Self-Criticism*, trans. G. Lock (London: New Left Books, 1976).
5. B. De Giovanni, *Hegel e il tempo storico della società borghese* [Hegel and the historical time of bourgeois society] (Bari: De Donato, 1970); but see also G. Vacca, *Scienza, Stato e critica di classe* [Science, state, and class criticism] (Bari: De Donato, 1970); and C. Luporini, *Situazione e libertà nell'esistenza umana* [Situation and freedom in human existence] (Florence: Le Monnier, 1942).
6. See the articles by P. A. Rovarotti, "L'autocritica degli althusseriani" [The Althusserians' self-criticism], *Aut-Aut: Rivista di filosofia e di cultura* 138 (November-December 1973): 65–73; and J. Rancière, "La nuova ortodossia di Louis Althusser" [The new orthodoxy of Louis Althusser], *Aut-Aut: Rivista di filosofia e di cultura* 138 (November-December 1973): 73–77.
7. Lenin, *Philosophical Notebooks*, 38:183.
8. Ibid., 38:200.
9. Ibid., 38:190–200.
10. Ibid., 38:201.
11. Ibid., 38:213.
12. Ibid., 38:211.
13. Ibid.
14. Ibid., 38:215–216.
15. Ibid., 38:216.
16. Ibid., 38:196.
17. Ibid., 38:201.
18. Ibid., 38:217–218.
19. Ibid., 38:218.
20. Ibid., 38:228.
21. Ibid., 38:233.
22. Ibid.
23. Ibid., 38:175, 274, 169.
24. He carries them with him in ideas . . . some notebooks had gone lost. See Colletti, introduction to Vladimir Ilyich Lenin, *Quaderni filosofici*, trans. Luigi Colletti (Milan: Feltrinelli, 1958), clxvii–viii.
25. The description of the trip to Russia can be found in L. Fischer, *The Life of Lenin* (New York: Harper and Row, 1964).

PART FOUR

The Economic Foundations of the Withering-Away of the State

Introduction to the Reading of
The State and Revolution

19

"WHERE TO BEGIN?"

L ET'S START READING *The State and Revolution*. What has been said so far is essentially an introduction to the discussion found in *The State and Revolution*. This work is at the heart of Lenin's thought and the reason why revolutionary workers will always be Leninist. Our reading is going to concentrate on chapter 5, entitled "Economic Basis of the Withering Away of the State." We will obviously read the previous chapters first to see how the question of the withering-away of the state, which is central to this work, is justified and developed. The edition I am using[1] has the advantage of also including the preparatory notebooks on *Marxism and the State*, where Lenin outlines his interpretation of Marx, Engels, and Kautsky. The notebooks are interesting because they help us reconstruct the genesis of Lenin's argument. Although *The State and Revolution* was written between August and September 1917, when Lenin was forced to flee to Moscow after the first failed insurrectionary attempt in July,[2] the notes on *Marxism and the State* that it uses were edited in Switzerland in the period prior to Lenin's return to Russia. In Switzerland, having been forced to flee Krakow (then part of Austrian-ruled Poland), Lenin develops three series of texts: the first series includes his philosophical studies gathered in his notebooks on Hegel; the second concerns a study on imperialism and the popular essay on this topic; finally, these reports on *Marxism on the State* are the last texts before the work of August

1917 began. These three moments represent the rediscovery and renewal of the method of dialectics, the analysis of imperialism, and the specific analysis of the state and the approach of the workers' revolution to it; we will demonstrate how they are closely connected. The history of the manuscript on *Marxism and the State* is rather peculiar. In short, it seems that Lenin had intended to write *The State and Revolution* in Switzerland or upon his return to Russia, but was not able to do so because he lost his notebooks during the journey; when he recovered them by a stroke of luck, while hiding from an arrest warrant, he finally wrote the text in August and September.

The notebook ends abruptly on chapter 6 and contains the following sections: the first concerns social classes and the state in general; the second is a reconstruction of Marx's writings on the revolution of 1848; the third is dedicated to the experience of the Paris Commune of 1871 and Marx's analysis of it; the fourth includes complementary explanations and follows Marx's and especially Engels's polemical writings on social democracy, displaying both agreement and criticism of them (the critique of the Erfurt and Gotha program are of particular interest to Lenin here); the fifth directly confronts the issue of the withering-away of the state and the material bases for its demise; the sixth is a ferocious attack on Plekhanov and Kautsky; and all that remains of the seventh is an outline entitled "The Experience of the Russian Revolutions from 1905 to 1907." The scheme on which *The State and Revolution* was reconstructed is as follows: it starts with Marx's debate on the origins of the state to arrive at the issue of class struggle and the experience of the struggles between 1848 and 1871; it then proffers a communist program that concerns both the analysis of the party positions and the issue of the withering-away of the state; finally, it returns to the polemic against "opportunists," Kautsky and Plekhanov. According to the original plan, the work was to end with an analysis of the experience of the Russian revolutions of 1905 and 1917 in order to show the currency of the communist program and demonstrate its use for the masses in the wake of the suggestions following from the analyses of 1848 and 1871. Chapter 7, the final chapter, where theory, history, polemics, and program would have come together and been reciprocally verified is greatly missed in the overall work. Let us read the idea for it:

1. New "creation of the people" in the revolution. Quid est? (Plekhanov 1906).
2. Lessons of 1905. (1906 resolutions of the Mensheviks and Bolsheviks.)
3. Eve of 1917 revolution: theses of X. 1915.
4. Experience of 1917. Mass enthusiasm, Soviets. (Their wide scope and their weakness: petty-bourgeois dependence.)
5. Prostitution of the Soviets by the S.R.s and Mensheviks: militia, arming of the people

   military department. "*Departments*" economic department.

   verification 3–5. VII

   authorities' "independence" of party organisations.
6. Kornilov revolt.

   Demoralisation of Mensheviks and S.R.s.

   Fraud of 14–19. IX.
7. "Messianism." Who will start? [or this in "conclusion"?]³

This would have been a consistent summary of the whole of Lenin's theoretical activity from a particular point of view: the preparation for insurrection. "Who will start" is the closing of the outline for chapter 7. In these notes, Lenin quotes from Engels's introduction to *The Poverty of Philosophy*: "But what in economic terms may be formally incorrect, may all the same be correct from the point of view of world history."⁴ "Where to begin" is a verification of the problem that we have addressed elsewhere as the inversion of the relation between organization and composition. "Messianism"? This is an ironic response to all of those who, in the *Western* Marxism of the Second International, insisted on the *Oriental*, Messianic character of Lenin's thought. In fact, Lenin here rejoins the strength of the dialectical subversion of determinate praxis (of class composition) toward the ends of the organizational enterprise: the withering-away of the state, the happiness of human beings, the subjectivity of the management of the process, the rooting of organization in the essential political needs of the proletariat. Lenin polemically adopts the term "Messianism" and uses it in inverted commas: "Who will start" is obviously the Russian proletariat, where the "Messianism" of organization has managed to trigger and regulate a mass movement, leading it to its essential and conscious political ends. On this premise, the Russian proletariat will succeed in facing the problem of the withering-away of the state. It would be easy for us, today, on the basis of the Russian experience of actual socialism, to heavily criticize Lenin and accuse him of utopianism. But what purpose would it serve? The accusation of utopianism and the crisis of the objective finality would never take away the subjective tension represented by this aversion to the state, which is also the operative matrix of every revolutionary mass movement. Departing from the realm of a utopia anchored to the subjective ability of the masses amounts to an abandonment not only of Lenin, not only of Marx, but also of any materialist foundation for revolutionary action and of the ability to understand its mature and actual tendency.

Let us start with the preface to the first edition of *The State and Revolution*, dated August 1917, and the postscript to the first edition, dated November 30, 1917.

> This pamphlet was written in August and September 1917. I had already drawn up the plan for the next, the seventh, chapter, "The Experience of the Russian Revolutions of 1905 and 1917." But except for the title I had no time to write a single line of the chapter; I was "interrupted" by a political crisis—the eve of the October Revolution of 1917. Such an "interruption" can only be welcomed; but the writing of the second part of the pamphlet ("The Experience of the Russian Revolutions of 1905 and 1917") will probably have to be put off for a long time. It is more pleasant and useful to go through the "experience of the revolution" than to write about it.[5]

This postscript is rightly famous. It locates the book that represents the theoretical nucleus of Lenin's political and practical experience of those days and provides it with an intensity that only the revolutionary process could give rise to.

The preface to the first edition states: "The question of the state is now acquiring particular importance both in theory and in practical politics."[6] Why is that? Because all the problems come together and are based on this question. Lenin has been convinced, since the beginning of the revolution, that the war crisis and its characteristics of capitalist development can be exploited; the war is the last phase of a cycle of capitalist development: "The imperialist war has immensely accelerated and intensified the process of transformation of monopoly capitalism into state-monopoly capitalism."[7] This is the first statement that is also the foundation of Lenin's position. He correctly identifies the problem: the phase that capital is undergoing is one where the monopolist structures of capital are being perfected, and their full symbiosis with the structures of the state, which is extraordinarily intensified by the war experience, is becoming deeper. We are at the tail end of a process that began with the great wave of workers' struggles that followed 1870 and the formation of social democratic parties, a process that launched the capitalist restructuring that continued and deepened in the nineteenth century until its "real" and not merely chronological end, which was signaled by the first great imperialist war. The capitalist restructuring that followed the "communard" attack has already been described in two important works: Hilferding's *Financial Capital* and Rosa Luxemburg's *The Accumulation of Capital*. The shift had been grasped: when workers attacked as they did at the end of the 1870s, both directly and en masse, the bases of capitalist production using the particular social figure of the poor and mass proletariat, which was the first technical composition that capital produced for manufacturing production, and as this offensive occurred between 1848 and 1870, capital hugely raised its level of organic composition, that is, the proportion between machine and labor, between variable and constant capital. To what purpose? To further separate the working class unified by the struggle, and to build the figure of the professional worker as one who possesses a higher level of productivity than previous workers and acquires the dignity of work, a higher conscience of work, a position separate from the proletariat as a whole. The possibility of this capitalist leap forward is created by a huge process of concentration and the safeguard of the conditions for monopoly, that is, the ability to determine the price of commodities unilaterally. But this creates the need to develop imperialistically a market that corresponds to the productive capacity of this higher determinate level of organic composition. This is the process correctly described by Hilferding and Luxemburg, and subsequently summed up in Lenin's theory of imperialism, with some adjustments that are not of interest to us here. What is of interest, instead, is the overall framework:

the initiative of workers' struggle in the period between 1848 and 1870, the leap forward of the overall capitalist structure geared toward the blockage of this level of struggles, and the restructuring of production and of the labor force in order to affect a rupture in the unity that had developed in the working class. This internal and vertical rupture that occurred at the end of the nineteenth century would mark the specific character of the European labor force until the crisis of 1929 and the innovations that followed.

The Russian revolution develops from this figure of the worker as the revolution of the professional worker with all of its specificity. It is the revolution of a worker linked to a particular ideology of work and a specific ideology of socialism. She turns that capitalist constriction into a revolutionary force. This always occurs and always must occur if it is true that the worker is variable capital before being revolutionary, if it is true that the worker is part of capital itself. The limits of the Soviet revolution lie far beyond the fact that it was bureaucratically managed or otherwise: they are determined by the particular history of capital, linked to a particular type of working-class composition. This understanding has allowed us, in the most recent phase of revolutionary experience, to consider the permanence of the revolutionary process as a fundamental aspect and the need to impose, upon the constant layering of different levels of workers' composition, a constant rupture of those layers: the permanence of the revolutionary process as such and the cultural revolution as a crucial element of the project and the program. We will return to these implications in greater depth later on.

Let us return now to the phase Lenin describes. The fundamental shift is the financial one. The capitalist leap forward took place through the financial concentration and the function of productive and direct intermediation assumed by the banks. Alongside this process, capital acts directly on the expansion of the market through two stages that Lenin aptly describes: the first is prevalently the export of commodities; the second is prevalently the export of capital, and thus the attempt to expand the capitalist market in its strict sense and the circulation of capital as such: "The imperialist war has immensely accelerated and intensified the process of transformation of monopoly capitalism into state-monopoly capitalism."[8] The third moment is a further perfecting of the imperialist model. The reality of command as concreteness and as power of concentration fully comes to light. To carry out this project, the capitalist needed to wear the mask of the state; now it is fully incentivized by the imperialist war. War is presented as a clash that occurs at the level of the division of markets, as a necessary outcome of the process initiated to reconfigure the command over the working class, a process that led to a new definition of the domination of the working class as part of capital. Now, the war makes the overall rationality of the system much deeper. The leap forward of capital becomes a somersault: in order to defeat the enemy within (the working class), capital is forced to proceed, by building financial capital, toward the imperialist conquest of markets, but this leads to clashes and anti-imperialist wars. The imperialist war is a war for the partition of markets that necessarily derives from the urgent need to dominate the inner enemy, the workers.

It is pointless to dwell on whether Lenin's scheme is correct or adequate to the actual reality of class struggle, the composition of capital and of the working class; equally pointless would be to underline the inadequacy of the scheme to the current situation. Today the crisis emerges within the realm of planning, which cannot be reduced to Lenin's analysis.[9] But this is not what we are interested in here.

Of interest to us instead is the fundamental dialectical passage found in Lenin: the acceleration of the imperialist processes and the acuteness of the contradictions clash directly with their class foundations. The external contradictions explode in order to become what they are again: general representations of internal, class contradictions. What imposes the war on the state is the need to legitimate and directly safeguard the kind of monopolistic operation being carried out, but in this it reveals its primary goal: the internal domination of the working class. The imperialist war has extraordinarily accelerated the process of transformation, as they used to say:

> Now the monstrous oppression of the toiling masses by the state, which is merging more and more with the all-powerful capitalist associations, is becoming ever more monstrous. The advanced countries are being converted—we speak here of their "rear"—into military convict prisons for the workers. The unprecedented horrors and miseries of the protracted war are

making the position of the masses unbearable and increasing their indignation. The international proletarian revolution is clearly maturing. The question of its relation to the state is acquiring practical importance.[10]

This is to say that the more capitalism embarks on a contradiction revealed
by mergers, imperialism, war, and the augmentation of the violence of the
antiworkers' oppression, the more it is possible to unmask the nature of this
process. As soon as a specific contradiction emerges, crisis becomes insuppressible. Marx writes this a thousand times: the crisis is manifest from the
standpoint of the workers because only the workers know the true nature of
the capitalist process. If the war crisis reinforces the state, this is only to fully
demonstrate how unsustainable the situation is for the workers. The revolution is proposed, from the outset, as a tendency toward an awareness of this
unsustainable situation from the standpoint of the masses.[11]

The "maturing of the international proletarian revolution"! Really, what an
adventurist our old comrade would be if we were to listen to those who glorify
his teachings today! Nonetheless, the distance of the object is not real: the
question of the international proletarian revolution is real and near because
Lenin perceives it as the product of a living subject that stands before him.

What is the attitude of this living, concrete, determinate subject toward
the state? This becomes a crucial issue because the attitude toward the state is
the main element of the question of the program. What does a revolution of
this state accomplish? The revolution is the seizure of power in the eminent
form of its presentation, of power as a structure and machine predisposed,
legitimately, to manage a violence geared to specific aims. What are these
aims? Why do we seize the state? What leap does the revolution require, and
what attitude must the proletariat have toward the state? Why does the proletariat want the state, why does it seize it? What is its immediate and determinate utility? Fundamental to all of this is the fact that this living subject,
bearer of the world revolution that advances, realizes its own task in all its
intensity, with the ferocious will that the hope for liberation from imperialist
domination, its misery and desperation, demands.

From this standpoint, the essential aim of the pamphlet is already clarified
in the preface where Lenin immediately attacks the "elements of opportun-

ism that accumulated during the decades of comparatively peaceful development": these

> have given rise to the trend of social chauvinism which dominates the official socialist parties throughout the world. This trend—Socialism in words and chauvinism in deeds— . . . is distinguished by the base, servile adaptation of the "leaders of socialism" to the interests not only of "their" national bourgeoisie, but precisely of "their" state—for the majority of the so-called Great Powers have long been exploiting and enslaving a whole number of small and weak nationalities. And the imperialist war is precisely a war for the division and redivision of this kind of booty.[12]

The demystification of the theory of the state derives its necessity from the fact that the social democratic leaders are so involved in the mechanism of capitalist concentration, which is that first collective form of the state predisposed to the sustenance of the development of capital in the imperialist perspective, that only a liberation from this ideological subjugation can allow for the free development of the proletarian revolutionary struggle and the definition of its aims. Capital and the state have penetrated each other to such a degree that any attitude that is subaltern to the state leads to positions of unconditional support for imperialism from the standpoint of capitalism against workers. Therefore, "the struggle for the emancipation of the toiling masses from the influence of the bourgeoisie in general, and of the imperialist bourgeoisie in particular, is impossible without a struggle against opportunist prejudices concerning the 'state.'"[13] Lenin's argument, by means of a reconstruction of Marx's texts on the state, tends to unmask the false theory of the state that had developed in order to participate in imperialism and earlier to support the nation-state.

> First of all we examine the teachings of Marx and Engels on the state and dwell in particular detail on those aspects of this teaching which have been forgotten or have been subjected to opportunist distortion. Then we deal specially with the one who is chiefly responsible for these distortions, Karl Kautsky, the best-known leader of the Second International (1889–1914),

which has met with such miserable bankruptcy in the present war. Finally, we shall sum up the main results of the experiences of the Russian revolutions of 1905 and particularly of 1917. . . . The question of the relation of the socialist proletarian revolution to the state acquires not only practical political importance but also the importance of a most urgent problem of the day, the problem of explaining to the masses what they will have to do in the very near future to free themselves from themselves from the yoke of capitalism.[14]

At this point it becomes clear that the absence of chapter 7 in Lenin's book is damaging, because there his reconstruction of the struggles would have undoubtedly displayed the same intensity and formidable ability to propose and analyze that distinguished Marx's writings on 1848 and 1870. This absence might cause a distorted view of the work as a whole. Its *doctrinal* character (in reference to the principles of Marxism and Marx and Engels's interpretations) appears to be exclusive, while in fact, as we have argued, it certainly isn't. This might legitimate illusionary *theoretical* readings detached from the emergence of the revolutionary subject as such. Moreover, the lack of a debate on the revolutions of 1905 and 1917 is felt because it affects the analysis and the categories it outlines are not sufficiently determined. We will see how this applies to the question of the withering-away of the state in particular. Therefore our reading will need to make up for this absence, and there are two ways it can do so: on the one hand, it can try to refer to Lenin's overall methodology and the political program he sustains in this period; on the other hand, it can try to make it current by asking "what *The State and Revolution* can do for us," in other words, how a theory built on the experiences expressed by the revolutions of 1848 and 1871, and the experiences implicit in the revolutionary process of Russia in 1905 and 1917, can be immediately assimilated to revolutionary Marxism today.

On this issue, we will probably come to a series of conclusions that break with the tradition of the workers' movement. Lenin's theoretical attempt is formidable, especially in relation to similar contemporary experiences, but it is fully determined. It consists in an attempt to theorize a specific phase of the discourse of the workers' movement on the state, determining and fixing the argument historically on the economic basis of the state, starting from Marx and Engels's analysis. From this economic determination of the revolutionary process emerges an indication of the specific elements that need to be destroyed in the process itself. But there we find a confirmation that this work is linked to the determinate phase of the revolution of the professional worker, of the revolutionary proposal of socialism. Reading *The State and Revolution* demands of us detachment and a questioning of what the withering-away of the state means today, what the transitory phase of the dictatorship of the proletariat is, what relation is established between the seizure of power and the extinction of the machine of capitalist domination, what function the organized working class occupies in this process. It means asking what struggles have to say on this project, because if struggles are really achieving levels, in Europe and America, that already point toward a direct attack on capitalist command, if struggles already see a refusal of all intermediary state formulas of capitalist domination over the working class, if proletarian movements radically refuse the organization of labor and its amelioration and tend toward the direct appropriation of existing wealth, if more and more of the existing wealth is conceived as the possibility to expand human faculties, well, what is, then, the dictatorship of the proletariat? What is this *act* of seizing power in general in relation to the struggles that already prefigure, within themselves (and the only possible preconfiguration is the struggle), the refusal of all delegation, a project of direct reappropriation of wealth, and a new development of the collective human energy that the working class represents? Given this, what is the dictatorship of the proletariat? As is known, in Lenin we find an intermediate phase that is defined as the dictatorship of the proletariat and practically consists in the construction of a planned society and socialism: well, at the level of the planned society of capital, what does transition mean? For Lenin too, the intermediate phase entails the identification of the automatic means of control over social production. Well, in a situation where all of this has already been set into motion by capital itself, what is the dictatorship of the proletariat? If you like, the problem becomes more radical: the question is whether we can still talk of a dictatorship or a *socialist* revolution, or whether, today, any *realistic* project of revolution needs to place itself on the terrain of *communism*, whether the Marxist project of the withering-away of the state entails communism as a minimal program or not, as the attempt to put into practice from the outset that exit of humanity from prehistory, as Marx defined it.

NOTES

1. See Lenin, "Plans of Chapter VII (Unwritten)," *Marxism on the State: Preparatory Material for the Book "The State and Revolution"* (Moscow: Progress Publishers, 1972).

2. On Lenin's absconding, see L. Fischer, *The Life of Lenin* (New York: Harper and Row, 1964); and Edward Carr, *The Bolshevik Revolution, 1917–1923*, vol. 1, *A History of Soviet Russia* (London: Macmillan, 1958).

3. Lenin, "Plans of Chapter VII (Unwritten)," 94–95.

4. F. Engels, foreword to *The Poverty of Philosophy*, by K. Marx (Moscow: Progress Publishers, 1955), 4.

5. V. I. Lenin, *The State and Revolution*, trans. S. Apresyan and J. Ryordan, in *Collected Works* (Moscow: Progress Publishers, 1964), 25:145.

6. Ibid., 25:1.

7. Ibid.

8. Ibid.

9. On this issue, see S. Bologna, P. Carpignano, and A. Negri, *Crisi e organizzazione operaia* [Crisis and workers' organization] (Milan: Feltrinelli, 1974); and L. Ferrari Bravo, *L'imperialismo e la classe operaia multinazionale* [Imperialism and the multinational working class] (Milan: Feltrinelli, 1975).

10. Lenin, *The State and Revolution*, 25:1.

11. Ibid., 25:1–2.

12. Ibid.

13. Ibid., 25:2.

14. Ibid., 25:2–3.

20

THE CONCEPT OF STATE IN GENERAL CAN AND MUST BE DESTROYED

"THE STATE IS the product and the manifestation of the *irreconcilability* of class antagonisms."[1] The very existence of the state shows that contradictions between classes are not reconcilable; the detection of a dialectical nexus, in the sense of antagonism, is found wherever there is a state. Providing the evidence of this thesis is a task that Lenin initially assumes as fundamental: "the *recovery* of Marx's real teachings on the state."

What does this definition mean? First of all, Lenin refers to Engels's theory on *The Origin of the Family, Private Property and the State*. According to Engels, the origin of the state is necessarily linked to the supersession of primitive communism, that is to say, of the immediacy of the social relation and its community form: only when this immediacy of relations is broken can the state emerge, as a mediation of this rupture in the sense that a power is exercised that is external to the community and the communist forces and tensions functioning in primitive society. Therefore the state is a power external to society, the product of the irreconcilability of the conflicts that emerge and preside over the formation of any kind of mature society whenever the initial stage of its development, characterized by a sort of primitive communism, is overcome. Engels's anthropological (romantic and positivist) soup, the mythical and fabulous, though rude and necessary, image of primitive communism can be true or false:[2] it is not up to us to either deny or confirm it.

We will simply point out that in fact we do not need to search for the origins of the state *in general* to establish with precision what the state is in capitalist society. All that interests us is that the state is defined in this antagonistic form in capitalist society as a product of the irreconcilability of classes. More than a product of the irreconcilability of classes in general, the state is the product of the irreconcilability of two opposing classes (the proletariat and the capitalist class, represented by the bourgeoisie or other political, managerial, or bureaucratic ranks). The proletariat is linked to the laws of dialectics of capitalist society, not to the laws of dialectics in the absolute. The dialectics of capitalist society is the dialectics of value, the extraction of the maximum wealth based on exploitation. This is the law of value that immediately turns into the law of reproduction and distribution of the overall accumulated value of any mode of production that sustains those who create this value on the one hand, and those who appropriate this value through the organization of its production on the other. In restoring Marx's real theory of the state there is no need to make recourse to grand anthropological questions, to ask what the state is when humans exit the mythical stage of primitive communism (which one doubts has ever existed: others verisimilarly suggest that the first stage of human life was much more violent and perhaps much more irreconcilable). In any case, Lenin hardly ever indulges in a verification of the correctness of Engels's approach and of the validity of its anthropological premises; he is interested in the foundation of the analysis of the definition of the state more than in the restoration of the theory in its overall aims. The reference to Engels's work pays homage to its formidable distribution and, perhaps, to the elegant natural right fiction underpinning the analysis of his present. (In Lenin's excerpts of Engels's work,[3] Lenin never refers to the passages on anthropology, while he underlines the theoretical definition of the state.)

What matters then is whether the definition of the state is adequate to the reality that Lenin confronts, and Engels is correct in this respect:

> Summing up his historical analysis, Engels says: "The state is, therefore, by no means a power forced on society from without; just as little is it 'the reality of the ethical idea,' 'the image and reality of reason,' as Hegel maintains. Rather, it is a product of society at a certain stage of development; it is the

admission that this society has become entangled in an insoluble contra-diction with itself, that it has cleft into irreconcilable antagonisms which it is powerless to dispel. But in order that these antagonisms, classes with conflicting economic interests, might not consume themselves and society in sterile struggle, a power, seemingly standing above society became neces-sary for the purpose of moderating the conflict, of keeping it within bounds of 'order'; and this power, arisen out of society, but placing itself above it, and increasingly alienating itself more and more from it, is the state."[4]

Marx and Engels use this kind of formula not only where the state is con-cerned, but also more generally to define the processes of reification, for-mation, and consolidation of the economic categories of capitalist exploita-tion as commodity and money, value and surplus value, profit, and so on. This definition of the state as perceived by Lenin has little to do with the anthropological issues of *The Origin of the Family, Private Property and the State*; on the contrary, it emerges directly from Marx's critique of political economy. We are therefore dealing with materialist and historical political categories rather than naturalist, abstract, and anthropological ones. In fact, the irreconcilability of classes that the emergence of the state points to is in itself dynamic: the more it deepens, the more explosive its antagonism. Lenin claims that there are several classical social democratic mystifications of this question and refers to two in particular that are based on the attempt to turn the apparent mediation of the state into a real one: general, the par-ticular interest interpreted by the state; internal (and thus effectively media-tory), the external function of state command. Lenin outlines two lines of mystification that share this common foundation. On the one hand, bour-geois and petit bourgeois ideologues who are "compelled under the weight of indisputable historical facts to admit that the state only exists where there are class antagonisms and the class struggle 'correct' Marx in such a way as to make it appear that the state is an organ for the *reconciliation* of classes."[5] Thus reality is ascribed to the appearance of generality, and the incontestable truth that the state is an organ for class domination is denied. The clumsiness of this position is efficacious nonetheless: their victory in 1917 in the Rus-sian revolution shows that this new *conciliatorism* was a testing ground for all social democratic revisionist and democratic positions; the apology of the *conciliatory* state had become a weapon of opportunists and the organization of a refusal of the revolutionary process.

Furthermore, Lenin claims:

> On the other hand, the "Kautskyite" distortion of Marxism is far more subtle. "Theoretically," it is not denied that the state is an organ of class rule, or that class antagonisms are irreconcilable. But what is lost sight of or glossed over is this: if the state is the product of the irreconcilability of class antagonisms, if it is a power standing above society and "*increasingly alienating* itself from it," then it is obvious that the liberation of the oppressed class is impossible not only without a violent revolution, but *also without the destruction* of the apparatus of state power which was created by the ruling class and which is the embodiment of this "alienation." As we shall see later, Marx very definitely drew this theoretically self-evident conclusion as a result of a concrete historical analysis of the tasks of the revolution. And—as we shall show in detail further on—it is precisely this conclusion which Kautsky . . . has "forgotten" and distorted.[6]

Apparently Kautsky does not forget the truth of Marx's analysis: not only that the state does not conciliate, but also that it is not a neutral space where the irreconcilability of the antagonistic interests of classes can develop. Instead, he forgets that the state machine is *necessarily* linked to the prevalence of a power that opposes society, transcending it the moment it pretends to be the general interest of society itself; and finally, he forgets that this necessary contradiction is constantly growing.

This dialectics of the state can only be explained with reference to Marx's theory of value and exploitation: it is impossible to arrive at a Marxist definition of the state without passing through *Capital*, where the relationship between the organization of labor and the despotism over labor is developed.[7] But an affirmation of the growing antagonism of the state also entails reading the history of capital *directly* from the standpoint of the proletariat and class struggle. This is Lenin's project. From the outset, Lenin underlines the exponential growth of exploitation and of the destructive power of capital at this stage of its development. But this also immediately points to an augmentation and intensification of the antagonistic nature of the state. The deepening of class struggle, then, also ascribes a radically subversive task to the proletariat. When we read Lenin's notes on Marx's theory of the state we can fully grasp this second element: the philosophical or anthropological deformation that seems to function as Lenin's Engelsian point of departure is only sporadic; in fact, for Lenin as for Marx, the irreconcilability derives not only from the development of the law in general, but from its specificity in class struggle. The struggle of the working class, of the active subject in the development, deepens the irreconcilability of the state function. Unsurprisingly then, Lenin goes back to Marx's arguments in the *Eighteenth Brumaire of Louis Bonaparte* and underlines them in preparation for these texts:

> But the revolution is thoroughgoing. It is still journeying through purgatory. It does its work methodically. By December 2, 1851 [the day of Louis Bonaparte's coup d'etat], it had completed one half of its preparatory work; it is now completing the other half. First it perfected the parliamentary power, in order to be able to overthrow it. Now that it has attained this, it perfects the executive power, reduces it to its purest expression, isolates it, and sets it up against itself as the sole target, *in order to concentrate all its forces of destruction against it.* And when it has done this second half of its preliminary work, Europe will leap from its seat and exultantly exclaim: Well grubbed, old mole![8]

Lenin sees a mechanism that he will further analyze as a cosubstantial element of the overall theory of the irreconcilability of classes in the state in general and in its political direction. This element emerges from Marx's text and consists in the specificity of the function of working-class struggle within and against the state. The extraneous position of the state is here the product of a function of workers' struggle and becomes exalted, isolated, and attacked. Let us read this again: "the revolution works methodically, . . . first it perfected the parliamentary power, in order to be able to overthrow it." These political upheavals and the mode of organization of the state are always a direct result of class struggle; the perfecting of the state structure is a direct effect of class struggle because it is given by the combination of the workers' offensive and the state's adequate responses to it. This process is neither indeterminate nor generic: workers' offensives always function with a specific aim. Hence the ability of class struggle to keep confronting its adversaries in a manner that is increasingly central, determinate, and punctual. Rather than the "cunning of reason," providence, or teleology, it is the determination of a collective subject, a collective praxis that determines the dialectics of struggle and changes its terrain and power relations. When we talk about capitalist restructuring, even in the technical terms of the restructuration of the mechanisms of value extraction, we are pointing precisely to this question. This is what we read in *Capital*; in the *Grundrisse* this notion is largely anticipated; and finally in all of Marx and Engels's historical and political writings we find the application of this perspective. So, let us go back to this question and outline its institutional terms.

Class composition comes to change within struggles and through subjective and objective comportments: this is the line of revolutionary Marxism. This is embodied in the wage when by wage we mean all the conditions that make the dialectical turnover of capital and the working class historical, determinate, and effective. Through different levels of wages the working class behaves subjectively, and we can there verify a dialectics that, in the different progressive phases of working-class composition determined by struggles and their historical results (of salaries), corresponds to different and increasingly advanced and perfected levels in the compositions of capital, that is, in the form of extraction of surplus and in the overall social organization of exploitation. This process can be projected onto institutional forms. Institutional forms are nothing but a large functional sheath that corresponds to the various degrees and forms of exploitation and that is dynamically predisposed to control, contain, and repress struggles, because now we know that institutions do not see the working class as passive: the irreconcilability refers to its subject, the working class. Dialectics teaches us that alongside the working class, which puts the capitalist process into action, there is a capital that tries to recuperate this process in order to modify itself both as a mechanism of direct exploitation and as a general, institutional sheath of this mechanism. Forgetting this means forgetting the ABCs of Marxism, and Kautsky has indeed forgotten it, and Kautskyism today forgets this even more, because if in the analysis of the *Eighteenth Brumaire* Marx could discuss this, and if Lenin could renew this description of such a process, we, today, see its most intense theoretical exaltation and our practice is forced, happily forced, to follow this rhythm.

Let us return to Lenin. Imagine the enthusiasm Lenin must have felt in his rediscovery of Marx's laws of revolutionary practice, when he perceives that in the theory of permanent revolution expressed in the *April Theses* and put into practice in the early phase of the revolution, it was possible to repeat not only Marx's spirit, but his words. The first phase of the revolution, the February insurrection, defeated the bourgeoisie and built parliamentary power, but only to allow this power to show its bourgeois nature, its substantial inefficacy, and force it to turn into executive power, that is, into a repressive fact as soon as it fakes representation. The action of the proletariat consisted in isolating power, giving it its purest form, and showing it in its most essential and accomplished stage in order to *bring it down*: this is the moment of the second phase of the revolution. The theory of permanent revolution arises from the dialectical perception of the effects produced by the revolutionary movement, its successes, as new obstacles. The February revolution was a democratic revolution: produced by proletarian struggle but always democratic. Now it is necessary to act again, move forward, in order to avoid repeating "all the revolutions which have occurred up to now perfected the state machine, whereas it must be broken, smashed."[9] Now, says Lenin while writing *The State and Revolution*, is the time for the definitive leap that can smash this machine!

Let us think about reformism today. In its various formulations, reformism repeats exactly the first of Lenin's alternatives, the opportunism in the theory of the state: the state is conceived as an organ of conciliation, but in a particular way, because conciliation today is carried out in a more integrated social fabric and thus conciliation and organization seem to become more and more involved in each other, almost juxtaposed. It seems that the capitalist state that retains the appearance of mediation and social conciliation only does so by unnerving social organization itself, and that there can only be a reformist capitalist state. The second revisionist alternative Lenin describes is the current communist alternative that functions in a reformist manner: it is a version of what is called the Kautskyian deformation of Marxism. This is certainly more subtle and entails a neutrality of power relations, a neutral state zone in which the game of proletarian forces might develop and determine structural changes in the power framework. The deformation is subtle because on the one hand it represents the historical experience of the working class, without a doubt, which consists in determining effective changes in the structure of the state, but on the other hand it mystifies the fact that the state as such is always the organ of the domination of a class over another, the result of a mechanism of overall production, and thus always a figure of the power relation as a whole. The entire position of reformism, both in its vulgar version and in its subtle one, still falls pray to Lenin's criticism, and today this is much more so, given the level of social integration that the state machine operates on, since they are much tighter than they were in the phase of Marx and Lenin's speculation on these questions.

The second paragraph of the first chapter of *The State and Revolution*, entitled "Special Bodies of Armed Men, Prisons etc.," is an example of the argument made so far. What does the power of the state consist in, this power that is born out of society but becomes extraneous to it, that, if anything, can be a fact of social organization only insofar as it is a despotism for society, that can appear as general interest only insofar as it is command, power, force, violence against the working class? Starting from Engels's work, Lenin returns to the description of military and bureaucratic formations in order to provide a physical image of the concept of the state as the ultimate and decisive reality of state power. We have little to add on this issue here. Lenin's argument could be returned to elsewhere to see how special corps are no longer simply places of armed men today, given the level of social integration of mature capitalism. Insofar as control spreads and separates itself even from the form of democratic representation, special corps are being established across all branches of state power (banks, financial organisms, planning, and so on).[10] Lenin's thesis on special corps is confirmed.

But if we stay on the paragraph we are reading here, it is interesting that Lenin deepens the analysis of a fundamental issue, the general theoretical thesis on the augmentation of the state contradiction in the 1890s, in the period that immediately precedes the revolution and prepares for the great imperialist war and the economic shift toward imperialism that is its condition. Lenin returns to the argument insistently.

> As early as 1891, Engels was able to point to "rivalry in conquest" as one of the most important distinguishing features of the foreign policy of the Great Powers, but in 1914–17, when this rivalry, many times intensified, has given rise to an imperialist war, the social-chauvinist scoundrels cover up the defense of the predatory interests of "their own" bourgeoisie with phrases about "defense of the fatherland," "defense of the republic and the revolution," etc.![11]

This is all very beautiful, if anything, for its style!

But is this definition of the state, as it is essentially formulated in terms of armed special forces, correct? It is correct, but actually partial. As we stated from the beginning, the state is a different thing, a specific sheath of the capitalist organization of labor. Paragraph 3 proposes to study the state as an instrument of exploitation and its organization. Exploitation is not an act; it is a complex machine where elements of command and organization, juridical and actual authority, and so on play out and take on different locations (depending on political and economic structures and class composition at a given historical time). Lenin's question grasps a particular phase of the development of the state as the organizer of exploitation that we have already described. Lenin goes to the concrete core of the issue: he sees that, beyond the general structure, the different proportion in which the moment of organization and the moment of repression are combined also depends on the intensity of class struggle, but at this stage, class struggle goes through insurrectional moments. For Lenin, the moment of direct violence is fundamental, given the specific conditions of its political work, and it is more than that as well. The nature of the state Lenin is faced with is imperialist and monopolistic: this represents one of the conditions of his argument. Such a state determines itself, at the threshold, as pure and simple eminence of the standpoint of violence. This is not only the case with war as the concluding phase of classical imperialism. We need to go back to the imperialist and colonial practice described in Rosa Luxemburg's *The Accumulation of Capital* to understand the situation Lenin is presented with. Under those circumstances, we cannot accuse Lenin's analysis of being exaggerated! But we cannot even forget that insofar as capital develops, its organized elements become more important than those of coerced participation, and the mystifying function of the general interest broadens. The capitalist state, as it develops, also more strongly integrates the working class, and this happens for material reasons, because development entails always-higher levels of socialization of the forces of production. The society becomes a factory as they say, and complex social interrelations are all played out in productive terms. From this standpoint, the function of the state becomes more organizational; and the more social integration progresses, the more despotism traverses the normal mechanisms of social development. This is not to say that violence is not manifest or that its pure and simple expression is not part and parcel of the armory of power. Violence is the necessary ingredient for the existence of the state, as it always has been. What has changed is the form of development of state violence. Undoubtedly, if we take the integration of these two paragraphs of *The State and Revolution* as essential (on the one hand the state as a special detachment of armed men and prisons, on the other hand the state as an organ of exploitation and a tool of the organization of exploitation), then we must keep in mind that these elements have different importance in different phases of development: progressively, command tends to become internal to the project and to social reality as a whole. All the changes undergone during the great reformation of capitalism that followed 1929 have been geared to link command to the need to socialize production.

Let us now return to our reading of the text. In the third paragraph Lenin reasserts his vigorous attack on bourgeois democracy. The latter is "the best political sheath for capitalism." There is no need to dwell on this assessment, which is so central to Lenin's thought. It is more interesting, for us, to return to the debate on the dialectical relation between proletarian struggles and the state form. The analysis of this relation is affirmed in the middle of the third paragraph. Quoting Engels, Lenin writes:

"Because the state arose from the need to hold class antagonisms in check, but because it arose, at the same time, in the midst of the conflict of these classes, it is, as a rule, the state of the most powerful, economically dominant class, which, through the medium of the state, becomes also the politically dominant class, and thus acquires new means of holding down and exploiting the oppressed class." The ancient and feudal states were organs for the exploitation of the slaves and serfs; likewise, "the modern representative state is an instrument of exploitation of wage-labor by capital. By way of exception, however, periods occur in which the warring classes balance each other so nearly that the state power as ostensible mediator acquires, for the moment, a certain degree of independence of both." Such were the absolute monarchies of the 17th and 18th centuries, the Bonapartism of the First and Second Empires in France, and the Bismarck regime in Germany.

Such, we may add, is the Kerensky government in republican Russia since it began to persecute the revolutionary proletariat, at a moment when, owing to the leadership of the petty-bourgeois democrats, the Soviets have already become impotent, while the bourgeoisie is not yet strong enough simply to disperse them.[12]

The analysis of the relation between struggles and the state form could not be more accomplished than this.

But we ought to be careful here because there has been a series of attempts to justify neo-Kautskyian theories on the basis of these passages. These claim that bourgeois democracy could represent a neutral state form in which class conflicts and forces could express themselves efficiently with the aim of changing structures. The claim is not that the nature of the state is different from that outlined by classical Marxists, but rather that the organized power of the large popular masses has imposed itself on capital and conquered real spaces of power. At the *institutional level* we would be faced with a sort of historical, permanent dualism of power. The state has become something different, not because its concept has changed, but because the workers' movement has modified its reality. Such a proposal has nothing to do with Leninism and even less to do with the stance defended in *The State and Revolution*. In fact, Lenin clearly rejects this position. When he deals with the issue of dual power, he does not define nor does he wish to define a model of the state: there is only one state, and it is a monopoly of power and dictatorship. The situations Engels outlines identify wholly transitory phases where he registers a momentary subtraction of power away from its sole source. In these situations, the only question is how to break the thread that still keeps the contradictions together. Lenin's response to theories of the state that defend the possibility of power relations that, at some point, turn the state into a place where equal and opposing forces manage to coexist is clear: this possibility does not exist. Because if there were equal and opposing forces, they could only define a moment of staidness; but when has this ever been the case with class struggle? These theories would have to reintroduce, with the notion of equal and opposing forces, a category of static conciliation, which is the opposite of the dynamics of class struggle, and in doing so they would fall back on the first alternative of revisionism. In fact, this concept hides the mystification of the agreement, of collaboration, and of the attempt to turn the state into the *real* rather than apparent interpreter of the general interest, thus denying the opposing interests of classes. On the contrary, dual power is always an absolutely momentary and transitory phase; without completely mystifying the dialectical nature of society, no notion of the state can be sustained on a static dialectics of opposing forces. Obviously the spaces conquered by the working class can be broadened, and the concession of universal suffrage can be a measure of the maturity of the working class and its overall conditions of life and struggle, but all of this is only part of the class ability to attack and a subordinate result of a struggle that does not seek reconciliation.

The third paragraph concludes with a quotation from Engels on the issue of the withering-away of the state:

> The state, then, has not existed from all eternity. There have been societies that did without it, that had no conception of the state and state power. At a certain stage of economic development, which was necessarily bound up with the cleavage of society into classes, the state became a necessity owing to this cleavage. We are now rapidly approaching a stage in the development of production at which the existence of these classes not only will have ceased to be a necessity, but will become a positive hindrance to production. They will fall as inevitably as they arose at an earlier stage. Along with them the state will inevitably fall. The society that will organize production on the basis of a free and equal association of the producers will put the whole machinery of state where it will then belong: into the Museum of Antiquities, by the side of the spinning wheel and the bronze axe.[13]

Lenin comments:

> We do not often come across this passage in the propagandist and agita-
> tional literature of present-day Social-Democracy. But even when we do
> come across it, it is mostly quoted in the same manner as one bows before
> an icon, i.e., it is done to show official respect for Engels, and no attempt is
> made to gauge the breadth and depth of the revolution that this relegating
> of "the whole machinery of state to the Museum of Antiquities" presup-
> poses. In most cases we do not even find an understanding of what Engels
> calls the state machine.[14]

NOTES

1. V. I. Lenin, *The State and Revolution*, trans. S. Apresyan and J. Ryordan, in *Collected Works* (Moscow: Progress Publishers, 1964), 25:7.
2. An example in favor of Engels's anthropological theses: two beautiful volumes by G. Thomson, *Aeschylus and Athens* (London: Haskell House, 1969), which recover Engels's theses in a particularly rich and fascinating historical development.
3. Lenin, *Marxism and the State: Preparatory Material for the Book "The State and Revolution"* (Moscow: Progress Publishers, 1978), 215–219.
4. Lenin, *The State and Revolution*, 25:7.
5. Ibid., 25:7–8.
6. Ibid., 25:9.
7. I tried to provide a broad analysis of this relation in my article "Rileggendo Pasukanis: note di discussione" [Rereading Pasukanis: discussion notes], *Critica del diritto* 1 (1974).
8. Lenin, *The State and Revolution*, 25:31.
9. Ibid., 25:33.
10. On this, the analysis of Marxist analysts of finance is extremely important, especially J. O'Connor, "Summary of the Theory of the Fiscal Crisis," in *Kapitalistate* (1973) 1:79–83 and the works cited there.
11. Lenin, *The State and Revolution*, 25:13.
12. Ibid., 25:14.
13. Ibid., 25:16–17.
14. Ibid., 25:17.

21

OPPORTUNIST AND REVOLUTIONARY CONCEPTIONS OF THE WITHERING-AWAY OF THE STATE

The proletariat seizes from state power and turns the means of production into state property to begin with. But thereby it abolishes itself as the proletariat, abolishes all class distinctions and class antagonisms, and abolishes also the state as state. Society thus far, operating amid class antagonisms, needed the state, that is, an organization of the particular exploiting class, for the maintenance of its external conditions of production, and, therefore, especially, for the purpose of forcibly keeping the exploited class in the conditions of oppression determined by the given mode of production (slavery, serfdom or bondage, wage-labor). The state was the official representative of society as a whole, its concentration in a visible corporation. But it was this only insofar as it was the state of that class which itself represented, for its own time, society as a whole: in ancient times, the state of slave-owning citizens; in the Middle Ages, of the feudal nobility; in our own time, of the bourgeoisie. When at last it becomes the real representative of the whole of society, it renders itself unnecessary. As soon as there is no longer any social class to be held in subjection, as soon as class rule, and the individual struggle for existence based upon the present anarchy in production, with the collisions and excesses arising from this struggle, are removed, nothing more remains to be held in subjection—nothing necessitating a special coercive force, a state. The first act by which the state really comes forward as the representative of the whole of society—the taking possession of the means of production in the name of society—is also its last independent act as a state. State interference in social relations becomes, in one domain after another, superfluous, and then dies down of itself. The government of persons is replaced by the administration of things, and by the conduct of processes of production. The state is not "abolished." It withers away. This gives the measure of the value of the phrase "a free people's state," both as to its justifiable use for a long time from an agitational point of view, and as to its ultimate scientific insufficiency; and also of the so-called anarchists' demand that the state be abolished overnight.[1]

The comment to this passage from Engels's *Antidühring* opens the fourth paragraph of the first chapter of *The State and Revolution*, concerned with "the withering-away of the state and violent revolution." This issue is at the heart of Lenin's discussion and here we find a synthetic and formidable preview of the development of the work as a whole: the preview is polemical and forces the pace of the argumentation but also connects the analytical moment to a political proposal and changes the direction of the whole debate. As we have already pointed out, the target of Lenin's attack is a gradualist notion of the revolutionary process: the withering-away of the state, as opposed to the anarchist notion of the abolition of the state, was understood as a "vague idea of a slow, equal, gradual change without leaps and storms." In the next conversation we will try to insist on the methodological and substantial aspects of Lenin's notion of dialectics as it emerges with great clarity in these words, and will highlight its subjectivist character in the insistence on the relation between the notion of the state and the notion of politics, the analysis of reality, and the forces of mass and revolutionary change. Before we look into these subjectivist aspects, we would like to dwell on the other side, the analytical and objectivist side, if you like, of Lenin's analysis, since this side of the analysis concentrates on the reality of the state and draws on its substantial features from the standpoint of revolutionary dialectics.

Lenin makes five fundamental remarks in his analysis of Engels.

The first concerns the impossibility of the proletariat recuperating the state of the bourgeoisie. Engels claims, and Lenin reasserts, that as soon as power is seized, the state is destroyed by the proletariat. The issue of the withering-away only concerns the "remains of the state" after the socialist revolution and refers to the "proletarian semi-state."[2] Only the destruction of the state as such can set into motion the revolutionary process of its withering-away. Clearly, this approach underlines an objective fact about the structure of the bourgeois state, a rigidity and totality that cannot be shaped by the proletarian forces. All of the reformist ideas, both prior to and, even more so, subsequent to Lenin, are ruled out on the grounds of a correct use of the dialectics of totality, rather than on the basis of an ideology. This is the totality of bourgeois domination and a conception of the state as an ensemble of means adequate to the sustenance of command. Reformism can only be functional to the development of the state totality, a totality of the bourgeois class. No structural concession can be made to the reformist effort of the good social democrats. On the other hand, the concept of destruction includes that of withering-away rather than vice versa, as the reformist would like to. The reduction of the state to a semistate and the breaking of its totality are a substantial act that cannot be given up on, one that needs to attack the rigidity and implacable centripetal tension of the state of the bourgeoisie. Reformist argumentations could only be sustained if they demonstrated that the current state is already a semistate: but would we ever find a reformist so mad as to consider this an affirmation worthy of any attention? This is clearly not enough.

In the second part of his commentary (on dictatorship), Lenin clarifies the rigid character of the state structure and brings it back to bear on a determinate apex around which the intensity of the revolutionary class relation can be measured. The state is a particular "apparatus of repression." It is a property, an exclusive and unilateral use of force for the domination of capital. It is the coerced outcome of the capitalist command over society. The revolution will aim at this determinacy of the state power of the bourgeoisie in order to destroy it. Again, here the issue is neither the withering-away nor the substitution of the state, if not as dialectical moments of the will to destruction. The moments of the process of substitution (the dictatorship of the proletariat is the substitution of the proletariat for the bourgeoisie in holding on to this special power of repression) are subordinate to the destruction of the unilateral and ferocious character of the capitalist centralization of power aimed at domination, and they are so with no illusions, according to the most neat and determinate figure of destruction, insofar as by destruction we mean violence proper, an equal and opposing violence that must be set into motion and can never be diluted in the process of the withering-away of the state. Let us note that there is no contradiction between the first and the second moment: the destruction of the bourgeois state and the dictatorship of the proletariat, the necessary violence of the proletariat and the process of the seizure of the state. These are not opposing elements: they are related as substance to form and absolutely complementary. The destruction of the state and the dictatorship of the proletariat are, in this form, a process!

And here we come to the third point (on "withering away"). The destructive determination of the revolutionary process and its punctual and extreme violence are mediated through the process of withering away. The latter loses its utopian and voluntarist features and becomes an effective framework for the revolutionary process. The withering-away of the state occurs after the seizure of power and the expression of the will to destroy the state: it is defined as a stage that can be embarked upon starting with the destruction of the specific function of the state of the bourgeoisie, that is, when the state in general, "the most complete democracy," has come into being as a result of the seizure of power, as the content of the dictatorship. The process of the withering-away of the state is not a dialectical synthesis (as in Hegel) of a triadic process, after an abstract thesis (the distinction of the bourgeois totality) and the punctual antithesis (the actual violence of the revolution as the appropriation of power and exercise of dictatorship): the only thing it shares with Hegel's dialectics is that it comes third! This is because each element of this process has its own full individuality, and because a potential continuity is founded on the leaps of the political will, on the alternating of the power relations, and finally, as we will amply argue, on the determinacy of material conditions. Given that these conditions decide in the last instance, we will later see how the timing and the modes of the phases of the process can be changed in continuity with the design and tendency of the stages Lenin defines here.

Two observations follow on from this in Lenin's commentary, and each of them approaches the issue from a different standpoint. They are still moments of the definition of the nature of the state in "objectivist" terms, part of a conception that moves forward explosively from the destruction of the state, to the dictatorship, and to the withering-away of it. But these are polemical remarks where the substance of the argument tends to emerge from a theoretical confrontation. Moreover, there is a paradoxical reclaiming of the anarchist notion against all the stances that have used the polemics against anarchists as a shortcut to arrive at reformism. Fourthly, Lenin comments, "after formulating his famous proposition that 'the state withers away,' Engels at once explains specifically that this proposition is directed against both the opportunists and the anarchists. In doing this, Engels puts in the forefront that conclusion, drawn from the proposition that 'the state withers away,' which is directed against the opportunists."[3]

The reformist social democrats theorized the "free people's state" as a Trojan horse for their insertion in the "present state": fine, but the state of democracy that follows, this state of structural reforms, is still a state. So, this conception is

> an opportunist slogan, for it expressed not only an embellishment of bourgeois democracy, but also failure to understand the socialist criticism of the state in general. We are in favor of a democratic republic as the best form of state for the proletariat under capitalism; but we have no right to forget that wage slavery is the lot of the people even in the most democratic bourgeois republic. Furthermore, every state is a "special force for the suppression" of the oppressed class. Consequently, every state is not "free" and not a "people's state." Marx and Engels explained this repeatedly to their party comrades in the seventies.[4]

In other words, the withering-away of the state is a form of its abolition where the abolition is not proclaimed as a miracle or immediate act; rather, it is the outcome of a process that stems from destruction to liberate, by means of the dictatorship, the forces of the withering-away, of the historical and efficient abolition of the state, *by* the state.

On the last point, Lenin defends the value of the anarchist notion of violence against that of the opportunists. He notes that "Engels' historical analysis of its role becomes a veritable panegyric on violent revolution. This, 'no one remembers'; it is not good form in modern Socialist parties to talk or even think about the significance of this idea, and it plays no part whatever in their daily propaganda and agitation among the masses. And yet, it is inseparably bound up with the 'withering away' of the state into one harmonious whole."[5] Lenin proceeds to comment on the following passage:

> That force, however, plays another role [other than that of a diabolical power] in history, a revolutionary role; that, in the words of Marx, it is the midwife of every old society which is pregnant with the new, that it is the instrument by the aid of which the social movement forces its way through and shatters the dead, fossilized political forms—of this there is not a word in Herr Dühring. It is only with sighs and groans that he admits the possibility that force will perhaps be necessary for the overthrow of the economic system of exploitation—unfortunately, because all use of force, forsooth, demoralizes the person who uses it. And this in spite of the immense moral and spiritual impetus which has resulted from every victorious revolution! And this in Germany, where a violent collision—which indeed may be forced on the people—would at least have the advantage of wiping out the servility which has permeated the national consciousness as a result of the humiliation of the Thirty Years' War. And this parson's mode of thought—lifeless, insipid, and impotent—claims to impose itself on the most revolutionary party that history has ever known![6]

If we try to evaluate the content of our overall discussion of Lenin's notion of the state, of the state in general, both here and in the preceding lessons, we can immediately note that his conception is articulate and complete. In fact, we are used to the absurd and mystifying notions of the state and right offered by bourgeois science, in our times but even more so during Lenin's, which claim that the state and right are always split and analyzed at two extreme poles, that of pure consensus and that of pure command. Juridical realism, normativism, pluralist and monistic notions are pitted against one another throughout the history of the theory of the bourgeois state. But their battle is ephemeral because their ideology is completely mystifying, because the state of the bourgeoisie, the state of the capitalist organization of labor, lives its own life in the constant synthesis of elements of organization and command. One is functional to the other; one is meant for the other, and vice versa. The figure of the capitalist state fully realizes the dialectics of organization and command, as well as that of cooperation and exploitation, that characterizes the whole process of valorization of capital. The state is a form of the capitalist process as a whole, the gigantic projection of the dualistic character of commodity fetishism. Above all, it is the centripetal acceleration of all capitalist exigencies of command over the overall process of the production and circulation of value. It is an accomplished form of the collective capitalist over the society of capital. Lenin fully comprehends this accomplishment and centripetal articulation of the state organization. Lenin's notion of the state is a chapter in Marx's theory of capital that is consistent with Marx's teachings and analysis in *Capital*.

Nonetheless, this theory of the state has hardly been understood. For many, Lenin's insistence on the state as violence and totalitarian command over society entails a normative and imperative option. After all, Lenin's ability to regard the workers' power to attack the state as a theoretical aspect relevant to the analysis of the state itself, or in any case, fundamental in the project of its destruction, has led to an emphasis on the organizational, institutional, and sociological aspects of Lenin's theory of the state. As a result, Marxist theory of right ended up reproducing internally the same dualism of the bourgeois tradition and its mystifying powers. Only a handful of authors, especially Pasukanis,[7] had the strength to reassert the complexity of Lenin's theory of the state, and they did not meet with much gratitude from the workers' movement. It is therefore necessary to return to Lenin's theory of the state with great determination: to learn to read the theory of the state inside the categories of commodity and capital.

Having said that, it cannot be denied that fundamental changes concerning the general conditions of capitalist development have intervened after, and because of, the October revolution. Undoubtedly, the reformed state of capital exalts the moment of organization and the social continuity of its command much more than it did during the tsarist aristocracy. Moreover, the socialization of the capitalist mode of production makes the determinations of command over society more extensive, mobile, and efficient. While we acknowledge this, the state is still a specific form of the synthesis between organization and command: it cannot give these up wherever they are and however they determine their synthesis. Violence is organic and substantial to social organization and will be so as long as there is exploitation. Lenin's teaching is that it must be seized and attacked, isolated and perfected for it to be fully exposed and ultimately destroyed. The fact that capitalist command is diluted into development does not change the grave reality of it: it only generalizes it and makes it so strong that its existence is mistaken as a natural occurrence. Today, prior to being confronted with the definition of the formal reality of the state, a revolutionary notion of the state that adopts Lenin's standpoint is faced with the problem of its destruction: what differentiates us from Lenin is the extent of the spread of the command that needs to be destroyed, not the will or need to destroy it.

We have now gone through the paradoxes of the political and juridical science of capital, only to approach our own paradox.[8] Let us assume that the capitalist will to mystify and its ability to organize reach a stage where the recognition of the function of command over society becomes invisible both as a result of its totality and for its inherence in the overall social organization. Who is going to identify the moment of its destruction, then? Workers' hatred will be sufficient, because the capitalist paradox has its integral reverse side: it will be possible to find, inside the relation of production, the power of the state of capital fully deployed, and to hit it and destroy it there. This *workerist* attitude is more Leninist today than that of the many who seek out in the "present state" the "state of the past."

NOTES

1. Lenin, quoting Engels's *Anti-Dühring*, in *The State and Revolution*, trans. S. Apresyan and J. Ryordan, in *Collected Works* (Moscow: Progress Publishers, 1964), 25:18.

2. Ibid., 25:20.

3. Ibid., 25:21.

4. Ibid., 25:22.

5. Ibid., 25:22–23.

6. Ibid., 25:23.

7. See my article on Pasukanis in *Critica del diritto* 1 (1974).

8. For a definition of paradox, see Negri, introduction to *Scienze Politiche: Feltrinelli-Fischer Encyclopaedia*, ed. Antonio Negri (Milan: Feltrinelli, 1971).

22

THE PROBLEM OF THE "WITHERING-AWAY" OF THE STATE

Against Equality

THE LAST PART of the fourth paragraph of the first chapter, a summary of the theses presented so far, interests us for two reasons: First, from a methodological standpoint. Lenin insists on the fact that only dialectics allows for a correct understanding of the stages of the revolutionary project. We know what the role of dialectics is for Lenin: on the one hand, dialectics makes it possible to understand the relation of continuity between structure and superstructure, institutional moment and materiality of political struggle, and to bring the terms of class struggle to bear on the theory of the political composition of the working class. On the other hand, for Lenin, dialectics allows this continuity to be made *discontinuous*, to invert the relation between composition and organization, materiality and revolutionary will. Let us return, from this perspective, to some of the issues we have dwelled on concerning Lenin's *Notebooks* on dialectics. The operative instruments of dialectics, as managed by Lenin, allow for an intervention into the continuity and the discontinuity of the revolutionary process while also uniting this duality in the process of the tendency. Perhaps there is no heavier accusation than the one Lenin levels against the authors and politicians of the Second International in this text:

Dialectics are replaced by eclecticism—this is the most usual, the most wide-spread practice to be met with in present-day official Social-

Democratic literature in relation to Marxism. This sort of substitution is, of course, nothing new; it was observed even in the history of classical Greek philosophy. In falsifying Marxism in opportunist fashion, the substitution of eclecticism for dialectics is the easiest way of deceiving the people. It gives an illusory satisfaction; it seems to take into account all sides of the process, all trends of development, all the conflicting influences, and so forth, whereas in reality it provides no integral and revolutionary conception of the process of social development at all.[1]

To fully understand this passage, we need to remember some fundamental moments in the process of development of Lenin's methodology and, as we have argued, how those different moments came together. The first moment dates back to the 1890s and is characterized by a definition of the concept of social formation, that is, the political composition of the working class as found in *The Development of Capitalism in Russia*. The second moment, of the years that immediately precede and overlap with the first imperialist war, sees an outline of the dialectics of the revolutionary leap and a definition of the radical discontinuity of the process, induced by the deepening of the contradictions of capitalist development. The synthesis of these moments cannot merely be reduced to an example of eclectic combination. On the contrary, these different moments unite in a dynamism that is as effective for the interpretation of the revolutionary process of the masses as it is founded on the collective will of the revolutionary subject. The combination is a function of the heat of the moment and the most explicit version of the standpoint of the workers in the history of revolutionary Marxism. On the other hand, the eclectic falsification of dialectics is a method typical of the political argumentation of reformists. The reality is complicated, they claim, so let us consider all the tendencies and countertendencies that agitate within it! This reality is inexhaustible and irreducible to the determinate "one-sidedness" of the workers' standpoint! Here eclecticism is opportunism. Of course, reality is inexhaustible in itself, but what affects it and makes it comprehensible is a class standpoint. For Marx and Lenin, society is mature enough for the revolutionary process insofar as a subjective force reduces it, simplifies it, and forces it into this fundamental class relation. Eclectic falsification reduces dialectics to a broom that sweeps away everything around it; it goes against the method of Marx and Lenin, which is one of a determined and close examination of the problem, of the solution to the basic antagonism in the problem, and of the elimination, or, rather, subordination, of all secondary elements to the fundamental contradiction: "The necessity of systematically imbuing the masses with *this* and precisely this view of violent revolution lies at the root of *all* the teachings of Marx and Engels."[2]

Now we come to the second reason for our interest in this last section of the first chapter of *The State and Revolution*, and take up another important element in Lenin's thought: namely, how everything that was presented in the Marxist tradition as a theoretical thesis is made immediately practical and determined. The method that is typically Marxian but takes on an absolutely new form in Lenin is the method of a tendency that grasps contradiction at its highest stage and describes the reality of capital from within the violent exasperation, from the standpoint of the workers, of a particular stage of development, thus overturning its determinacy into a project of workers' offensive. The materiality of the tendency is turned into the materiality of the project. From this perspective, theory changes its meaning too: the practical determination of Lenin's discussion, the subjective dimension and the party project, and his ability to see reality "directly" in its moments of transformation require a close examination of the nuances of the differences between Marx and Lenin. Althusser[3] noted this, observing that while Marx's discourse essentially runs through historical structures (for instance, in the definition of the shift between different stages of manufacture, from simple cooperation to large industry) and describes the overall tendency in this continuity, Lenin makes use of immediately scientific structures. It is important to avoid a hypostasis of this difference: in Marxism the coexistence of these two tendencies is precisely what characterizes dialectics. Undoubtedly the operative character of Lenin's categories is an enrichment of dialectics; the fiber of Lenin's thought is a complex theoretical and practical activity and does not use successive horizontal structures, but vertical ones that represent, time and again, the threshold, the cutoff point of a determinate historical formation. His practical insistence on these levels of understanding condenses revolutionary will onto an immediately practical plane. Demystification immediately becomes an operational scheme; understanding is a condition of and always subordinate to operability. The subjective will of the party must succeed in interrupting this historical series at any point: this is the conclusion and one of the specific elements of Lenin's thought.

From this standpoint, our own Marxism is enriched, and it would be useful to develop our analysis, on the basis of these points, and verify its richness in fields of investigation that are closer to us. For instance, it would be very beautiful if we started to open up the analysis of the development of the capitalist mode of production (of the process of restructuration) here in a direction similar to the one initiated in Italy in sporadic moments during the 1960s. This analysis could be opened to include the identification of a series of new scientific definitions that bear on the comportments of workers and masses, not merely as they are qualified with reference to their internal historical modifications, but also as the emergence of punctual subversions and ruptures in the continuity of development.[4] It would be interesting to launch this kind of analysis again, especially taking into account the events that are occurring, the prevalence of stagnation of development, and consequently perhaps also the prevalence in workers' comportments of stable structures rather than dialectical rhythms accentuated in the relation between class and capitalist development. Obviously, it is always a case of relative points of view and evaluations, because all of these elements always move hand in hand, and the historical body of the working class we are confronted with is extremely compact and singularly united. However, it is necessary to highlight the acceleration or deceleration of the overall process, privileging adequate tools accordingly. Going back to Leninism, in this sense, is opportune and necessary.

But let us return to Lenin's text. Here the practical rupture of the historical continuum is determined by specific contents: what is specific is not only the method but also the content of its application. Lenin concludes and sums up his argument thus: "The supersession of the bourgeois state by the proletarian state is impossible without a violent revolution. The abolition of the proletarian state, i.e., of the state in general, is impossible except through the process of 'withering away.'"[5] The analysis does not conclude with a practical and decisive inversion of the historical situation as it came to be determined: as we have seen, the development of imperialism and its war exasperate the figure of the state as an antiworkers' function of command. Here the violence of the state becomes its determinate content. The analysis grasps and almost exasperates the fixing of this figure: against the violence of the state, only workers' and proletarian violence are valid. What allowed us to directly trace the shape of reality as a function of an attack on it was not a simplification of it, but its scientific reduction. The destruction of the state is a condition for any further step. The abolition of the state starts from the exercise of power, because the exercise of proletarian power fundamentally entails the realization of a formidable transfer of power to class, to the masses. The destruction of the state is the condition for the withering-away, for the proletarian positive process of reappropriation of power as society as a whole. At this point, instead of following the order of Lenin's exposition, I will jump to chapter 5 of *The State and Revolution*. Chapters 2, 3, and 4 are close examinations and philologically accurate recuperations of Marx and Engels's texts on this question. Lenin reconstructs the debate on the revolutionary process and communism as it developed in the theory of the classics. The second chapter concerns the teachings of Marx and Engels on the revolution of 1848–1851; the third chapter focuses on the experience of the Paris Commune of 1871 in Marx's analysis; the fourth chapter dwells on Marx and Engels's texts from 1870 onward and on the polemics internal to social democracy, especially the question of the program (Erfurt and Gotha). We will return to these chapters later.

What interests us at this stage is seeing exactly what "withering away" means beyond its mere theorization, although Lenin wishes for theory to be organized around a determinate and continuous experience as much as in terms of a political program. This text, in fact, does not simply emerge from a theoretical need, but from a need for theory to be linked to a revolutionary practice with the aim of overcoming the democratic phase of the Russian revolution. This text is characterized by revolutionary passion; it is traversed by it and left incomplete because, as Lenin claims, it is more interesting to make the revolution than write about it. Let us see how the question of the economic conditions for the withering-away of the state, and thus the question of the program, is confronted by Lenin.

Here we come to the fifth chapter of *The State and Revolution*, on "The Economic Basis of the Withering-Away of the State."

Before reading and closely following Lenin's argumentation here, we will highlight some of its fundamental characteristics because this moment is as central to Lenin's discourse as it is problematic, especially to those of us who read *The State and Revolution* from the standpoint of the workers and must therefore confront our urgent needs with Lenin's. Lenin's discussion on the economic basis of the withering-away of the state returns to Marx's discussion on the level of development of the forces of production and the identification of the tendency of class struggle as it presented itself in the second half of the nineteenth century. Lenin's problem consists in establishing the dictatorship of the proletariat as a shift to a socialist phase that is still dominated by the need for organizing labor and wages. Obviously we are first and foremost interested in recuperating the *form of the revolutionary process* described by Marx and Lenin. But while we are interested in the form of this shift and its dialectical reality (in this lies the permanence of the teachings of the classics), we are also forced to confront its contents and ask whether and to what extent Marx and Lenin's discourse, in different situations, is valid to us, or whether these definitions are now insufficient and contradictory. The basic problem concerns the relation between revolutionary workers' power (as it is expressed through the insurrectional shift and the establishment of the dictatorship) and the organization of social labor. Confronted with this problem, we can ask, today, whether the overall maturity of the productive forces has reached the levels described in the pages of Marx's *Grundrisse*, where communism becomes the main point and content of proletarian dictatorship, where by communism we understand the destruction of the organization of wage labor rather than simply the socialist perfecting of this organization. In Lenin, the debate is still entirely linked to the problem of socialist organization of labor, and he recognizes this shift in the whole of the revolutionary Marxist tradition of the nineteenth century. Therefore, is it possible to manage within an analogous form of dialectics a problem that is based on such different conditions (for us and for the workers' science familiar to Lenin)? Can *The State and Revolution* teach us anything in this respect?

I think it can, because like Marx, Lenin goes to the core of the question. He announces it in the premise of chapter 5:

Marx explains this question most thoroughly in his *Critique of the Gotha Program* (letter to Bracke, May 5, 1875, which was not published until 1891 when it was printed in *Neue Zeit*, Vol. IX, 1, and which has appeared in Russian in a special edition). The polemical part of this remarkable work, which contains a criticism of Lassalleanism, has, so to speak, overshadowed its positive part, namely, the analysis of the connection between the development of Communism and the withering away of the state.[6]

The main issue is an analysis of the nexus between the development of communism and the withering-away of the state. What is the figure of this shift?

The analysis basically follows the *Critique of the Gotha Program*, which was already largely investigated in the fourth chapter and becomes here a fundamental text (the Gotha program is the proposal for the program of German social democracy, and takes its name from the city that hosted the congress).[7] Here Marx confronts a series of problems that are introduced in a discussion of social democracy. In particular, the Gotha program was strongly influenced by the social democratic faction that regarded Lassalle's theoretical position as the foundation of their project.[8] They reflected on the possibility of an alliance between the working class and the Prussian state to isolate the class of landowners that had until then enjoyed a prominent position in the management of the Prussian and German state machine. This marginalization and alliance would have facilitated the recognition of the working class as the motor of development. The main issue in Lassalle's theory that finds its way into the Gotha program is that of "equal wages." In the particular German situation, the state administration played a huge role in the acceleration of the development of German industry in the second half of the nineteenth century: Germany turned from being a country marginalized from capitalist development into the power that had all its papers in order to enter the imperialist phase, and this process took place thanks to the determinate mediation of the state. The process of the unification of Germany was made possible by the ability of the Prussian state to insert itself into the production process and directly function as the capitalist brains of development.[9] In this situation, Lassalle's reasoning is as follows: a political alliance between the working class and the progressive forces of the state is desirable because it would allow for the progressive elimination of parasitical revenues (of landed estates and their related political powers) and the constitution of a highly productive society where rent is reduced to zero. Here we can see the law of value perfectly in force. But what is the law of value? It is the law according to which the capitalist product, profit, is seen as a relation between necessary labor time and surplus labor, and thus as a relation of ratios of relative wages corresponding to ratios of labor supplied, where profit is not understood in bourgeois terms as an interest ratio of capital expenditure, but as a surplus directed toward the overall reproduction of capital. From this perspective, the wage is "strictly" understood as a rate paid to the laborer for a labor directed to the greater overall reproduction of capital: when capital reproduces itself at a more advanced level of development, wage quantities and relations must be revised and renewed always as integral rates and revenues of the labor supplied. Here revenue becomes a socialist function. From Lassalle onward, socialist planning would be more or less set in these terms. Lassalle's operation can be more clearly understood in political terms. Exploitation obviously remains unchanged for the working class, and profit, as a global quantity of capital that is renewed and augmented, is based on a rule of exploitation and constituted by a surplus value that augments itself. But for Lassallian socialists, the main problem lies in the definition of a scheme of reproduction wherein wage distribution (of capital and labor) is always commensurate to the laws of development and its needs. Exploitation is regarded as a necessary function of this process: there is no development without labor exploitation because there is no development without labor, so the question is how to eliminate the overexploitation arising from ratios of revenues that have a completely different status, that is to say, parasitical rent.[10]

Marx and Lenin offer a strong critique of these positions when they concentrate on the overcoming of the law of value, the demystification of the "equal wage," and the building of the economic bases of communism: the dialectics applied to these questions is a crucial motif and workers' theory still refers to it today. Like Marx, Lenin claims that equality, the function of the law of value (that is, the exclusion of the surplus profits of particular classes), and equal wages (as wages that are integral to labor in a society that functions in socialist terms) have nothing to do with the withering-away of the state and the transition to communism. Lenin presents a radical critique of Lassalle and brings it to bear on the terrain of a definition of the transitory phase. This is the crucial point of the fifth chapter of *The State and Revolution*. I believe that this is one of the highest expressions of Marxian theory, only equaled, perhaps, by some of the passages found in Marx's *Grundrisse*, which was unknown to Lenin in 1917. Only in the *Grundrisse* do we find an anticipation of the communist critique of the rule of equality and of the definitive destruction of these lurid utopias in effectively materialist terms (unless we wish to go back to the fervid allusions of Marx's early writings). This is the definitive dissolution of any relationship between the communist struggle and the struggle of the radical bourgeoisie in whatever form it manifests itself; this is also the definitive dissolution of any relationship between the idea of freedom and the idea of communism, of any continuity, however generic, between liberal forces and the definitions of a communist realm.

In future conversations we will return to these issues. Now it is most useful to note some of the limitations of Lenin's text. In fact, despite its power, in this text Lenin's intuition is still expressed in terms of an analysis and critique of the state superstructure of liberalism and of socialist radicalism, rather than as an analysis that grasps the society founded on labor as the essential moment of the material organization of labor. The reason for this limitation is also the strength of Lenin's intuition, because it organizes the subjective will to break through and disrupt the material limits and the organization of social labor as they present themselves in the determinate level of development of his times. A radical examination and interpretation of these tendencies from the standpoint of the workers are only possible today and starting from the highest levels of capitalist development, from the most advanced watchwords developed by workers in struggle. For this reason, these pages of *The State and Revolution* must be integrated not so much with the formal completion of this or that issue, but rather with all of the moments where theory leaps forward and turns into a practical ability to recuperate the new fabric of class and struggle as it presents itself. The limit of Lenin's discourse might be necessary, understood as arising from the formidable contemporary ability to allude to more advanced contents of communism through a critique of equality! The problem of equality is not one of formal identity or abstract equivalence between different people: it is a question of building a communist society. Rather than recognizing an identity or an equality that does not exist and can never exist in the capitalist process, the issue is building an equality that is a constitutive, equalizing, and liberating activity, rather than a utopia, a process of destruction of the state as the hierarchical rule of exploitation. It is no surprise that this libertarian apotheosis of Leninism has always caused greater scandal in the good reformist socialist tradition than, for instance, the issue of violence: in fact, the Oriental and Blanquist ideology that Lenin has been attacked for consists in this radical critique of the concept of equality played at the rhythm of the law of value.

NOTES

1. Lenin, *The State and Revolution*, trans. S. Apresyan and J. Ryordan, in *Collected Works* (Moscow: Progress Publishers, 1964), 25:24.
2. Ibid., 25:25.
3. See, especially, L. Althusser, *Reading Capital*, trans. B. Brewster (London: New Left Books, 1970); Althusser, *For Marx*, trans. B. Brewster (London: Penguin, 1969).
4. This analysis was carried out during the 1960s by researchers publishing in the reviews *Quaderni Rossi* [Red notebooks], *Classe Operaia* [Working class], *Contropiano* [Counter plan], and *Potere Operaio* [Workers' power].
5. Lenin, *The State and Revolution*, 25:25.
6. Ibid., 25:99.
7. It was first published in 1891 and can now be found in *Marx and Engels Collected Works* (Moscow: Progress Publishers, 1989), 24:75–99.
8. There is an ample bibliography on Lassalle in Germany, unequalled elsewhere and in Italy; it would be worth studying him a little again.
9. On the development of Germany and its ideologies, see my old book and its ample bibliography: Negri, *Studi sullo storicismo tedesco* [Studies on German historicism] (Milan: Feltrinelli, 1959).
10. We slightly forced the expression of Lassalle's and Prussian socialist thought here, but it is useful to reintroduce their debate into our own to highlight the unchanged rupture between revolutionaries and opportunists.

23

FIRST APPROACH TO A DEFINITION OF THE MATERIAL BASES OF THE "WITHERING-AWAY"

Against Work, Against Socialism

I N THE FIFTH chapter of *The State and Revolution*, Lenin still extensively focuses on a critique of the Gotha program, before approaching the issue of the withering-away of the state and the first phase of communism. At first, this long introduction seems different and less effortless in the context of the economy of his debate, but it is not so. In fact, this discussion is necessary for him to link again the issue of the withering-away of the state with its materialist dimension, which entails an assault on and destruction of the law of value, or, rather, its exasperation and overcoming. His critique of the state is also a critique of socialism.

Lenin begins with the scientific, materialist presentation of the problem at the heart of it:

The whole theory of Marx is the application of the theory of development—in its most consistent, complete, considered and pithy form—to modern capitalism. Naturally, Marx was faced with the problem of applying this theory both to the forthcoming collapse of capitalism and to the future development of future communism. On the basis of what facts, then, can the question of the future development of future communism be dealt with? On the basis of the fact that it has its origin in capitalism, that it develops historically from capitalism, that it is the result of the action of a social force to which capitalism gave birth.[1]

Therefore, the issue of the transition from capitalism to socialism must be framed in the context of an investigation of the material basis of the transition, by which we mean the dialectics of class relations. Here we perceive an ambiguity: this dialectics, so long as it functions, serves as mediation between the capitalist ability to produce and reproduce capital and the labor force that is dialectically internal to it and thus also capable of presenting itself as an antagonistic force. Therefore, material basis also means revolutionary subject, where the latter is produced as such by capitalist development but is also its spring and core, unless it manages to express its will to make this development hegemonic in antagonism and to push it to the threshold of the revolutionary leap by means of struggle. So long as this does not happen, so long as the labor force inhabits the capital relation (whatever power relation it establishes with command and the organization of capitalist accumulation), so long as accumulation is not interrupted and the working class is not freed from capital, there can be no communism. The hegemony of development is not liberation from development at this stage. Here, one could define the phase where Lenin sees the need for a dictatorship of the proletariat as one of working-class hegemony over development. But a series of problems arises at this point, and we need to confront them immediately. The working-class hegemony over development means socialism, that is to say, the main rules of the capitalist process of production and reproduction are sustained, and to them a criterion of equality and the establishment of the political forms of "democracy" are added (as Lenin observed) because they affirm the dictatorship of the majority of the people (the proletariat) over all other social strata and classes. It is important to note that here socialism means development, and development refers to the capitalist mode of production, the law of value, the proletariat as the basis of the potential and eventual but future communist society. Marx and Lenin are aware of this conditioning of the material basis, which leads them to introduce a particular notion of transition from capitalism to communism.

The realism of Marx's and Lenin's analyses leads them to regard the transitory phase as necessarily dominated by the revolutionary dictatorship of the proletariat and as a socialist phase too. Rightly so, because the historical framework in which they both live is one where there must be a long phase of development of capitalism and an affirmation of socialism as hegemony over development and democracy of labor. But this historical framework was never overcome in Marx or Lenin in terms of a political proposal, while it was overcome from the standpoint of a theoretical forecasting of a further phase where communism can develop in synchrony with the paces and forms of struggle, adequate to the structure of workers' needs as they emerge in struggles, and thus represent the definitive revolutionizing of the conditions of production. In other words, affirmation and critique of socialism go hand in hand in both Marx and Lenin, and cannot but be joined. Similarly, affirmation and critique of the dictatorship of the proletariat go together (and can only go together), just as, when we started discussing the material basis, we could not disjoin the affirmation of development from the identification of a revolutionary subject against the development of capital. Undoubtedly, Marx and Lenin are correct in this analysis of the situation. In fact, the overall condition of the relations of production and of the forces of production, in the absence of a workers' figure capable of overcoming the limits of professionalism and thus of the concrete relation with fixed capital, made it impossible to forecast a different outcome. A different and politically potential outcome could only emerge when the social unification of the proletariat in terms of abstract labor and the affirmation of a mass productivity through the collective homogeneous practice of the proletariat became the material basis of production. We will return to this later. In Lenin we inevitably see this problem expressed as one of the discrepancy and lack of homogeneity between the communist urge for liberation and the effective possibility of building a socialist state. It is absolutely crucial for this to happen. *The State and Revolution* is the text of communist restlessness. Socialism is not enough; on the contrary, it is a situation that is as necessary as it is necessary to overcome it. Lenin is fully aware of this and we can find the same awareness in every perceptive proletarian theory, because the transition continues to be a situation of struggle. So long as this bourgeois state exists, whether or not the bourgeoisie is the dominant subject, whether or not its rules are pushed to turn into rules of equality and norms against bourgeois domination, the situation is still absolutely dramatic.

After Lenin, both Stalin and Mao[2] interpreted and described, in a manner that was theoretically correct, the situation, and they emphasized the possibility (and necessity?) of an intensification of the struggle between classes in a period of transition. This effectively seems to correspond to the experience of the revolutionary dictatorship of the proletariat far more than do the gradualist and reformist versions offered by other theories and practices. Maoist theory in particular advances on these premises correctly by articulating a framework of the contradictions of the phase of transition that follows the seizure of power and regulating its contents; in the period of the cultural revolution, it finally and genially overturned the terms in which Stalinism had posited and failed to solve the question of the deepening of class struggle and therefore of the state's resolve against the bourgeois class with the bureaucratic distortions of revolutionary development: the Chinese Communist Party launched the struggle of the masses against the state and completely opened up the revolutionary process to a process of reappropriation of the proletariat's capacities for leadership again.[3] These are very different images from the sweet pictures painted by other theories and practices of the phase of the dictatorship of the proletariat and its relation with the first experiences of the withering-away of the state. It is very important in this respect to recall the Yugoslav Councils' theory, also for the unfair destiny it had to face. In this theory, the intensification of class struggle is mystified, and the function of the working class is denied and drawn into the people, with no distinction between the particularity of proletarian interests and the general interests of society.[4] Similar theories emerge everywhere in the climate of the betrayal of Leninism and of the triumph of renewed capitalist practices in so-called socialist countries.[5] The freedom and spontaneity of the process is opposed to the harshness of class struggle; in Lenin's words, "the expression 'the state withers away' is very well-chosen, for it indicates both the gradual and the spontaneous nature of the process."[6]

This is pure mystification: when Lenin insists on these expressions, he insists on the simplicity and easiness of the shift, and we find plenty of similar statements in the second paragraph of the fifth chapter. But we must be careful when interpreting them because they in no way replace the harsh need for a dictatorship of the proletariat and workers' command. When Lenin confronts these issues, he is always considering the discontinuity of the process between the rupture of the bourgeois state machine, the seizure of leadership, and then, starting from this, the actualization of the material conditions for the withering-away of the state form itself. Lenin insists on this discontinuity, and we must see it as a definitive feature of his theory. Neglecting this discontinuity means falling into the great mess of theories that see the upsurge of spontaneity as continuity and the withering-away of the state as something caused by the proletarian seizure of power. These theories of the continuity of struggle, the seizure of power, and the phase of dictatorship and withering-away of the state present the idealist and utopian image of a march forward and fail to see the real process of building communism, that is, the fact that the withering-away of the state only goes through the determination (and the struggle for the determination) of favorable and mature material conditions.

What are these conditions in Lenin's program? In the third paragraph of the fifth chapter, Lenin clarifies his point of view; but before coming to these, let us read two passages that reinstate the concepts we have underlined here and introduce our discussion on the material bases:

> No, forward development, i.e., towards Communism, proceeds through the dictatorship of the proletariat, and cannot do otherwise, for the resistance of the capitalist exploiters cannot be broken by anyone else or in any other way. And the dictatorship of the proletariat, i.e., the organization of the vanguard of the oppressed as the ruling class for the purpose of suppressing the oppressors, cannot result merely in an expansion of democracy. Simultaneously with an immense expansion of democracy, which *for the very first time* becomes democracy for the poor, democracy for the people, and not democracy for the moneybags, the dictatorship of the proletariat imposes a series of restrictions on the freedom of the oppressors, the exploiters, the capitalists.[7]

And he goes on to write: "Democracy for the vast majority of the people, and suppression by force, i.e., exclusion from democracy, of the exploiters and oppressors of the people—this is the change democracy undergoes during the *transition* from capitalism to Communism."[8]

So far so good: proletarian violence discriminates and attacks its adversaries, annihilating the formal criteria of bourgeois democracy; this occurs in the first phase, the phase of destruction. But this is not enough—communism is difficult and class struggle intensifies:

> Furthermore, during the *transition* from capitalism to Communism suppression is *still* necessary; but it is now the suppression of the exploiting minority by the exploited majority. A special apparatus, a special machine for suppression, the "state," is still necessary, but this is now a transitional state; it is no longer a state in the proper sense of the word; for the suppression of the minority of exploiters by the majority of the wage slaves of yesterday is comparatively so easy, simple and natural a task that it will entail far less bloodshed than the suppression of the risings of slaves, serfs or wage laborers, and it will cost mankind far less.[9]

In fact, our historical experience has shown how horrible and tragic the repressive conditions of this shift can be, but we cannot forget the place of this writing in the great wave of the revolution of 1917, and we cannot deny that it is animated by great enthusiasm and the feeling that an objective was within reach. However, even from such optimism, it cannot be deduced that there is an organic continuity in the process. Being realistic, we would be better off remembering the miserable and tragic outcomes of many failed experiences than pretending they are irrelevant to the workers' perspective. If nothing else, because capital makes us pay with our own for every failed experience and every betrayal of the international workers' movement.

What material conditions make the transition to communism possible? In what way does the proletarian hegemony over development determine these conditions so that a communist society can be born? In my view, the third paragraph of this chapter ought to be read in full:

> In the *Critique of the Gotha Programme*, Marx goes into detail to disprove Lassalle's idea that under socialism the worker will receive the "undiminished" or "full product of his labor." Marx shows that from the whole of the social labor of society there must be deducted a reserve fund, a fund for the expansion of production, a fund for the replacement of the "wear and tear" of machinery, and so on. Then, from the means of consumption must

be deducted a fund for administrative expenses, for schools, hospitals, old people's homes, and so on.[10]

Basically, Marx insists on the absolute need to draw a surplus from the labor supplied. This surplus must be directed toward the costs of reproduction of capital and labor force. Even on pure accounting grounds, Lassalle's theory of socialism (as an integral revenue for the worker) does not work. However, this initial reasoning only touches on the substance of the problem. Lenin continues:

> It is this communist society, which has just emerged into the light of day out of the womb of capitalism and which is in every respect stamped with the birthmarks of the old society, that Marx terms the "first," or lower, phase of communist society. The means of production are no longer the private property of individuals. The means of production belong to the whole of society. Every member of society, performing a certain part of the socially-necessary work, receives a certificate from society to the effect that he has done a certain amount of work. And with this certificate he receives from the public store of consumer goods a corresponding quantity of products. After a deduction is made of the amount of labor which goes to the public fund, every worker, therefore, receives from society as much as he has given to it. "Equality" apparently reigns supreme. But when Lassalle, having in view such a social order (usually called socialism, but termed by Marx the first phase of communism), says that this is "equitable distribution," that this is "the equal right of all to an equal product of labor," Lassalle is mistaken and Marx exposes the mistake. "Hence, the equal right," says Marx, in this case still certainly conforms to "bourgeois law," which, like all law, implies inequality. All law is an application of an equal measure to different people who in fact are not alike, are not equal to one another. That is why the "equal right" is violation of equality and an injustice. In fact, everyone, having performed as much social labor as another, receives an equal share of the social product (after the above-mentioned deductions). But people are not alike: one is strong, another is weak; one is married, another is not; one has more children, another has less, and so on. And the conclusion Marx draws is: " . . .

With an equal performance of labor, and hence an equal share in the social consumption fund, one will in fact receive more than another, one will be richer than another, and so on. To avoid all these defects, the right instead of being equal would have to be unequal." The first phase of communism, therefore, cannot yet provide justice and equality; differences, and unjust differences, in wealth will still persist, but the exploitation of man by man will have become impossible because it will be impossible to seize the means of production—the factories, machines, land, etc.—and make them private property. In smashing Lassalle's petty-bourgeois, vague phrases about "equality" and "justice" in general, Marx shows the course of development of communist society, which is compelled to abolish at first only the "injustice" of the means of production seized by individuals, and which is unable at once to eliminate the other injustice, which consists in the distribution of consumer goods "according to the amount of labor performed" (and not according to needs). The vulgar economists, including the bourgeois professors and "our" Tugan, constantly reproach the socialists with forgetting the inequality of people and with "dreaming" of eliminating this inequality. Such a reproach, as we see, only proves the extreme ignorance of the bourgeois ideologists. Marx not only most scrupulously takes account of the inevitable inequality of men, but he also takes into account the fact that the mere conversion of the means of production into the common property of the whole society (commonly called "socialism") does not remove the defects of distribution and the inequality of "bourgeois laws" which continues to prevail so long as products are divided "according to the amount of labor performed." Continuing, Marx says: "But these defects are inevitable in the first phase of communist society as it is when it has just emerged, after prolonged birth pangs, from capitalist society. Law can never be higher than the economic structure of society and its cultural development conditioned thereby." And so, in the first phase of communist society (usually called socialism) "bourgeois law" is not abolished in its entirety, but only in part, only in proportion to the economic revolution so far attained, i.e., only in respect of the means of production. "Bourgeois law" recognizes them as the private property of individuals. Socialism converts them into common property. To that extent—and to that extent alone—"bourgeois law" disappears. However, it persists as far as its other part is concerned; it persists in the capacity of regulator (determining factor) in the distribution of products and the allotment of labor among the members of society. The socialist principle, "He who does not work shall not eat," is already realized; the other socialist principle, "An equal amount of products for an equal amount of labor," is also already realized. But this is not yet communism, and it does not yet abolish "bourgeois law," which gives unequal individuals, in return for unequal (really unequal) amounts of labor, equal amounts of products. This is a "defect," says Marx, but it is unavoidable in the first phase of communism; for if we are not to indulge in utopianism, we must not think that having overthrown capitalism people will at once learn to work for society without any rules of law. Besides, the abolition of capitalism does not immediately create the economic prerequisites for such a change. Now, there are no other rules than those of "bourgeois law." To this extent, therefore, there still remains the need for a state, which, while safeguarding the common ownership of the means of production, would safeguard equality in labor and in the distribution of products. The state withers away insofar as there are no longer any capitalists, any classes, and, consequently, no class can be suppressed. But the state has not yet completely withered away, since the still remains the safeguarding of "bourgeois law," which sanctifies actual inequality. For the state to wither away completely, complete communism is necessary.[11]

No commentary on the understanding of the text and the consistency of its premises is needed.[12] But a first difficulty confronts us here, if we wish to interpret *The State and Revolution* in contemporary terms, and it is the same difficulty we find reading Marxian and Leninist texts. The problem is that we are faced with an entirely different situation from that in which they raise these question, especially when it comes to the law of value or the rule of equality; their function has changed because the socialization of production has changed; and the transformation of the relation between overall labor force and machinery has changed with the emergence, already under a capitalist regime, of a new generic productivity of capitalist labor, a new general productivity of social labor that can no longer be measured in terms of effectively supplied labor. In the *Grundrisse* Marx had already identified this situation as it developed within the most advanced capitalism;[13] there he defined as "miserable" the calculation relative to the labor supplied when compared with a capital that defines its reproduction no longer in a determinate relationship with single labor, but with the overall social force of production. When it comes to abstract labor, abstracted from its concrete determinations, Lassalle's idea is no longer even plausible. What interests us, however, is that Marx's and Lenin's idea of the state as a bourgeois state and the hypothesis of the possibility, for the proletariat, of appropriating the bourgeois state and using its laws and norms to manage the dictatorship of the proletariat no longer hold. In fact, the bourgeois state no longer exists, in the terms in which Marx and Lenin described it, as a state that applies the laws of the market, the—materially defined—rule of the wage of the exchange between labor power and revenue. Insofar as every relation between individual labor and total mass of products disappears, the classical rule of bourgeois law as one founded on the exchange of wage labor and exchange as it links to the law of value also disappears. What state are we confronted with today, then? A state where the dictatorship of capital is infinitely stronger and more developed than could be seen in the classical bourgeois state; a state where the rule of wage distribution is no longer based on the interchange between labor power and capital, but on the internal organization of the need to reproduce this command, here simply consisting in a rational hierarchy of functions intended for the perpetuation of domination. But while the situation has made the state in general more monstrous and stronger, the state must also allow for the presence of some of the fundamental conditions for the transition to communism and the revolutionary socialization of the proletariat.

From this standpoint, Lenin's text must be further investigated. In the following paragraph Lenin insists that "so long as the state exists there is no freedom."[14] We are far from the social democratic ideology here, very far from any reformist mystification. Militant and revolutionary communism verifies anarchism: "When there will be freedom, there will be no state."[15] And, again, the power of the program invests and transforms workers' needs, translating them into projects:

> The economic basis for the complete withering away of the state is such
> a high stage of development of Communism that the antithesis between

mental and physical labour disappears, when there, consequently, disappears one of the principal sources of modern *social* inequality—a source, moreover, which cannot on any account be removed immediately by the mere conversion of the means of production into public property, by the mere expropriation of the capitalists. This expropriation will create the *possibility* of an enormous development of the productive forces. And when we see how incredibly capitalism is already *retarding* this development, when we see how much progress could be achieved on the basis of the level of technique now already attained, we are entitled to say with the fullest confidence that the expropriation of the capitalists will inevitably result in an enormous development of the productive forces of human society. But how rapidly this development will proceed, how soon it will reach the point of breaking away from the division of labour, of doing away with the antithesis between mental and physical labour, of transforming labour into "the prime necessity of life"—we do not and *cannot* know.[16]

The first condition for this chance to massively develop the productive forces is the abolition of the division between intellectual and manual labor. The second condition is the development of the productive forces, because expropriation alone will already pave the way for a giant quantitative development of the productive forces, which capital is slowing down. The third material condition (included in the first and second affirmation) is the potential qualitative change implicit in the development of the productive forces, which is a socially unified transformation of its effects, given that the product of labor is already presented as associated labor, as manual, physical, and intellectual labor. Only on this premises can the problem of the withering-away of the state become a real one. We have a first definition of the material bases that need to be built in order to wither away the state, and only from this point on can Lenin conceive of the dissolution of the dictatorship.

In our times, this part of Lenin's analysis must be accepted, and we will start from it to see what has changed. That is to say, in what sense has the development pushed by struggles, this history of the workers' dictatorship as we have recorded it in recent years, before the formal and state dictatorship of the workers, already radically changed the conditions for a shift to communism? In what sense are the questions of insurrection and dictatorship today relevant to those who look at the question of the withering-away of the state?

NOTES

1. Lenin, *The State and Revolution*, trans. S. Apresyan and J. Ryordan, in *Collected Works* (Moscow: Progress Publishers, 1964), 25:100.
2. J. V. Stalin dwells on the issue of the contradictions of the phase of the dictatorship of the proletariat in the writings collected in *Problems of Leninism* (Peking: Foreign Language Press, 1976). His views were taken up and corrected in the practice and theory of the Chinese Communist Party.
3. Many are the writings on the Cultural Revolution in China, but it is not important to point to them here: we are more interested in the political significance of the echo of the Chinese experience in the European proletariat.
4. The Yugoslav theory of Councils and its suggested alternatives of transition are some of the most vulgar products of "socialist" theory since the World War II.
5. "Socialism with a human face" and other similar formulas are a revisionist and liberal ideology (in bureaucratic terms, obviously) spreading in popular democracies and, in lesser numbers, in the Soviet Union. Capitalist restoration and demagogy are both features of this ideology.
6. Lenin, *The State and Revolution*, 25:106.
7. Ibid., 25:105.
8. Ibid., 25:106.
9. Ibid., 25:107.
10. Ibid., 25:109.
11. Ibid., 25:111–113.
12. For a bibliography on transition and a comment on Marx's writings on it, see D. Zolo, *La teoria comunista dell'estinzione dello stato* [The communist theory of the withering-away of the state] (Bari: De Donato, 1974).
13. For an analysis of this issue, see lesson 24 in this book.
14. Lenin, *The State and Revolution*, 25:114.
15. Ibid.
16. Ibid.

24

MARX'S ANTICIPATION OF THE PROBLEM OF "WITHERING-AWAY"

Against the Law of Value

THIS LESSON IS, so to speak, a parenthesis in the unfolding discussion, and a paradoxical one too, because we suggest that in order to understand Lenin and offer a reading of his works that throws light on contemporary issues, we need to take a further step back. In Marx, we want to read a Marxist prediction of our present that is consonant with Leninist thought.

Marx confronts the question of "withering away" especially in the *Grundrisse*, in the framework of an analysis of the capitalist laws of development and mode of production. Obviously, the discussion is broached schematically and by way an analysis and prediction of the liminal points of capitalist crisis, or the critical relationship between the development of the capitalist mode of production and the capitalist control of the conditions and productive forces of this development. But it would be mistaken to regard the pages we are going to read as a mere "potential future" or an objectivist extrapolation of some real data: the *objectivism* of Marx's discourse is always dialectically connected to the emergence of workers' antagonism and sets a trend and affirms itself as the outcome of class struggle.

From this standpoint, our reference to Marx, meant to throw light on the present might seem less paradoxical. Combining the pages of the *Grundrisse* with those of *The State and Revolution* can enable us to come closer to what interests us here: a critique of the issue of "transition" from the standpoint of contemporary class relations.

First, a further premise of our reading of the *Grundrisse* is called for. We now have an excellent translation of this collection of texts written in preparation for *Capital*, and also some commentaries in Italian.[1] Well, this is an extremely important work because it reveals a cross section of Marx's thought and shows the dynamics of his theory: it is the laboratory wherein elements of critique come to combine. Its most important aspect is that the standpoint of the working class, workers' *subjectivity*, is here liberated at every turn, beyond all preoccupations with the system, and in an entirely explicit manner. This might be the reason for the long silence that has hitherto surrounded this work, and this is certainly the reason why these pages of the *Grundrisse* become enormously important in the face of our present problems and the current significance of the emergence of the workers' subject. Therefore, we would add that Marx managed to describe the mechanism of the elements that make up the workers' theory of crisis, and to reveal it as a determination and effect of workers' struggles, rather than as *fall and catastrophe*, in this work more comprehensively than anywhere else.

Beyond these premises, let us come to the core of the issue. How is the problem of *withering away anticipated* in Marx? Can this term be ascribed to the issue of crisis and fall in Marx? Can Marx's and Lenin's issues be drawn together, and how? In order to answer these questions, I think that it is necessary to recount some of the terms of Marx's discussion. Marx's definition of the problem of crisis and the overcoming of the capitalist system starts with an analysis of the changing tendencies of the conditions of production. The analysis touches on both objective and subjective aspects of this process.

OBJECTIVE ASPECTS

But in the degree in which large-scale industry develops, the creation of real wealth becomes less dependent upon labor time and the quantity of labor employed than upon the power of the agents set in motion during labor time. And their power—their *powerful effectiveness*—in turn bears no relation to the immediate labor time which their production costs, but depends, rather, upon the general level of development of science and the progress of technology, or on the application of science to production.[2]

Science is immediately incorporated into productive labor at the pace of the reduction of labor time: "invention becomes a business, and the application of science to immediate production itself becomes a factor determining and soliciting science."[3] Therefore, on the basis of these conditions, "real wealth manifests itself rather—and this is revealed by large-scale industry—in the immense disproportion between the labor time employed and its product, and similarly in the qualitative disproportion between labor reduced to a pure abstraction and the power of the production process which it oversees."[4]

At the objective level, when we are faced with this limit of the capitalist development of large-scale industry, three fundamental contradictions emerge. The first contradiction pertains to the relationship between the unity and extensiveness of abstract labor and the power of the overseen process of production. The second consists in the fact that, within this process, capital, on the one hand, strives to "reduce labor time to a minimum, while, on the other hand, positing labor time as the sole measure and source of wealth."[5] Third, the contradiction that reveals the absurdity of capitalist command is that capital "diminishes labor time in the form of necessary labor time in order to increase it in the form of superfluous labor time; it thus posits superfluous labor time to an increasing degree as a condition—*question de vie et de mort*—for necessary labor time."[6]

SUBJECTIVE ASPECTS

Given the critical conditions just defined, the contradiction becomes such that it reveals the working class as the historical subject of the tendency, not only (no longer) as mere antagonistic activity, but as the *possibility* of subversion: above all, it shows it to be a world of new subjectivities that are taking shape in a social, communist manner, beyond the capitalist revolutionizing of the conditions of production. *First*, as antagonistic activity, capital:

On the one hand . . . calls into life all the powers of science and Nature, and of social combination and social intercourse, in order to make the creation of wealth (relatively) independent of the labor time employed for that purpose. On the other hand, it wishes the enormous social forces thus created to be measured by labor time and to confine them within the limits necessary to maintain as value the value already created. The productive forces and social relations—two different aspects of the development of the social individual—appear to capital merely as the means, and are merely the means, for it to carry on production on its restricted basis. *In fact*, however, they are the material conditions for exploding that basis.[7]

Second, and fundamentally, the working class is now seen as engaging in an activity of reconstruction and a real and present possibility of communism:

No longer does the worker interpose a modified natural object as an intermediate element between the object and himself; now he interposes the natural process, which he transforms into an industrial one, as an intermediary between himself and inorganic nature, which he makes himself master of. He stands beside the production process, rather than being its main agent. Once this transformation has taken place, it is neither the immediate labor performed by man himself, nor the time for which he works, but the appropriation of his own general productive power, his comprehension of Nature and domination of it by virtue of his being a social entity—in a word, the development of the social individual—that appears as the cornerstone of production and wealth. The theft of alien labor time, which is the basis of present wealth, appears to be a miserable foundation compared to this newly developed one, the foundation created by large-scale industry itself. As soon as labor in its immediate form has ceased to be the great source of wealth, labor time ceases and must cease to be its measure, and therefore exchange value [must cease to be the measure] of use value. The surplus labor of the masses has ceased to be the condition for the development of general wealth, just as the non-labor of a few has ceased to be the condition for the development of the general powers of the human mind. As a result, production based upon exchange value collapses, and the immediate material production process itself is stripped of its form of indigence and antagonism. Free development of individualities, and hence not the reduction of necessary labor time in order to posit surplus labor, but in general the reduction of the necessary labor of society to a minimum, to which then corresponds the artistic, scientific, etc., development of individuals, made possible by the time thus set free and the means produced for all of them.[8]

TO SUM UP

We could add further evidence to these passages of the *Grundrisse*, but for the time being it is not important.[9] From these sections of the *Grundrisse*, we highlight the fundamental assumption that *Marx posits the issue of fall as one of withering away*; the *objective* aspects are only presented as *subjective*. Marx chases and defines a contradiction that concerns the law of value itself. He shows how the law of value, which ought to represent the rationality of exploitation (and be the scientific key to its interpretation), must lose its rationalizing and legitimating plausibility within the very development of the capitalist mode of production. Marx shows how the demise of the function of the law of value simultaneously corresponds (as cause and effect) to the enormous and formidable growth of the productive, free, and innovative potential of the proletariat, and this simultaneity must be underlined. Hence there emerges the revolutionary contradiction between this new reality of class and any representation of the law of value and its functioning (even in its planned or socialist guise). The issue of the demise and the issue of withering away coincide at this point. The withering-away refers to the law of value-labor as a law of exploitation, whereby labor is—materially—fully emancipated from the residual legitimating rationality of capitalist development. From the capitalist standpoint, the demise of the functioning of the law of value corresponds to its subjective use in terms of maintenance of the mechanism of appropriation and alienation. It is necessary to rebel against this, and to move from the recognition that capital is no longer the regulation of development inside exploitation toward a struggle against capital as a pure and simple development of exploitation. For every subject and for all those who are exploited by capital, the content of this materialist prediction becomes both a material commitment to subversion and the materialist indication of the objectives of communism, as rooted in the comportments and the historical reality of class.

But let us return to the issue of "withering away" proper. For Lenin, and for Marx before him, the political conditions of the withering-away entail an articulation of insurrection, dictatorship, and socialism that allows for these shifts to determine not only a violent abolition of privilege but also a subsequent spontaneity of the process of withering away, when the large majority of the proletariat has consciously, that is to say, materially, reappropriated the conditions of the production of wealth. Marx predicts this spontaneity of the shift to communism very precisely, when he defines, at the level of the critique of political economy, the characteristics of that great "social individual" produced by the development of capital, in the accomplished abstraction of labor, the overcoming of the division of labor, and the fall of the conditions of subsistence of the law of value. In the *Grundrisse*, Marx anticipates Lenin with his definition of the most advanced stages of the shift to communism. But the viewpoints are wholly identical. Lenin neither corrects nor revises Marx's propositions; he simply reinvents them, because he could not have read the *Grundrisse*, and because he does so in continuity with the revolutionary method of dialectical Marxism, which he is such a master of.

However, it must be said that even in the dark years, for theory, of the Second International, this implicit framework of Marx's analysis had not been forgotten. Engels explicitly drew on it and developed an analogous theme, albeit from a standpoint of the theory of the state rather than from a general theoretical one. Let us recall this: on the basis of the social democratic traditionalism of the Second International, we move from a definition of the state as found in the *Manifesto* ("The executive of the modern state is but a committee for managing the common affairs of the whole bourgeoisie"; "the organized power of one class for oppressing another")[10] to the later definition in *The German Ideology* that conceived of the synthesis of civil society in the state form. However, those who had not embarked on the Marxian path in the direction of a critique of the law of value could go no further than this.

Unless you understood the critique of the state at the level of the critique of political economy, you could certainly not go any further—one cannot forget that the state is, for Marx, one chapter of *Capital*: "the whole is divided into six books: 1. On Capital (contains a few introductory Chapters). 2. On Landed Property. 3. On Wage Labor. 4. On the State. 5. International Trade. 6. World Market."[11] Despite all this, Engels did do so and, from his privileged position as Marx's reader, alluded to his analysis and the most advanced point of workers' science. Taking up Marx's suggestion (the state intervenes in the tendency in order to maintain "private production without the control of private property"),[12] Engels identifies a stage when the bourgeoisie demonstrates its "incapacity . . . for managing any longer modern productive forces." Here Engels posits the figure of the state as "the ideal personification of the total national capital": "the more it proceeds to the taking over of productive forces, the more does it actually become the national capitalist, the more citizens does it exploit."[13] And this happens because "the transformation, either into joint-stock companies, or into state ownership, does not do away with the capitalistic nature of the productive forces. In the joint-stock companies this is obvious. And the modern state, again, is only the organization that bourgeois society takes on in order to support the general external conditions of the capitalist mode of production against the encroachments as well of the workers as of individual capitalists."[14] In state-owned industries "the workers remain wage-workers—proletarians. The capitalist relation is not done away with. It is rather brought to a head."[15] Rather than being suppressed, the law of value is pushed to the limit of the mystification it induces: "The modern state, no matter what its form, is essentially a capitalist machine, the state of the capitalists, the ideal personification of the total national capital."[16]

Out of the entire Second International, only Lenin was able to read and recuperate this lesson in *The State and Revolution*. The revolution needed to approach the seizure of the state to fully expose the dirty philology of power. "So long as the state exists there is no freedom," he wrote.[17] So long as the law of value exists, in whatever form, the proletariat will not free itself. Only revolutionary practice could reinvent Marx, and this is what happens in *The State and Revolution*. Here, the fabric of the critique of political economy, from the critique of the law of value, is fully grasped and developed. This is a formidable Marxist paradox: only the standpoint of class struggle can invent a scientific reading of reality in order to propose it as the object of destruction, as what must be destroyed in order to be liberated! Therefore, the direction we need to move toward is from the construction of socialism to the destruction of the law of value and its functioning whatever the form and of exploitation under any guise (even socialist). The anarchic barbarity of Leninism is here the highest and most refined point of the Marxian critique of political economy—in spite of all the professors!

The condition of the working class is such today that the growth and expansion of the tendency described by Marx are given in an accomplished form. A contemporary reading of *The State and Revolution* must intensify and develop these aspects even further. And this is what we intend to do in the forthcoming lessons.

NOTES

1. *Lineamenti fondamentali della critica dell'economia politica*, trans. E. Grillo, 2 vols. (Florence: La Nuova Italia, 1968–1970). For commentaries, refer to R. Rosdolsky, *The Making of Marx's Capital*, trans. P. Burgess (London: Pluto Press, 1977); and V. S. Vygodski, *The Story of a Great Discovery: How Karl Marx Wrote Capital*, trans. C. S. V. Salt (Kent: Tunbridge Wells, 1974), published in Italian in 1971 and 1974.

2. Karl Marx, *Grundrisse*, trans. M. Nicolaus, in *Marx and Engels Collected Works* (Moscow: Progress Publishers, 1986), 29:90.

3. Ibid.

4. Ibid., 29:91.

5. Ibid.

6. Ibid., 29:92.

7. Ibid.

8. Ibid., 29:91.

9. Those who wish to dwell on this analysis can refer to Antonio Negri, "Crisis of the Planner State," in *Books for Burning: Between Civil War and Democracy in 1970s*, ed. T. S. Murphy, trans. A. Bove, E. Emery, T. S. Murphy, and F. Novello (New York: Verso, 2005).

10. Marx and Engels, *Manifesto of the Communist Party*, in *Marx and Engels Collected Works* (Moscow: Progress Publishers, 1978), 6:486.

11. K. Marx, *Letters*, in *Marx and Engels Collected Works* (Moscow: Progress Publishers, 1978), 40:268.

12. K. Marx, *Capital*, vol. 3, in *Marx and Engels Collected Works* (Moscow: Progress Publishers, 1978), 37:436.

13. F. Engels, *Anti-Dühring*, in *Marx and Engels Collected Works* (Moscow: Progress Publishers, 1978), 25:265. [Translator's Note: "The ideal personification of the total national capital" is the English translation of *ideeller Gesamtkapitalist*, rendered in the Italian as "the ideal collective capitalist," a definition that has sparked much debate in Marxist literature.]

14. Ibid., 25:266.

15. Ibid., 25:265.

16. Ibid.

17. V. I. Lenin, *The State and Revolution*, trans. S. Apresyan and J. Ryordan, in *Collected Works* (Moscow: Progress Publishers, 1964), 25:473.

25

TOWARD A PROBLEMATIC VIEW OF TRANSITION

Impossible Socialism and the Coming Communism

I N THE LAST lesson we examined the way Marx's *Grundrisse* offers important anticipations of the functioning of the law of value in advanced capitalism. These anticipations are now a reality. In our situation, a mystification of (and transition to) socialism has been fully experienced by capital itself, and capital has transfigured the functioning of the law of value: today the so-called first phase of communist society, or more properly the socialist phase where the law of value needs to function, is not so much a sign of the perpetuation of inequality, but one of its impossibility. Insofar as the law of value ceases to function, *socialism is impossible*.[1]

Our problem is not to merely define the transitory nature of the dictatorship of the proletariat and of socialism as a first step: in fact, Marx's and Lenin's forecasting of socialism becomes ever less realistic as the law of value cannot function. Marx states that capitalist production produces this kind of contradiction within itself, by taking the productive forces to such a level of productive potential, as they are socially integrated and constitute the mass of fixed capital, that its relationship with living labor becomes insignificant. At a certain stage of the development of capitalist society, we are confronted with a total disproportion between the material substance of this society as a sum of machinery and as socialization of the productive forces, on the one hand, and living labor, that is, labor that produces surplus value in direct relation with machinery, on the other. Socialism, as an apology for equality and as a proposal for the realization of the law of value that follows the rule of giving to each according to her labor, is confronted with the impossibility of determining any quantitative, incontrovertible, or scientific term as a criterion of wage redistribution. At this level of the overcoming of the law of value, wage redistribution occurs according to purely political norms, norms that express command and no longer have anything to do even with the fiction of equality that is interpreted by the law of value. At this point, we are confronted with our greatest problem: *What does "transition to communism" mean today?* What is the content of the dictatorship of the proletariat? What forms and times are given for the formation and development of the effective conditions for the withering-away of the state?

In both Lenin and Marx (as confirmed in the *Grundrisse*), transition means verification, realization of the law of value, to the point of wholly unfolding the ambiguity it interprets as a threshold model of formal justice and thus substantial injustice. The path to communism entails two preparatory phases: first, smashing the state machine; second, realizing this unjust socialism (unjust insofar as it is socialism, because there is no just socialism). Today, it is materially impossible to embark on this path. Some of the shifts have already occurred within capitalist development, in a last phase that has subsumed a function of socialism in it: capitalist development has determined conditions of income distribution that have practically burned the rule of the law of value and thus pose a series of questions on the transitions; these questions are entirely new, and revolutionaries' critical attention must turn to them.

Let us analyze this more closely: for Lenin, the content of the dictatorship of the proletariat is the repression of the minority of exploiters first and the preparation of the conditions that should lead to a new gigantic development of the productive forces and thus to the threshold of communist freedom and the withering-away of the state by means of the destruction of the division of labor and the one-sided development of individuals. He theorizes these principles very clearly in the fourth paragraph of the fifth chapter of *The State and Revolution*:

> So long as the state exists there is no freedom. When there is freedom, there will be no state. The economic basis for the complete withering

away of the state is such a high state of development of communism at which the antithesis between mental and physical labor disappears, at which there consequently disappears one of the principal sources of modern social inequality—a source, moreover, which cannot on any account be removed immediately by the mere conversion of the means of production into public property, by the mere expropriation of the capitalists. This expropriation will make it possible for the productive forces to develop to a tremendous extent.[2]

When questioning the transition today, we need to recognize that our situation is different. Why? Clearly, the repression of the minority of expropriators is fundamental: in fact, the more the law of value ceases to apply, the more absurd and terrible does the law of command seem. But what does preparing the conditions for liberation today refer to? Obviously it does not merely refer to the fact that the ownership of the means of production becomes common, or to the realization of the law of value; from within the moment of the dictatorship of the proletariat today, we can think of "something more," something that is already operative today and neither awaits the maturation of other conditions nor refers to a higher stage of development. This "something more" is not the destruction of the kind of division of labor founded on the unjust application of the law of value, but an assault on capitalist command as such. Today, the expropriation of the expropriators must contain in itself the possibility of destroying every form of command immediately, and of the liberation of class from labor (that is, from the law of value): communism does not follow on from any preceding phase.

Let us look at this in more concrete terms: it is thinkable today, inside capitalist society, to have a form of management of the means of production that makes private interest and all the forms of income that are not directly founded on industrial production superfluous, and it is thinkable today that the division of labor, as a traditional one between intellectual and physical labor, is outmoded. There is no logical difficulty in seeing this as the given situation. Capitalist reformism, even in the crisis it is forced into by class struggle, entails a continuous perfecting of this process. What is the only moment of irrepressible contradiction in a development that reproduces the whole condition of misery and inhumanity which capitalist development carries with it and that exasperates it the more it faces class struggle? It is the rule of command based on the self-preservation of capitalist production, on the preservation of the system of wages. For this reason today, the revolutionary process knows no intermediate phases within which to build the conditions of possibility of communism: today, breaking down the command of capital and the state does not necessitate opening up an intermediate phase to build conditions adequate to the development of communism; it means putting into action immediately the possibility of a communist existence. The conditions are built inside capitalist society by the communist class struggle of the proletariat. Obviously, this is given a distorted shape, as Marx and Lenin point out in their analysis of the last phase of the construction of communism. Science, technique, machinery, and the dead labor that was consolidated in capitalist production and that created formidable conditions for the production and great development of the individual (the development of a one-sided capacity for human expansion): all of this was consolidated in a distorted way, and this raises a series of question. Of what use is this dead capital to us in transition? Is it possible to "use" it? Can we conceive of a process of transition dominated by a necessary relation with the existing fixed capital, from a *continuous and one-sided* conception of the development of science and technique? I doubt that a generation of revolutionaries, having seized power, could regard science, technique, machinery, existing factories, and the entire armory of dead labor as immediately of use for the growth of communism. Probably the act of destruction of the state, the Leninist breaking point, must be levered against the whole of dead labor as it exists now. Workers' comportments today do verify this perspective when the struggle is waged on advanced objectives: the spreading of nontraditional forms of struggle such as sabotage and the destruction of plants and materials as well as of the science and technique one-sidedly used and decisively subordinated not to the mythical permanence of the law of value, but simply to the irrationality of command. These forms of struggle are neither neo-Luddism nor cheap anarchism; they attest to a political declaration of extraneousness to the whole of capitalist development. Today it is unimaginable for a revolutionary movement not to take on the problem of the destruction of the state machine, as well as that of the destruction of dead labor as it has accumulated and been organized around the exploitation of humankind. Science, technique, machinery, and dead labor have become moments of a one-sided and irresistible theory and practice of capitalist command as such. Here proletarian dictatorship must prove itself and find the key to a further deepening of class struggle.

Now we can approach a further problem with transition. So far, we have seen how the dissolution of the law of value at a certain stage of capitalist development determines the impossibility of conceiving of an intermediate stage based on socialism. Second, we have considered how the massive presence of dead labor in the physical and material structure of capitalist command turns the moment of dictatorship into a need to push the "rupture" against these objects. The third problem we need to confront now is a revision of the *linear progress* from socialism to communism found in both Marx and Lenin, to an extent. How is this process conceived of? The process is described in the following terms. First moment: insurrection, that is the ability to smash the state machine; second: determination of the intermediate phase entailing the socialization of the means of production, common ownership, and the establishment of the law of value as a socialist, though unjust and necessary, norm; third moment: opening up a further phase through this dictatorship that facilitates the massive growth of the productive potential and that on this basis builds the shift to communism, that is, the dissolution of the state and of law, the affirmation of a state where each human will have according to her needs rather than her labor: a conscious dissolution of the law of value and labor in the communist phase. Notably, this shift from socialism to communism is implicitly a continuous process in both Marx and Lenin. There is a continuity of accumulation of productive capacities, of transformation of man and woman as a subject of this accumulation and as a subject of the objective transformation, and this proceeds at a continuous pace. All of this seems to slightly contradict Marx and Lenin's method, which is strongly dialectical, as well as their awareness of the actual mechanism of class struggle and the real role of workers' subjectivity in future history:

> By what stages, by means of what practical measures humanity will proceed to this supreme aim we do not and cannot know. But it is important

to realize how infinitely mendacious is the ordinary bourgeois conception of socialism as something lifeless, rigid, fixed once and for all, whereas in reality only socialism will be the beginning of a rapid, genuine, truly mass forward movement, embracing first the majority and then the whole of the population, in all spheres of public and private life.[3]

Furthermore, Lenin insists on the relative difficulty of facing the question of transition as a whole, and he invites caution, "because there is no material for answering these questions."[4] Nonetheless, the image one can draw from it is one of an excessively one-sided and linear tendency. Obviously, the boorish and mystifying orthodoxy of reformism has exalted these motives. Because of this, the continuity of the shift from socialism to communism must be questioned both theoretically and historically. It is obvious that, if accumulated dead labor has allowed for this enormous development of the productive potential of human labor, it is equally true that in capitalist development this new economic base takes on an absolutely distorted form, which is that of capitalist command. The moment of rupture must therefore turn not simply toward the juridical form of the state, but also against the overall accumulation of dead labor, which includes machinery as well as the shape of the *brain* that people have had to forge when coming in contact with capitalist science and the need to reproduce the capitalist mode of production. Far from being continuous, the shift from socialism to communism could only entail a "permanent cultural revolution," the continuous destruction of objective criteria of orientation and knowledge. The process points to a route that is as difficult as it is dramatic. In this process one can only foresee a deepening and reproducing of class struggle in forms that no longer have anything to do with property relations, but with relations of command wherever they present themselves, and they will probably present themselves more forcedly in the organization of scientific knowledge. This can be said from the theoretical point of view.

From a historical perspective, the critique of the continuity of the shift must be even stronger. The fact that the need for this critique was neglected caused so-called socialist countries to reproduce the radical nature of its object. These are "so-called" socialist countries not because they are not socialist, but because they are as socialist as capitalist countries. After the proletariat's seizure of power, phenomena grossly defined as the formation of a state bureaucracy—the state organization of command, whose roots are much deeper—are linked to the persistence of dead labor, the colossal pressure that it exerts against the liberation of living labor, against the force of proletarian invention, against every revolutionary possibility of collective praxis, in other words, against any chance to develop new forms of life. It must be said: Stalin and Mao identified this kind of difficulty very well, and the Stalinist solution for this problem was undoubtedly incorrect, but this cannot lead to the denial that this problem exists and to the fiction that the shift from socialism to communism is continuous. What was Stalin's mistake? It was not that he identified this discontinuity; it was that he tried to solve it by means of state dictatorship. The Maoist solution to the problem is the opposite, and in this it is correct: it goes through the liberation of the mass power against the state.

In any case, we face a different problem today. The discontinuity is not measured as a persistence of the state and bourgeois right—"It follows that under communism there remains for a time not only bourgeois law, but even the bourgeois state, without the bourgeoisie!"[5] It is rather measured against socialism, democracy, and the persistence of the power and command of dead labor over living labor. This discontinuity is much graver and dramatic. In Lenin, breaking the state machine meant substituting the ruling class through the armed expropriation of the expropriators, and there the issue of socialism and democracy ensued. But what does this rupture consist in today? It cannot be mere expropriation; it cannot be the armed realization of equality according to the law of value. Breaking the nexus between the development of the productive force and its capitalist form is the question today. But this accentuates beyond measure the discontinuity and difficulty of the process, because at this point there can only be class struggle and "cultural revolution." The "democracy of armed workers" must be immediately realizable. The constitution of a "single state syndicate" and the use of economic calculation and control:[6] this is the heavy legacy of capitalist development. But for us this does not represent the first phase, but the *first act* of the revolutionary process. This stage was reduced to an act, to a decree that was so immediately realizable because it represented the conclusion of a development of struggle. In his analysis of his conditions, Lenin adds a consideration that is perhaps the most heavily characterized by the need for continuity: "But this 'factory' discipline, which the proletariat, after defeating the capitalists, after overthrowing the exploiters, will extend to the whole of society, is by no means our ideal, or our ultimate goal. It is only a necessary *step* for thoroughly cleansing society of all the infamies and abominations of capitalist exploitation, *and for further* progress!"[7]

Well, this is our starting point. This step is reduced to an act and the situation is not linear because the armed proletariat cannot stop at dominating a social factory that neither relates to its needs nor can relate to development as a determination of the conditions for communism. The "rupture" cannot limit itself to a seizure of power but must extend inside and against the social factory and inside the very composition of class. The rupture is directed to the positive content of class liberation. Here, in the intensity of a dramatic and deep dialectics, begins a truly "forward movement"[8] of communist society against the dead and petrified society of alienation.

The fourth great problem concerns the modality of the transition. It is another side of the critique of the continuity of the shift from socialism to communism and can present itself as a problem of critique and verification of the spontaneity of this shift. In Marx and Lenin, the shift from socialism to communism is described as an effect of a sort of gushing and immediate spontaneity: with the dictatorship, the "semistate" is no longer even a "state," and Lenin recalls that Engels suggested that "the word 'state' be eliminated from the programme altogether and the word 'community' (*Gemeinwesen*) substituted for it. Engels even declared that the Commune was long a state in the proper sense of the word."[9] Now, this spontaneity is consistent with the notion of continuity and derives from the fact that there are three stages— the rupture, socialism, and communism—which are conditional upon one another. But in our situation these stages have been inverted (and we already have socialism not as the rule of the law of value but as the capitalist possibility of determining the social levels of its own reproduction that are valid within the rule of command and of fully revealing the inhumanity of socialism and of any application of the law of value). This means that what was defined as the first moment, the rupture, will still be a first element, but its tension will be altogether different. It will have to coincide with a process of withering away that in its turn is located inside the whole dialectics of the distorted form of socialization that the social production of capital has brought about. Thus, this overlapping of rupture and withering away, this foundation of one term upon the other, hardly gives rise to spontaneous and felicitous effects. Stalin and Mao identified this dramatic view of the intensification of class struggle at the very moment when we approach communism according to the rules of revolutionary dialectics: clearly spontaneity and happiness are very far from being given. But beyond Stalin and Mao, the same applies to us. The more the socialist phase is elided and rupture and withering-away overlap, the more the dialectics of class struggle eliminates spontaneity from the process and grasps the transition as struggle. The problem is here extremely serious because it concerns more or less all of the modalities of the revolutionary process: first and foremost, the figure of the revolutionary party as the ability to constantly reproduce, from within class and for class, the power to keep breaking class relations and equilibrium as they come to be determined; and with it, the ability to be vanguard and use all the means of violence to seize power. This ability does not emerge from Lenin's concept of an external vanguard that negates and destroys in order to plan and create socialism, but it rises up from class as an adequate and determinate function: insofar as socialism is impossible, planning is the first thing to defeat, communism is the minimal program.

These problems emerge directly from the review and practical objective we need to consider, on this important chapter of *The State and Revolution*, in light of the current condition of class struggle. To sum up, the issues we think need to be reviewed are: First, a deeper critique of socialism and a full review of the times, the scheme, and the general model of revolutionary development. Second, the debate on the "rupture," and by this we understand that we are not simply dealing with juridical formulas and institutional dynamics, but with the whole, massive reality of dead labor as machinery, science, and social organization of production. Third, the problem is one of the objective discontinuity of the shift from socialism to communism. Fourth, and finally, the issue of the critique of the spontaneity of this shift, with the implications it entails in terms of a definition of the subjective revolutionary power of the workers that organizes existing practice. These are the problems that, in this final phase, we will try to analyze individually not only to propose a solution but also to lead toward a correct approach to the problem of transition that is so crucial today in Marxism.

NOTES

1. The current literature on transition is wholly inadequate. The question of transition is always approached in terms of Marx's "political" stance being radically separate from his critique of political economy, hence the inadequacy. In fact, the question is how to posit the relation between transition and the theory of value, something attempted by Rosdolsky, in continuity with a tradition that begins with the first period of Bolshevism. Here, theorists of value (Rubin and the like), and theorists of right (Pasukanis and others), and theorists of planning (Preobraschensky and the like), and theorists of the state and imperialism (Bucharin and the like) had perceived this nexus.
2. V. I. Lenin, *The State and Revolution*, trans. S. Apresyan and J. Ryordan, in *Collected Works* (Moscow: Progress Publishers, 1964), 25:473.
3. Ibid., 25:477.
4. Ibid., 25:474.
5. Ibid., 25:476.
6. Ibid., 25:477.
7. Ibid., 25:479.
8. Ibid., 25:477.
9. Ibid., 25:462.

26

ON THE PROBLEM OF TRANSITION AGAIN

The Word to the Masses

W E ARE NOW returning to the issue of transition as framed by Lenin to confront it with the urgent theoretical and practical questions that face us today, and we will eventually return to the four specific fundamental issues outlined previously. First, we need to consider other general questions, in particular about the safeguard against the dangers of utopianism as we find it in Lenin. This danger is particularly present in discussions of the issue of transition; we might go as far as to say that in the socialist tradition the problem of transition emerges as a response to real and impatient questions and develops along the lines of a prefiguration. From the outset, the origin of the problem of transition, the prefiguration of the conditions, and the values of a communist society take root in the conscience of those who revolt and spring from and sediment in a consciousness of misery and in the ferocious and fantastic will to insurrection. Struggle, hope, and utopia are enmeshed in a single tension throughout centuries of proletarian insurgency. The power of the image of a future society that drags the struggle forward is a correlative of misery—on the one hand, something to be liberated from, on the other, in formidable tension and continuity, something that liberation moves toward, something to be liberated. While the prefiguration of the future is a force that directly acts on the organization of the revolt, it also characterizes the organization of those who rebel. The image of a communist society, in order to be seized, requires a communistic organization, and so on.[1]

Guarding against the dangers of unbridled hope, the shift from utopia to science directly influences the concept of organization and the definition of the timing and the forms of the revolutionary process. Therefore, the particular solution to the problem of transition is relevant not only at the level of analysis and political forecasts, but above all for a definition of the figure of the party: the revolutionary process and the figure, concept, and theory of the party are configured in relation to the kinds of obstacles and steps envisaged in this process, to the extent that the party represents the material interests of the proletarian masses in relation to goals to achieve and obstacles to overcome.

A party founded on the insuppressible hatred for the existing power of capital is different from one based on the love for communism. A party founded on the need to destroy and dissolve the present order of things will need, in Marxian terms, to be politically equipped to carry out this activity, and thus will need to exclude from its core any motivation that pushes this harsh present need into oblivion by means of beautiful words and dreams.

Let us return to the initial question: how are the dangers of prefigurations and utopia guarded against in Lenin's *The State and Revolution*, which is so engaged in the definition of transition of its times and its contents? To answer this question, it is not sufficient to refer to the Marxian realism of Lenin's theory, for, seen in the context of Lenin's experience of social democratic opportunism, this is not a one-sided realism; on the contrary, it is double- and triple-edged. In fact, Marxian realism is such only when seen for what it is: a realistic analysis of the insurgence of the revolutionary subject as a proletariat, and a scientific consciousness of a revolutionizing process that results from development and its deadly contradictions. Clearly, in Marx's and Lenin's view, any possible prefiguration emerges from the activity of the masses; the party is the negation of prefigurations and utopia insofar as its role is to be an effective organizer of this activity. If Marxism is a revolutionary materialism, this is the only view it can possibly sustain.

As we have seen, the only way to avoid the danger of utopian prefigurations is to posit the question of transition when a determined and effective inversion of the relation between class composition and class organization is given. The revolutionary activity of the masses asks the question of transition realistically, and only the revolutionary activity of the masses can prefigure communism. Going back to the specificity of the question of transition in Lenin, let us try to analyze its other features and limits. I believe that it is possible to state something with a degree of certainty: insofar as the inversion of the relation between composition and organization posits this question, the way Lenin resolves it is strictly and rightly linked to his analysis of class composition and to the determinate social and political structure of this analysis. An extraordinary basic coherence emerges between Lenin's analytical framework and the theoretical and practical consequences he derives from it. Therefore, Lenin's definition of determinate class composition objectively dominates even this aspect of his communism and outlines, outside of utopian dangers, its dimensions and its contents. Inevitably, on this premise, Lenin's thought, as it necessarily results from his refusal of utopia and the effectiveness of the discourse of the masses, presents the limits and problems we analyzed in the previous lecture.

Having said that, let us question whether there are further limits and inconsistencies in this system. Let us question whether our analysis can move beyond a comparison between our needs and those of the class composition of his times and detect potential inconsistencies in Lenin's model in relation to the real situation he recorded and adapted to from time to time. The continuity of the revolutionary process from socialism to communism that characterizes Lenin's definition of transition has been one of the main objects of the criticism coming from militants of the workers' movement, from Stalin to Mao Zedong, and can certainly not be imputed to an inconsistency in Lenin's thought. Although it is a fundamental limitation of Lenin's theory, this linear continuity of the revolutionary process is also closely tied to the particular class composition to which his theory is addressed. The continuity of the process of accumulation persists even after the revolutionary rupture and the growth of the material bases adequate to communism; in Lenin's situation, a rupturing in order to plan was a necessary moment—a rupture functional for planning and developing the continuity of the process of accumulation and its increasing and ever more extensive reproduction, because only on these material bases could the demand for communism come to take shape.

The other element we have pointed to is harder to understand: for Lenin, the notion of development is not only linear and continuous, but also spontaneous, pacific, and automated; here the process seems to move with a natural force, and this is an inconsistency and an idealist limitation of Lenin's theory. In fact, Lenin knew perfectly well the workers' spontaneous opposition to labor. The initial years of the revolutionary process in Russia confronted him with the massive and generalized flight from work of the workers. Under those conditions and that composition of class relations, the revolutionary process appeared to have nothing to do with the workers' spontaneous dedication to work. In such a process, well beyond spontaneity, one needed to implant a specific dialectics, which Lenin soon interpreted and applied with the introduction of the NEP (New Economic Policy); these were an attempt to put into motion a dynamic of class struggle for development, for the determination of the conditions of the shift from socialism to communism in transition. The reactivation of the market and, in the market, the concession of trust in entrepreneurial freedom amounted to the state putting into action the mechanisms of class struggle: then the trade union reappeared as a negotiator of the price of the labor commodity, as the class pressure for socialism and the permanent revolution.[2]

Undoubtedly, the image Lenin provides for the process of transition in *The State and Revolution* presents some utopian undertones when it comes to the definition of the spontaneity of the shift, and this can be entirely understandable, given the political enthusiasm surrounding the writing of this work; yet it still represents a real and effective inconsistency in his theory. It is inconsistent not only in relation to us, but in relation to the rest of Lenin's argument. It is strange that in the description of the fundamental shift from socialism to communism in *The State and Revolution*, Lenin's dialectical insights seem to be lost; we are confronted with moments of evolutionism and gradualism, in the philosophical "tradition" of materialism in the widest sense of the term, rather than with the teachings of the *Philosophical Notebooks* on Hegel. The dialectical thread that emerges in later works and that plays as crucial a role as the previous traditional materialism seems to be underestimated in relation to this issue, and this is all the more surprising, given the chronological and thematic continuity between the *Philosophical Notebooks* and *The State and Revolution*.

Nonetheless, this is certainly not the most substantial limitation of Lenin's work; rather, the greatest limitation is the almost-exclusive and extreme emphasis on the institutional aspects. This means attention to, on the one hand, the juridical property relation as a fundamental moment against which the rupture must be directed and to, on the other hand, the figure of the state as an abstract political-juridical institution present in the whole issue of transition: this is the greatest limitation. But this is a limitation to the internal consistency of Lenin's theory. Who, more than Lenin, had developed the concept of political and juridical institutions in the analysis of class composition since the 1890s? Who more than him had insisted on the very interpenetration of the development of the productive forces with the figure of the state, drawing from it a notion of the state that, far from being merely juridical and institutional, was actually embedded in the analysis of the process of production and its direct and immediate form? On this issue, let us look at two classical works— *The Development of Capitalism in Russia* and *Imperialism as the Highest Stage of Capitalism*—that complete the arch of Lenin's theoretical analysis from the 1890s to 1917. Both of these works present a conceptualization of the state as the organizer of the exploitation of work in proper terms, that is, not a statical but as a coordinated and functional force affecting the changes of labor organization during the period that goes from large manufacture to imperialism. In this perspective, the state is the form of overall capital, the effect and engine of development, the necessary relation and the figure of capital as the organizer of social exploitation on larger and larger scales. From this standpoint, it would have been important and consistent to further develop this issue in *The State and Revolution*; instead, the whole point is entirely missing, and Lenin simply emphasizes the juridical and institutional aspects of the state. Hence the impossibility of showing that the struggle against the state is a struggle against work: this is the limitation we insist on. From the standpoint of the revolutionary process, the hegemony of this aspect of the state wherein it immediately organizes labor only comes to prominence beyond the general conditions of accumulation in a stage of direct and general subsumption of labor under capital. But the Russian autocracy is such a burdensome and inevitable form of self-legitimating and traditional power that it in some respects justifies Lenin's emphasis on the political and juridical institutional aspect of the state and his relative underestimation of the direct relation between the state and the organization of productive processes. Moreover, a close examination of the strategic and practical reality and an analysis of the particular state of disarray of the Russian state in the war period, when Lenin wrote this work, would plausibly demonstrate that there are justifiable reasons for his emphasis: when it comes to the direct organization of labor, insurrectional action develops precisely in the context of an accentuation of the complete disarray of the state not only in general terms, but also in terms of the infrastructure of industrial development, from railways to postal services, and of the coordination of social labor overall.

These justifications notwithstanding, this lack and internal limit in Lenin's theory has heavily influenced the way in which the question of transition has subsequently been developed. Therefore, forms of voluntarism and subjectivism, institutional or parainstitutional, have been put forward when discussing the issue of the revolutionary process, and these pages in Lenin have been used as their justification.

Here, we need to take our discussion further both in terms of a critical evaluation and in the comparison of Lenin's with our situation. First of all, let us propose some of the elements of the debate on insurrection. The issue of insurrection has rarely received the attention it deserves in discussions of transition. On the basis of a given class composition and given limits to development, on the basis of a necessary externality of the vanguard insofar as it is not merely regarded as an intellectual vanguard of theoretical consciousness but is instead a properly workers' vanguard, the issue of insurrection clearly unfolds in the direct imputation of the responsibility for the insurrection to the vanguard alone. Clearly, insurrection is discontinuity and an explosion of a concentrated subjective will, born out of an overall structure that allows for the continuous creation of spaces that can or cannot be used by the revolutionary brain. In this class composition, the party only crafts the revolution insofar as it plays its own initiative in the overall disequilibrium of the process of accumulation and institutional restructuring of the accumulation of the bourgeois state. Insurrection is an art, and in Lenin's theory, the party is a bearer of the art of insurrection: undoubtedly, the concept of "rupture," as proposed in *The State and Revolution*, traces this notion of the revolutionary process. At this point, a question arises: when the relation between the break-

ON THE PROBLEM OF TRANSITION AGAIN

ing of the state machine and the withering-away of the state as the organizer of labor is posited directly and no longer linked to some spontaneity in the process, but rather to the deepening of class struggle—in other words, when we can begin to think the revolutionary process only on the basis of this tight relationship—what is left of Lenin's notion of insurrection? What is, then, insurrection? The revolution today can only be crafted as a material ability to build a mass power that, step after step, time after time, destroys the reality of the capitalist state as a work state. This has no longer anything to do with insurrection as an eminent and explosive moment: the revolutionary process develops and can only develop as an overall process of revolutionizing. What does appropriation mean, after all, and what does it mean to wither away the state as the overall organizer of power in the working class, if it does not emerge from a determined ability to carry forward a process that is at once a molecular, determined, and continuous destruction of all the facets of the state organization and, simultaneously, also the actual seizing of this wealth and this materiality of power that confronts us?

If this is the situation, the limitations of the argument in *The State and Revolution* concerning its analysis of the relation between the state and the organization of labor really seem to force us to deeply revise the argument. This revision requires that we confront the organizational relation with the current terms of class struggle. In this light, the revision of the concept of the party is crucial. The party, this form of adjustment of ends and means that must develop the ability of organizing both the "rupture" and the "withering-away" (as the proletarian seizing of wealth), is a privileged object of the theoretical and practical inquiry of the masses. But in addition to this, other questions are raised. In the previous lecture, while discussing rupture, we showed that the question needed to be reviewed in light of the capitalist integration of the state form and the form of dead labor, which is so severe today that the problem, as indicated by class struggle, is probably one of materially distributing wealth not because it is wealth, but because it is presented in an entirely distorted way. We have seen how it is impossible to think that the existing machinery, science, and overall accumulation of dead labor can be used as it is in the development of communism. We are thus faced with a paradox: on the one hand, the development of the workers' capacity for rupture cannot rely on a mythical moment but can only sustain itself on the desire for existing wealth, on the ability to immediately reappropriate it; on the other hand, this reappropriation must be completely subordinated to the ability to destroy and the need to build new conditions for a new world. This paradox represents a huge difficulty, and the misery of the political practice that reformism accentuates is difficult and makes our analysis even more difficult. But, faced with this difficulty, we must be Marxist and Leninist until the end. This entails that when issues arise that cannot be resolved, and when there is a terrible responsibility of committing potentially tragic mistakes, we must first of all think that our artisan tools are wholly inadequate and that the issues raised by the masses, in class struggle, must be solved by the masses through class struggle.

The same applies to the issue of organization: the activity of the masses manages to determine it time and again. And the same applies also to the determination between appropriation, destruction, and liberation of the power of mass invention.

I think that at this stage, and from this standpoint, we can begin to read the pages on the Commune that Lenin attaches to his treatment of the question of transition.[3] Following Marx's method, Lenin teaches us that the form of the organization can only be found in the movement of the masses. We are obviously entitled to carry out a more specific analysis of the commiseration between the organizational means and the ends of the movement, while keeping close, theoretically, to the specific terms of class composition. But we cannot forget that every time an actual organization arises, it does so because of the activity of the masses. To recognize the mass character of organization as a "recovered" form that the proletariat time and again moulds and discovers in itself is both the question and the solution. The Paris Commune is, from this standpoint, a formidable theoretical fact beyond all its ingenuity and mistakes, and it is a perfect moment of the proletarian expression of its ability as a subject to give an adequate form to its organization. This kind of analysis must move beyond the example of the Paris Commune.

Currently, in March 1973, the workers at Mirafiori are accomplishing their own theoretical miracle and discovering a form of military mass organization inside the factory; they are finding the right terrain of a new relation of struggle for appropriation and power. We will need to test ourselves on these grounds and remember that the problems our reading raises can only find, as Lenin intimates, a definitive solution at the level of practice. To the masses go the first and, always, the last word.[4]

NOTES

1. On the role of utopianism in the determination of the revolutionary movement during precapitalist stages of development, there is a vast and important literature. For a generic view, see the works of Ernst Bloch, in particular, his crucial text on *Thomas Münzer*. For subsequent works, see also the entry on "Utopia," in *Scienze Politiche: Feltrinelli-Fischer Encyclopaedia*, ed. Antonio Negri (Milan: Feltrinelli, 1971).

2. On this issue, see R. Di Leo, *Operai e sistema sovietico* [Workers and the Soviet system] (Bari: Laterza, 1970); C. Bettelheim, *Class Struggles in the USSR, 1923–1930* (New York: Monthly Review Press, 1998); F. I. Kaplan, *Bolshevik Ideology and the Ethics of Soviet Labor, 1917–1920: The Formative Years* (London: Peter Owen, 1969), as well as, of course, E. Carr, *History of Soviet Russia* (London: Macmillan, 1958–1978).

3. Lenin's writings on the Paris Commune of 1871 repeat, with renewed enthusiasm, Marx's appreciation of it.

4. See on this, Negri, "Articolazioni organizzative e organizzazione complessiva: il partito di Mirafiori" [Organizational developments and overall organization: The Mirafiori Party], in *Crisi e organizzazione operaia* (Milan: Feltrinelli, 1974), 189ff.

27

TRANSITION AND
PROLETARIAN DICTATORSHIP

The Particular Interests of the Working Class

W E HAVE ALREADY seen how Marx's and Lenin's formidable feats were to use the method of the masses and raise the question of transition from the standpoint of the workers. What interests us is that this entailed a positing of the question from a political perspective and thus, preliminarily, from outside an economicist or related perspective. I think that this is extremely important and needs to be underlined. In fact, such framing of the question eventually disappeared from the discussion of the workers' movement: we would have to wait something like fifty years, until the actions of the Chinese Communist Party in the second half of the 1960s, for the political issue of transition to be rediscovered. The rest of the literature gathered under the rubric of "the issue of transition" is economicist and excludes that the working class has a primary role in the management of the transition from socialism to communism. We might go as far as to say that the problem of transition actually became the most fertile terrain on which to develop a series of extremely formalized attempts at planning in the treatment of political economy of the self-styled Marxists. The paradox of the theory of transition as it developed prior to the revolutionary rediscovery of the Chinese Communist Party was that it began with *The State and Revolution* and ended up with a theory of economic calculus. From Lenin to Leontiev, ironically; from a theory of permanent revolution to a theory of equilibrium; from the definition of growing factors of revolutionary insubordination to the *inputs-outputs* of the system! Moreover, the theory of transition was entirely developed by economists within the remit of the theory of labor. After Lenin, reformism could only conceive of the period of transition in terms of value theory, a theory of exploitation. The issue of the shift to communism and of the abolishment of the law of value and of the economic system gradually became obscured until it was completely set aside, apart from the opportune addition of adequate mystifications, especially during the Stalinist period, when the fact that the Soviets had seized power seemed in itself sufficient for a notion of the withering-away of the law of value. These were propaganda operations, pure and simple. Probably they were based on what seemed to us the greatest limitation of Lenin's theory, that is, the inability to express clearly an identity of tendency between communism and the fall of the law of value, and therefore between communism and the suppression of labor itself, which in Lenin was due to the sociopolitical structure he operated in. If this can be read between the lines in Lenin, it is not explicit but rather imposed, and the problem of transition as it emerges in 1917 in Russia cannot be detached from the general backwardness of Russian society and its economic basis at the time. This insufficiency is the mystified foundation of the passive, reactionary, and conservative motivations found in the later development of the theory of transition.

But let us be clear about this: this is a purely philological game and foundation. The later mystification can find its justification neither in the overall political framework of Lenin's theory nor in his positing of the working class as the subject of change. In Lenin we find a ponderous example of a theoretical anticipation of reality, and the failures that often occur in the shift from the theoretical to the historical party (a shift that is always so terribly painful and grave, especially in the dramatic situation of revolutionary Russia) do not diminish its power. We always find, in Lenin, some element that makes it impossible to reduce his thought to economism. This element consists in an appreciation of the political theory of transition based on the assumption of the working-class subject as an absolute foundation: such an aspect resists any perturbation of the question in economicist terms. In the years that followed Lenin's death, political staff and Menshevik economists, the same people who during the great crisis moved to the West and joined its large planning offices, seized Soviet planning and turned it into a capitalist machinery: this also highlights the irreducibility of Lenin's thought to their practice.

Having said this, we can now move on to a further observation, secondary but useful for introducing a new element in the reconstruction of Lenin's overall theory. This concerns the role of anticipation and forecasting. When we spoke of Lenin's method in the first part of these lectures, perhaps we placed an excessive emphasis on the correspondence between his thought and the historical and political practice of his times, the determinate composition of the working class and its historical formation. This helped us show an important feature of his mode of proceeding and focus on the inversion from a theory of composition to a theory of organization. But things are more complicated than that. If we limited ourselves, even for a moment, merely to the level of composition theory, we would have to recognize that both the populists and the Mensheviks were right on this, insofar as, paradoxically, they reflected more intelligently the high degree to which political operations were possible in Russia. What characterizes Lenin's theory, in this case, is simply the fact that his is the best understanding of the *objective* moments of the situation. If we take into account the two works that we have focused on—*The Development of Capitalism in Russia* and *What Is to Be Done?*—we can immediately note that they also display a formidable sensitivity to the moment of the tendency, since they both point to the action of a historical subject (in this case, the working class) as the drive, push, and traction that could impose progress toward mature capitalism on Russian society. The focus on the structure of the party as defined in *What Is to Be Done?*—on the hegemonic and driving function of a workers' vanguard that carries with it the proletariat and some of the peasants and the small bourgeoisie, who are involved in a series of mediations such as progressive democracy and the parliamentary system—displays an ability not only to grasp some of the general characteristics of the situation, but to confront them with a driving function and winning tendency that thus presume a historical subject of the whole process. It is impossible to think of a historical tendency without also conceiving of a need for a determinate historical subject. This is certainly a historical product, but is still a subject. Only from this standpoint can the anticipation work, without being either cerebral or prefiguring: rather than a mechanical necessity, it is a necessary tendency planted in the ability of a historical subject to move in a given direction. When this determination is recuperated, the party becomes history and makes history. That subject must be led and subjected to a political class leadership. The same mechanism applies to what concerns the tendency of the transition in *The State and Revolution*. In this case, Lenin expresses an absolutely preliminary emphasis on the revolutionary subject, and this is the revolutionary subject that Lenin finds before him, and whose movement Lenin feels the intensity and reality of. Lenin's theory concentrates on this subject, and his anticipation is only possible on the basis of the recognition of the role of the working class. This is an extremely important aspect of Lenin's thought from the point of view of method: in this way Lenin deals decisively with economism and subjectivism, which are always experienced within the communist movement. The antagonistic duplicity of economism and subjectivism, or idealism and materialism conceived statically and nondialectically, is overcome by the identification of a subject that is material and avoids the possibility of falling into these opposing formulas of mystified solutions to the problem. The theoretical overcoming of the dualism is not practical: only organization can help the practical side, and when it comes to revolutionary organization, *The State and Revolution* presupposes it. In fact, in Russia, beyond the attempts of the NEP, planning was developed in purely economistic terms and exasperated the populist tradition of Russian Marxism, turning it into a vulgar Marxism where the subject of agency changes.[1]

We did not have a working class as such, as a subject leading the movement; instead, we started seeing as a subject the whole of the hypotheses of populism, the people, the nation, while planning was gradually reduced to economic calculus. Clearly this does not mean that economic calculus ought to be excluded from planning or that the growth and extension of the material basis can be denied because of the emergence of the project and will of the class. Rather, it simply suggests that we need to recall an absolutely fundamental moment in Marxism, that of the hegemony of the political, which is the hegemony of a consideration of class relations, levels of consciousness, needs and necessities, and everything that concerns, in the last instance, the political will of the masses and of the ruling class. Only from this perspective can the problem of anticipation in Lenin acquire clarity. And this also clarifies the fact that economism and reformism have heavily appropriated the issue of transition and turned it into a grim ideology that can in no way be recuperated in a classical Leninist framework.

This was a long parenthesis to recover the methodological design of Lenin's theory. It is now appropriate to return to the text, *The State and Revolution*, and analyze the purely historical and polemical chapters that we have not yet considered. Chapters 2 and 3 analyze, respectively, the experience of 1848–1851 and that of the Paris Commune of 1871. Chapter 4 continues on the same issue to offer a deeper analysis of the state in classical texts, and chapter 6 essentially engages in a polemic with Kautsky and Plekhanov. I think that Lenin's analysis in these chapters can now be better understood, because the expressive form of *The State and Revolution* slightly betrays the animus and intention of the work.

As we have argued, the main intention is to grasp the essential shift of the Russian revolution and propose to the workers' subject the task of creating the proletarian dictatorship in order to bring about communism and wither away the state. The other chapters provide a series of elements that have already been outlined in the general introduction of the first chapter, and are concentrated in chapter 5, where the political perspective becomes more current and the project is outlined in practice.

Let us look into chapter 2. This is an interpretation of the *Manifesto* supported by a reading of Marx's historical writings on the period. Starting from what we have argued so far, we will see that, rather than being an introduction or a stage toward chapter 5, which is undoubtedly fundamental, this second chapter can be regarded as its simplification. In other words, Lenin's polemical needs and the opportunity to refer to the authority of classics as a foundation of his thought in no way represent a hindrance to the impact of the text. The reference to classics has the role of providing evidence in this as in other chapters. But it is worth underlining how in these chapters what matters is not so much the continuity, the systematic repetition of the presentation of the concept of the state, but the relevance of Lenin's methodology, what we have named the Leninist anticipation of communism, as it is practically embodied in this phase of the Russian revolution.

First, it is worth noting the insistence, in the analysis of the *Manifesto* in chapter 2, on the concept of the dictatorship of the proletariat: this is not an abstract concept but a particular and determinate function that must immediately be placed in a stage of development of the revolutionary process under analysis, that is, in the chapter on the economic bases of transition:

> In depicting the most general phases of the development of the proletariat, we traced the more or less veiled civil war, raging within existing society up to the point where that war breaks out into open revolution, and where the violent overthrow of the bourgeoisie lays the foundation for the sway of the proletariat. . . . We have seen above that the first step in the revolution by the working class is to raise the proletariat to the position of the ruling class to win the battle of democracy. . . . The proletariat will use its political supremacy to wrest, by degree, all capital from the bourgeoisie, to centralize all instruments of production in the hands of the state, i.e., of the proletariat organized as the ruling class.[2]

Reclaiming the revolution as an element of the concept of the state here entails reclaiming the dictatorship as a primary aim of the revolution. This is why this theory was forgotten, because, as usual, the method of mystification has intervened in that of scientific analysis: "This definition of the state has never been explained in the prevailing propaganda and agitation literature of the official Social-Democratic parties. More than that, it has been deliberately ignored, for it is absolutely irreconcilable with reformism, and is a slap in the face for the common opportunist prejudices and philistine illusions about the 'peaceful development of democracy.'"[3]

Mystification and demystification are economic categories, let us not forget that. Unfortunately these terms are now used as a substitute for "false" and "true." But in Marxism mystification does not mean false, as opposed to true: a mystification can be true insofar as it exists and is given and real; there are mystifications that are infinitely more real and true than many other things. Mystification is not ungraspable; it is a reality linked to a particular utility and particular interests, and thus always determined by its class nature. From this perspective, the process of demystification is none other than the constant revelation of the interests behind an affirmation (or oblivion or neglect) and, in this case, behind a forgetting that is not secondary, because it affects the *Manifesto*, a crucial text for the whole of the communist tradition. These are the interests behind the mystification of the nature of the state:

> The exploiting classes need political rule to maintain exploitation, i.e., in the selfish interests of an insignificant minority against the vast majority of all people. The exploited classes need political rule in order to completely abolish all exploitation, i.e., in the interests of the vast majority of the people, and against the insignificant minority consisting of the modern slave-owners—the landowners and capitalists. The petty-bourgeois democrats, those sham socialists who replaced the class struggle by dreams of class harmony, even pictured the socialist transformation in a dreamy fashion—not as the overthrow of the rule of the exploiting class, but as the peaceful submission of the minority to the majority which has become aware of its aims. This petty-bourgeois utopia, which is inseparable from the idea of the state being above classes, led in practice to the betrayal of the interests of the working classes, as was shown, for example, by the history of the French revolutions of 1848 and 1871, and by the experience of "socialist" participation in bourgeois Cabinets in Britain, France, Italy and other countries at the turn of the century.[4]

Of equal relevance is the method of mystification, which entails the notion of workers' particular interests as a power and a foundation of the dictatorship. On the one hand, there is the mystification of the concept of the state in the name of particular nonproletarian interests; on the other hand, there is its demystification in the name of the particular interests of the proletariat as a "particular class":

> The overthrow of bourgeois rule can be accomplished only by the proletariat, the particular class whose economic conditions of existence prepare it for this task and provide it with the possibility and the power to perform it. While the bourgeoisie break up and disintegrate the peasantry and all the petty-bourgeois groups, they weld together, unite and organize the

proletariat. Only the proletariat—by virtue of the economic role it plays in large-scale production—is capable of being the leader of all the working and exploited people, whom the bourgeoisie exploit, oppress and crush, often not less but more than they do the proletarians, but who are incapable of waging an *independent* struggle for their emancipation.[5]

Let us now return to chapter 2. Lenin immediately adds: "Marx's theory of 'the state, i.e., the proletariat organized as the ruling class,' is inseparably bound up with the whole of his doctrine of the revolutionary role of the proletariat in history. The culmination of this rule is the proletarian dictatorship, the political rule of the proletariat."[6] The term "dictatorship of the proletariat" only appears later—in the *Manifesto* the paraphrase "the proletariat organized as a ruling class" is featured—but this does not change anything, because the other expression qualifies the paraphrase and allows for the concept of "particular class" to emerge. This is very important because Marx here overcomes the definition of the proletariat he had previously offered, where, soaked with the theories of the left Hegelians, the proletariat featured as a *general class*, as the universality of human interests. This view is still Hegelian and idealist, and is overcome insofar as the proletariat is no longer seen as a human, metaphysical, philosophical subject, but as the product of capitalist development. Here its particularity and that of its interests, as opposed to the social generality of capital, become the key to overturning the process, and it is clear that scientific communism can only be born out of this concept of particularity because only in this case can the dialectics be exercised on the subject, its independence, and the particularity of its immediately antagonistic interests: "Only the proletariat—by virtue of the economic role it plays in large-scale production—is capable of being the leader of all the working and exploited people, whom the bourgeoisie exploit, oppress and crush, often not less but more than they do the proletarians, but who are incapable of waging an independent struggle for their emancipation."[7]

This notion of autonomy of proletarian emancipation, born out of the particularity of the subject, had to be discovered as a refusal of any preconceived generality, any burden of idealism and humanism that could be ascribed to the proletariat as such. Lenin's affirmation of this notion gave great intensity to his Marxism, but this concept of the proletariat as a particular class was completely forgotten after Lenin, by social democrats and Marxist theorists alike, with their watered-down versions at the service of the pacific road to socialism. Sometimes this was done astutely, for instance, when, accompanying theoretical declarations in honor of the classics and tradition, they placed their emphasis on the general emancipating function of the actions of the proletariat. And from this, they moved toward the issue of alliances, the reaffirmation of the generality of workers' comportment. But this is all false, practically and theoretically. The particularity of workers' interests, the autonomous particularity of the interests of the working class, is absolutely irreducible and can only increase its autonomous particularity and turn into dictatorship. The interests of other sections of the proletariat (the large masses of *all workers*)—in other words, all of those interests that fall under the umbrella of the concept of working class as industrial productive labor, whether directly or indirectly—are not part of the revolutionary subject. Marx's and Lenin's concept of the working class has no appendix. The other proletarian interests can only be subjected to and dominated by the particular interest of the working class, and only then can the notion of alliance find meaning, insofar as these interests are dominated and used politically from outside, outside of any strategic confusion, and not from inside the workers' interests, which are isolated, autonomous, particular, and sectarian. The notion of workers' dictatorship that is taking shape in these passages is clear beyond any doubt: "The proletariat needs state power, a centralized organization of force, an organization of violence, both to crush the resistance of the exploiters and to lead the enormous mass of the population—the peasants, the petty bourgeoisie, and semi-proletarians."[8] Here, even the concept of violence seems to be a direct result of the particularity of workers' interests: alliance is always a violence exercised against both exploiters and exploited; the interests of the exploited in general only coincide with those of the working class if one makes them coincide with the use of workers' violence for the organization of the entire movement.

These ideas bring us straight to the core of the Marxist-Leninist theory of proletarian dictatorship and are extremely important for the theory of transition too: it seems clear to us that a theory of transition based on the issue of large alliances, for instance, and on structural reforms and reformist steps forward can acquire legitimacy in whomever's theory but it has no foundation in the tradition of Marxism and Leninism. On the contrary, for Marxist and Leninist traditions, each problem always comes to be reduced to the essential issues of the emergence of the particular interests of the workers and the recognition that only violence can be an instrument of mediation in the revolutionary process.

From this standpoint, we will have to develop, as we do in the next lesson, the specific determination that requires a reunification of the particular interest with the exercise of violence. But the second chapter does not provide new insights into this. The only issue of note there is that Lenin also retraces Marx's historical writings following the period of the *Manifesto of the Communist Party*, especially *The Eighteenth Brumaire of Louis Bonaparte*, and quotes two crucial passages concerning the interpretation of the overall process of proletarian revolution, especially in relation to the issue of bringing to light the revolutionary subject as it stands before him. In particular, at the beginning of the second paragraph of chapter 2, Lenin quotes what I think is one of the most beautiful of Marx's passages, which begins thus: "But the revolution is thoroughgoing. It is still journeying through purgatory. It does its work methodically. By December 2, 1851 [the day of Louis Bonaparte's coup d'état], it had completed one half of its preparatory work. It is now completing the other half. First it perfected the parliamentary power, in order to be able to overthrow it."[9] So the development of bourgeois political institutions is seen as the result of the workers' struggle: "Now that it has attained this, it is perfecting *the executive power*, reducing it to its purest expression, isolating it, setting it up against itself as the sole object, *in order to concentrate all its forces of destruction against it*. And when it has done this second half of its preliminary work, Europe will leap from its seat and exultantly exclaim: well grubbed, old mole!"[10] After all, "all revolutions perfected this machine instead of smashing it."[11] This is another crucial point: while it is true that institutional revolts and capitalist restructurings are the result and the effect of workers' struggle, this perfecting still belongs to capital. Hence the constant paradox of capitalist development: that as it perfects itself, it becomes increasingly isolated and exposed to workers' attacks; as it burns down all mediations and all developed forms of control over social movements, it becomes reduced to the executive, to the mere capacity of command and self-reproduction. The perfecting of capitalist development becomes its own precariousness as a rule: the more capital perfects itself, the more it approaches the revolutionary moment.

We have already seen this in different contexts, but it was important to have this conversation to see how Lenin's notion of proletarian dictatorship loyally recovers Marx's theory and uses it in a polemic against reformism, and, above all, to identify the need and urgency for a shift taking place in the Russian revolution. This is what we have highlighted in this lesson.

NOTES

1. We ought to be cautious when thinking about NEP. Di Leo regards it as a sort of cultural revolution that could have caused a rehabilitation of the mechanism of capitalist development and a resurgence of class struggle in Russia. See R. Di Leo, *Operai e sistema sovietico* [Workers and the Soviet system] (Bari: Laterza, 1970); and Di Leo, "Massa, avanguardia: gli operai e Lenin" [Vanguard mass: workers and Lenin], *Critica Sociologica* 12. There is also good documentation on the issue in general in Kaplan, *Bolshevik Ideology and the Ethics of Soviet Labour, 1917–1920: The Formative Years* (London: Peter Owen, 1969).
2. Marx and Engels, as cited in V. I. Lenin, *The State and Revolution*, trans. S. Apresyan and J. Ryordan, in *Collected Works* (Moscow: Progress Publishers, 1964), 25:406.
3. Ibid., 25:407.
4. Ibid., 25:408.
5. Ibid., 25:409.
6. Ibid.
7. Ibid.
8. Ibid.
9. Ibid., 25:410.
10. Marx, as cited in ibid., 25:410.
11. Ibid., 25:411.

28

TRANSITION, MATERIAL BASIS, AND EXPANSIVENESS OF THE WORKING-CLASS GOVERNMENT

T O SEEK FURTHER confirmation of our interpretation of some of the most important issues in Lenin's text, in this lesson we are going to concentrate on the third chapter of *The State and Revolution*, entitled "Experience of the Paris Commune of 1871: Marx's Analysis."

In this chapter, three main theoretical issues arise and need to be interpreted. The first emerges from a reading of Marx's historical writings and his notion of the revolutionary shift in the context of Lenin's polemic against the vulgar social democratic conception of it. Lenin refers to Marx's text on the *Civil War in France* and to the last preface to the German edition of the *Manifesto of the Communist Party*, dated 1872. He highlights Marx and Engels's correction in this preface, quoting the following text: "One thing especially was proved by the Commune: that 'the working class cannot simply lay hold of the ready-made state machinery and wield it for its own purposes.'"[1] Moreover, in 1871, in a famous letter to Kugelmann, a Hamburg doctor and friend of his, Marx writes:

> If you look up the last chapter of my Eighteenth Brumaire, you will find that I declare that the next attempt of the French Revolution will be no longer, as before, to transfer the bureaucratic-military machine from one hand to another, but to *smash* it [Marx's italics—the original is *zerbrechen*],

and this is the precondition for every real people's revolution on the Continent. And this is what our heroic Party comrades in Paris are attempting.[2]

What we are interested in pointing out is not so much that Lenin recovers Marx's stance on this issue, but that in his own polemic with revisionists he raises a fundamental question that introduces us to a debate that is also very much alive in the workers' movement today. This helps us verify the currency of *The State and Revolution* in the spirit in which we have done so far: "Here it will be sufficient to note that the current, vulgar 'interpretation' of Marx's famous statement just quoted [that is, from the 1872 Preface] is that Marx here allegedly emphasizes the idea of slow development in contradistinction to the seizure of power, and so on. As a matter of fact, *the exact opposite is the case*. Marx's idea is that the working class must *break up*, *smash* the 'ready-made state machinery,' and not confine itself merely to laying hold of it."[3] How did revisionists interpret the passage we have just read? Let us read it again: "one thing especially was proved by the Commune: that 'the working class cannot simply lay hold of the ready-made state machinery and wield it for its own purposes.'" What was the revisionist interpretation of this? If we cannot simply and purely lay hold of the state machinery, we must create the general conditions to seize it. The process becomes one of complex and articulated development: a process that entails *reforming the structure*. But in fact, according to Lenin, the opposite is the case: Marx thinks that the working class must break and smash the state machinery as it is ready-made, rather than simply get hold of it. Lenin's interpretation is confirmed by Marx's text; the revisionist reading is only based on words and does not hold water.

But we are not interested in mere philology. We want to grasp the implicit issue here, which concerns the development of struggle and the seizure of power. Clearly, for revisionists the concept of development is primary and counterposed to that of power. Despite its many variants, this is their scheme. In the context of the class composition recorded between 1870 and 1917, revisionists conceived of political development as being the same as economic development: political development and economic development are almost completely juxtaposed and the economic aspect becomes fundamental. From the classical social democratic perspective to the current communist one, revisionism has centered on a strategy of structural reforms and still upholds the hegemony of the economic instance: change in the economic structures is a condition of the seizure of power. This ends up reinforcing the economist and opportunist perspective and thus imposes an attitude that takes responsibility for the bourgeois state, which is a collaborationist and participatory stance. Methodologically and substantially, Lenin insists on a revolutionary notion that is formed by an emphasis on rupture, on smashing up; this becomes all the more relevant as the development and place of class struggle change in the economic context.

In no way does Lenin neglect the question of the relationship between development and the ability to break with it: he posits it in dialectical terms, and the discontinuity of the process does not elude but rather insists on the complexity of relations, choices, and alternatives. This insistence characterizes all of Lenin's activity. We find it in the first period, during the 1890s; it emerges when he raises the issue of the insurrections of 1905, and especially after 1905, in his political work, when he gathers together his previous ideas and develops them theoretically in the *Philosophical Notebooks*. The relation between development and rupture, the definition of a *discontinuous continuity* of the revolutionary process, is one of the most important aspects of Lenin's thought. Grasping this particular root as it rises up from a dialectical analysis offered in Marx's writings on the Commune and recognizing its importance in the polemic against revisionism only reinforce our conviction that this is a fundamentally current and preliminary motif in Marx's and Lenin's thought.

A second fundamental aspect that requires some clarification in our reading is illustrated in other sections of the third chapter, in the context of another polemic. It might seem strange, but Lenin's thought often emerges from polemics to which he offers a response—and what an odd response! Lenin's response is not constrained by the object of the polemic; it is projected forward. It does not accept the operative field of the provocation; it subverts it as it responds to it. In any case, the second main aspect concerning us here is spurred by Bernstein's critique of Lenin's concept of power and of the organization of power after the revolution. On the basis of Marx's discussion of the example of the Commune, Lenin claims that the withering-away of the state emerges from the possibility that all workers, organized as a ruling class, directly partake in the management of power. Bernstein and revisionists oppose Lenin on this and accuse him of "primitive democracy," of not taking into account the complexity of advanced capitalist societies and so on.

How many times have revisionists leveled this accusation! But in Lenin, beyond the scientific definition, we also find the sensation and the idea that it is precisely the development of the capitalist base as a complex material one that allows for the direct management of power. The problem is always one of standpoint. When things are seen from the workers' standpoint, the fact that the complexity of industrial development turns the labor force into a unified element, an abstract capacity whose function is totally interchangeable, allows for the overall direct control of economic and political development:

> Capitalist culture has *created* large-scale production, factories, railways, the postal service, telephones, etc., and *on this basis* the great majority of the functions of the old "state power" have become so simplified and can be reduced to such exceedingly simple operations of registration, filing, and checking that they can be easily performed by every literate person, can quite easily be performed for ordinary "workmen's wages," and that these functions can (and must) be stripped of every shadow of privilege, of every semblance of "official grandeur." All officials, without exception, elected and subject to recall *at any time*, their salaries reduced to the level of ordinary "workmen's wages"—these simple and "self-evident" democratic measures, while completely uniting the interests of the workers and the majority of the peasants, at the same time serve as a bridge leading from capitalism to socialism. These measures concern the reorganization of the state, the purely political reorganization of society; but, of course, they acquire their full meaning and significance only in connection with the "expropriation of the expropriators" either being accomplished or in preparation, i.e., with the transformation of capitalist private ownership of the means of production into social ownership.[4]

Nobody can fail to notice the overbearing tone of Lenin's affirmation here. It is not a utopia but the affirmation of a new humanity at the highest level of scientific prediction ever developed or construed by revolutionary Marxism;

this is because there is a constant link to the material basis and to the subversion of capitalist development.

At this stage many problems might arise in relation to the distorted form of this shift. But we have already criticized this and recognized that there is much optimism in Lenin's notion of the transition. Yet we know that Lenin's illusion can be recovered when a high level of development has determined an adequate material basis and thus a capable labor force, to the degree that its labor, or its refusal of labor, can produce communism. This is affirmed again when Lenin writes:

> There is no trace of utopianism in Marx, in the sense that he made up or invented a "new" society. No, he studied the birth of the new society out of the old, and the forms of transition from the latter to the former, as a mass proletarian movement and tried to draw practical lessons from it. He "Learned" from the Commune, just as all the great revolutionary thinkers learned unhesitatingly from the experience of great movements of the oppressed classes, and never addressed them with pedantic "homilies."[5]

Again, the polemical attitude against economism is as deep in Marx as it is in Lenin. It often seems that prefiguration is an enemy: theoretical delegation is completely shifted onto collective praxis. Theory comes to determine the need for the shift, but its forms and the new and highest modes of its organization are nothing but the practice that defines them: it is the movement that "discovers the forms of its organization":

> Marx deduced from the whole history of socialism and the political struggle that the state was bound to disappear, and that the transitional form of its disappearance (the transition from state to non-state) would be the "proletariat organized as the ruling class." Marx, however, did not set out to *discover the political forms* of this future stage. He limited himself to carefully observing French history, to analyzing it, and to drawing the conclusion to which the year 1851 had led, namely, that matters were moving towards *destruction of the bourgeois state machine*. And when the mass revolutionary movement of the proletariat burst forth, Marx, in spite of

its failure, in spite of its short life and patent weakness, began to study the forms *it had discovered.* The Commune is the form "at last discovered" by the proletarian revolution, under which the economic emancipation of labor can take place. The Commune is the first attempt by a proletarian revolution to smash the bourgeois state machine; and it is the political form "at last discovered," by which the smashed state machine can and must be replaced. We shall see further on that the Russian revolutions of 1905 and 1917, in different circumstances and under different conditions, continue the work of the Commune and confirm Marx's brilliant historical analysis.[6]

The main aspect here is the relation between the base and the revolutionary movement: a different way of addressing in material terms the continuous discontinuity that had seemingly configured a purely logical process. The "shift to communism" is a "leap" that starts on the springboard determined by capitalist development; the role of theory is to mediate the reality that confronts us by means of a "historical-natural" method with no utopian undertones, even though the method projects our intelligence and our practical activities onto moments and realities that seem defeated in everyday practice. But the tendency—the scientific moment of the mediation between reality, objectivity, and subjectivity, between what confronts us and what the working class will do—grasps, indeed scientifically and beyond appearances, this irresistible revolutionary process. Contrary to the reformists, who claim that the leap is something unpredictable and purely subjective, Lenin thinks that the discontinuity of the process is embodied in reality, in the material basis, and must be recognized and analyzed. This material basis is as stable as it is great: the large industry, the factory, the social infrastructure of industry, and, from an upturned standpoint, the worker that this production determines. Today human beings can be used as producers beyond any qualification outside of what they are bearers of as commodity labor, because they are born, built, and instructed in this society, and thus become an entirely interchangeable element of its function as a whole. But the worker, while being inside this reality, also has the ability to dominate it in terms of elementary registers and controls, not simply by virtue of the reality of her proletarianization and the relation with the material basis that is open to her, but rather because this proletarianization equalizes everyone at the highest level of capitalist production. Capitalist production today is already open to this possibility and now only mystifies it in terms of command, hierarchical development, and the reproduction of the existing structure. But this basis, from both an objective and a subjective point of view, was determined in antagonistic and potentially revolutionary terms. This is another methodological aspect that the third chapter offers to our understanding of the fifth chapter, which it complements.

The third and last element concerning us in this chapter is even more important: it gathers together a series of fundamental motives for the theory of the revolutionary shift as well as the theory of the party. Let us read the last passage that Lenin quotes from Marx:

> The multiplicity of interpretations to which the Commune has been subjected, and the multiplicity of interests which expressed themselves in it show that it was a thoroughly flexible political form, while all previous forms of government had been essentially repressive. Its true secret was this: it was essentially *a working-class government*, the result of the struggle of the producing against the appropriating class, the political form at last discovered under which the economic emancipation of labor could be accomplished. . . . Except on this last condition, the Communal Constitution would have been an impossibility and a delusion.[7]

"A thoroughly flexible political form": proletarian dictatorship becomes here identical with the shift from state to nonstate. In Marx and Lenin, parallel to the affirmation of the particular process of insurrection, dictatorship, and withering-away, a tripartite formula, we find allusions to a binary formula that is much more realistic and true in practice, and now serves as the basis of our political discourse. If the problem of the abolition of labor is fundamental, then the binary formula is adequate to it. The Commune is not simply a dictatorship; it is a thoroughly flexible political form, an ongoing transition from state to nonstate. Here Lenin's political position is impatiently exposed through an interpretation of this important quotation from Marx, where the shift is seen as the action of a proletarian engaged in an advanced level of struggle: in this, the binary formula of the immediate withering-away of the state is the correlative, both the cause and the effect, of the immediate expansiveness of the seizure of power of the proletariat. The opposition between this flexible political form and all other previous forms of government that had been unilaterally repressive is almost Lenin's preventive self-criticism of the dictatorship of the proletariat, where the proletariat is conceived in a static and repressive way as a dogma of the shift. The dictatorship of the proletariat is a crucial and essential shift, but nothing could be more damaging than seeing it as inessential, and nothing could be more dangerous than seeing it as static and nondialectical, that is, conceiving of it outside of the logic of the continuous discontinuity and thus outside of the relation between the material basis and the development of subjectivity (or we might say outside of the Maoist interpretation of the concept of the dictatorship of the proletariat as a permanent revolution).

In addition to the other beautiful things that can be found in chapter 3 of *The State and Revolution*, these three issues seem fundamental. Let us summarize them. The first is Lenin's critique of the revisionist and social democratic understanding of the relation between development and revolution. Lenin clarifies, through Marx, that this is a relation of discontinuity and rupture. He does so in polemical terms, and this becomes more important as revolutionary convictions mature alongside the power of the working class in capitalist society. The second fundamental issue concerns the relation between the material basis and the possibility of a direct government of class: contrary to reformist discourse and practice, the direct government of workers is confirmed by the development and maturation of the formation of the material basis. On the premises of the previous two, the third aspect concerns the flexible political form of workers' government as an ability to immediately develop the process of withering away, of liberation from labor, as soon as the state is smashed. These moments converge on the reaffirmation of the essential nature of the revolutionary shift inside and against development, while they help us define this shift as a binary process, wherein the process of the withering-away of labor there can immediately begin. Today our analysis confirms Marx's "illusion" and Lenin's "optimism."

NOTES

1. Marx and Engels, as cited in V. I. Lenin, *The State and Revolution*, trans. S. Apresyan and J. Ryordan, in *Collected Works* (Moscow: Progress Publishers, 1964), 25:419.
2. Marx, as cited in ibid., 25:420.
3. Ibid., 25:419.
4. Ibid., 25:425–426.
5. Ibid., 25:430.
6. Ibid., 25:437.
7. Marx, as cited in ibid., 25:436.

29

A PROVISIONAL CONCLUSION

Lenin and Us

CHAPTER 4, ON "Supplementary Explanations by Engels," keeps to the themes of the third chapter and reinstates the question of the smashing of the state with an eye to Engels's writings after 1871. From our point of view, not much can be recovered from it, because it consists in a series of repetitions and philological points on questions that were already expressed, with no new elements of note.

One interesting point for us, both methodologically and substantially, is found in the fourth paragraph, entitled "Criticism of the Draft of the Erfurt Program." Here Lenin raises the issue of the economic basis of communism and the relation between forms of capitalist development and planning. This is one of the few points made on this issue, and it is interesting to see how it is developed. Lenin writes:

We shall note in passing that Engels also makes an exceedingly valuable observation on economic questions, which shows how attentively and thoughtfully he watched the various changes occurring in modern capitalism, and how for this reason he was able to foresee to a certain extent the tasks of our present, the imperialist, epoch. Here is that observation: referring to the word "planlessness" (*Planlosigkeit*), used in the draft program, as characteristic of capitalism, Engels wrote: "When we pass from joint-stock companies to trusts which assume control over, and monopolize, whole industries, it is not only private production that ceases, but also planlessness." Here we have what is most essential in the theoretical appraisal of the latest phase of capitalism, i.e., imperialism, namely, that capitalism becomes monopoly capitalism.[1]

The comment on this quotation points out an important aspect of the theory of transition. Lenin is commenting on Engels's polemic against the definition of capitalism as "planlessness" and approaches the concept of "collective capital," or planned capital. If capitalism cannot be planned for the editor of the Erfurt, the revolutionary shift concerns a planned society. The shift to planning, for him, is a shift to socialism. Rightly, both Engels and Lenin oppose this definition. In fact, the process of planning can easily concern capital itself. The whole of capitalist development is geared toward this aim. Shareholders' societies, trusts, and monopolies are large collectors of capital that gradually build up to the figure of the planned collective capital. Far from being the essence of socialism, planning is a typical feature of capital as it reaches its hegemonic maturity. If this is true, the transition does not coincide with planning, but with the destruction of the wage-labor relation. If this is true, then all the theories—and there are many of them—that have persecuted us with their privileging of planning as the field of the transition must be attacked. In particular, we must demystify and undermine the framework of the ideology of planning that has been fervidly sustained in the socialist and communist movement until now. Moreover, if planning is a weapon of capital, if capital has come to apprehend it and constrain it in itself so forcefully that it has become natural to it, then we can derive a methodological indication of the need to keep refounding the communist program of destruction of the state and focus on the most advanced level of capitalist development as it unfolds.

And here we come to another side of the same coin: the fact that capital assumes forms of management and socialization proper to the socialist movement, far from demonstrating the overcoming of socialism, is in fact a process of approaching and approximating a more advanced phase from which to attack and ground the distinction between the state and the capitalist organization of labor. This growing socialization of capital, rather than appearing as an end and a radical transformation or subversion of the capitalist system, actually displays an opposed and antagonistic side, demonstrating that within this mode of production the working class is taking shape and undergoing a metamorphosis that makes it see communism closer insofar as its own socialization as a class and its own place in the instrumentalism (rationalized, centralized, and simplified) of capitalist command allow for a direct shift to the seizure of power. The progress of capitalist socialization is not a transformation of the capitalist regime in itself, but simply an opening for new possibilities for the revolutionary offensive of the working class:

> But however much they do plan, however much the capitalist magnates calculate in advance the volume of production on a national and even on an international scale, and however much they systematically regulate it, we still remain under capitalism—at its new stage, it is true, but still capitalism, without a doubt. The "proximity" of such capitalism to socialism should serve genuine representatives of the proletariat as an argument proving the proximity, facility, feasibility, and urgency of the socialist revolution, and not at all as an argument for tolerating the repudiation of such a revolution and the efforts to make capitalism look more attractive, something which all reformists are trying to do.[2]

Both Engels and Lenin attack and destroy the question of state socialism carried forward by the Second International, the direct premonition of the social democratic betrayal of the first imperialist war.

In the sixth chapter on "The Vulgarization of Marxism by Opportunists," we find a harsh polemic against Plekhanov and Kautsky and a position in favor of so-called left radicalism (especially that of Pannekoek). We have little to add to this. The main aspect of this chapter is the strong polemical character of the dictatorship of the proletariat against opportunists. This is also used against anarchists, but the content of the anarchists' demands (when they were not presented in Proudhon's terms, that is, in terms of autonomy, decentralization, and small artisan experimentations) is always assumed as a fundamental part of the revolutionary project of left-wing communism. Against the anarchists, Lenin insists on the issue of the "leap" and the "break" of proletarian dictatorship as a moment for revolutionaries to concentrate on; but then, he uses the anarchists against the reformists, because Bolshevism—that is, the communist notion of the party and the state (as autonomous realities, one in terms of the overall mediation of the revolutionary process, and the other as the adversary and thus essentially as an object against which to turn the revolutionary force)—has nothing to do with reformism. From the anarchists, Lenin recuperates, holds forcefully, and makes credible the antistate stance, the hatred for any form of exploitation of human beings.

We have come to the end of our reading of *The State and Revolution*. This is a precious book, and reading and rereading it is the least we can do with it. Obviously, at every reading one needs to choose a standpoint on which to insist and focus. We have essentially tried to identify the issue of transition from a political standpoint, one of a critique of political economy, rather than insist on the prediction of some formal and sometimes ideological characteristics of the future communist state. This reading might have remained blocked in the idea initially declared at the beginning of our conversations. This idea was that Lenin's Marxism is the most perfect instrument the communist tradition has left us: an instrument, a method. Thus nothing would be less Leninist than putting *The State and Revolution* on a pedestal and treating it as a text on which to mould the solutions that we provide, time and again, to the practical and theoretical problems of class struggle. Lenin's method is the most refined form Marxist method because it is based on a series of extremely effective and politically determined concepts: these are, for instance, the concept of determinate historical formation, which can be translated into one of class composition; the concept of tendency, which is a theoretical and practical anticipation; the configuration of the revolutionary process as a product of a mass workers' subject located inside the power relations that are time and again redetermined with other strata of the proletariat and eventually with other classes, from within which this relation is resolved into a definition of both strategy and tactics. Lenin's method is the method of this subject, and the concept of the party as mediation between spontaneity and subjectivity, between mass movement and offensive movement, is nothing but the determinate form of this mass method.

Beyond the limitations of this essay, which we have, I think, strongly underlined, we can observe that the so-called Marxism of the 1960s, the Marxism that we have contributed to by practically developing and defining it as a new theoretical and revolutionary fabric and that is now affirmed as a fundamental part of the movement, can legitimately refer to Leninism. Undoubtedly, the reformists, having made Lenin vulgar, now try to recuperate the Marxism of the 1960s and, with books, anthologies, and conferences, with small bureaucratic support operations, try to make it meek and locate it within reformism. But this is a waste of time! The Marxism of the 1960s is vaccinated against this recuperation. In fact, this Marxism started from the position of a strong polemic against Lenin, and this is why, among other reasons, it could not read Lenin outside of the stringent orthodoxy into which communist parties had forced it, a stringent and mortifying orthodoxy that prevented one from grasping the constructive and expansive aspects of the Leninist method. Lenin was known as the author of *Imperialism*, but we know very well now that this "popular essay" does not correspond to the situation of imperialism we find ourselves in, to our thoughts or actions. Lenin was defined as the theoretician of the centralized party, of the rigid, instrumental, and bureaucratic relation with the union and workers' struggles, but the struggles have decided to break with this relation of subordination. Lenin, finally, was defined as a theoretician of the unprincipled alliances determined by reformism.

Now, on these premises, in the context of the first phase of development of Marxism in the 1960s, critique could not help but involve Lenin's thought. The elements of strength that the new Marxism had outlined—especially the formidable discovery of this revolutionary subject with new characteristics, a working-class subject that has completely changed its power relations with the rest of society insofar as the socialization of capital has proceeded and the whole of society was posited against the working class—globally undermined the way social democracy and the Third Internationalism had used Lenin. Thus, the attack waged against Leninism was positively aimed at destroying the fetishistic definition of the current force of capital as a state monopoly, as reformists were imposing this emerging definition as a doctrinal image. The theory of the party was attacked because it was a theory of the extraneousness and subordination of the proletariat; the theory of alliances and all the dirt it carried with it was also attacked; and so on.

But the experience of the Marxism of the 1960s allowed us to recover Lenin and find fertile ground in him, because this recovery completely discounted the critiques that were leveled in the past and found in Lenin's method the basis, the support, and the instrument to carry them out. Perhaps Lenin operated, in relation to the Second International, the same shift that the Marxism of the 1960s forced in relation to the Third International. His initial reasons derived not only from a theoretically superior intelligence, but also and especially from a braver and more advanced positioning of class struggle: Leninism and our Marxism find a formidable path to take in this compactness of theoretical and practical thought.

Lenin is our new teacher, always alive and adequate, because Leninism, as an instrument and a method, is born not only out of its place inside the composition of the working class, or simply out of its ability to describe and analyze class experiences and generalize them in order to turn them into a weapon. And Leninism does not simply emerge from the shift from the weapons of critique to the critique of weapons in a determinate class composition. It also and above all is able to keep measuring up to and verifying the "leaps" determined by the revolutionary process. Lenin's thought represents the paradox of an absolutely consistent theoretical continuity based on key concepts and on an elasticity that is ready to continuously adapt to new situations. This paradoxical characteristic is also typical of Marx's thought, at least where Marx confronts the level of politics and history; but Lenin takes this all a step up. The Marxism of the 1960s will be able to consolidate its hegemony in communist theory, in Italy and in all advanced capitalist countries, when it rids the scene of all the archaic residues of traditional Third Internationalism, and recovers and develops this Leninism.

To conclude: today our fundamental task is comforted by reading Lenin's texts. Our task is to carry out a systematization not only of the main concepts but also and above all of their relation to collective practice that, for the first time, we can now regard as a mature aspect of the communist project. The great changes our Leninism needs are not dependent on Lenin's limits; they derive from the revolutionary and communist maturity of class.

Leninism today will demonstrate this ability to traverse the masses into the class and subordinate any theoretical approach to what the direct practice of revolutionary struggle is. It is no longer possible to move thought forward outside a relation of this kind. This is a provisional conclusion that we accept, reread, use, critique, and recognize ourselves in Lenin; but beyond all this, Lenin *made* his revolution. This is crucial. Any conclusion must take this into account and can only be provisional until *our own revolution* measures up to the classics.

NOTES

1. V. I. Lenin, *The State and Revolution*, trans. S. Apresyan and J. Ryordan, in *Collected Works* (Moscow: Progress Publishers, 1964), 25:447.
2. Ibid., 25:448.

PART V

Appendix on
"Left-Wing" Communism

A Conclusion and a Beginning

30

A DIFFICULT BALANCE

"L EFT-WING" COMMUNISM, AN *Infantile Disorder* is a party manual, a manual for a party that has won and has begun to develop a strategic and tactical plan to build the model of the workers' international, which subsequently became the foundation of the international organizational structures for the defense, the expansion, and the control of the expansion of the Soviet revolution: "I shall begin with our own experience—in keeping with the general plan of the present pamphlet, the object of which is to apply to Western Europe whatever is of general application, general validity and generally binding force in the history and the present tactics of Bolshevism."[1]

Although it is a party manual, *"Left-Wing" Communism* "exports" the model of a movement, that is, the model of the "Soviet," of the socialist revolution grounded in the shift that occurred through the radicalization of the workers' and the democratic struggle:

> Now we already have very considerable international experience which most definitely shows that certain fundamental features of our revolution have a significance which is not local, not peculiarly national, not Russian only, but international. I speak here of international significance not in the broad sense of the term: not some, but all the fundamental and many of the secondary features of our revolution are of international significance

in the sense that the revolution influences all countries. Now, taking it in the narrowest sense, i.e., understanding international significance to mean the international validity or the historical inevitability of a repetition on an international scale of what has taken place in our country, it must be admitted that certain fundamental features of our revolution do possess such a significance. Of course, it would be a very great mistake to exaggerate this truth and to apply it not only to certain fundamental features of our revolution. It would also be a mistake to lose sight of the fact that after the victory of the proletarian revolution in at least one of the advanced countries things will in all probability take a sharp turn, viz., Russia will soon after cease to be the model country and once again become a backward country (in the "Soviet" and the socialist sense). But at the present moment of history the situation is precisely such that the Russian model reveals to all countries something, and something very essential, of their near and inevitable future. Advanced workers in every land have long understood this; and more often they have not so much understood it as grasped it, sensed it, by revolutionary class instinct. Herein lies the international "significance" (in the narrow sense of the term) of Soviet power, and of the fundamentals of Bolshevik theory and tactics.[2]

Furthermore, this manual offers the model of the action of the Russian party as a driving and fundamental example, but the validity of this model is brought to bear on the ability of the masses to verify it:

The experience of the victorious dictatorship of the proletariat in Russia has clearly shown even to those who are unable to think, or who have not had occasion to ponder over this question, that absolute centralization and the strictest discipline of the proletariat constitute one of the fundamental conditions for victory over the bourgeoisie. This is often discussed. But not nearly enough thought is given to what it means, and under what conditions it is possible. Would it not be better if greetings in honor of Soviet power and the Bolsheviks were *more frequently* attended by a *profound analysis* of the reasons *why* the Bolsheviks were able to build up the discipline the revolutionary proletariat needs? As a trend of political thought and as a political party, Bolshevism [has existed] since 1903. Only the history of Bolshevism during the whole period of its existence can satisfactorily explain why it was able to build up and to maintain under most difficult conditions the iron discipline needed for the victory of the proletariat. And first of all the question arises: how is the discipline of the revolutionary party of the proletariat maintained? How is it tested? How is it reinforced? First, by the class consciousness of the proletarian vanguard and by its devotion to the revolution, by its perseverance, self-sacrifice and heroism. Secondly, by its ability to link itself with, to keep in close touch with, and to a certain extent, if you like, to merge with the broadest masses of the toilers—primarily with the proletariat, *but also with the non-proletarian* toiling masses. Thirdly, by the correctness of the political leadership exercised by this vanguard, by the correctness of its political strategy and tactics, provided that the broadest masses have been convinced *by their own experience* that they are correct. Without these conditions, discipline in a revolutionary party that is really capable of being the party of the advanced class, whose mission it is to overthrow the bourgeoisie and transform the whole of society, cannot be achieved. Without these conditions, all attempts to establish discipline inevitably fall flat and end in phrase-mongering and grimacing. On the other hand, these conditions cannot arise all at once. They are created only by prolonged effort and hard-won experience. Their creation is facilitated by correct revolutionary theory, which, in its turn, is not a dogma, but assumes final shape only in close connection with the practical activity of a truly mass and truly revolutionary movement.[3]

From this perspective, *"Left-Wing" Communism* is highly problematic from the outset and its main concern is striking a balance between the model it presents and its verification by mass action: the realization of a revolutionary process of international scope.

But there is more to it than a search for a static equilibrium reliant on structural conditions that are predictably long-term and stable, as evidenced in the analysis carried out in individual countries experiencing situations different from that of 1920. The Bolshevik program needs to be measured up against the parameters of class composition and the model of subjective and party initiative: each phase of the program had achieved a sort of stability in terms of prediction and had worked out an adequate model to resolve the relation between the organizational form and the initiative of the masses. But a *highly problematic equilibrium* is proposed in a *dramatic situation* wherein the triumph of the Bolshevik revolution provoked the response of all national bourgeoisies, one that, in a period of deep crisis, began to make itself adequate to the need for an offensive restructuring. The difficulty of the relation between a revolutionary model and the initiative of the masses, both in its generality (as connected to the very nature of the problem) and its particularity (as connected to national situations), here is multiplied by the exceptionality of the period of class struggle at a continental level, by the harshness of the struggle itself, and the terrible decision of both contenders.

Lenin describes with lucidity this second aspect of the question, concerning the exceptionality and harshness of this period of class struggle:

> The dictatorship of the proletariat is a most determined and most ruthless war waged by the new class against a *more powerful* enemy, the bourgeoisie, whose resistance is increased *tenfold* by its overthrow (even if only in one country), and whose power lies not only in the strength of international capital, in the strength and durability of the international connections of the bourgeoisie, but also in the *force of habit*, in the strength of small production. For, unfortunately, *small production* is still very, very widespread in the world, and small production *engenders* capitalism and the bourgeoisie continuously, daily, hourly, spontaneously, and on a mass scale. For all these reasons the dictatorship of the proletariat is essential, and victory over the bourgeoisie is impossible without a long, stubborn and desperate war of life and death, a war demanding perseverance, discipline, firmness, indomitableness and unity of will.[4]

In addition to their emphasis on the exceptional ruthlessness of class struggle, did Lenin and the leadership of the Communist International recognize the exceptionality of the ongoing transformations of those years? The Soviet revolutionary model was entrusted to the experience of the masses in a period of extreme accentuation of class struggle, fine: but was there a perception of the *dialectical shift that the victory of the Soviet revolution had set off at the world level*, and of the intensity of the response of both national bourgeoisies and single capitalists?

In fact, from October onward in more or less time the bourgeoisie tried to gather its own forces to respond to the Bolshevik challenge multiplied by the workers' initiative on a world scale, and to use the entire armory at its disposal to this end. The bourgeois dictatorship reorganized itself and alternated despotic (fascist) forms with reformist means, armed with a growing awareness and an implacable anti-Bolshevik hatred. This reorganization touched on levels that were both structural and of social command (the state) as well as on the mechanism of social production. The Russian revolutionary initiative found an equal and opposite response from the side of capitalism. As always, the dialectics of workers' revolution met its powerful reverse in capitalist restructuring; the workers' revolutionary initiative had to measure itself up against this new level of power relations, and inevitably renew itself.[5] Does *"Left-Wing" Communism* address these questions? Does it offer *a model that is adequate to the new conditions of working-class struggle as it developed after the October revolution* in capitalist restructuring? In this situation, is the equilibrium powerfully determined in Lenin's thought between the Bolshevik model and the Soviet and revolutionary initiative sustained, or does it break down?

If we read *"Left-Wing" Communism* as an attempt to respond to these questions, undoubtedly the text throws up a number of ambiguities. On the one hand, the presentation of the Soviet and Bolshevik model is extraordinarily powerful and thus embodies an absolutely valid revolutionary tension; on the other hand, the equilibrium between the subjective tension of the model and the new structural conditions of class struggle at the world level does not seem to be entirely adequate. *"Left-Wing" Communism* represents the beginning of a consideration and analysis of party relations on the international scale (of the relation, that is, between subjective initiative and political class composition), and this is an enthusiastic beginning, but still extremely skewed toward the Russian experience. This is the beginning of a new problem emerging, and ending, in the exposition of an old model, presented as a *conclusion* to the Russian experience.

Let us analyze this question more closely. What is the barycenter, the main indication, of this pamphlet? It is the example of the Russian Bolshevik Party:

> Having arisen on this granite theoretical foundation, Bolshevism passed through fifteen years (1903–17) of practical history which in wealth of experience has no equal anywhere else in the world. For no other country during these fifteen years had anything even approximating to this revolutionary experience, this rapid and varied succession of different forms of the movement—legal and illegal, peaceful and stormy, underground and open, circles and mass movements, parliamentary and terrorist. In no other country was there concentrated during so short a time such a wealth of forms, shades, and methods of struggle of *all* classes of modern society, and moreover, a struggle which, owing to the backwardness of the country and the severity of the tsarist yoke, matured with exceptional rapidity and assimilated most eagerly and successfully the appropriate "last word" of American and European political experience.[6]

Therefore, the whole Bolshevik strategy is taken up here, but tactical and strategic indications do not emerge out of nothing: they arise from an analysis of the political composition of class, from the political labor on the general conditions of a determinate proletariat, the Russian one in particular. Here all forms of struggle have been used and all revolutionary means experimented with. Time and again, the selection of the most adequate means was established by the party and verified by the masses. Bolshevism is not simply an openness to use all forms of struggle, but a commensuration of these weapons with an objective in light of the program and experience of the masses. The decisive question is thus: how can the instruments be commensurate with the objectives and adequate to the political composition of the working and proletarian class? The decisive question concerns the relation between the party and class composition, the revolutionary experience of the masses. The Bolshevik Party always managed to establish some equilibrium between these elements, until its victory.

Well, on what grounds can this analysis of the comportment and line of the Bolshevik Party be extended? On what basis does it become a model?

Given what we have argued in our attempted reconstruction of the main movements and modalities of Lenin's thought, the only ground where it is possible to exemplify the Bolshevik scheme into a model requires an analogy to the political situations and class composition. Lenin is right on this: we will later see how little he can be accused of scheming, and how attentive he is to the particularity of the situations instead. There is nothing schematic about the model he proposed. It is essentially and fundamentally a political fact. The extension of the Bolshevik revolution can rely on a fundamental analogy to individual class compositions for a very simple reason: because the subjective power of the Russian revolution pivots on the movement of the masses, is connected to a determinate model, and is sustained by the example of proletarian dictatorship. This is the point: offering the model now, in 1920, means discovering a crucial dimension of the working-class composition at the world level. Herein lie both Lenin's greatness and the fascination with *"Left-Wing" Communism*.

But *"Left-Wing" Communism* is more than this. This new equilibrium between the organizational proposal at the international level and the subjective aspects of the political composition of the international proletariat was extremely fragile. We have seen why this was so: the equilibrium was mined by the capitalist ability to respond and was inevitably limited to the short term of a growing revolutionary tension. Paradoxically, the Bolshevik model was not presented as a figure of stabilization of the movement, but as an element of growth, a record of the offensive. Lenin's synthesis, in this case, is entirely a *synthesis* of the offensive, of the attack related to the (short-term) terms of the offensive and burned by the impelling defense of the Soviet regime. Because of this, the synthesis is fragile. The expansion of the communist movement necessitated other means at this stage: above all, it needed to be able to forecast capitalists and workers' comportments, the necessarily new configuration of the power relations between classes. Here *"Left-Wing" Communism* falls; and not only does it fall, it also attempts, as we shall see, an ideological and false exit from the difficulties confronting it.

For now, we will simply hint at this. We have seen Lenin's gaze move onto the character of power tout court, with its powerful abstraction, in order to single it out as the exclusive object of hatred and the target of the attack.

But these emphases on the "autonomy of the political," as determined as they were by the particular figure of Russian autocracy, had become exclusive to him. Here, instead, in the difficult situation of 1920, the analysis seems heavily tilted to this side. As we shall see, the attack on extremism or "left-wing" communism essentially moves from the defense of the "autonomy of the political" and is sustained by a demand for a formal position of the party before the structures of the state. As we shall see, Lenin exasperates particular and one-sided aspects of the global discourse in his particular situation, given the urgency of defending the Russian revolution.[7]

What does it matter? They can be subverted later! The sectarian singularity of their attitude innervates the overall strategy of the Bolsheviks. But one needed the strength to do that, to build continuity between a sequence of tactical moments and a strategic design. That did not happen. From this standpoint, *"Left-Wing" Communism* contains the residue of a "Leninism" that is not singular and becomes characteristic of a historical phase of international communism: over time, the "autonomy of the political" would turn into an ideology fixed in the "political" perspective of the International that sees the interests of power as primary. And so far, so good! (But this is a different issue.) The terrible thing, the real, deep betrayal of Leninism, the subversion of the continuity between Marx and Lenin, occurs when this ideology of power becomes unhinged from an analysis of the political class composition and dissolved into a mystification of capitalist power as something capable of an indeterminate variation of antiworkers' responses. The nexus between class action and capitalist restructuring is destroyed and organization becomes a fetish. The forecasting of capitalist comportments is flattened into sociological analysis in the recovery of economism. The naturalism and anarchist utopianism of the notion of the state become characteristic of the international communist movement, on the left and, more frequently, on the right. The exigencies of 1920 end up barring an understanding of capitalist development and of the transformations of working-class composition in the 1920s and 1930s. In the hands of the Dimitrovs and Togliattis, *"Left-Wing" Communism* becomes a reactionary weapon.

In the following conversations we will explore, on one side, the limits and mystifications that were to befall *"Left-Wing" Communism* and, on the other,

Lenin's formidable ability to see in 1920 a tactical shift like the disciplined defense of the dictatorship of the proletariat as a fundamental moment of proletarian armament, for the revolution, for communism.

Thus we must remember that the margin of equilibrium internal to *"Left-Wing" Communism* is minimal: the structural difficulty of the Leninist synthesis is here exposed to capital's restructuration and fails to sustain its impact. Or rather, it only sustains it insofar as Lenin turns a situation of need into a moment of offensive; but it does not sustain it insofar as other necessary tactical shifts are turned into ideology and mystified in the strategy of the revisionists' International.

NOTES

1. V. I. Lenin, *"Left-Wing" Communism, an Infantile Disorder* (Peking: Foreign Language Press, 1970), 36.
2. Ibid., 1.
3. Ibid., 5–6.
4. Ibid., 5.
5. On this issue, see various authors, *Operai e stato* [Workers and the state] (Milan: Feltrinelli, 1972); and K. H. Roth, *Die "andere" Arbeiterbewegung* (Munich: Schriften zum Klassenkampf, 1974).
6. Lenin, *"Left-Wing" Communism*, 8.
7. Carr's theses are fundamental in this respect and need to be revisited.

31

A DEFINITION OF "LEFT-WING" COMMUNISM, AND SOME (ADEQUATE?) EXAMPLES

L ENIN'S PAMPHLET STARTS with an irrefutable definition of left-wing communism, a definition that is still valid today, if we substitute some of its terms, and that is grounded in the experience of struggle of the Russian party outlined in both its material origins and its theoretical and practical character. Let us read the definition:

It is far from sufficiently known as yet abroad that Bolshevism grew up, took shape, and became steeled in long years of struggle against *petty-bourgeois revolutionism*, which smacks of, or borrows something from, anarchism, and which falls short, in anything essential, of the conditions and requirements of a consistently proletarian class struggle. For Marxists, it is well established theoretically—and the experience of all European revolutions and revolutionary movements has fully confirmed it—that the small owner, the small master (a social type that is represented in many European countries on a very wide, a mass scale), who under capitalism always suffers oppression and, very often, an incredibly acute and rapid deterioration in his conditions, and ruin, easily goes to revolutionary extremes, but is incapable of perseverance, organization, discipline and steadfastness. The petty bourgeois "driven to frenzy" by the horrors of capitalism is a social phenomenon which, like anarchism, is characteristic of all capitalist countries. The instability of such revolutionism, its barrenness, its liability to become swiftly transformed into submission, apathy, fantasy, and even a "frenzied" infatuation with one or another bourgeois "fad"—all this is a matter of common knowledge. But a theoretical, abstract recognition of these truths does not at all free revolutionary parties from old mistakes, which always crop up at unexpected moments, in a somewhat new form, in hitherto unknown vestments or surroundings, in a peculiar—more or less peculiar—situation. Anarchism was not infrequently a sort of punishment for the opportunist sins of the working-class movement. The two monstrosities were mutually complementary. And the fact that in Russia, although her population is more petty bourgeois than that of the European countries, anarchism exercised a relatively negligible influence in the preparations for and during both revolutions (1905 and 1917) must undoubtedly be partly placed to the credit of Bolshevism, which has always combated opportunism ruthlessly and uncompromisingly. I say "partly," for a still more important role in weakening the influence of anarchism in Russia was played by the fact that in the past (in the seventies of the nineteenth century) it had had the opportunity to develop with exceptional luxuriance and to display its utter fallaciousness and unfitness as a guiding theory for the revolutionary class. At its inception in 1903, Bolshevism took over the tradition of ruthless struggle against petty-bourgeois, semi-anarchist (or dilettante-anarchist) revolutionism, the tradition which has always existed in revolutionary Social-Democracy, and became particularly strong in 1900–03, when the foundations for a mass party of the revolutionary proletariat were being laid in Russia. Bolshevism took over and continued the struggle against the party which more than any other expressed the tendencies of petty-bourgeois revolutionism, namely, the "Socialist-Revolutionary" Party, and waged this struggle on three main points. First, this party, rejecting Marxism, stubbornly refused (or, it would be more correct to say: was unable) to understand the need for a strictly objective appraisal of the class forces and their interrelations before undertaking any political action. Secondly, this party considered itself to be particularly "revolutionary," or "Left," because of its recognition of individual terror, assassination—a thing which we Marxists emphatically rejected. Of course, we rejected individual terror only on grounds of expediency, whereas people who were capable of condemning "on principle" the terror of the Great French Revolution, or in general, the terror employed by a victorious revolutionary party which is besieged by the bourgeoisie of the whole world, were ridiculed and laughed to scorn already by Plekhanov, in 1900–03, when he was a Marxist and a revolutionary. Thirdly, the "Socialist-Revolutionaries" thought it very "Left" to sneer at comparatively insignificant opportunist sins of the German Social-Democratic Party, while they themselves imitated the extreme opportunists of that party, for example, on the agrarian question, or on the question of the dictatorship of the proletariat.[1]

The lack of method in the revolutionary analysis of the political composition of class; the tendency toward fanatical and individualist leftism and terrorism; opportunism and the absence of a party perspective on crucial questions: these are the features Lenin ascribes to extremism and they are still current. Its origins are all petit bourgeois, its motivations desperate, and its extraneousness to the dialectics of collective practice total. The rogue character of extremism could not be better defined than by an explicit association with the definition of the material condition of uprootedness and precariousness of the petty bourgeoisie, of the "small masters" in whatever figure they present themselves: Lenin underlines its difference from the political comportment of the working class efficiently and truthfully. Our experience of these years and beyond has verified the validity of Lenin's definition.[2] The greatest danger for communism is failing to follow and carry out a class analysis of its motivations when it is politically necessary, or failing to develop the most rigorous and constant procedure of its criticism and self-criticism.

Lenin's argument proceeds and extends in the rest of the pamphlet, tracing the reconstruction of two experiences of struggle against left-wing deviations within the party from the definition of extremism and a recounting of the struggle against social revolutionary extremism outside the party. The two examples recalled are a discussion from 1908 on the question of participation in an ultrareactionary parliament and in the legal societies subjected to ultrareactionary laws, and the debate in 1918 (the Brest peace) on the question of allowing for some compromises. Lenin's analysis of these two cases develops the criteria of the definition of "extremism" outlined earlier. In both instances, the deviation consisted in failing to reconnect the ability of decision and the political line with a determinate analysis of class composition, and in subsequently giving rise to comportments and perspectives, in the case of the comrades fallen into deviation, of adventurism and opportunism.

The first case concerns the question of sabotage. In 1905 Bolsheviks had boycotted parliament:

> At that time the boycott proved correct, not because non-participation in reactionary parliaments is correct in general, but because we correctly gauged the objective situation which was leading to the rapid transformation of the mass strikes into a political strike, then into a revolutionary strike, and then into uprising. Moreover, the struggle at that time centered on the question whether to leave the convocation of the first representative assembly to the tsar, or to attempt to wrest its convocation from the hands of the old regime. When there was no certainty, nor could there be, that the objective situation was analogous, and likewise no certainty of a similar trend and rate of development, the boycott ceased to be correct. The Bolshevik boycott of "parliament" in 1905 enriched the revolutionary proletariat with highly valuable political experience and showed that in combining legal with illegal, parliamentary with extra-parliamentary forms of struggle, it is sometimes useful and even essential to reject parliamentary forms. But it is a very great mistake indeed to apply this experience blindly, imitatively and uncritically to *other* conditions and to *other* situations. The boycott of the "Duma" by the Bolsheviks in 1906 was, however, a mistake, although a small and easily remediable one. A boycott of the Duma in 1907, 1908 and subsequent years would have been a serious mistake and one difficult to remedy, because, on the one hand, a very rapid rise of the revolutionary tide and its conversion into an uprising could not be expected, and, on the other hand, the whole historical situation attending the renovation of the bourgeois monarchy called for combining legal and illegal activities. Today, when we turn back at this completed historical period, the connection of which with subsequent periods is fully revealed, it becomes particularly clear that the Bolsheviks *could not have* in 1908–14 preserved (let alone strengthened, developed and reinforced) the firm core of the revolutionary

party of the proletariat had they not upheld in strenuous struggle the view-point that it is *obligatory* to combine legal and illegal forms of struggle, that it is *obligatory* to participate even in a most reactionary parliament and in a number of other institutions restricted by reactionary laws (sick benefit societies, etc.).[3]

Clearly the crux of the argument is established in the relation between class composition and revolutionary objectives, the keeping of the main means of revolutionary action.

The same applies to the analysis of the second case, the discussion on Brest in 1918.[4] Lenin's argument digs deeper into the terms of the definition of extremism and reinstates the more general aspects of its methodology and political critique. The certainty of the analysis of its character and the power relations of the political composition of the Russian proletariat determines adequate steps and adequately defines not only the currency of these devia-tions but also some important lines along which they can reproduce them-selves: "But anyone who set out to invent a recipe for the workers that would provide in advance readymade solutions for all cases in life, or who promised that the policy of the revolutionary proletariat would never encounter difficult or intricate situations, would simply be a charlatan."[5] Having examined Lenin's definition of the concept of extremism in relation to the politics of the Russian party, we move closer to the core concern of the pamphlet. This is a polemic against the extremism of the comrades in Western Europe and a clarification of the equilibrium between the Bolshevik model and the revolutionary pro-gram adequate to the political class composition in Western Europe. In light of this statement and of all of Lenin's method, the analysis and polemic are intended to be internal, commensurate, and adequate to the object, which is the revolutionary movement in Europe. The definition of extremism based on the model and past history of the Bolshevik Party must become exemplary of the current vicissitudes of communist internationalism. By "exemplary" we mean the realization of a party line that is rigorous but not schematic. Does Lenin's exemplification achieve its aim? This is what we need to ask.

The first target of Lenin's polemic is the line of left-wing communists in Germany.[6] It is not difficult for him to approach their kind polemically: too much talk, doctrine, intellectually rigid alternatives, and utopianism. Lenin's black beast, the focus of his polemic, is clarified soon enough: it is the absurd and ridiculous subversion operated by left-wing communists of the right polemics against the corrupt heads of social democracy (the representatives of the labor aristocracy) and the counterpositing of the dictatorship of the masses to the dictatorship of the leaders. The consequences are extremely serious, since they imply a simultaneous underestimation of the power of the adversary that leads to the renunciation of the only valid means of struggle, the centralized Bolshevik Party, as well as to an overestimation of the power of the masses, of their spontaneity and closeness to communism:

Repudiation of the party principle and of party discipline—such is the opposition's *net result*. And this is tantamount to completely disarming the proletariat *in the interest of the bourgeoisie*. It is tantamount to that petty-bourgeois diffuseness, instability, incapacity for sustained effort, unity and organized action, which, if indulged in, must inevitably destroy every proletarian revolutionary movement. From the standpoint of Communism, the repudiation of the party principle means trying to leap from the eve of the collapse of capitalism (in Germany), not to the lower, or the intermediate, but to the higher phase of Communism. We in Russia (in the third year since the overthrow of the bourgeoisie) are going through the first steps in the transition from capitalism to Socialism, or the lower stage of Communism. Classes have remained, and will remain everywhere *for years after* the conquest of power by the proletariat. Perhaps in England, where there is no peasantry (but where there are small owners!), this period may be shorter. The abolition of classes means not only driving out the landlords and capitalists—that we accomplished with comparative ease—it also means *abolishing the small commodity producers*, and they *cannot be driven out*, or crushed; we *must live in harmony* with them; they can (and must) be remolded and re-educated only by very prolonged, slow, cautious organizational work. They encircle the proletariat on every side with a petty-bourgeois atmosphere, which permeates and corrupts the proletariat and causes constant relapses among the proletariat into petty-bourgeois spinelessness, disunity, individualism, and alternate moods of exaltation and dejection. The strictest centralization and discipline are required within the political party of the proletariat in order to counteract this, in order that the *organizational* role of the proletariat (and that is its *principal* role) may be exercised correctly, successfully, victoriously. The dictatorship of the proletariat is a persistent struggle—bloody and bloodless, violent and peaceful, military and economic, educational and administrative—against the forces and traditions of the old society. The force of habit of millions and tens of millions is a most terrible force. Without an iron party tempered in the struggle, without a party enjoying the confidence of all that is honest in the given class, without a party capable of watching and influencing the mood of the masses, it is impossible to conduct such a struggle successfully. It is a thousand times easier to vanquish the centralized big bourgeoisie than to "vanquish" the millions and millions of small owners; yet they, by their ordinary, everyday, imperceptible, elusive, demoralizing activity, achieve the very results which the bourgeoisie need and which tend to restore the bourgeoisie. Whoever weakens ever so little the iron discipline of the party of the proletariat (especially during the time of its dictatorship) actually aids the bourgeoisie against the proletariat.[7]

This is beautiful passage. Here Lenin comes to the realization that the process of the withering-away of the state is one of the destruction of the mechanisms of the production and reproduction of the power of capital at a level that was not found even in *The State and Revolution*. But are the application of the Russian model and its exemplification really adequate to the German situation?

The polemic against the left-wing communists, whether German or not, moves onto another level: "Should revolutionaries work in reactionary trade unions?"[8] Now Lenin does not mystify in any way the debate on the union. We know these passages and have often gone back to them in our conversations: that "certain reactionary character" of the union; or worse, that Mensheviks and social chauvinists, who represented a "*craft-union, narrow-minded, selfish, casehardened, covetous, petty-bourgeois 'labor aristocracy,' imperialist-minded, imperialist bribed and imperialist-corrupted,*"[9] were nested in the unions as real "*labor lieutenants of the capitalist class*" (to use Daniel

De Leon's terms), cannot be denied. But why draw from this recognition a renunciation of practice? Why reject the Bolshevik teaching to "imperatively *work wherever the masses are to be found*"?[10] And, worst of all, why use nonsensical arguments, such as the proposal of radically new and radically democratic means, in the mass reality of the union? In this case, as in the polemic against the "leaders," tactical mistakes are followed by strategic and theoretical ones, the underestimation of the enemy and the overestimation of one's own strengths:

And we cannot but regard as equally ridiculous and childish nonsense the pompous, very learned, and frightfully revolutionary disquisitions of the German Lefts to the effect that Communists cannot and should not work in reactionary trade unions, that it is permissible to turn down such work, that it is necessary to leave the trade unions and to create an absolutely brand-new, immaculate "Workers' Union" invented by very nice (and, probably, for the most part very youthful) Communists, etc., etc. Capitalism inevitably leaves Socialism the legacy, on the one hand, of old trade and craft distinctions among the workers, distinctions evolved in the course of centuries; and, on the other hand, trade unions which only very slowly, in the course of years and years, can and will develop into broader, industrial unions with less of the craft union about them (embracing whole industries, and not only crafts, trades and occupations), and later proceed, through these industrial unions, to eliminate the division of labor among people, to educate, school and train people with an *all-round development and an all-round training*, people who *know how to do everything*. Communism is advancing and must advance towards this goal, and *will reach it*, but only after very many years. To attempt in practice today to anticipate this future result of a fully developed, fully stabilized and formed, fully expanded and mature Communism would be like trying to teach higher mathematics to a four-year-old child. We can (and must) begin to build Socialism, not with imaginary human material, nor with human material specially prepared by us, but with the human material bequeathed to us by capitalism. True, that is very "difficult," but no other approach to this task is serious enough to warrant discussion.[11]

Lenin's writing is powerful for its realism and argumentative force. We must emphasize that he is attempting to present his own material investigation while faced with the roughness and soliciting coming from the left-wing communists of Western Europe. Lenin always tries to take into account the new situation of transition when facing both Russian and European debates, and is highly aware of the identity of the overall power relations dominating both camps. Let us read two more passages from this text:

> After the first socialist revolution of the proletariat, after the overthrow of the bourgeoisie in one country, the proletariat of that country *for a long time* remains *weaker* than the bourgeoisie, simply because of the latter's extensive international connections, and also because of the spontaneous and continuous restoration and regeneration of capitalism and the bourgeoisie by the small commodity producers of the country which has overthrown the bourgeoisie. The more powerful enemy can be vanquished only by exerting the utmost effort, and *without fail*, most thoroughly, carefully, attentively and skillfully using every, even the smallest, "rift" among the enemies, of every antagonism of interest among the bourgeoisie of the various countries and among the various groups or types of bourgeoisie within the various countries, and also by taking advantage of every, even the smallest, opportunity of gaining a mass ally even though this ally be temporary, vacillating, unstable, unreliable and conditional. Those who fail to understand this fail to understand even a particle of Marxism, or of scientific, modern Socialism *in general*. Those who have not proved by *deeds* over a fairly considerable period of time, and in fairly varied political situations, their ability to apply this truth in practice have not yet learned to assist the revolutionary class in its struggle to emancipate all toiling humanity from the exploiters. And this applies equally to the period *before* and *after* the proletariat has conquered political power.[12]

Therefore:

> As long as the bourgeoisie has not been overthrown, and after that as long as small-scale economy and small commodity production have not entirely

disappeared, the bourgeois atmosphere, proprietary habits and petty-bourgeois traditions will hamper proletarian work both outside and inside the
working-class movement, not only in one field of activity, parliamentary,
but inevitably in every field of social activity, in all cultural and political
spheres without exception. And the attempt to brush aside, to fence oneself off from *one* of the "unpleasant" problems or difficulties in one sphere
of activity is a profound mistake, which will later most certainly have to
be paid for. We must study and learn how to master every sphere of work
and activity without exception, to overcome all difficulties and all bourgeois
habits, customs and traditions everywhere. Any other way of presenting the
question is just trifling, just childishness.[13]

If all these issues are rejected, if one refuses to use all means and move in
every field or rejects the long battle *internal* to the ranks of the proletariat to
change the current power relations, then one will "think it possible to '*solve*' the
difficult problem of combating bourgeois-democratic influences *within* the
working-class movement by such a 'simple,' 'easy,' supposedly revolutionary
method, when in reality they are only running away from their own shadow,
only closing their eyes to difficulties and only trying to brush them aside with
mere words."[14]

But is this new exemplification of the Bolshevik proposal for Europe, one
that implicitly dwells on the issues pertaining to Bolshevik theory and dramatically points to the commonality of the problem of the transition in Russia as in
Europe, adequate to the needs of the German and European comrades?

The question becomes serious, and it is appropriate for us to try to answer
it. From a relatively personal point of view, I must immediately clarify that
from the first readings of *"Left-Wing" Communism* I have always had the
impression that, despite everything, there lies in the roughness of the German
comrades a dark prediction of a state of class struggle that was irreducible
to the Bolshevik experience. In fact, German communists struggled against
a social democracy that was not only a conglomerate of corrupt leaders, a
whole of representatives of the labor aristocracy, but also a formidable mechanism of capitalist integration, a direct instrument for the social reproduction of capitalist relations that had very relevant functions, a slow but sure

step in the capitalist pace toward its restructuring into social capital. In fact, German, Dutch, and English communists could not fight, along the ridge of tradition, for the democracy that followed: unions, parties, and other representative institutions were actually becoming necessary moments of integration, moments of a system of new formation of the social legitimacy of capital. Only by directly putting a strain on the mechanisms of representation, breaking them, opening a political space directly to the action of the workers' variable could they hope to seize, in the medium-to-long term, a dimension of offensive and adequate revolutionary theory. What could the polemic of *"Left-Wing" Communism* mean to these comrades? Didn't it end up configuring, for them, when they were faced with the problems that arose from the capitalist response, a position external to the needs gathered from the working-class composition in which they operated? Didn't *"Left-Wing" Communism* present itself to them more as a conclusion to the Russian debate on insurrection than as the beginning of a determinate analysis of the opening of the revolutionary process in Western Europe?

And wasn't it the case that the ongoing capitalist initiative could only be anticipated by insisting precisely on the new form of organization of the base, on the opening-up of a process of struggles not in the union, but antiunion? Wasn't the refusal of the centers of state political mediation, either as centers of denunciation or as centers of propaganda, actually setting off a process of reappropriation and a mass defense of spaces of power?

This is one impression. If this were the case, *"Left-Wing" Communism* would be a dead work; its efficacy would simply amount to the moralist appeal to and soliciting of the activism of the militant cadres. But this is not the case. *"Left-Wing" Communism* is also something else: the attempt to accelerate the pace of the revolutionary process through the revolutionary exporting of a victorious model, the attempt to invert the relation between composition and organization in the countries of Western Europe. Above all, *"Left-Wing" Communism*, for Lenin, is the will to play out, in the short term, the process of the international revolution. From this standpoint, the serious limitations of its prediction are obvious, as are the limits of its adequacy to the single class compositions in the short term. But this does not mean that these limits were not *real*, and that, once Lenin's own ability to directly lead the project waned, these would not come to the fore and determine significant conditions in the tragedy of the years of the 1920s and the 1930s.

In the long term, the correctness of the definition of "left-wing" communism as a petty bourgeois phenomenon ended up being confounded with ambiguous exemplifications and, beyond Lenin's direction of the Communist International, was undoubtedly reduced to an instrument of repression. This became confused, and again, anarchism came to represent "a sort of punishment for the opportunist sins of the working-class movement."[15] Today, however, we are in the position to recover the correctness of Lenin's definition of extremism as a petty bourgeois ideology without falling into the quicksand of traditional exemplifications. And the more we recover this radical cleaning operation in Leninism, the more we will take into account another series of motivations of *Left-Wing" Communism* that leads to defining the most profound and truest moments of Bolshevism as a weapon of proletarian subversion.

NOTES

1. V. I. Lenin, *"Left-Wing" Communism, an Infantile Disorder* (Peking: Foreign Language Press, 1970), 16–18.

2. For a series of references to *"Left-Wing" Communism*, some adequate and matured in a long vicissitude of struggles, see A. Bordiga, *"Estremismo malattia infantile del comunismo," Condanna dei futuri rinnegati* [*"Left-Wing" Communism, an Infantile Disorder: a condemnation of futures disowned*] (Milan: Edizioni Il programma comunista, 1973).

3. Lenin, *"Left-Wing" Communism*, 20. On the boycott, see also p. 122ff.

4. Ibid., 22, and also, on the question of "compromises," p. 62ff.

5. Ibid., 24.

6. Ibid., 26–35.

7. Ibid., 32–33.

8. Ibid., 36–48.

9. Ibid., 42.

10. Ibid., 44.

11. Ibid., 40–41.

12. Ibid., 67.

13. Ibid., 125.

14. Ibid., 121.

15. Ibid., 17.

32

TOWARD A NEW CYCLE
OF STRUGGLES

"L EFT-WING" COMMUNISM IS not only a correct definition of a petty bourgeois adventurist and terroristic deviation; it is not only the proposal of a Bolshevik model and the attempt to push for, in this way and in the short term, a formidable acceleration of the pace of the revolutionary process; it is not only even a series of exemplifications or applications of the Bolshevik model to the vicissitudes of class struggle and organization in Western European countries with the difficulties this entails. *"Left-Wing" Communism* is also the start of a *new theme*, the voluntary and decisive foreboding of a new cycle of struggles, the beginning of a discussion of the strategy, tactics, and organization of the international communist movement, not only as a repetition of the dialectical adventure of the capsizing and inversion of the relation between composition and organization or in the sense of, as we have already pointed out, an acceleration of the revolutionary pace in the short term on the basis of Lenin's realization of the subjective transformations introduced by the Soviet triumph over class composition in advanced capitalist countries. There is more to it than this. We would like to trace, in *"Left-Wing" Communism*, a *second* stratum in his political proposal and analysis that coexists with what we have argued so far but is not homogeneous to it, because instead of assuming the question of the international revolution as a *conclusion* to be drawn from the Bolshevik model, Lenin develops his discussion starting from an original *novum*, from the new international working-class composition. From this standpoint, *"Left-Wing" Communism* contains cues for an analysis and proposal whose fecundity we can only fully appreciate today.

I am not trying to exaggerate Lenin's new awareness, but he certainly has no doubts about the fact that the historical period from the Paris Commune to the First Soviet Socialist Republic has come to a close.[1] There is more to this:

> After the proletarian revolution in Russia and its victories on an international scale, which were unexpected for the bourgeoisie and the philistines, the whole world has changed, and the bourgeoisie has changed everywhere too. It is terrified of "Bolshevism," incensed with it almost to the point of frenzy, and, precisely for that reason, it is, on the one hand, accelerating the progress of events and, on the other, concentrating attention on the suppression of Bolshevism by force, and thereby weakening its position in a number of other fields. The Communists in all advanced countries must take into account both these circumstances in their tactics.[2]

For this reason: "Unless we master all means of warfare, we may suffer grave, often even decisive, defeat if changes beyond our control in the position of the other classes bring to the forefront forms of activity in which we are particularly weak."[3]

"Violence" and new "forms of activity" of the class adversary: on these terrains the communists, as the vanguard of the working class, must face the new cycles of struggle. Lenin's possibilism has nothing to do with unilateral availability in questions of organization (with an obligatory complement of theoretical cynicism), but it is the armed awaiting for the opening of a new cycle.

If these are the terms of the question, then the strategic perspective and the theoretical outlook need to completely open up again and retrace the whole dialectical path of the program. Lenin's insistence on the need to develop and reconstruct the particular character of the international strategic design[4] must be read as being very different from the bureaucratic order of specializations mandated by the central committees of external offices.

This insistence, preoccupation, and instance are rather an attempt to found, again, in the new situation of the initiative, an idea of class composition and to ground again the unique international task of communists in this idea of class composition and *the concrete modes* of its expression. If we return to Lenin's study of dialectics, we could call this a search for the new "essence" of the movement, where by movement and essence we do not simply mean connection and coordination, but a new production of the revolutionary struggle. The conditions of the process are wholly material and consist in national particularities, and their driving force lies in the power of the working class. As Lenin writes: "The big, advanced capitalist countries are marching along this road *much more rapidly* than did Bolshevism, which history granted fifteen years to prepare itself, as an organized political trend, for victory."[5]

To reinstate this: we are not exaggerating Lenin's awareness. We are retracing a second stratum in his thought that is often suffocated by other exigencies. But there is a hugely fascinating element in this text. Not only, in a more or less determinate way, is the theoretical stance turned toward the refoundation of class composition as the fundamental and exemplary yet not paradigmatic term of the revolutionary process; the analysis also wants to become internal to this refoundation and focus on the decisive shift immediately:

Now all efforts, all attention, must be concentrated on the *next* step, which seems, and from a certain standpoint really is, less fundamental, but which, on the other hand, is actually closer to the practical carrying out of the task, namely: seeking the forms of *transition* or *approach* to the proletarian revolution. The proletarian vanguard has been won over ideologically. That is the main thing. Without this not even the first step towards victory can be made. But it is still a fairly long way from victory. Victory cannot be won with the vanguard alone. To throw the vanguard alone into the decisive battle, before the whole class, before the broad masses have taken up a position either of direct support of the vanguard, or at least of benevolent neutrality towards it, and one in which they cannot possibly support the enemy, would be not merely folly but a crime. And in order that actually the whole class, that actually the broad masses of the working people and those oppressed by capital may take up such a position, propaganda and agitation alone are not enough. For this the masses must have their own political experience. Such is the fundamental law of all great revolutions, now confirmed with astonishing force and vividness not only in Russia but also in Germany. Not only the uncultured, often illiterate, masses of Russia, but the highly cultured, entirely literate masses of Germany had to realize through their own painful experience the absolute impotence and spinelessness, the absolute helplessness and servility to the bourgeoisie, the utter vileness of the government of the knights of the Second International, the absolute inevitability of a dictatorship of the extreme reactionaries (Kornilov in Russia, Kapp and Co. in Germany) as the only alternative to a dictatorship of the proletariat, in order to turn them resolutely toward Communism.[6]

Despite the indeterminacy of the argument and its methodological tone, from stitching up the fabric of class composition some important indications of the struggle of the new cycle emerge. The first element is "the political experience of the masses"; the second is the insistence on the "last and decisive struggle" to which the masses are called and to which they must come. Behind these indications a *new subject* begins to emerge *in relation to* the Russian experience and the Bolshevik model, and this subject is a mass subject capable of communism. The modes of the tactics then must start from this new composition and a more mature subject that is to be transformed by it. Lenin's attention increasingly moves from observation and suggestions relative to tactical shifts between democratic struggle and socialist struggle, between economic and political struggle, to an extremely robust and destructive concept of anticapitalist workers' struggle.

In starting from the new workers' subject, what interests Lenin is not the disquisition over democracy and socialism that typified the previous cycle of struggle: here workers' struggle can strike at the heart of capital and use the crisis against it. An anticapitalist use of the crisis to the end:

The fundamental law of revolution, which has been confirmed by all revolutions, and particularly by all three Russian revolutions in the twentieth century, is as follows: it is not enough for revolution that the exploited and oppressed masses should understand the impossibility of living in the old way and demand changes; it is essential for revolution that the exploiters should not be able to live and rule in the old way. Only when the "*lower classes*" *do not want* the old way, and when the "upper classes" *cannot carry on in the old way*—only then can revolution triumph. This truth may be expressed in other words: revolution is impossible without a nation-wide crisis (affecting both the exploited and the exploiters). It follows that for revolution it is essential, first, that a majority of the workers (or at least a majority of the class-conscious, thinking, politically active workers) should fully understand that revolution is necessary and be ready to sacrifice their lives for it; secondly, that the ruling classes should be passing through a governmental crisis, which draws even the most backward masses into politics (a symptom of every real revolution is a rapid, tenfold and even hundredfold increase in the number of members of the toiling and oppressed masses—hitherto apathetic—who are capable of waging the political struggle), weakens the government and makes it possible for the revolutionaries to overthrow it rapidly.[7]

But this is not sufficient. Retracing this second stratum of *"Left-Wing" Communism*, one comes to think that the rules of tactics and strategy change radically not only in the face of the main moments of the crisis (workers' use of the crisis, direct communist struggle), but also in their entire development. In the new cycle of struggles, on the basis of a new workers' subject, the gradualism of tactics and the party seems to wane. The inversion of the relation between composition and organization given in October seems by now to be embodied in the new class composition. Therefore it is the accumulation of *struggles* and their adding-up to become a cycle, all against capital and not focused on various shifts but on the *decisive shift*, that is what interests Lenin. Workers' struggle matures the capitalist shifts and exposes capital to the harshest of offensives: "Victorious tsardom is compelled to accelerate the destruction of the remnants of the pre-bourgeois, patriarchal mode of life in Russia. The country's development along bourgeois lines proceeds with remarkable speed. Extra-class and above-class illusions, illusions concerning the possibility of avoiding capitalism, are scattered to the winds. The class struggle manifests itself in quite a new and more distinct form."[8] Hence the "astonishing richness of content"[9] of the struggles explodes and turns to directly revolutionary objectives:

> Because in the era of imperialism generally, and especially now, after the war, which was a torment to the peoples and quickly opened their eyes to the truth (viz., that tens of millions were killed and maimed only for the purpose of deciding whether the British or the German pirates should plunder the largest number of countries), all these spheres of social life are being especially charged with inflammable material and are creating numerous causes of conflicts, crises and the accentuation of the class struggle. We do not and cannot know which spark—of the innumerable sparks that are flying around in all countries as a result of the economic and political world crisis—will kindle the conflagration, in the sense of specially rousing the masses, and we must, therefore, with the aid of our new, communist principles, set to work to "stir up" all and sundry, even the oldest, mustiest and seemingly hopeless spheres, for otherwise we shall not be able to cope with our tasks, we shall not be comprehensively prepared, we shall not master all arms and we shall not prepare ourselves to achieve either the victory over the bourgeoisie (which arranged all sides of social life—and has now disarranged them—in its bourgeois way) or the impending communist reorganization of every sphere of life after that victory.[10]

Tactics and strategy are rooted in a new subject capable of communism and of the last and decisive shift. The emphasis is on spontaneity, development, and a variety of forms of struggle, on the cumulative character they reveal in the middle term, on the destructive character they make explicit in periods of crisis. What about organization? We have two considerations on this issue. The first is what Lenin regards as "fully completed," the historical period in which "the opinion we have always advocated, namely, that revolutionary German Social-Democracy, . . . *came closest* to being the party which the revolutionary proletariat required in order to attain victory."[11] The second consideration is that "now the idea of Soviet power has arisen *all over the world* and is spreading among the proletariat of all countries with extraordinary speed."[12] Well, organization must change to reflect these considerations.

We must not repeat the "dialectical errors" committed by the leaders of the Second International:

> They fully appreciated the need for flexible tactics; they learned themselves and taught others Marxist dialectics (and much of what they have done in this respect will forever remain a valuable contribution to socialist literature); but *in the application* of these dialectics they committed such a mistake, or proved in practice to be so *un*-dialectical, so incapable of taking into account the rapid change of forms and the rapid acquiring of new content by the old forms, that their fate is not much more enviable than that of Hyndman, Guesde and Plekhanov. The principal reason for their bankruptcy was that they were "enchanted" by one definite form of growth of the working-class movement and Socialism, they forgot all about the one-sidedness of this form, they were afraid of seeing the sharp break which objective conditions made inevitable, and continued to repeat simple, routine, and, at a first glance, in contestable truths, such as: "three is more than two." But politics is more like algebra than arithmetic; and still more like higher mathematics than elementary mathematics. In reality, all the old forms of the socialist movement have acquired a new content, and, consequently, a new sign, the "minus" sign, has appeared in front of all the figures; but our wiseacres stubbornly continued (and still continue) to persuade themselves and others that "minus three" is more than "minus two"![13]

Organization must change too and become adequate to the new contents of class composition. Obviously, on this second stratum of *"Left-Wing" Communism*, the linearity of the argumentation is often suffocated by the needs of the movement, such as when Lenin places trust in the hope that old organizations can be seized again:

> The old forms have burst asunder, for it has turned out that their new content—an anti-proletarian and reactionary content—had attained inordinate development. Today our work has, from the standpoint of the development of international Communism, such a durable, strong and powerful content (for Soviet power, for the dictatorship of the proletariat) that it

can and must manifest itself in every form, both new and old, it can *and must* regenerate, conquer and subjugate all forms, not only the new, but also the old—not for the purpose of reconciling itself with the old, but for the purpose of making all and every form—new and old—a weapon for the complete, final, decisive and irrevocable victory of Communism.[14]

But this cannot hide the intensity and novelty of the dialectical path, from new composition to new organization, which, if not described, is at least alluded to in this second stratum of *"Left-Wing" Communism*. Again, once the Bolshevik ability to anticipate and lead has ceased, workers' struggle has to accomplish the philological labor of reading Lenin and filling his allusions with explosive contents. Our philology, too, is grounded in this new workers' struggle, in this new cycle of struggles, and in its new organization.

NOTES

1. V. I. Lenin, *"Left-Wing" Communism, an Infantile Disorder* (Peking: Foreign Language Press, 1970), 19ff.
2. Ibid., 106.
3. Ibid., 101.
4. Ibid., 95.
5. Ibid., 94–95.
6. Ibid., 96–97.
7. Ibid., 86.
8. Ibid., 11.
9. Ibid., 10.
10. Ibid., 105–107.
11. Ibid., 19.
12. Ibid., 14.
13. Ibid., 108–109.
14. Ibid., 110.

33

FROM "LEFT-WING" COMMUNISM TO WHAT IS TO BE DONE?

T HE BURDEN OF proof of the difficult equilibrium of *"Left-Wing" Communism* fell on the development of class struggle in two ways. First, by exposing its negative side, the vicissitudes of the Communist International could not be more implacable evidence of the grave deviations "to the right" provoked by that polemic against "leftism," so much so that the actual continuity of the international workers' movement was definitively broken, with no possibility of turning back and restoring it. Secondly, it exposed its positive side in the interpretation of the new workers' struggles around the world. In this respect, we should note that the moments of the second stratum, where Lenin tries to reinterpret some of the positions of "extremists," found wide expression and affirmation through the struggles. In any case, the scission between the two sides of *"Left-Wing" Communism* was aggravated and made extreme by the development of class struggle.

Some people who are aware of this have treated Lenin as an empty shell to discard. Is it right to do so? If we were to keep to the reasons of tradition, to its respect and the habitual function of the institutional continuity of the workers' movement, it would be right to do that. But from the dialectical standpoint it would not, because the two sides of the difficult Leninist equilibrium are real moments, not only present in the institutional history of the workers' movement, but above all active in and inside the political composition of the working class. Here the victory of the institutional side was revealed to be ephemeral, and the tendency to develop the second side, through a new communist political class composition, became unstoppable. Our task will not consist in engaging in anti-Leninist polemics, but in trying to dig deep into workers' struggles and make the tendency Lenin hints at emerge in a way that can win organizationally. It is a case for moving back from *"Left-Wing" Communism* to *What Is to Be Done?* and to Lenin's refoundation of the new strategic project of the new political composition of the working class. The revolutionary task is to discover this undefeatable dialectical element. But this task cannot be proposed ambiguously again. I remember that starting in 1969 in the realm of the most apprised vanguards of the revolutionary movement, the rallying cry was, "Let's start saying Lenin." What came of it? A clumsy repetition of some aphorisms, the mechanical reproduction of a bureaucratic schema, theoretical reflux, and an accommodation of the positions of reformism. This is certainly not the trend we wish a resumption of Leninism to follow. It cannot sway between formalism and empiricism; it must rigorously become a substantial Leninist adherence to collective practice, to the political composition of the working class.

We need a historical reconstruction of the vicissitudes of class struggle from Lenin's times to ours. How many and which periods of struggle have gone past? Certainly the period of that difficult equilibrium between workers and party, in which the figure of the mass worker, through spontaneity, compensated for the lack of a party leadership of the offensive: today, what new development is determined between the insuppressible movement of leadership "from below" of mass actions and the functions of the offensive? To use Lenin's terms, how are "the movements of the left and the right arm" articulated? The historical crisis of capital that we are immersed in and that promises a repressive development in the long term tries out new mechanisms of class restructuration: how can the capitalist initiative be anticipated on this terrain and in this perspective? Moreover, in this new historical period of class struggle, how are the various components of the proletarian movement recomposed and restructured? What is the relationship between autonomy and leadership? We have often insisted on the importance attributed by the new political class composition to the movements of proletarian autonomy insofar as they anticipate and chase after the operations of capitalist power along internal and vertical lines: But how can a sense of direction be recomposed in this movement? How is it necessarily built from below and from within? We have insisted on the proletarian tendency toward direct reappropriation and the establishment of a dualism of power on these grounds in the medium term: how, given this situation, are the moments of the workers' and proletarian dictatorship for communism established and built?

These are only some of the questions facing us and looking for a solution in the practice of the masses. In fact, even the question of a new "what is to be done?" is terribly complex, because, as Lenin taught us, the totality of the questions conditions and inseparably unites content and form. Now, the process of class reorganization starts from a series of crucial premises, the first of which is the urgency for class to reappropriate its own organization and immediately make it an instance of power. The problem of organization emerges and develops, in a Leninist way, from a total adherence to these fundamental comportments. The working class displays an impressive maturity, and the tendency of organization comes to affirm itself amid a burst of comportments of liberation and power struggles, a condensed and powerful mass looking for a new expressive force. As we are confronted with this violence of mass processes, this "geological explosion" of the movements, of what use can old aspirations and icons be? Again, from the standpoint of Leninist dialectics, we must recognize the new dialectical shift as it is determined not only by the domination of the totality over single contents and forms, but also by the self-productive power of the process, its violence and radical nature. The new "what is to be done?" is written by the masses today: Lenin alluded to this task when he dedicated the second stratum of his *"Left-Wing" Communism* to the masses and the violence of the international revolutionary process.

Note that what we are talking about is not old spontaneism or being "at the tail of the masses." The continuous experimentation with organization of the new left and the constant risk of making relevant to the masses what the material movements of class built are subjective tasks; but they are "tasks," not "delegations"! When the working class took delegation away from the institutional workers' movement, it took it away from everyone. It was not simply the denunciation of the "betrayal" of the institutional movement, but a radical and substantial modification of the political composition of class. And if we wish to speak of "betrayal," we need to clarify that it did not consist in failing to be loyal to the original model of Bolshevism but in failing to mediate, through a constant revolution of organization, the two elements of the difficult equilibrium Lenin had tried to mediate in *"Left-Wing" Communism*. Continuity could only amount to permanent transformation, the subjective risk of anticipating and revealing what the masses came to build into their process of liberation and power struggle. It is neither "delegation" nor "betrayal." There can be no "delegation," even to identify the terrain of a new organizational synthesis, but only the risk of theoretical and practical anticipation, and thus the development of a specific function of the mass movement itself.

How are we to move forward if the only practice of "what is to be done?" permitted today is one of intensification of all moments of autonomy? How is the shift to unity—not only unity of program but also unity of timing— given the "ultimate and decisive" moment that Lenin recognizes as our right commitment and that his last work places the greatest emphasis on? In other words, how is the materialist definition of the essence as connection and coordination turned into a definition of the movement as production, which is typical of Lenin's materialist dialectics? Or in other words again, how can we configure, today, when faced with a determinate political class composition, that Leninist practice of the revolutionary inversion of the relation "composition-organization" into "organization-composition"?

We only have fragments of the needed answers to these questions, which are sparse but rooted in the comportment of the masses. Workers' and proletarian autonomy is the fundamental fabric these comportments are rooted in, and from an *internal* analysis of workers autonomy, the chapters of a "what is to be done?" founded on the present composition of class unfold. At the level of tactics, it moves in the intermittent but continual shift from *communist* (radically egalitarian) *demands* on wages and salaries to *actions of direct reappropriation*, to movements of organization and management of *power*. At the level of organization, it is found in the development, in leaps and yet uninterrupted, from the pluralism of points of organization and the contemporary plurality of all forms of struggle (in the Leninist sense: both legal and illegal) to the *coordination of* the overall initiative and the accumulation of moments of clash. Workers' autonomy has learned to manage a permanent organizational revolution. It does not fear the danger of a possible dispersion of its strength because it knows that this molecular fabric lives off irreducible power relations. Instead, it refuses all forms of gradualism in the management of the struggle because this destroys its strength and entails the delegation and representation of a power that the class knows it can manage. The highest realization of the working class today is that power does not come into being in representation and delegation, but is established in class itself. Strategy, the path toward a qualitative leap demanded by revolutionary dialectics, is in no way analogous to the process of representation.

This is a discontinuity that needs to be posited inside class, in its immediacy and particularity. The essence must be recognized as productive and denied as a connection.

Having said this, no problem has been solved; we only reframed the question from the standpoint of the political comportments of class. The mechanism of a solution can only emerge if one digs deeper into the mix of the power relations that constitute class composition, into the analysis of the indissoluble nexus that ties together the comportments of class and capitalist development. The relationship between the theory of *Imperialism* and the strategy of insurrection outlined by Lenin during the first imperialist war is a perfect model of the path of revolutionary thought that is adequate to its times. Now as then, the analysis must retrace the interconnections between struggles and capitalist development, between struggles and crisis, restructuration, and so on. Insofar as struggles have imposed development upon capital, their immanence in the material structure of power has become stronger. Hence the need for a punctual analysis that is always fixed on the class standpoint and always mobile in the interrelations of power. Today we have the chance to read, from our standpoint, what capital can no longer read from his. Schematics, formalism, and irrationalism permeate the human and social sciences of capital; they are no longer able to even describe the effects of exploitation, something that bourgeois radicalism had traced at points, and they no longer allow capital to restructure and intervene in the way that it managed to do until the 1930s. Only from the class standpoint can the current situation of power relations be explained. Capital can, and is forced to, come to this recognition only when it has the chance to preventively and repressively manipulate the forces that constitute the working-class standpoint. We could give many examples of this: inflation, the play of multinationals, and so on. But this is not the place for it. Here we only want to recover Lenin's teaching in an intentional and informal manner: we must turn the analysis that capital twists to control development, leading to the deepening of the crisis.

With this, we come close to Lenin's operation of the inversion of practice. The dialectical shift pivots on the crossing of revolutionary will and capitalist crisis, one that only the scientific class standpoint can outline. In this perspective, Leninism is the ability to turn Marxian scientific analysis into a weapon of the proletariat and the armory of the masses. We have seen, studied, and experienced moments when this happened. Criticism and self-criticism must now carry out the task in continuity with a new Leninist exegesis that is all practical and all mass-based. In fact, what we experienced in European countries and especially in Italy during the 1960s represented a formidable preparatory experience for a revolutionary process that will later mature into an offensive. But only if we deepen the critical and self-critical analysis of our 1905, only if we do this at the level of the masses, can the process of revolutionary organization adequately grow.

Terrible times lie ahead of us. The capitalist terrorist use of crisis, the repressive transformation of the state, the definitive change in the rule of development, and the fall of the law of value: we see all this and we will see it more and more heavily turned against us. We will have to resist. We will rediscover, with Lenin, that all of the weapons of the proletariat must be used, especially those that are most heavily denied to us by a tradition of defeat and betrayals. To this, we must add that Marx and Lenin's definition of our task of destruction of the state for communism will only be given within the recognition of a newly recomposed strategic project, and in a subsequent cycle of international workers' struggles.

It is your task, workers and students, all of us marching under the flags of communism, to solve, in subversive practice, the question of insurrection and liberation.